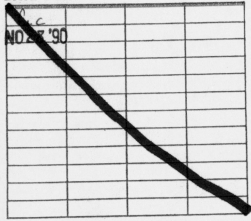

Techniques
of Teaching
Vocabulary

Techniques of Teaching Vocabulary

Edgar Dale

Professor of Education
College of Education
The Ohio State University

Joseph O'Rourke

Research Associate
College of Education
The Ohio State University

Special Consultant

Henry A. Bamman

Professor of Education
Sacramento State College

Field Educational Publications, Incorporated

A Subsidiary of Field Enterprises, Incorporated
Palo Alto, California   Addison, Illinois   Atlanta
Dallas   Ocean, New Jersey   Portland, Oregon

Acknowledgments

Grateful acknowledgment is made to the following sources for permission to reprint copyrighted material:

29: "The Highwayman" from the book *Collected Poems* by Alfred Noyes. Copyright, 1906, 1934, 1947 by Alfred Noyes. Reprinted by permission of J. B. Lippincott Company and John Murray (Publishers) Ltd. 38: Charles H. Judd, *Reading: Its Nature and Development.* Copyright 1918 by The University of Chicago. Reprinted by permission of The University of Chicago Press. 221: Excerpt from "Chicago" from *Chicago Poems* by Carl Sandburg. Copyright 1916 by Holt, Rinehart and Winston, Inc. Copyright 1944 by Carl Sandburg. Reprinted by permission of Holt, Rinehart and Winston, Inc. 223, 252, 262: Selections from *The Adventures of Huckleberry Finn* by Mark Twain. By permission of Harper & Row, Publishers, Inc. 245: Excerpts from *Dorp Dead* by Julia Cunningham. © Copyright 1965 by Julia Cunningham. Reprinted by permission of Pantheon Books, a division of Random House, Inc. 247: Reprinted by permission of Charles Scribner's Sons from *The Wind in the Willows* by Kenneth Grahame. 252: "I Have a Rendezvous with Death" from *Poems* by Alan Seeger, reprinted by permission of Charles Scribner's Sons. 270: "The Vision of Sir Launfal" from Volume 9 of *The Complete Writings of James Russell Lowell,* reprinted by permission of Houghton Mifflin Company. 323: Lillie Pope, *Handbook for the Volunteer Tutor,* 1969. Reprinted with permission of the International Reading Association and the author.

Preface

In this book we present techniques that the teacher can use to help students develop vocabulary and language skills. We stress a planned, systematic approach that makes use of the relationship between many words and concepts in order to apply prior knowledge of vocabulary to learning new words.

The book makes three key points:

1. Vocabulary development is concept development. Vocabulary growth and language growth go hand in hand.

2. Vocabulary development comes from a variety of experiences — touching, tasting, smelling, seeing, hearing — and through our emotions.

3. Vocabulary development occurs within the context of a communication triad: (a) reading and writing, (b) speaking and listening, and (c) visualizing and observing.

Our objectives are to provide the teacher with teaching techniques that will help the students to

a. broaden and enrich their language experiences
b. see words as the names of experiences
c. bring almost-known words into sharp focus
d. use the principle of transfer by analyzing words and key word parts
e. be aware of external and internal context clues
f. learn to enjoy language
g. sharpen their reading skills

The research related to this book was financially supported for many years by the Payne Fund, headed by Mrs. Frances Bolton of Cleveland, Ohio. The writers acknowledge the assistance of Lytton Beeler and are indebted to Elizabeth Chapin for her help over the years.

Table of Contents

1

Introduction

The aim of this book is a simple one—to help you as an instructor develop a plan to teach students how to improve their vocabulary at an accelerated pace. We say "at an accelerated pace" because everyone increases his vocabulary daily. He learns the name of a new food, reads a new place-name in the news, hears about a new disease, corrects his pronunciation of a word or learns to use it more precisely. Indeed, the range and depth of a person's vocabulary is the best single index of his mental development. Developing a rich vocabulary is not chiefly a matter of looking up words in the dictionary. On the contrary, a rich vocabulary comes basically from experiences and from the organizing and reorganizing of these experiences.

But most persons, from child to adult, have not developed an organized, systematic way to improve their vocabulary. It may be hit-or-miss. It may lack well-defined objectives. Without a plan, their vocabulary grows sporadically at best.

For example, it is likely that you now take the monthly word tests in the *Reader's Digest*. Is this a systematic, organized approach to vocabulary development? It really isn't. There are twenty words presented each month. You probably already know half of them, and of the remaining ten, you could vaguely know five more. After you correct your test, you find, let's say, that there were seven words you didn't know. These words have no meaningful relationship to each other and you may not remember their meanings long unless you have an unusually retentive memory. Taking the test may be a pleasant, interesting diversion, but it does not lead to a systematic growth in vocabulary.

What about the value of the many books with such intriguing titles as *Word Power, Vocabulary Made Easy, Increase Your Word Power, Thirty Days to a More Powerful Vocabulary?* Are they likely to be helpful?

Many of these books contain helpful hints for increasing your vocabulary. But the weakness of many such ambitious approaches to word development is cited in Lloyd and Warfel's volume *American English in Its Cultural Setting.* In Chapter 27, "Thirty Years to a More Powerful Vocabulary," the authors point out that "the road to a big vocabulary is a long one." Moreover, many of these books tend to mislead us by intimating that there is "something deficient about our vocabulary and lead us to think that a few more words tossed into it will fix everything up."[1] But such books do not provide an organized program for vocabulary study.

Teacher Interest

An effective program usually requires teachers who are actively interested in, indeed excited about, vocabulary development. The writers of this book have found, in developing vocabulary study materials for elementary and high school classes, that if the teacher is excited about vocabulary development, both he and the students rate the study materials more favorably. Teacher enthusiasm, moreover, tends to compensate for any weaknesses in the materials.

[1]Donald J. Lloyd and Harold R. Warfel, *American English in Its Cultural Setting* (New York: Alfred A. Knopf, Inc., 1956).

Concept Development

A systematic program of vocabulary development is not an "extra." Indeed, vocabulary development is conceptual development—a basic educational aim of any school or college. Each subject has key concepts. Some of these are stated as single words. In mathematics, some of the key terms are *add, divide, subtract, multiply, fraction, decimal,* and *set.* In economics, some of them are *supply, demand, gross national product,* and *rediscount rate.* A student of sociology learns such terms as *acculturation, diffusion,* and *ecology.* The psychologist talks about *reinforcement, conditioned reflexes, structuralism, behaviorism,* and *cognitive behavior.*

Most fields of study have extensive, specialized vocabularies. For example, the authors H. B. English and A. C. English have prepared a 594-page book (*A Comprehensive Dictionary of Psychological and Psychoanalytical Terms*) that deals solely with psychological terms. There are medical dictionaries, political science dictionaries, and dictionaries for many other fields.

Plan and Program

We present here what we have found to be a workable, efficient program for vocabulary development. The program is organized so that it can be easily used in the classroom. Basically, we want teachers to become more sensitive to the difficulty levels of words: to know what words are generally known at a given grade level and what word parts can be taught successfully at each level. We want to show them how they can make their students word-conscious and extend their use of words.

There are several levels of comprehension involved in word knowledge. They may follow these stages:

1. I never saw it before.
2. I've heard of it, but I don't know what it means.
3. I recognize it in context—it has something to do with ...
4. I know it.

We suggest that teachers and students concentrate on stages two and three in an attempt to move as many "almost-known" words as possible into stage four.

These are some of the learning principles guiding us as we developed these lessons.

1. In each lesson the learning objectives are specific and clear-cut. The form of the lesson and the principles involved are as significant as the content. Using the form suggested, the teacher may add his own content, although each lesson includes adequate illustrative material for immediate use.

2. Through self-inventory, self-checking, review, and recall tests, we try to establish motivation for learning new words.

3. There is immediate knowledge of results (answers are provided).

4. The capabilities of the learners are considered.

5. The relationship of vocabulary to conceptual development in various fields is stressed.

6. The exercises maximize the transfer of present knowledge of words, roots, prefixes, and suffixes.

7. The content is so varied that the teacher, choosing the appropriate materials, can help the student find the proper level of material for his need. The assignments can be fitted to class needs through our programmed-teaching approach.

8. We suggest ways to encourage students to apply their knowledge, to note and remember new words in their reading.

9. We set up systems of learning new words which utilize the concepts of generalization and discrimination.

10. The teacher has easy access to adequate illustrative material, which saves him the trouble of searching for additional words or sentences to support the principle involved.

11. Planned review is an integral part of the program.

12. The Appendix provides lists of roots, prefixes, and suffixes, as well as a short list of English words derived from Latin. These lists of words can be used by the teacher to formulate lessons or as a reference in general word study. The lists represent a composite of information garnered from several sources, including technical dictionaries.

Familiarity of Words

We have familiarity scores on most of the words in the lessons. Having grouped many words by their common roots, suffixes, and prefixes, we were able to discover which words containing these roots were already known at the different grade levels and which were not.

For example, note below the words already known by the sixth-grader. He does not know *biography* well, but he will when he is in the eighth grade. *Biography* is well known at the eighth-grade level, but *graphic* (from the same root) is not commonly known at the twelfth-grade level. *Stenographer* is not well known at the eighth-grade level. The student is not generally taught to associate *biography* and *stenographer* with other *graph* words he knows, such as *paragraph*, *autograph*, and *telegraph*.

What is the purpose of singling out the *graph* root (or other roots) in the known words in the sixth grade? First of all, it will fix the meaning. Second, it will fix the spelling. Third, it will make the root available for transfer to more difficult words.

Percentage of Word Recognition

Word	Grade 6	Grade 8	Grade 10	Grade 12
photograph	88			
photographer	88			
paragraph	89			
autograph	87			
biography	61	90		
telegraph	94			
phonograph	92			
graph		92		
graphic				51
graphite			73	
stenographer		66		
bibliography			70	
autobiography	89			

The Need for a Planned Vocabulary Program

Vocabulary development in school must be a planned program. The research in the field indicates that this is a sound principle. Incidental teaching, alone, tends to become accidental teaching.

Beginning in the early grades, the teacher can introduce the student to vocabulary study habits that should increase transfer potential. For example, children can begin early to develop a mental filing system—a variety of ways to classify. They can learn to group words under general topics, first by a gross filing system, later through a finer system of discrimination. This approach was successfully used by the Enrichment Unit Project Staff of the Columbus, Ohio, Public Schools.

The development of vocabulary must be seen as a part of the major communication program of the school. All education is vocabulary development, hence conceptual development; we are studying words and symbols all the time. But we do need a special period at least once a week to review words and their parts, to develop principles and generalizations relating to word analysis and synthesis, and to classify and discuss words.

A systematic program of vocabulary development will be influenced by age, by sex, by income, by native ability, and by social status. A ninth-grade girl does not talk about her *dolly*. A fourth-grader does not know what a *second semester* is. A disadvantaged child may not know anything about *à la carte* or *table d'hôte*. Boys usually are unfamiliar with the colors *champagne* beige, *flamingo* pink, or *holly* green.

Geographical factors also affect vocabulary development. There are "farm" words as well as "city" words, "Southern" words as well as "Northern" words. Minority groups have special, vivid vocabularies. Any systematic program of vocabulary development must consider these factors. Since words are the names given to experiences, it is obvious that students need rich experiences to develop their vocabulary. A study trip to a farm, a museum, a planetarium, a department store, or a summer camp, attending a concert, and a ready supply of easy-to-read books all help in this respect.

Consolidation of vocabulary skills is an important part of reading. In the reading process, the student brings to and gets ideas from the printed page. He associates sound, symbol, and meaning. In reading, symbols convey meanings that are synthesized into related ideas. These symbols are words. They are perceived, understood, reacted to, and combined with previously known ideas. That is, the reading process leads from the known to the unknown. Effective vocabulary study must proceed in the same fashion: from known to unknown words, as from *helicopter* to *lepidoptera*.

A planned vocabulary program provides the student with ample opportunity to build new concepts upon old ones. Such a program presents appropriate study materials that make effective use of the principle of transfer. Early in his education, the student must be encouraged to see relationships and make associations, be provided with the opportunity to notice that learning the word *hateful* is not like learning a completely new word if he already knows *hate*. He learns that *hate* may undergo inflectional change: that by adding suffixes to *hate* he may form such words as *hated, hater, hating, hateful, hatefully,* and *hatefulness*. With skillful guidance, the student can, at another level, make the transition from *repeat* to *repetitious*, from *imply* to *implicit* — if the word-analysis habit is fixed.

Thus greater attention to the systematic presentation of known words that take on new meanings with inflectional change can help the student learn the principle of generalization. This principle, according to Eric H. Lenneberg,[2] is one of the three major means of language acquisition.

Systematic Approach

We noted earlier that the weakness of the typical approach to vocabulary development is that it is unsystematic. Let us suppose that today a senior class in high school learns *euphoria, antebellum,* and *monotheism*. Tomorrow they learn *euphonious, ante meridiem,* and *monocular*. The third day they learn *eupeptic, antediluvian,* and *monomania*. This approach is unsystematic and there is likely to be little transfer. A systematic approach would be to teach *ante meridiem, antediluvian,* and *antebellum* as one group; *euphoria, euphonious,* and *eupeptic* as a second group; *monotheism, monocular,* and *monomania* as a third. With this approach the student gets the benefit of transfer of learning.

Teaching for transfer can be begun in the early grades. For example, building on the word *telescope* (known by 87 percent of fourth-graders), the teacher can point out other words made from *scope* (from Greek *skopein,* to watch or look): *microscope, periscope, radarscope, gyroscope, horoscope, kaleidoscope*.

[2]Eric H. Lenneberg, *Biological Foundations of Language* (New York: John Wiley and Sons, Inc., 1967), p. 332.

Using this book the teacher can help the student form the habit of analyzing many words systematically to get clues to their meaning. For example, he might analyze *telescope* and several other *scope* words thus:

Tele means distant, far away; *scope* means see, look. When you look through a telescope you are able to see an object far away. Note also *television, telephone, telegraph,* and *telemetry,* all referring to distance.

Look at *microscope* (*micro,* small + *scope*). Germs are *small, minute,* or *microscopic.* With a microscope we see small forms of life.

A submarine has a *periscope.* Before surfacing the commander uses it to look around. The Greek prefix *peri-* means all around. What's another use for a periscope? (to look around corners) Note also *perimeter, periphery,* etc.

A *kaleidoscope* is a tube containing loose pieces of colored glass and two mirrors. If you turn the tube you see changing patterns of attractive colors. (*Kalos* is Greek for "beautiful"; *eidos* means "form.") So *kal* + *eido* + *scope* give us the word *kaleidoscope*—an instrument for seeing colored glass form beautiful designs, or, more generally, a changing pattern or scene.

Maximal Transfer Potential

A systematic program of vocabulary mastery helps the student develop a flexible mental file for storing and retrieving words. A new word isn't of much value if it is filed and lost. So a mental filing system must be active. This mental file can become a lightning-fast computer to help remember and figure out the meaning of words. The student should learn firsthand the benefits of such mental filing.

Note, for example, these words: *atypical, atheist, acentric, apathy, amoral, agonic, agnostic.* What is a useful way to file them? Actually, a dual filing system can be used. First, one learns that the prefix *a-* means not or without. Thus *atypical* means not typical. So *acentric* means not on center; *amoral* means without morals. The second file is for the root meaning, e.g., *atheist* (from *theos,* meaning God), *apathy* (not feeling), *agonic* (without an angle), *agnostic* (not knowing). Therefore, the more prefixes and roots the student has mastered, the greater his capacity for filing, remembering, and figuring out the meaning of words.

Unconsciously, the student may already have a way of filing certain words such as *apathy, sympathy, empathy,* and *pathology;* or *polygon, trigon, pentagon,* and *hexagon.* But a systematic approach to the study of vocabulary instills a conscious awareness of the associative elements in these words—the meaningful roots *path* (feel) and *gon* (angle). Knowing the element *ectomy* (cut out) helps you make associations between *tonsillectomy, appendectomy, gastrectomy,* and *neurectomy.* And knowing the root *tom* (cut) lets you see the relationship between words such as *anatomy* and *atom* (which people once thought could not be cut).

The Twilight Zone

Another fruitful way of organizing and filing words is to think of them as not known, partly known, or well known. If we visualize our vocabulary as a series of concentric circles with loose boundaries containing the words we know in varying degrees, this idea becomes clearer. We learn our new words, and thus enlarge our vocabulary, largely by sharpening the focus of those words at the edges of our knowledge, the words in the twilight zone.

The authors believe that any motivated individual can increase his working vocabulary by 10 percent. This will be, in part, a result of bringing into sharp focus these words, parts of words, and expressions which are now only partly known.

A student's score on vocabulary tests would increase sharply if credit were given for partly knowing a word, even when there was some confusion about the exact meaning. It is the daily task of the teacher to help students become more skillful in moving words from their twilight zone of confusion and partial knowledge to the broad daylight of clear understanding.

Many of the units of this text are closely interrelated. For example, the units on roots, prefixes, and suffixes can be used interchangeably both to analyze and to synthesize word parts that may form "twilight zone" words for the student. The authors stress the association of both internal and external context clues as a means of strengthening concepts.

Basic Vocabulary

It is helpful to know how a child learns his first three or four thousand words. In our study of the vocabulary of inner-city children, we found that three fourths of them had a vocabulary of fifteen hundred words by January and February of their first year of school. We noted that most of these words (a) can be sensed, (b) are necessary to speak almost any sentence, (c) are in the everyday vocabulary of most people, (d) are ones which have been experienced and internalized and will never be forgotten.

How did the children learn them? First, they heard them from parents, older children, and playmates, on television and radio, on the playground and at the store. Second, they experienced them—they said things, they ate things, they touched things, they smelled things, they drank things. Their vocabulary was circumscribed only by their experiences and by the available models.

If these children had grown up in a wealthy suburb, with more opportunity to attend nursery school or kindergarten, to accompany their parents when they shopped, and to spend more time at exhibits, zoos, parks, and children's theaters, their vocabulary would reflect their wider variety of experience.

Vocabulary and Life

When you organize and provide a vocabulary development program, you are changing the lives of students. Vocabulary growth is not at the periphery of our lives; it is central, focal. It can lead the student forward to broader experiences, which in turn generate more new experiences in logarithmic fashion.

Learning a new word carries within itself an explosive effect. We might visualize such new words as seeking further applications, nagging us to look further, study deeper. For example, when you learned the word *serendipity* (the faculty of making happy and unexpected discoveries by accident) did you then become aware of serendipities in your own life and in other people's lives? Did you become serendipity-sensitive? Perhaps you first became conscious of the word *bursitis* through having had it. Soon you discovered other people who had it and you commiserated with them on the painfulness that accompanied it.

Learning new words is a dynamic process that involves getting compound interest. New words in one's repertoire of responses are incremental, intrusive, propulsive, apparently pushing the possessor on to search for new applications. When our words change, we change.

Vocabulary and Mental Ability

That a student's vocabulary level is a good index of his mental ability has been a generally accepted fact. Over fifty years ago, research prompted Lewis M. Terman to note that his vocabulary test (one of a series of tests to provide an intelligence quotient) alone "will give us an intelligence quotient within 10 percent of that secured by the entire scale."[3] In addition, vocabulary tests have been found to correlate highly with tests of reading ability. Of course, one might ask whether we have a big vocabulary because we are born with high intelligence or whether we develop that intelligence by developing a big vocabulary. No neat answer is possible, but there is little doubt that rich experiences plus careful attention to naming will favorably influence the mental abilities of children.

Students need to realize that vocabulary is an index of the nature and quality of their lives. It reflects what they have studied, where they have been, the subtleties and refinements of their mind. A good mind means a good vocabulary and a good vocabulary means a good mind. Which comes first? Which causes the other? It is more accurate to say that they are interactive—each is an inseparable part of the background and abilities of the learner.

Words are a part of a language system, integrated in syntactical patterns. Words are often related hierarchically, like grandfather, father, and son. Like colors, they may be arranged in various systems. Would your students know that the following colors are presented in this order—

[3]Lewis M. Terman, *The Measurement of Intelligence* (Cambridge: The Riverside Press, 1916).

violet, indigo, blue, green, yellow, orange, red — to represent the spectrum?

Sometimes our combinations and systems call for opposites: *optimism* and *pessimism*, *hot* and *cold*, *ameliorative* and *pejorative*, *systole* and *diastole*. Sometimes they are grouped according to their similarities — *feverish, inflamed, burned up*. The point we are making is simply that learning words is not an isolated activity. It is an on-going part of life — the never-ending process of conceptualizing.

Vocabulary Development and Conceptual Development

It is necessary to see vocabulary development as conceptual development. Even though every word is a concept, the term *concept* is both broader and deeper than *word*. If you learn the French word *l'eau* for water, you don't have a new concept but another name for a familiar concept. However, since translations are never exact there may always be some conceptual difference. For example, the word *pain* in French connotes something different from our word *bread* because the French have a different concept of bread. Further, "the bread of life" means something more than the separate meanings of the words. Concepts are developed both by generalization and by differentiation. We learn to separate "dogs" into "collies," "bulldogs," and "dachshunds." We learn to group "apples," "oranges," and "cherries" under "fruit."

Ordering Concepts

Vocabulary development means more than adding new words to your repertoire of experience. It means putting your concepts in better order or into additional orders or arrangements. To change your vocabulary is to change your life.

One big job of vocabulary development is to help students see likenesses and differences that they never saw before. They can easily learn that *believe* and *belief* are related. One is a verb and the other a noun. Indeed, one of the important gains in concept development is learning the rules for changing words from one part of speech to the other. Some are easy — *boy* to *boyish, zest* to *zestful*. Some are harder — *pygmy* to *pygmean*. But how do you make an adjective out of *uncle*? *Unclean* won't do. How about *uncular*? Actually we have to make a big jump — from *uncle* to *avuncular*. Do you know what a *tress* is? Do you get a good clue by learning that it is the singular of *tresses*?

How do we designate a man from Norway? Do we call him a Norwayan even though we do call a man from America an American? No simple rule applies here. Instead we used the word *Norwegian*. The point is that one's vocabulary may be inert. But it need not be. Through the use of known key prefixes, suffixes, and roots, we can daily make small and eventually large changes in our stock of words.

Although certain words are carefully fenced in—the denotative words of a science, for example—these words tend to slip away from their fenced-in denotations and acquire new meanings, or connotations. Space words become metaphorized: *pad, countdown,* and *blast-off.* Baseball expressions move into common talk and are changed in the process: *fielding questions, batting a thousand, struck out, didn't get to first base.*

We hope that you and your students get a quickening sense of the vitality of the English language—learn to enjoy the zest of newly minted slang terms, learn to play with words as well as work with them. One of the authors asked a Philadelphia taxi driver, "Who has the right-of-way on a traffic rotary?" He replied, "We call that a 'much-right.' One driver has as much right on the rotary as another."

Subtleties and Nuances

Philosophers have spent much of their time dealing with the meaning of words like *true, good,* and *beautiful.* This analysis has a long tradition. The Jewish Torah is part of a vast literature produced by rabbis who have debated more than two thousand years over the meanings of words, phrases, and sentences in the Old Testament. The question "What do you mean?" often focuses attention on the fact that words do not mean the same thing in different places. In Britain the word *compromise* is a good word. In the United States we often think of *compromise* as a bad word—to compromise in a conflict is to give up one's principles.

The word *pride* is used in both favorable and unfavorable ways. "Pride goeth before a fall." Pride is one of the seven deadly sins. But shouldn't we take pride in the quality of our work, pride in accomplishment? Shouldn't we be proud that we are Methodists, Catholics, Americans, Chinese, Republicans, Democrats, or skeptics? Actually, it may be more useful to say "arrogance" when we are talking about pride that has gone beyond its rightful boundaries.

So in vocabulary study we may not be thinking of the new word or the big word but the right word. Throughout this book you will notice many opportunities provided for your students to make discriminating judgments about the choice of the right word.

What about "hard" words in literature and poetry? Should every hard word be looked up in the dictionary? Shakespeare, Dickens, Fielding, Austen, and other well-known writers use dated words such as *reticule, mews,* and *glebe.* These words are worth looking up if their meanings are pivotal to a broader understanding. However, if you are reading your own paperback, it may be enough to look carefully at a hard word, underline it, and try to guess its meaning. Of course, you might also wish to look it up. At any rate, if you read widely, it is quite likely that you will see the word again.

Typically, unfamiliar words we have carefully noted will turn up in future readings. One of the authors noticed that the word *reticule,* for instance, occurs in both Dickens and Twain. Twain describes Huck Finn, dressed up as a girl, carrying a *reticule.* When the author looked up the word *reticule,* he discovered it came from Latin *rete* (a net) and *reticulum* (a little net)—descriptive of the net handbag carried by women shoppers.

Using the Dictionary

When should the teacher ask the student to look up the meaning of a word? Teachers may overemphasize the value of having the students look up and write meanings for long lists of words. The general rule is to reduce the amount of sheer drudgery that the youngsters go through so that their mastery of vocabulary remains an interesting as well as useful experience. For example, instead of asking an entire class to look up the same word, you might have each student look up two or three words. The student need not report to the teacher or class on all of these words, but from time to time you might ask each student to refer to his notebook to see who has found an interesting word or word origin. Some students can make visual presentations with the overhead projector or use chalkboard drawings to illustrate such words as *corral, mustang, maverick.*

The value of defining a word by writing it in a sentence has been greatly exaggerated. Typically, the technique has been that of looking up a series of words in which students have no particular interest and writing a sentence on each one. You did not learn most of your vocabulary this way, neither did the authors, and neither will the students whom you teach. This is boring and futile and will develop an unfavorable, negative attitude toward your whole vocabulary program. Use of the dictionary is discussed in Unit 13.

Programming Material for Study

In this book we have often programmed the material. This is significant, because in programming we consider (a) the student's need, (b) the student's performance in relation to that need, (c) the terminal behavior of the student who works through the program, (d) the learning steps involved: small, large; easy to hard; known to unknown; spaced practice (review); recall tests. In addition, the student is offered a consistent method of internalizing words and concepts. Further, he gets the opportunity (through the process of grouping likes and opposites and the systematic study of roots and affixes) to generalize from one word to another and from one idea to another.

Word Analysis and Synthesis

One of the key techniques offered in this book and indeed in studying words in general is to break them up into their component parts. Once the meaning of the parts is known, they can be synthesized into a final meaning. This process of analyzing and synthesizing makes up the totality of word study. For example, let us analyze the word *circumspect*. It has two component parts: *circum* (Latin "around") and *spect* (from Latin *spectare*, "to look at"). Hence, a circumspect person is watchful on all sides or careful, cautious, prudent—always looking over his shoulder. In addition, the student learning either of these word parts can then analyze and synthesize other words such as *circumnavigate, circumpolar, spectacle, inspect, reinspection,* and *retrospection.* Indeed, he might for his own amusement combine prefixes, suffixes, and roots to create new words.

In pre- and post-test analyses of inner-city junior high school students, we found that they made exceptional vocabulary gains from material we had prepared using Latin and Greek roots. These students were also able to coin meaningful words of their own:

grapher
  (writer, recorder)

audvision
  (can see and hear)

graphometer
  (measures, records)

scalegraph
  (records weights)

phonomatic
  (makes sounds by itself)

autometer
  (self-measuring device)

retrometer
  (measures reentry thrust)

telescript
  (written telegram)

barophone
  (measures weight by sound waves)

monoscript
  (written once)

scriptograph
  (written recording)

solarscope
  (sun viewer)

jector
  (hurler)

astrometer
  (measures stars)

astrocraft
  (spaceship)

armobile
  (armed vehicle)

The Contextual Relationship of Words

As we have already pointed out, we do not learn most of our words by looking them up in the dictionary. Rather, we learn them through context (spoken and written), and we often approach a new word with partial knowledge of it. A student, for example, may know the word *octopus* (an eight-legged sea creature) from biology and the word *octagon* (an eight-sided figure) from math. When he encounters the word *octave* (a series of eight notes) in music, he already knows it has something to do with *eight*. And when he reexamines *October*, a word he already knows, he may be motivated to discover that it was the eighth month in the Roman calendar. He has thus used an internal context clue to determine the meaning of an unfamiliar word.

We see, therefore, that the analysis or synthesis of words is no simple mechanical matter. It is incremental, generative; something that is going on all the time. One of the tasks of the teacher is to help develop the habit of observation of words in this manner so that the student can use context more effectively.

We wish to emphasize that noting internal clues is an important part of the context-clue method of word attack; that this is a natural, highly fruitful method of learning words. We suggest also that unless these key meanings are clarified and generalized at some stage of development in the mind of the learner, he may fail to understand new words in their contextual setting because he does not have the added skill of being able to analyze word parts. Therefore, we think of word analysis and synthesis as an integral part of the context-clue method of learning and using words.

Words and Critical Thinking

The central human issue for teachers and students is whether they are in charge of their own lives. To what extent can we resist those who would manipulate us for their own ends? How can we learn to think for ourselves? Certainly a grounding in vocabulary and in the study of the nature of persuasion (rhetoric) may help us think more clearly. Many words carry slanted, emotion-laden connotations far beyond their denotative meanings: *school, democratic, childhood, teacher, discipline, arithmetic, vacation, examination, parents, identity*. Many have strong favorable and unfavorable connotations. The critical reader and thinker is aware of these aspects of word influence and reacts accordingly. One goal in vocabulary development is to sharpen the student's critical thinking processes.

Word Development Techniques

Seventeen different categories of word development appear in this book. Under each heading we provide from three to five examples of techniques for study within a given area. Our purpose has been to furnish you with ideas and materials which are specific enough and extensive enough to be used immediately. These categories include:

Testing as Teaching (Unit 2)
Context Clues (Unit 3)
Synonyms, Antonyms, Homonyms (Unit 4)
Word Origins (Unit 5)
Prefixes (Unit 6)
Suffixes (Unit 7)
Roots (Unit 8)
Pronunciation and Spelling (Unit 9)
Semantics (Unit 10)
Figures of Speech (Unit 11)
Literature and Vocabulary Development (Unit 12)
Using the Dictionary (Unit 13)
Word Games (Unit 14)

Procedure

The teacher can help the student understand the general principles of vocabulary study involved in each exercise. Later the student can apply these principles to new situations. Some students, of course, will infer these principles without help; others will need direct guidance.

What is the best order for teaching these exercises? We placed Unit 3, *Context Clues,* near the beginning of the book because it is closely related to the processes of word perception, syntactic relationship, and reading. However, the teacher may wish to change the order to meet the needs of his class.

How many exercises should each pupil do under each category? Here, too, the immediate goals of the teacher and the background of the students will influence this decision. Some exercises may be too hard for the pupils, others too easy. The teacher may use as many exercises as are found useful and improve on them by relating the principle involved to whatever content is appropriate to the class objectives. Some teachers may use a few lessons; others may find some use for all of them. We hope that the teachers using these materials will carefully preview the material and use the most productive lessons first. If pupils are successful at the onset, their continuing interest will be assured.

The attitude of the teacher toward these exercises is critically important. We have found again and again that the teacher's enthusiasm or lack of it is caught by the class. Interest in vocabulary is both taught and caught.

The first step is to test to find out where your students are in terms of vocabulary development. This does not involve the use of complicated diagnostic measurement. Rather, it merely means having the students take frequent self-inventory tests, self-checking tests of words, parts of words, and word usage. We want to find out where the student is but not leave him there.

15

Some words are completely unknown to us, some almost known, some are well known. Teachers can help students make great vocabulary gains by helping them bring their almost-known words into sharp focus. These are words they could and would use, given a little guidance and encouragement.

But first, the student needs to be aware of what words he knows or doesn't know well. As we have already pointed out, the student can build this awareness by underlining unfamiliar words in newspapers, magazines, and books which he owns. Even so, a student's judgment about his word knowledge may be faulty. To help the student make an accurate inventory of his vocabulary, the teacher can choose key words related to the subjects studied by the student and present them in a variety of test forms. We present several of these test forms in *Testing as Teaching*, Unit 2. It is essential that the student learn how to check his own understanding of words—what he knows and doesn't know.

The Role of Audio and Visual Experiences

Language develops out of direct and indirect experiences. The three thousand or so words that children learn before they enter formal schooling are mainly a result of direct sensory experiences: touching, tasting, smelling, seeing, and hearing. As they learn to read, children associate these direct experiences with indirect experiences in the form of symbols—the letters that form our written words. Often this association is a difficult one and needs to be reinforced with imagery—another form of indirect experience.

Images can be visual—pictorial material (projected and nonprojected), maps, graphs, charts, diagrams, etc.—or they can be auditory—drama, simulations, demonstrations. Both types involve condensation of a direct experience that bears some similarity to it. This is why children learning to associate the word *pencil* with the actual object may be aided by an accompanying picture (visual image) of a pencil. More difficult concepts, like *pet,* can be mastered with the aid of audio and visual images that reinforce associations with, and hence knowledge of, the written and spoken word.

Using Audiovisual Materials To Teach Vocabulary

Many of the lessons in this text can be taught more effectively with the use of devices such as overhead projectors, slides, filmstrips, moving and still pictures, records, and tapes. Students should be encouraged to play an active role in the preparation of materials for presentation. For example, they can make illustrations for projection, word cards for display on bulletin boards, and tape recordings to illustrate word pronunciation and usage. They can collect interesting, unfamiliar, or unusual words found in books, newspapers, and other media, for their own personal use, or present them to the class for discussion.

Illustrations like the simple drawings below can sometimes help the teacher get across small differences in meaning. These drawings can be used on flash cards with the prefixes written on the back, or they may be displayed in conjunction with a particular lesson.

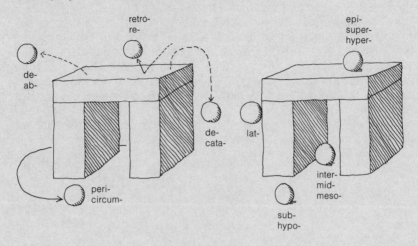

Or, students can be encouraged to discover the meaning of unfamiliar words by inferring their meaning from illustrations:

caudal   acaudal   bicaudal
(a = without)   (bi = two)

Another approach illustrates the use of one prefix in several words:

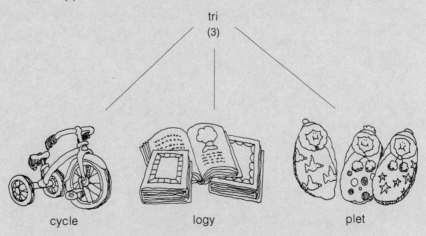

tri
(3)

cycle   logy   plet

17

Although it is not the authors' purpose to present an in-depth study of audiovisual techniques, we strongly recommend that teachers, particularly in the lower grades, use whatever resources are available to them in teaching vocabulary to their students. Many school systems have audiovisual specialists who can assist in the development of vocabulary lessons. Teachers can work in conjunction with the art and shop departments to make display items: boards, flash cards, etc. On the county level, the audiovisual department of the county superintendent's office provides, by subject area, lists of films and filmstrips that are available to the teacher. The same office is, moreover, usually equipped with a professional library containing many of the current texts on the subject of audiovisual techniques.

In the final analysis, however, it is the inventiveness of the teacher that will determine the most effective use of audiovisual devices.

2

Testing
as
Teaching

Testing is a highly useful vocabulary technique because (1) the student must pay close attention to complete the exercise correctly, (2) the answers to the questions are clear-cut, (3) the student is actively involved, (4) the student senses the importance of the exercise, for his ability is being measured, (5) the exercises are generally brief, and (6) the teacher has a quick measurement of the student's progress.

There are four main ways to test vocabulary: (1) *Identification*—the student responds orally or in writing by identifying a word according to its definition or use. For example, a word may be identified as a synonym of another word. (2) *Multiple-choice*—the student selects the correct meaning of the tested word from three or four definitions. (3) *Matching*—the tested words are presented in one column and the matching definitions are presented out of order in another column. This is another form of multiple-choice test. (4) *Checking*—the student checks the words he knows or doesn't know. He may also be required to write a definition of the words he checked. Within these four groups the teacher can use a variety of techniques to test and teach vocabulary.

A self-test is a useful one. Here the student, by checking the words he knows or doesn't know, makes an inventory of his stock of words to find out the strengths and weaknesses of his vocabulary. Below are some examples of easy-to-construct and easy-to-take vocabulary inventory tests.

Testing Method 1: Self-Inventory Checklist

In a list of words in easy-to-hard sequence, the student merely checks the words he knows (or doesn't know), thus determining, to an extent, his word knowledge. He may or may not be asked to define several of the words checked. Later he may consult a dictionary to see how accurately he determined his knowledge of the words he checked. The purpose is to alert the student to the state of his word knowledge.

A variety of lists may be constructed, preferably having some relationship to the student's area of study or interest. For example, the teacher may present a list of business terms, such as the following (the student checks the blank):

___ bank	___ premium
___ credit	___ debit
___ savings	___ mortgage
___ teller	___ fiscal
___ account	___ economy
___ overhead	___ consumer
___ profit	___ corporation
___ loan	___ compound interest
___ revenue	___ bankruptcy
___ contract	___ stockholder
___ bond	___ overdraft
___ deposit	___ dividend
___ finance	___ cashier

Testing Method 2: Discriminative Self-Inventory Checklist

Using the symbols +, √, −, O, the student indicates, on a chosen list of words, how well he knows each word.

+ means "I know it well, I use it."
√ means "I know it somewhat."
− means "I've seen it or heard of it."
O means "I've never heard of it."

The teacher may list words related to a subject to be studied, such as health:

___ muscle		___ calories	
___ diet		___ nutrition	
___ energy		___ calcium	
___ vitamin		___ cholesterol	
___ protein		___ thiamine	
___ carbohydrate		___ strength	

The same technique may be used diagnostically by an English teacher, for example, to measure the literary adequacy of the class. Words might include:

___ drama		___ simile	
___ Victorian		___ personification	
___ couplet		___ metaphor	
___ sonnet		___ hyperbole	
___ allegory		___ metonymy	
___ lyric		___ irony	
___ essay		___ soliloquy	

Testing Method 3: Finer Discrimination in Word Choice

The multiple-choice technique may be used to point up the distinctions between word meanings. For example, the high school student may be asked to check the best word to complete such sentences as the following:

1. It was a hot day with a great deal of moisture in the air. The day was (parching___, stifling___, balmy___).
2. While washing dishes, Mary broke a plate. "You're a big help," her mother said. Mary's mother was being (ironic___, sarcastic___, satirical___).
3. Judging from the number of burned trees on the hill, the forest ranger (implied___, inferred___) that soil erosion would soon be a problem.

Reasons for word choices should be discussed after the exercise has been completed.

Testing Method 4: Matching

The teacher may make the exercises self-corrective by including the answers at the end or on the left (to be covered with a mask and progressively disclosed after the student completes each item).

A. Matching words with definitions.

1. __b__ mobile   a. cut in two   f. cut apart
2. __a__ bisect   b. movable   g. yearly
3. __d__ octagon   c. one hundred years
4. __c__ century   d. an eight-angled figure
5. __f__ dissect   e. a ten-sided figure

B. Matching roots with definitions.

1. __b__ aud   a. look   f. sound
2. __c__ graph   b. hear   g. call
3. __a__ spect   c. write
4. __f__ phon   d. angle
5. __d__ gon   e. side

C. Matching prefixes with definitions.

1. __b__ penta   a. one   f. three
2. __d__ di   b. five   g. nine
3. __a__ mono   c. six
4. __e__ quad   d. two
5. __f__ tri   e. four

D. Matching words with related phrases.

Testing the general meaning of given words by matching these words with other words or phrases (*not* definitions) that refer to them. The student draws a line from the word to the word or phrase that is generally associated with it.

a. owl	flies high	e. canine	puppy
eagle	called wise	feline	kitten
b. carat	diamond	f. spider	web
caret	editing	bee	honey
c. Chihuahua	large	g. lions	covey
St. Bernard	small	quail	pride
d. dogs	gaggle	h. elephant	memory
geese	kennel	snake	fangs

General List of Vocabulary Testing Methods

(Methods previously described are marked with an asterisk.)

*1. Have students check known words from an easy-to-hard list of words.

*2. Use matching test (with definitions) on words, roots, prefixes, and suffixes.

3. Have students write out the definition(s) of a word. (Use sparingly. It is easy to overdo this approach.)

4. Have students classify words under given topics: *short* (brief, curt, terse, laconic, etc.).

5. Test students' knowledge of names of countries, rivers, towns, key products, etc. (multiple choice).

6. Present words for division into prefixes, roots, suffixes.

7. Have students define roots, prefixes, suffixes in given words.

8. List grammatical or literary terms for students to define:
Antonyms are _____. A *couplet* is _____.

*9. Have students form words from given roots, prefixes, suffixes.

*10. Manipulate word elements to form words. Use roots in three positions:

*graph*ite	geo*graph*ic	tele*graph*
(prefix position)	(root position)	(suffix position)

11. Have students write as many words as possible from a given root, e.g., *aud* (hear): *aud*ience, *aud*itorium, *aud*it, *aud*ition, etc., before consulting a dictionary. Then, have them use the dictionary to add to the list those words known but not recalled the first time. (Avoid long, meaningless lists.)

12. Have students derive the meaning of words from external context clues. Infer the meaning of the italicized word from its relationship to other words in the sentence:
They had lemons, oranges, *pomegranates,* and other kinds of fruit.

13. Have the students derive the meaning of words from internal context clues. Infer the meaning of the word from the meaning of its component parts (*in-, un-, pre-, post-,* etc.):
Incapable means not capable . *Inaccurate* means not accurate .

Then reverse the procedure:
A word meaning *not capable* is incapable .

14. Present a scrambled list of words to be arranged alphabetically. (This provides practice in the use of the dictionary.)

15. Have students complete comparisons or analogies:
Black is to white as hot is to cold .
Zenith is to nadir as apogee is to perigee .

16. Present a paragraph with some words underlined. Ask students to infer the meaning of these words. Discuss the use of internal and external context clues.

17. Have students write
a. synonyms for words: *small* <u>minute</u>
b. antonyms for words: *microscopic* <u>macroscopic</u>

18. Before and after they study a chapter of one of their texts, check students' understanding of key words by multiple-choice tests. Students may be asked to help prepare these tests.

19. Ask the students to give their own definitions for a list of words. Also do the reverse: give definitions and ask students to supply the words defined, e.g., *substance used in pencils* (graphite). Clues may be added: g r _ _ _ _ _ e.

20. Test the meaning of words in famous quotations:
1. pledge, allegiance, republic, indivisible
2. fourscore, conceived, proposition
3. events, dissolve, assume, self-evident
4. preamble, insure, domestic, tranquility
This may be done by multiple-choice or matching tests. .

21. Have students infer the document, speech, literary or historical character from several key words in a quotation:
countrymen, lend, bury, praise _____
students write source

allegiance, republic, indivisible _____

course, events, dissolve, bands _____

22. Match names and places:
1. Tokyo   a. Illinois
2. Chicago   b. New York
3. United Nations   c. Japan

23. Have the students cross out the word that doesn't belong (classification tests):
1. centurion   senate   Caesar   Mikado
2. agora   Shinto   acropolis   amphitheater
3. cuneiform   sphinx   Cicero   pharoah

24. Have students cross out the picture that doesn't belong in the group (pictorial variation of classification tests):

cat   tiger   leopard   dog

25. Present a grid, like the one below, containing key prefixes and roots in vertical and horizontal format. The student is to combine them to form words (marked "X" in the grid). The idea is to discover the transferability of key word parts.

	a duc(t) (lead)	b tract (draw)	c dic(t) (say)	d cycle (wheel)	e pel (push)	f pod(e) (foot)
1. mono				X		X
2. bi				X		X
3. tri				X		X
4. ab(s)	X	X				
5. pro	X	X			X	
6. uni				X		X
7. ex		X			X	
8. contra			X			

Answers

1d, monocycle	3d, tricycle	5a, product	6f, unipod
1f, monopode	3f, tripod	5b, protract	7b, extract
2d, bicycle	4a, abduct	5e, propel	7e, expel
2f, bipod	4b, abstract	6d, unicycle	8c, contradict

26. Present a list of key roots that the student can combine to form words:

Word Parts

1. alti	8. mega
2. anemo	9. meter
3. arch(y)	10. micro
4. aud	11. mit
5. auto	12. mon(o)
6. demo	13. crat
7. graph(y)	14. phon(o)

Words

altimeter	1 + 9
anemometer	2 + 9
monarchy	12 + 3
phonograph	14 + 7
autograph	5 + 7
democrat	6 + 13
demography	6 + 7

27. Have students substitute the correct word for these italicized "boners":

Answers

eligible	1. He's not *legible* for the army.
delusions	2. The speaker was suffering from *allusions* of grandeur.
punctured	3. My tire is *punctuated*.
rheumatic	4. My sister had *romantic* fever.
undulant	5. He was suffering from *indolent* fever.
sect	6. The crusaders belonged to a religious *sex*.
rickshaw	7. In China, he rode in a *kickshaw*.

Other words frequently confused: *angle, angel; cavalry, Calvary; persecute, prosecute; respectively, respectfully; precede, proceed; arraign, arrange*. (For additional confused pairs see Unit 9, *Pronunciation and Spelling*).

28. Test inflectional variations in words to see if the student sees the relationship between words of the same root. A list of composite words is presented in one column and the student is asked to provide a simple word from which each is derived. (If the teacher wishes, students may check themselves by using an answer key like the one on the left.)

Answers

palace	1. palatial	_____
		student supplies word
sign	2. signify	_____
person	3. personification	_____
whole	4. wholly	_____
weary	5. wearisome	_____
waste	6. wastrel	_____

Selected words will depend on students' level of attainment. Other words that might be included:

absentee, absent	erasure, erase
authenticity, authentic	erroneous, error
collegiate, college	partition, part
demolition, demolish	persuasive, persuade
denunciation, denounce	pilgrimage, pilgrim
domesticity, domestic	plurality, plural
habitual, habit	pollinate, pollen
humanitarian, human, or humanity	pretense, pretend
indicative, indicate	quietude, quiet
exemplify, example	rarity, rare
pervasive, pervade	reality, real
evasive, evade	remedial, remedy
competitive, compete	responsive, response
debutante, debut	simplify, simple
decisive, decide	sobriety, sober
deprivation, deprive	truism, true
elephantine, elephant	typical, type

3

Context
Clues

By using context clues, the reader can often figure out the meaning of an unfamiliar word without looking it up in a dictionary. In the following lessons we discuss various kinds of context clues, the strengths and weaknesses of context-clue methods of word attack, and examples of effective and ineffective context-clue exercises.

Kinds of Definitions

Formal Definition

The meaning of the word is expressed in a direct statement. Examples:

a. *Charades* is a game in which players must guess the meaning of a word from watching other players act out a dramatic representation of it.
b. A *word* is a sound or group of sounds that has meaning and is an independent unit of speech.
c. A *phoneme* is one of a group of distinct sounds that make up the words of a language.

Definition by Example

A definition by example can further clarify the formal definition. To define *charade* by example, we might add the following to sentence "a" above:

"Thus, if we dramatize a woman wearing something *gray* and *eating*, the answer would be *ingratiate*." (In gray she ate.)

To sentence "b" we might add:
"Thus, *th* is not a word but *the* is."

It is possible to define by example alone:

a. An example of a phoneme is the *p* in *pan* or the *n* in *pan*.
b. The beginning *p* in *pip* and the final *p* in *pip* differ slightly in pronunciation but belong to the one phoneme *p*.

Sometimes we not only define exactly but also give examples:

a. Many words are *doublets* (two forms of the same word), for example, *canal* and *channel*, *warden* and *guardian*, *fragile* and *frail*.
b. We get an alloy by melting two or more metals together; for example, *brass* is an alloy of bronze and zinc.

Sometimes the context clue is not for a single word but for a group of words or an idea, for example:

People often wrongly attribute human characteristics to animals. For example, the owl is not wise, the sloth is not lazy, the vulture is not bad.

There are other kinds of definition by example, though sometimes less precise. Note the two sentences below. Which most helps the inexperienced reader?

a. *Epics* are poems like *Beowulf*.
b. *Epics* are long narrative poems telling in dignified style the deeds of a hero or heroes. For example, some epics are *Beowulf, The Aeneid*, and Milton's *Paradise Lost*. However, *Paradise Lost* is a literary epic as contrasted with *Beowulf*, an English national epic.

Definition by Description

It is sometimes possible to define a word by describing the physical qualities or characteristics of the object for which the word stands. It may answer the questions *who, what, when, where, why*, etc. For example:

a. *Sweden* is a country in Europe, east and south of Norway.
b. An *orange* is a round, reddish-yellow, juicy fruit.
c. A *hook* is a curved piece of metal, wood, or other stiff material for hanging things on.

The principal fault with the descriptive context-clue method as illustrated in the above sentences is that it often does not distinguish a word from others in the same class. In the sentences above, notice that Sweden is only one of the countries in Europe that fits the description. Similarly, the description of an orange may fit that of a tangerine or a pomegranate; that of a hook could apply to anything from a clothes tree to a gallows.

What is defined in the following statement? "A _____ has four legs and a back, and you sit on it." Is it a chair? Yes, that fits the definition, but it could also be a horse or a camel. To give a more exact definition, one would have to add more details, such as the fact that the missing word is an article of furniture.

Definition by Comparison and Contrast

This method gives an author an opportunity to stretch the meanings of words and to be creative in his descriptions. Thus comparative definitions often extend beyond simple comparisons to implied ones, using various figures of speech. The comparison clue may range from a simple simile, "the moon is shaped like a ball," to Shakespeare's personification, "the inconstant moon, that monthly changes in her circled orb."

Hence, an author may use simile as a way of defining: "Some roads were once Indian paths. A road, in fact, is like a wide path." Or, like Alfred Noyes, in "The Highwayman," he may use metaphor: "The road *was a ribbon of moonlight*."

Defining by contrast may help the reader by telling him what a word is not. On the whole it is a helpful device, but it does not give the reader an exact meaning of the word being defined. For example:

a. A whale is not a fish.

Although this clue tells us not to classify whales with tuna, sharks, and swordfish, it does not tell us what a whale is, how long it is, what it looks like. However, in a paragraph describing the whale, this clue helps the reader remember to file whales under mammals rather than under fish.

b. One difference between a fish and a bird is that the fish does not have lungs.

You could not describe a fish or a bird from this clue; but you can infer that because a bird has lungs it is adapted to an air environment, and that a fish, without lungs, is not. Thus the effectiveness of the contrasting clue nearly always depends on the reader's experience. Note these sentences:

a. A tomato is not a vegetable.
b. Cleopatra was not an Egyptian.
c. Regular interplanetary travel is not likely to come in this century.

These negative clues do not tell the reader what a tomato is, what nationality Cleopatra was, or when interplanetary travel is likely to come. But it often is enough to give the reader a hint that he has been mistaken in his assumptions, that he must question statements he hears or reads.

Defining by Synonyms and Antonyms

Although a synonym for a word may not have the exact meaning of the defined word, it is often one of the best and shortest defining devices. For example, *bondage* may be defined as "servitude, slavery, serfdom," even though each defining word carries its own particular connotation. It must be remembered that a synonym, to be useful, must be closer to common usage than the original word is. Knowing that *bondage* and *servitude* are synonyms does not clarify the meaning of either word. A simpler synonym should be used, such as *slavery*. Other examples of synonym definitions:

a. *Somnambulism* is the state of sleepwalking.
b. A *gosling* is a young goose; a *gossoon* is a boy.
c. To *expire* is to die.
d. *Archaic* words are old-fashioned.

In addition to learning words through synonyms, the reader can extend his vocabulary and his reading skills by noticing the opposites of words. Authors often use antonyms to show the extremes of objects or ideas: *beginning, ending; alpha, omega; prologue, epilogue; large, small; minimum, maximum; microcosm, macrocosm*. Note the following examples:

a. The boy was *gaunt*, but the girl was *obese*.
b. He was *willing*, but she was *loath* to walk to the game.
c. Even a *prudent* person sometimes makes *rash* judgments.
d. He remembered two lines from *Julius Caesar*:

"*Cowards* die many times before their deaths;
The *valiant* never taste of death but once."

Synonyms and antonyms are therefore concise devices for presenting comparative and contrastive clues, for helping the reader note nuances, and for comparing and classifying concepts. They give a quick means of seeing similarities and differences.

Definition by Apposition

A noun placed next to another noun or pronoun to identify it is called an *appositive* (from Latin *ad*, to + *positus*, put). The appositive clue is a parenthetical word or phrase used to clarify or define. (We do not always use parentheses for a parenthetical expression, although the parentheses are understood to be there.) Usually the reader can easily identify appositive constructions. They are usually set off by commas: "Mr. Hart, *our football coach*, emphasizes good sportsmanship." If appositives are closely tied to the word they explain, no commas are needed: "My *sister Kate* is a tomboy."

Authors often use appositives to avoid verbosity. For example, using an appositive, the writer may make one sentence out of two or three.

a. Abraham Lincoln was our sixteenth president. He was assassinated by John Wilkes Booth in a theater. Booth was a Shakespearean actor.

With appositional phrases, this becomes:

b. Abraham Lincoln, *our sixteenth president*, was assassinated in a theater by John Wilkes Booth, *a Shakespearean actor*.

The appositive context clue may be a word or a group of words that help the reader discriminate between the meanings of unfamiliar words:

a. *Jute*, the *plant*, is grown in India.
b. *Jute*, the *fiber*, is obtained from the jute plant.
c. India exports *jute*, *a long, shiny fiber used to make gunny sacks*, to Europe and America.
d. The *Jutes*, an *early Teutonic tribe*, conquered Britain in the fifth century A.D.

Thus, appositive constructions provide an easily recognized means of defining or clarifying words in context without breaking the flow of the reading content.

Definition by Origin

An explanation of the history of a word can fix its meaning by providing a setting in which the word can be placed and remembered. It is an additional memory device, a filing system in which key words can be stored and from which they can easily be retrieved. For example, we may better remember the expression *table d'hôte* if we also learn that during the Middle Ages most travelers and people who ate at an inn had to sit at "the table of the host (*table d'hôte*)," that is, eat the meal offered at a fixed price.

Learning the origin of a word or phrase helps us file the word in a certain category: medicine, sports, politics, etc. For example, *pork barrel* refers to a government appropriation which benefits only a special group. This dipping-in fund gets its name from the custom of keeping open pork barrels in country stores. Certain customers occasionally helped themselves to the contents of the pork barrel.

The words *lilliputian* or *gargantuan*, used to describe a tiny or a huge object, evoke greater imagery if the reader knows about the Lilliputians in Swift's satiric novel *Gulliver's Travels* and if he remembers Rabelais' *Gargantua and Pantagruel* or knows that Gargantua was originally a helpful giant in French folklore.

In short, it often adds to the connotation of a word to know its origin. It helps the reader to know that *ghastly* is related to *ghost* (from Old English *gast*), that *ambush* is related to *bush* (from Old French *embuscher*, to hide in the bushes), and that the *Mercury, Gemini, Atlas, Saturn,* and *Apollo* spacecraft were named after characters in ancient mythology.

Learning To Recognize Context Clues

Students grow in their ability to use context clues if they practice recognizing the various kinds. The teacher can construct several sentences to illustrate each kind of clue or he may point out random context clues in passages the class may be reading.

The teacher may use several methods. We suggest two: (1) presenting groups of sentences to illustrate one kind of clue, or (2) presenting sentences that typify various kinds, letting the student explain which kind of clue each sentence represents.

The teacher may wish to write several different example sentences defining the same concept (as we have done in the first sentence of each category below), or he may wish to present the sentences in a paragraph containing various kinds of context-clue definitions.

Depending on the level of the student, the teacher might use some of the illustrative sentences below:

Formal Definition

a. *Sportsmanship* is the ability to get along with people not only in athletic competition but in daily life as well.
b. *Filigree* is delicate, ornamental, lacelike work in gold and silver wire.
c. *Latitude* is the distance north or south of the equator measured in degrees.
d. A *plow* is a farm implement used to cut and turn the soil in preparation for planting seed.
e. A *seesaw* is a balanced plank on the opposite ends of which persons sit and move alternately up and down.

Description

a. A good *athlete* usually combines physical skill with strength, alertness of mind, enthusiasm, and teamwork.
b. Through a telescope, *Saturn,* the second largest planet, looks like a big yellow star surrounded by rings.
c. The *griffin* was a mythological monster with an eagle's wings, head, beak, and a lion's body, legs, and tail.

d. A *butterfly*, which is often brightly colored, is a flying insect with four wings, two long feelers, and a sucking beak.
e. The *giant anteater*, which has a tube-shaped head, a long snout, and a large, bushy tail, is about seven feet long.

Example

a. *Sportsmanship* is often demonstrated by two opposing players who shake hands after a contest.
b. Violins, banjos, cellos, harps, lutes, and zithers are *stringed instruments*.
c. Modern airplanes are powered by various kinds of *engines:* piston, fan jet, turbojet, turboprop, and ramjet.
d. *Ant colonies* contain three classes—queens, workers, and males.
e. The following lines constitute a *couplet:*

"O, young Lochinvar is come out of the west!
Through all the wild Border his steed was the best."

Sir Walter Scott, "Lochinvar"

Synonyms

a. *Sportsmanship* is fair play, winning or losing gracefully.
b. *Peanuts* are also known as groundnuts, groundpeas, and goobers.
c. To *matriculate* is to enroll or register, particularly in a college or university.
d. *Flowers* (the blossoms of plants) may bloom in damp ground, deserts, lakes, and oceans.

Comparison

a. A *good sport*, like a modest person, does not seek praise or try to attract attention.
b. *Porpoises* are mammals that look somewhat like small whales.
c. In *As You Like It*, Jaques says, "All the *world's* a stage."
d. The *map of Italy* is shaped like a boot.
e. "Day after day, day after day,
We stuck, nor breath nor motion;
As *idle* as a painted ship
Upon a painted ocean."

Samuel Taylor Coleridge, *Rime of the Ancient Mariner*

Contrast

a. A person who boasts, behaves in a disorderly fashion, or offers excuses in competition is not a good *sport*.
b. Technically, the *peacock* is not the female of the species.
c. The *Latin sentence*, unlike the English sentence, does not depend on word order for meaning.
d. The *size of a plant* is not determined by the size of its seed.

Origin

a. *Sports* probably began as part of training for battle.
b. The Italian word for "fresh" is *fresco*, which gives us the name of a painting done on fresh plaster.
c. The *diesel engine* is named after Rudolf Diesel, a German engineer.
d. The *Magna Carta* (Latin for "Great Charter") is a document signed by King John at Runnymede in 1215 to give the English barons constitutional rights and privileges.
e. *Bisect* means cut in two (*bi*, two + *sect*, cut); *dissect* means cut apart (*dis*, apart + *sect*, cut).

Apposition

a. *Sports*, games or activities that give us pleasure and exercise, are enjoyed by young and old.
b. The word cereal is from *Ceres,* the Roman goddess of grain.
c. *Winston Churchill*, a great British statesman, said, "I have nothing to offer but blood, toil, tears, and sweat."
d. *Sir Walter Scott*, a Scottish novelist, also wrote excellent poetry.
e. *"Wild Bill" Hickock*, an American frontier scout, was a great marksman.

Rating the Effectiveness of Context Clues

The ability to infer the meaning of a word from its context depends on the clues given. For example, in the entry on Daniel Boone in the 1970 *World Book Encyclopedia*, the following sentence appears: "His hair was long and tied in a *queue* (pigtail)." The parenthetical definition insures that the student will know what the word *queue* means.

However, in the expression "the water was gelid," there is only a slight chance that the meaning *frozen* will be correctly inferred. (Of course, related sentences may also contain context clues.)

The following is a series of quotations from Dickens. As you read each item, estimate the chance (high, medium, low) that a student would be able to infer the meaning of the italicized word:

From *The Mystery of Edwin Drood:*

1. Then, follow white elephants *caparisoned* in countless gorgeous colours. (high _____, medium _____, low _____)

2. The choir are getting on their *sullied* white robes.
   (high _____, medium _____, low _____)

3. her flowing brown hair tied with a blue *riband*
   (high _____, medium _____, low _____)

4. Get off your *greatcoat*, bright boy, and sit down here in your own corner. (high _____, medium _____, low _____)

From *Martin Chuzzlewit:*

5. ... but in a very short time the punch within them and the healthful air without, made them *loquacious*, and they talked incessantly.
(high _____, medium _____, low _____)

6. quarts of almonds; dozens of oranges; pounds of raisins; stacks of *biffins*; soup-plates full of nuts
(high _____, medium _____, low _____)

7. Never surely was a pocket-handkerchief taken in and out of a *flat reticule* so often as Mrs. Todger's was, as she stood upon the pavement by the coach-door.
(high _____, medium _____, low _____)

8. "Here am I, sir!" shouted Mark, suddenly replying from the edge of the *quay*, and leaping at a bound on board.
(high _____, medium _____, low _____)

9. "There ain't nothing the matter. I've brought home Mr. Chuzzlewit. He ain't ill. He's only a little *swipey*, you know." Mr. Bailey reeled in his boots, to express intoxication.
(high _____, medium _____, low _____)

Note: After checking these items, the teacher will note that context alone does not always help the reader. In the case of *biffins* (item 6), meaning "red apples," the reader gets a hint of the general meaning of the word by classifying it with the other fruits (oranges, raisins, etc.).

Internal Context Clues

In addition to the external clues discussed above, students should be taught to look for internal ones. Our studies indicate that many students from the fourth to the twelfth grades have not learned to use internal clues to help figure out word meaning. The internal context-clue method is not used because students are not taught early and regularly that prefixes, roots, and suffixes have meaning. However, through a systematic approach to the study of roots and affixes at various grade levels, the student can learn a number of key word parts; he can easily acquire the habit of analyzing whole words by breaking them into their meaningful parts. Much lip service has been paid to word analysis, but little has been done on a systematic basis.

A student who is led to discover that the prefixes *non-, un-,* and *in-,* mean "not" immediately gets the idea of negation when he sees the words *nonvoter, nonreligious, nonfiction; unable, unfit, unalterable; inactive, inappropriate, inalienable.* Likewise, the student can be taught to notice key roots in words. For example, *scrib* or *script* in a word gives the reader a clue that the word has something to do with writing, as in *scribe, inscribe, postscript, scripture,* and *prescription.*

Learning key word parts from words already known, such as *auto-*

(self) in *auto*mobile, is an effective way of using transfer of knowledge to other words: *autograph, autobiography, automotive, automatic, autocratic*—all carrying the meaning of *self*.

Knowing the key suffixes can also give a clue to the general classification of a word. Once the student learns that *-less* at the end of a word may mean *without*, he can apply the concept to many words: *heartless, penniless, senseless, beardless*.

The importance of learning to use the internal context clue can be seen by scanning typical material read by elementary, high school, and college students. As the material becomes more abstract, and therefore more difficult, the number of words that are compounds of key roots and affixes becomes greater. Names of inventions, the areas of politics, medicine, etc., often use Greek or Latin words, or compounds of Greek and Latin combining forms (roots): *television* (Greek *tele-*, distant + Latin *vis-*, see); *appendicitis* (from Latin *appendic-*, hang on + Greek *-itis*, inflammation); *bursitis* (from Latin *bursa*, purse, sac + Greek *-itis*).

The authors believe that the skillful, systematic presentation of key roots and affixes can, over a period of time, increase the general level of vocabulary by half a grade.

Teaching students to use internal context clues to deduce the meaning of unfamiliar words is one way to sharpen the student's understanding of word inflection.

Our study of children's knowledge of words indicates that, in general, students are not making associations between such words as *reduce* and *reduction, receive* and *reception*. Our studies show that 74 percent of fourth-graders know *pretend;* but *pretense*, the noun form of *pretend*, is not commonly known until the twelfth grade (at a score of 78 percent). Therefore students need more practice in writing inflectional endings and adding plural and possessive suffixes (*-s, -es, -'s, -s'*): *boy, boys, boy's, boys'; church, churches, church's, churches'*.

Additional writing exercises might include using the past tense of regular verbs (*-d, -ed, -t*): *agree, agreed; show, showed; dream, dreamed* (or *dreamt*); or the participial endings (*-ing, -ed, -en, -n*): *show, showing; play, played; forget, forgotten; bite, bitten; draw, drawn.* In short, the student needs to learn early that by understanding these changes (inflections) he can recognize whether an event is taking place or has taken place, or that one or more persons or objects are being discussed.

Lessons can easily be presented that show how inflection changes the following:

1. Case
Nominative	girl
Possessive	girl's
Nominative	who
Possessive	whose
Objective	whom

2. Number
Nominative	girl, girls
Possessive	girl's, girls'

3. Person
First person	go
Third person	goes

4. Tense
Present	show
Past	showed
Present participle	showing
Past participle	shown

5. Gender
Male	Female
lion	lioness
god	goddess
Francis	Frances
Louis	Louise
Joseph	Josephine

The teacher might present an exercise involving gender by pointing out that one of the uses of inflection is to change masculine nouns to feminine nouns. One of the most common endings for feminine nouns is -ess: prince, princess; duke, duchess; actor, actress; emperor, empress.

Practice in using inflectional suffixes such as the plurals s and es, the y in fizzy, or the ly in happily helps students adjust to the habit of using derivational suffixes (derived from another language), for example, the French diminutive -ette, meaning "little," as in statuette.

Knowing useful suffixes can make the difference between verbosity and concise speech and writing. For example, if the student knows the suffix -oid (shape, form), instead of saying that an object is "shaped like a sphere," he can say "spheroid." Instead of saying "a person who is skilled in biology," he can say "biologist," for the Greek suffix -ist indicates a person who is skilled in or who practices a specified activity.

Frequent guided practice in using suffixes is a step forward in generalizing and conceptualizing. By using suffixes the student classifies objects according to a general characteristic. For example, a small kitchen can also be called a kitchenette. Thus the student can learn to categorize other words ending in -ette as referring to something small: dinette, novelette. The student can easily learn to use additional suffixes meaning "small," such as -let (streamlet, booklet, droplet); -ling (duckling, gosling, sapling, suckling); and -cule, -ule, -icle (molecule, globule, particle).

As we have previously suggested, exercises that help the student classify help him conceptualize. The learner categorizes before he discriminates. The small child may call all women mama (he categorizes) before he distinguishes between his mother and his aunt (he discriminates). We can help the student gain vocabulary skills by organizing some of his learning in advance and setting up a learning system for him. Once the student recognizes the meanings of key suffixes such as diminutives in words he knows, he will use less energy learning other words formed from the same suffixes.

Context Clues and Reading Skills

As we have pointed out, the particular meaning of a word generally depends on its relationship to other words in a phrase or sentence—its context. Therefore, the student needs to learn how to use the various kinds of context clues discussed previously to determine meanings of words in reading, thus bringing meaning to the printed page to get meaning out of it.

But, we should not assume that using context clues to determine word meaning will solve most vocabulary problems. Some teachers overestimate the power of context clues to reveal word meaning. Sometimes context does not help, as in the sentence "The boy spoke with alacrity." Alacrity might mean bitterness, sympathy, cheerfulness—any number of things.

Throughout this book we stress the need for attention not only to the context within which words are found but also to the structure and analysis of the word itself. The relative importance of the word *per se* as pointed out by Charles H. Judd many years ago still holds true:

> It has been said that a word which does not call up some past experience is an utterly barren item in the pupil's mental life. The truth is that many words when first heard do not arouse interpretive experiences. It is enough in these cases if the word becomes a motive for seeking an idea. If the pupil is aroused by a word to look for further experiences to attach to it, then the word which is at first without meaning may be a very potent instrument of instruction.[1]

One of the fundamental aims of an effective vocabulary program is to draw the student's attention to words. Heavy reliance on context clues alone as a word-study method may defeat this purpose. Therefore, we suggest that in teaching vocabulary the teacher needs to be aware of many ways of making students word-conscious, of helping them develop a conscience about word discrimination and precision somewhat in the way they develop a spelling conscience.

In developing word sensitivity the student needs to make use of context clues in relation to other methods of vocabulary study. He needs to see the relationship existing between cognates, derivatives, and word families. He needs to learn the significance of word inflection, the process of word formation by means of roots, prefixes, suffixes, and compounds. And he needs to be aware of the roles of the various parts of speech, such as connectives (prepositions and conjunctions) that relate ideas and concepts.

Teaching the Use of Context Clues

The following lessons provide specific techniques for teaching students how to use context clues. A variety of approaches is suggested. The teacher may wish to use the content in the lessons provided or to use the form of the lesson and supply his own content. The content included here is not aimed at a specific grade level.

If someone says "It's cold in here. Shut the _____," the student can guess that the missing word is *door* or *window*, because the words *cold* and *shut* give him a clue. If he is reading the sentence "My uncle has an *orchard*. We'll stop and get some _ _ p l _ _ and _ _ _ c h _ _," both *orchard* and the letters *pl* and *ch* give him clues to the missing words.

The exercises that follow test the student's ability to supply a missing or partially missing word, given a context containing external and internal clues. Using the underlined clues in the sentences below, the student fills in the right word:

1. On the day Bill became <u>ten</u> our neighbor gave him a b i r t h d a y party.
2. Mary likes <u>music</u>. She's getting a job with an o r c h e s t r a.
3. Mrs. Jones likes <u>plays</u>. She's joining the d r a m a t i c s club.
4. The Indians used c a n o e s to travel on <u>rivers</u>.

[1]Charles Hubbard Judd, *Reading: Its Nature and Development* (Chicago: The University of Chicago Press, 1918), p. 178.

5. Using a d e r r i c k the workman raised a huge stone slab to the top of the building.
6. At the boarding school the boys slept in a d o r m i t o r y.
7. Government by the people is called d e m o c r a c y.
8. At the museum we saw the skeleton of a prehistoric animal—the d i n o s a u r.

Context Clues Used with Root or Affix Meanings

The student uses external context plus root or affix clues to fill in the blanks. He covers the answers in the margin and checks his own work.

Answers

reversed

telegraph

audience

vision

intersection

exports

monochromatic

microscope

1. The halfback *ran to the opposite side of the field.* The halfback _ _ v e r s e d his field.
2. Morse invented *a device to send messages to distant places by wire.* Morse invented the _ _ _ _ g r a p h.
3. The speaker was pleased by the applause of *the people listening to him.* He was pleased by the applause of the a u d _ _ _ _ _.
4. Bill needs glasses because of the poor *condition of his eyes.* Bill's v i s _ _ _ is not good.
5. The car slowed as it neared the *place where the roads crossed.* The car slowed at the i n _ _ _ s e c t _ _ _.
6. The United States *sends* wheat *out of* the country. The United States _ _ p o r t s wheat.
7. Ann's painting used *tints and shades of one color.* The painting's color scheme was _ _ _ _ c h r o m a t i c.
8. Scientists look at germs through an *instrument that magnifies small objects.* They look at germs through a _ _ _ _ _ s c o p e.

Programming Exercises (Self-Instructing, Self-Correcting)

The ease with which students do each of the following exercises will depend on the number of learning steps used. Less able students will require more letter clues than abler students. These exercises are meant particularly for the upper grades. Some best fit high school seniors. But the form of the lesson, with easier content, can be used for the elementary grades.

In the sample exercise below, the student reads the sentences and fills in the blanks. He covers the answers on the side and checks his answers as he proceeds.

Answers

flood

flooded

flooded

temple

1. The high water *inundated* the countryside. High waters often cause a f l _ _ _.
The countryside was probably f _ _ _ _ _ d.
Inundated means f _ _ _ _ _ _.
2. The Chinese worshiped in an ancient *pagoda.* A pagoda is probably like a *church* or a t _ _ _ _ e.

At this point the teacher might point out that certain words often give clues to the meaning of other words. For example, in sentence 1 above, the phrase "high waters" gives a clue to the meaning of *inundate*. In sentence 2, "worshiped" helps us figure out the probable meaning of *pagoda*.

However, clues to the meaning of words are not always present. For example, in the sentence "He walked reluctantly to the store" there are no clues to help us figure out the meaning of *reluctantly*. Does it mean slowly, quickly, cheerfully, angrily, eagerly, hopefully, willingly, or unwillingly?

Students may practice looking for context clues in the following sentences.

Answers

sad	1. Mary was crestfallen at the low grade she received. *Crestfallen* means downhearted or s _ _.
critical	2. The carping critic didn't like the play and said so. He found fault with the actors' performances. He was severely critical. *Carping* means highly c _ _ _ _ _ _ _.
lack	3. The teacher was worried about John's *apathy*. She wanted to know what caused his l _ _ _ of interest in his studies.
indifference	His _ _ _ _ _ _ _ _ _ _ _ _ disturbed her. Lack of interest
apathy	toward something can be called indifference or a _ _ _ _ y.
short	4. "If you fail, it's your own fault," Jim said. "If," Bill replied *laconically*.
laconically	Bill wastes no words. He speaks briefly. His answers are s _ _ _ t and to the point. Bill answered l _ _ _ _ _ _ _ _ _.
secret	5. Cicero's enemy, Catiline, had a *clandestine* meeting with a band of conspirators in a secret place. Catiline did not want the meeting publicized.
clandestine	Catiline wanted to keep the meeting a s _ _ _ _ _.
	A secret meeting is often called c _ _ _ _ _ _ _ _ _ _.

At the conclusion of the exercise, the teacher might discuss with the class the "clue words" that give some hint about the meaning of the italicized words. For example, in item 4, clues to the meaning of *laconic* are "wastes no words," "briefly," "short," and "If."

Words in Various Contexts

The student is presented with words in context and asked to identify their meaning. The answers are underlined for the teacher's convenience.
   The student underlines the best choice:

1. The *Pentagon* building in Washington has
   a. four angles   b. six sides   c. <u>five angles</u>   d. three sides
2. An *ephemeral* thought lasts
   a. <u>a short time</u>   b. a long time   c. forever   d. for years
3. An imperious person is
   a. inactive   b. <u>commanding</u>   c. mysterious   d. watchful

Note that the context doesn't offer any clues to the meaning of the italicized words. Unless the reader knows *penta* (five) or *gon* (angle), no internal clues are offered. Thus the appearance of the word in context does not automatically indicate meaning to the reader.

4. The *culpable* manager finally admitted that the error was his. *Culpable* probably means
   a. freed   b. <u>guilty</u>   c. sorry   d. grieving
5. At the burial a *dirge* was sung. *Dirge* means
   a. lullaby   b. chant   c. <u>funeral song</u>   d. tune
6. A man who is *intransigent* is
   a. <u>uncompromising</u>   b. traveling   c. ineffective   d. frail
7. Caesar's *pugnacious* warriors were
   a. cowardly   b. homesick   c. <u>fond of fighting</u>   d. hungry
8. Monkeys are *arboreal* animals that live
   a. on the ground   b. <u>in trees</u>   c. in water   d. in deserts
9. The students' themes never seemed to suit the *captious* professor. *Captious* means
   a. respected   b. diligent   c. witty   d. <u>faultfinding</u>
10. We had to agree with him. His argument was *irrefutable*. *Irrefutable* means can't be
   a. logical   b. <u>disproved</u>   c. proved   d. expressed

Now the student is asked to match column A with column B to further test his understanding of these words out of context.

Answers	A	B	
1 c	1. culpable	a. relieved	k. fond of fighting
2 e	2. ephemeral	b. commanding	l. can't be disproved
3 h	3. pentagon	c. guilty	m. abundant
4 j	4. dirge	d. of trees	n. faultfinding
5 g	5. intransigent	e. not lasting	
6 k	6. pugnacious	f. reluctant	
7 d	7. arboreal	g. uncompromising	
8 b	8. imperious	h. five-angled	
9 n	9. captious	i. doubtful	
10 l	10. irrefutable	j. funeral song	

Compounds

A single word takes on various meanings when used as part of a compound. In the following exercises, the student chooses from lists the best word for each blank. He should be able to defend his choice through the contextual clues provided. The most probable answers are given in the blanks. Follow-up discussion of this type of lesson will help students refine their techniques for recognizing context clues. (Note: The tests increase in difficulty from Section A to Section C.)

41

Section A

The student chooses from the list below.

1. birdhouse
2. firehouse
3. statehouse
4. playhouse
5. treehouse
6. dollhouse
7. henhouse
8. schoolhouse
9. farmhouse

1. The _statehouse_ is located in the capital city.
2. In the early days, many children went to a little red _schoolhouse_.
3. Billy fetched the eggs from the _henhouse_.
4. The boys enjoyed playing Tarzan in their _treehouse_.
5. Having put out the fire, the men rode back to the _firehouse_.
6. The children pretended they were grownups in the _playhouse_.
7. The little girl enjoyed playing with the _dollhouse_.
8. When our dog barked the wren flew straight to the _birdhouse_.

Section B

The student writes the best word in each blank.

1. glasshouse
2. courthouse
3. snowhouse
4. bunkhouse
5. teahouse
6. guardhouse
7. smokehouse
8. warehouse

1. Many useful articles such as jars and glasses are made in a _glasshouse_.
2. The factory stores its material in a _warehouse_.
3. We were impressed by the beauty of the Japanese _teahouse_.
4. An igloo is a _snowhouse_.
5. After a hard day on the range, the cowboys retired to the _bunkhouse_.
6. Soldiers who go AWOL usually end up in the _guardhouse_.
7. A place for curing meat is called a _smokehouse_.
8. A place where lawsuits are tried is called a _courthouse_.

Section C

The student chooses the best word for each blank.

1. clearinghouse
2. doghouse
3. slaughterhouse
4. greenhouse
5. powerhouse
6. hothouse
7. icehouse
8. clubhouse
9. roundhouse
10. coffeehouse

1. An unbeaten football team is often called a _powerhouse_.
2. The engineer drove the locomotive into the _roundhouse_.
3. A man whose wife is irked with him is in the _doghouse_.
4. Before refrigerators were invented the _icehouse_ was very important.
5. Samuel Johnson often met his witty friends in a London _coffeehouse_.
6. A great number of magazines are sent to a _clearinghouse_ for distribution.
7. Leaving the eighteenth green, the golfers went into the _clubhouse_.
8. Another name for a hothouse is a _greenhouse_.
9. Another name for a _slaughterhouse_ is an abattoir.

Confused Pairs

The student often needs context clues to distinguish between certain words. For example, the words below are sometimes confused because they may sound somewhat alike. The student puts the correct word in the blank. The teacher may wish to remove the answers before duplicating material.

1. dual—duel
   Fighting a _duel_ is against the law.
   John has _dual_ mufflers on his hot rod.
2. whether—weather
   We must go _whether_ we like it or not.
   I hope the bad _weather_ doesn't delay our train.
3. formally—formerly
   The boy who won the 440 was _formerly_ a miler.
   Everyone at the ball was _formally_ dressed.
4. stationery—stationary
   It isn't difficult to hit a _stationary_ target.
   She used her best _stationery_ for writing personal letters.
5. except—accept
   He will probably _accept_ the invitation.
   Except for girls, nothing seems to interest him.
6. all together—altogether
   His understanding of the matter is _altogether_ wrong.
   They were _all together_ for the first time in ten years.
7. complement—compliment
   Miss Brown paid me a _compliment_ about my work.
   Their different points of view _complement_ each other.
8. illegible—eligible
   His writing is _illegible_.
   She was not _eligible_ for the contest.
9. illusion—allusion
   His _allusion_ to Achilles' heel was lost on us.
   A nightmare is only an _illusion_ and not reality.

Connective Words and Phrases in Context

One reliable test of a person's reading skill is his ability to understand the meaning of a conjunction or a preposition as it appears in context. Often we must study the context of the sentence to know what meaning to ascribe to prepositions and conjunctions. Note the following examples given below.
1. He went home *for* (to get) his baseball mitt.
2. He went home *for* (because) it was getting late.

The word *for* may be a preposition or it may be a conjunction. Some writers avoid using the word *for* meaning "because" to avoid this ambiguity.

The words *since* and *as* also cause ambiguity. What does the following sentence mean?

"*As* John was visiting his hometown, he stopped in to see the mayor."

Here two meanings of *as* are possible: (1) John stopped in to see the mayor *because* he was in town, and (2) John stopped in to see the mayor *during the time that* he was in town.

Such discriminations may not become apparent without considerable practice. Teachers are therefore advised to present these conjunctions or other connecting words in a variety of contexts until their students can read and use them effectively. For example, students should learn that *for* may mean "because," "in place of," "in honor of," "in spite of," "suited to," depending on the context. The following is a short list of such connectives that the teacher can use as an illustration.

Word	Meaning	Context
1. for	because	The scouts hurried back to camp <u>for</u> it was getting dark.
	in place of	Around the campfire, the boys used tree stumps and logs <u>for</u> stools.
	in honor of	The boys had a surprise birthday party <u>for</u> Don.
	in spite of	<u>For</u> all his embarrassment, he really enjoyed the party.
	suited to	He was happy with his present—a book called *Indian Tales <u>for</u> Boys*.
2. since	from then until now	I have not seen him <u>since</u> Christmas.
	because	I have not seen him <u>since</u> Christmas is the only time we get together.
3. yet	still	He is there <u>yet</u>.
	nevertheless	He is there, <u>yet</u> he does not enjoy it.
4. whatever	exactly what	<u>Whatever</u> are you doing?
	no matter what	<u>Whatever</u> you are doing, please put it aside for a moment.
	at all	He is doing nothing <u>whatever</u>.
5. before	previously	He had been there <u>before</u>.
	in front of	<u>Before</u> him stood the judge.
6. but	only	He was <u>but</u> a little child when his parents were imprisoned.
	except that	I would love to go to the movies, <u>but</u> I don't have enough money.
	yet	She was uneducated <u>but</u> a wise judge of people.

Another way to introduce these connectives is to present the following diagrams. After discussing them, the teacher might test the students by presenting the diagrams *without the words,* asking the students to use a connective that describes the drawing. Advanced students might be asked to supply an illustration of their own.

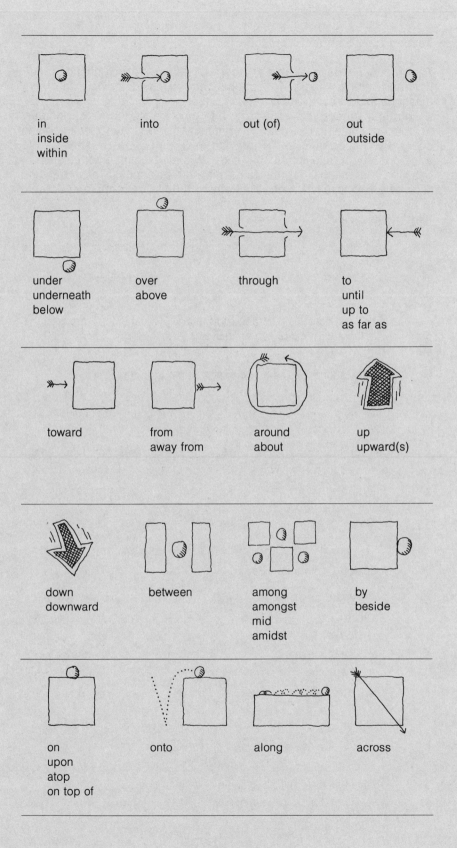

in
inside
within

into

out (of)

out
outside

under
underneath
below

over
above

through

to
until
up to
as far as

toward

from
away from

around
about

up
upward(s)

down
downward

between

among
amongst
mid
amidst

by
beside

on
upon
atop
on top of

onto

along

across

45

Testing for Conjunctive Meaning

The student needs to be able to recognize a variety of conjunctions, their use, and their meaning. The critical reader must be aware that conjunctions show how ideas are related.

For the teacher's convenience and to give the student an opportunity to conceptualize the variety of conjunctions, we have classified the connectives according to the function they perform in the sentence. In addition to being classified, the material is programmed so the student can find out whether he has used the correct connective (immediate knowledge of results). If he is incorrect, he can correct his own work.

Part I: Added Ideas

The student chooses the conjunction that introduces an added idea to the one stated first.

Answers

1. John was glad he had gone to the zoo. The animals were exciting.
b   ___, there was lots of candy and ice cream to eat.
   a. But   b. Besides   c. So   d. Thus

c   2. He was strong, ___ he could easily lift the big rock.
   a. though   b. but   c. and   d. although

d   3. John started down the road, ___ Jack came running along behind him.
   a. if   b. whether   c. although   d. and

a   4. Joe and Mary went to the lake to fish. ___, they went horseback riding.
   a. In addition   b. While   c. For instance   d. Though

c   5. Jim did well in his classwork. ___, the teacher told him his homework had been excellent.
   a. So   b. However   c. Furthermore   d. As

Part II: Choosing Conjunction Pairs

c   1. ___ Mary ___ Judy broke the glass, but no one knew which one did it.
   a. Both—and   b. Neither—nor   c. Either—or
   d. Not only—but also

a   2. Because of the rain, ___ Joe ___ Peter was able to go to the game.
   a. neither—nor   b. whether—or   c. either—or   d. either—and

c   3. There were ___ many clowns at the circus ___ many exciting wild animals.
   a. either—or   b. as—as   c. not only—but also   d. both—and

b   4. ___ Jane ___ Ann are twelve.
   a. Neither—nor   b. Both—and   c. Either—or   d. But—also

a   5. I cannot say ___ Bill ___ Henry is the taller boy.
   a. whether—or   b. neither—nor   c. both—and   d. since—and

Part III: Contrast

Here the student chooses the conjunction that expresses a difference or contrast between ideas.

Answers

a   1. It was eight o'clock in the evening, ____ there was still some light in the sky.
   a. but   b. thus   c. because   d. besides

c   2. The children enjoyed eating the large birthday cake. ____, many of them woke up the next morning with a stomach ache.
   a. But also   b. Thus   c. However   d. Otherwise

b   3. It was a difficult tune to play. ____ Howard played it without making any mistakes.
   a. Besides   b. Nevertheless   c. Consequently   d. So

a   4. Edward had had a good night's sleep. ____ he was very tired in the morning.
   a. Still   b. And   c. Since   d. Otherwise

c   5. Aunt Mary gave the baby his bottle, ____ he continued to cry.
   a. therefore   b. so   c. yet   d. besides

   6. There were many happy people in the stadium enjoying the game.
a   ____ there were also many sad fans outside who had not been able to get in.
   a. On the other hand   b. For instance   c. Otherwise
   d. Besides

Part IV: Example, Explanation

The student chooses the conjunction that expresses an example of a previously stated idea.

Answers

c   1. Many exciting things happened at the game. ____, the Cardinal manager was thrown out of the game for arguing with the umpire.
   a. However   b. In addition   c. For instance   d. So

b   2. Prepositions are connectives, ____, they show the relationship between a noun or pronoun (the object) and some other word in the sentence.
   a. while   b. that is   c. however   d. except

a   3. Owning a car can be very expensive. ____, you have to buy gas, insurance, new tires, and keep the car in good condition.
   a. For example   b. Moreover   c. So   d. Yet

d   4. The boys enjoy many winter sports ____ ice fishing, skating, skiing, and tobogganing.
   a. but   b. except   c. likewise   d. such as

Part V: Result

The student chooses the conjunction that introduces the result of an idea stated earlier.

Answers

b   1. Eddie had run all the way up the hill, ___ he was very tired when he reached the top.
      a. but   b. so   c. though   d. because

a   2. Jim felt tired after the game, ___ he decided not to go to the movies with the other boys.
      a. hence   b. because   c. still   d. besides

c   3. All the lockers looked alike. ___ it was difficult for Don to decide which one was his.
      a. But   b. Since   c. Therefore   d. Unless

a   4. The speaker held the attention of the audience throughout. ___ he was able to get his points across easily.
      a. Thus   b. Because   c. But   d. Although

c   5. There were many children at the party but Tom did not know any of them. ___, he felt very lonely.
      a. Yet   b. Nevertheless   c. For that reason   d. Otherwise

b   6. Philip had borrowed Tom's baseball mitt. ___ Tom could not play ball when Fred asked him.
      a. Still   b. Consequently   c. Provided that   d. Yet

Part VI: Condition

The student chooses the conjunction that helps express a condition under which an event will happen.

Answers

b   1. ___ you will cook the meal, I will buy the groceries.
      a. Because   b. If   c. Since   d. Although

a   2. Harry won't go ___ Mary goes with him.
      a. unless   b. but   c. still   d. yet

a   3. Joe said he would go on vacation ___ he could earn enough money.
      a. if   b. and   c. although   d. even though

d   4. Tom's father will buy the bicycle ___ Tom pays half the cost.
      a. even though   b. because   c. consequently
      d. provided that

b   5. He said the tour would leave sharply at nine ___ enough people were there on time.
      a. except that   b. provided   c. still   d. although

Part VII: Causation, Purpose

The student selects the conjunction that indicates the cause or purpose expressed in the first part of the sentence.

Answers

b   1. Tom was angry ___ Jim had broken the electric train.
        a. although   b. because   c. and   d. besides

c   2. Mary opened the door ___ her dog could come in out of the rain.
        a. otherwise   b. but   c. so that   d. even though

b   3. ___ Jerry didn't come on time was a mystery to Bill.
        a. Because   b. Why   c. If   d. Whether

d   4. The ground was still wet ___ it had rained the night before.
        a. and   b. so   c. although   d. since

c   5. Dick could not see the parade ___ he was standing behind a lamppost.
        a. yet   b. although   c. as   d. or else

a   6. He didn't know ___ Bob was so late.
        a. why   b. as   c. since   d. whether

b   7. The lawyer said his client was not guilty ___ he had been home the night of the robbery.
        a. whether   b. since   c. still   d. so

Part VIII: Choice or Alternative

The student chooses the conjunction that best expresses a choice between ideas or consequence of an idea.

Answers

a   1. Either Mike ___ Dave took the bat, but we don't know who did it.
        a. or   b. and   c. otherwise   d. but

d   2. It's a good thing they ran home ___ they might have been caught in the rain.
        a. but   b. whether   c. besides   d. or else

a   3. He must study ___ he will fail.
        a. or   b. accordingly   c. in addition   d. though

d   4. You had better leave now, ___ you will be late.
        a. if   b. even though   c. besides   d. otherwise

d   5. John's only line in the battle scene was: "We must stand together ___ we will be conquered."
        a. even though   b. although   c. still   d. else

c   6. She kept eating candy ___ she was dieting.
        a. besides   b. since   c. although   d. whether

Part IX: Concession

The student chooses the conjunction that shows or indicates a concession (a yielding), a choice, or an exception to the main idea stated.

Answers

d   1. Andy didn't care ___ Peter came or not.
      a. until   b. although   c. except   d. whether

a   2. Roy didn't want to go swimming ___ it was a nice, warm day.
      a. even though   b. if   c. because   d. besides

d   3. The president gave a good speech, ___ there were times when he lost his place.
      a. because   b. if   c. since   d. although

d   4. He studied hard for the test ___ he would rather have been at the game.
      a. furthermore   b. however   c. so   d. although

d   5. It doesn't matter to me ___ Bill brings his friend to the party.
      a. while   b. since   c. although   d. whether

a   6. Mary came to the party ___ she didn't like the hostess.
      a. even though   b. when   c. whether   d. still

4

Synonyms
Antonyms
Homonyms

Synonym, antonym, and *homonym* are words formed from the Greek root *onym* meaning "name." Synonym, from *syn* (together, like) + *onym* (name), means a word grouped with other words in the same classification according to general meaning: *repeat, iterate; walk, saunter; weaken, enervate.*

Synonyms not only help us convey general ideas, they also help us make fine distinctions between the meaning of words. Although the words *under, below,* and *beneath* are generally synonymous, we do not say we are living "beneath a democratic form of government"; we say "under a democratic form of government." A suspect is not "below the protection of the police"; he is "under the protection of the police."

Contrasted with the synonym is the antonym (*anti* or *ant,* against), a word that means the opposite of another word: *weak, strong; near, far; typical, atypical.* Like the study of synonyms, the study of antonyms can help students learn words through the process of classification.

Words that sound the same are called homonyms (*homo,* same): *sight, cite, site; bear, bare.*

Synonyms in Vocabulary Development

Studying synonyms is an excellent time-saving approach to vocabulary study. Comparing synonyms helps the student see the relationship between words of similar meaning. It also helps the student generalize and classify words and concepts.

Synonyms are substitute words. They allow us to express the same idea in a variety of ways, although the overall context, the setting, the mood, the tone of the speaker (or writer) may dictate the choice of the synonym to be used. Although the study of lists of synonyms helps the student to classify general concepts (large and small, high and low, etc.), of greater value is the development of the student's ability to make fine distinctions between one synonym and another.

But making fine distinctions is not easy. Students can best learn to distinguish the fine shades of meaning of words by (1) noting words that belong to certain classes or groups such as "big" (*large, great, huge, bulky, massive, corpulent, monumental, prodigious, titanic, elephantine, herculean, leviathan, behemoth, macroscopic, cyclopean, gargantuan, Brobdingnagian*), and then (2) using them as the situation demands.

Denotation and Connotation

The study of synonyms offers the teacher an excellent opportunity to teach concepts relating to the denotative and connotative aspects of vocabulary development. Dictionaries generally list the denotation (literal meaning) of a word. Such definitions (approximate at best) may be expanded by illustrative material such as pictures and synonyms.

But definition by synonym is useful only if the synonym is less difficult than the word being defined: density is thickness (the latter word is easier). David Berlo points out, in regard to denotative defining, that "when words are equally unfamiliar, we have gained nothing—and we probably have lost the receiver in the process."[1]

The denotative meaning of a word is often stretched to the connotative —an added meaning that the word implies. For example, *dense,* meaning thick, may be extended connotatively to mean *dense,* thick-headed.

As opposed to the denotation, the connotation of a word is the circle of ideas and feeling surrounding that word and the emotions that the word evokes. We can see the difference between denotation and connotation in the synonyms for a given word. Each of the following synonyms for *prison,* for example, carries a different connotation: *house of correction, workhouse, jail, lockup, dungeon, hoosegow, calaboose, jug, pokey, clink, penitentiary, correctional facility.*

Note also that these connotative meanings involve varying experiences. Each synonym for *man,* for example, has, in addition to its denotation, its own special connotation: *male, husband, father, son, uncle, grandfather, brother, widower, gentleman, fellow, chap, beau, buddy, guy, blade, rake.*

Making Discriminations

It is clear that students cannot easily make fine distinctions between one synonym and another without a great deal of experience and practice. In vocabulary study, it is impractical to assume that fine discriminations can be made before gross discriminations are conceptualized.

Therefore, we suggest that the student be provided with ample opportunity to make gross discriminations. He needs to hear and see broad relationships between synonyms, see how words can be classified in broad categories or filing systems. He needs to work with various forms of classification exercises.

This means that groups of like words must be presented so that the student can classify them under general topics. For example, synonyms for *govern* may be listed: *rule, direct, manage, control, conduct, lead, regulate, guide, steer, supervise, oversee, legislate, administer, take charge, head up.* This gives the student a general storage and retrieval device for remembering words. Choice of synonym and finer discrimination will come with practical application. For example, in an essay assignment, the student may want to differentiate between *govern* and *rule.* Research will reveal to him that while both *govern* and *rule* imply authority, *govern* connotes knowledge and ability in judgment; *rule* suggests an unquestioned use of power, an exercise of the will. *Govern* also connotes *stability, wisdom, uprightness; rule* may connote *dictatorship, autocracy, arbitrariness,* even *tyranny* or *despotism.* Out of context, *govern* connotes "goodness"; *rule* connotes "badness."

[1]David Berlo, *The Process of Communication* (New York: Holt, Rinehart & Winston, 1960), pp. 193–194.

In general, the connotation of *govern* is good. It implies knowledge, temperance, discretion. Thus metaphorical extension of *govern* allows us to say that we govern our passions, govern our actions, etc. On the other hand, the general connotation of *rule* is bad. A despot rules others. Subjugated people live under the rule of a foreign power. Such distinctions make it necessary to choose appropriate synonyms, a process that takes considerable time to learn. There is need, therefore, for much discussion in class concerning the connotations of various synonyms. Classifying words that are alike in their general denotation can begin a process of examining a synonym from general to finer shades of meaning.

The use of word lists in the lessons that follow (1) introduces the student to certain words and their general use, and (2) gives him a way of filing, remembering, retrieving, and using synonyms without undue emphasis at first on exact meaning. Familiarization with connotative meaning will come with practice in contextual framework, the use of models of writing, and class discussion of fine distinctions and shades of meaning. The general procedure in vocabulary development, in language development, is usually from the general to the specific.

Classifying Synonyms

The process of classification such as we find in a thesaurus allows the student to see at a glance the variety of synonyms used to express a given idea. It can be an effective prelude to and motivation for dictionary study.

Presenting groups of synonyms representative of a general concept also gives the student the added advantage of seeing comparative relationships and fine dissimilarities between words having a narrower, more specific meaning than the broad topic under which they are classified. Under the general term *little*, for example, the reader will note more specific concepts such as *small, tiny, minute, diminutive, undersized, miniature, microscopic, dwarf, elf, pygmy, mote, jot, iota, smidgen, molecule, Lilliputian,* etc.

On his own, or as a part of class activity, the student consulting the dictionary for the different shades of meaning conveyed by these words finds that both *little* and *small* refer to size and are often used interchangeably. But in general, *little* refers to degree of quantity, whereas *small* refers to number, measure, or bulk. We do not say "She has *small* money," we say "She has *little* money." The word *diminutive*, from Latin *minus* (less), particularly refers to size in relation to some other object, a size less than normal, or smaller than it ought to be. For example, a dwarf is a *diminutive* person.

The general meaning of *little* can be expressed in many ways:

A far-distant ship may be described as a *speck* on the horizon.

The lengthy speech was summed up *in a nutshell*.

There was not a *particle* of truth or a *grain* of truth in what he said.

A person may care not a *jot* or not a *whit* for your opinion.

Small details are often called *minutiae.*

There was only a *scintilla* of hope left.

There was a *touch* of sarcasm in his reply.

There is more than a *modicum* of truth in Franklin's aphorisms.

A *sprinkling* of wit brightens a speech.

A *tinge* of yellow will add color to the somber tones.

"One *touch* of nature makes the whole world kin."
  —Shakespeare, *Troilus and Cressida*

He was just a *snip* of a boy.

They considered her small contribution as a widow's *mite.*

Let's not discuss *minor* matters.

"She leet no *morsel* from hir lippes falle,
Ne wette hir fingers in hir sauce depe."
  —Chaucer, "The Prioress," *Prologue to the Canterbury Tales*

A *drop in the bucket*

The arrangement of synonyms for study encourages the student (1) to generalize and (2) to make distinctions between one word and another, resulting in discriminating choice. But studying synonyms is more than making generalizations and fine distinctions. By working with synonyms the student becomes involved in effective dictionary study, noting usage, connotations, word histories, allusions to prose and poetry, historical and fictional characters, and historical and current events. Thus the study of synonyms is more than the study of words of similar meaning. It is also the study of the relationships of words and, therefore, the relationship of concepts. It includes the connotative qualities, the subtle ideas and emotions surrounding words as interpreters of experiences.

The exercise below can help students build discriminative vocabularies. Additional pairs of words are provided for discussion.

Instructions: The student puts a check next to the word in each pair that usually has a bad connotation.

1. __ leave
   _X_ abandon

2. __ pacify
   _X_ appease

3. _X_ flatter
   __ praise

4. _X_ arrogance
   __ pride

5. __ humanitarian
   _X_ do-gooder

6. __ thrifty
   _X_ stingy

7. __ subtle
   _X_ crafty

8. __ sensitive
   _X_ thin-skinned

9. _X_ retreat
   __ withdraw

10. _X_ sanctimonious
    __ devout

11. __ visionary
    _X_ seer

12. __ bold
    _X_ reckless

55

Additional Pairs

flighty	big eater	postpone	prisoner
giddy	glutton	procrastinate	jailbird
squeamish	abdomen	aid	slender
dainty	belly	abet	skinny
scheme	drug	comply	plump
plan	dope	agree	fat
senile	overripe	cheap	short
elderly	rotten	inexpensive	squat
advantage	two-faced	jailer	immature
upper hand	insincere	guard	green
beg	beast	foul	cleanse
petition	creature	unclean	purge
discipline	debate	eat	advanced
punish	argue	devour	precocious
loiter	nose	clever	arty
linger	snout	sly	artistic

Antonyms in Vocabulary Development

Another effective way to help students' vocabulary skills is through the study of *antonyms*. Although the term *antonym* might not be used in the early grades, first- and second-graders can master the concept of opposites—*up, down; hot, cold; high, low.* Antonyms can range from easy words such as *dirty, clean; praise, blame* to harder ones such as *maculate, immaculate; eulogy, dyslogy; supernal, infernal.*

Just as no two synonyms are exactly similar in meaning, few antonyms are the exact opposite of other words. But just as we can conveniently group synonyms according to their general meaning, we can also classify certain terms as being opposite or nearly opposite in meaning. Moreover, helping students learn the "concept of opposites" helps them extend the concept of negativism in language, the concept first met in the use of conjunctions such as *but, however,* etc. Classifying antonyms, therefore, helps the student to think in terms of contrasting or contradictory concepts and statements.

In learning a new word the student should, whenever possible, learn the opposite of that word. Thus *female* would be taught with *male, wife* with *husband, feminine* with *masculine, lady* with *gentleman, nannygoat* with *billygoat, doe* with *buck, peahen* with *peacock.* At a higher level we would teach *pessimism* with *optimism, substructure* with *superstructure, omega* with *alpha, perigee* with *apogee, diurnal* with *nocturnal, postlude* with *prelude, eutrophy* with *dystrophy, Brobdingnagian* with *Lilliputian.*

Studying antonyms can be a part of word analysis. For example, the teacher might present pairs of words to illustrate how their antonymy evolves from the addition of certain prefixes and suffixes to roots or to base words. Some antonyms formed from prefixes are listed below.

Prefixes Forming Antonyms

The student is given one word in a word-pair and is asked to supply its antonym.

indoors—*out*doors
inflate—*de*flate
inhale—*ex*hale
inhibit—*ex*hibit
underfed—*over*fed
underhand—*over*hand
underrate—*over*rate
prepaid—*post*paid
pretest—*post*-test
ante meridiem—*post* meridiem
prewar—*post*war
antebellum—*post*bellum

prefix—*suf*fix (*sub* + *fix*)
exhume—*in*hume
progress—*re*gress
propel—*re*pel
prologue—*epi*logue
moral—*a*moral; *im*moral
subscription—*super*scription
subordinate—*super*ordinate
subhuman—*super*human
immigrate—emigrate
explode—*im*plode
exit—*ad*it

Suffixes Forming Antonyms

worth—worth*less*
bearded—beard*less*
useful—use*less*
guilty—guilt*less*

hopeful—hope*less*
graceful—grace*less*
colorful—color*less*

Suffixes Denoting the Opposite Gender

lion—lion*ess*
emperor—empr*ess*
host—host*ess*
widow—widow*er*
hero—hero*ine*

Paul—Paul*ine*
Joseph—Joseph*ine*
Robert—Roberta
Charles—Charl*ene*
sultan—sultan*a*

Note: Purists may suggest that a true antonym must be formed from a root word rather than through the addition of affixes. For example, it might be said that an antonym of *kind* is *cruel*, not *unkind*; that an antonym of *happy* is *sad*, not *unhappy*. However, the majority of persons view *unhappy* as an antonym of *happy* and on the whole have chosen through usage to disagree with the purists.

Notice, however, that the prefix *in-* does not always mean "not." *Inactive* is the opposite of *active*, but *infix* is not the opposite of *fix*. In the words *inside* and *income*, *in-* means "in" or "within." *Invaluable* is not an antonym of *valuable*, since it means "valuable beyond measure." Here the *in-* is called an *intensive* (an emphasizer of the root word *valuable*).

Using antonyms as a part of word analysis involves continual use of transfer and review, relating one concept to another, making associations, building new knowledge on old. Using the concept of opposites, the teacher can emphasize the idea of comparing through contrasting. Several approaches are suggested in the lessons that follow. One suggested method is to list words the student needs to know in English, health, history, and other subjects and to include or discuss antonyms for them. An exercise in health, at various levels of learning, might include noting the difference between: *healthy, ailing; sane, insane; robust, frail; sanitary, unsanitary; nutrition, malnutrition; aseptic, septic; eupepsia, dyspepsia; eugenic, dysgenic; eutrophy, dystrophy.*

Antonyms might also be studied as adjectives: *early, late; smooth, rough; strong, weak; merry, gloomy; sweet, sour; humble, proud; thin, fat; generous, selfish.*

Therefore, to increase vocabulary size and sensitivity, we suggest regular, guided practice in the use of like and unlike concepts. The teacher can best encourage the use of synonymy and antonymy as a method of vocabulary study by presenting the student with ample and varied examples.

Recognizing Antonyms in Context

Students can sharply increase their ability to recognize words by noting not only words that are similar but also words that are dissimilar. In these exercises, they are to choose the word that, in general, conveys the opposite meaning of the other words in the group. Exercises may be presented in the context of word groups or in sentences. The exercises below are suitable for elementary students. The student underlines the *antonym* in each group:

Answers

tiny	1. big	huge	tiny	large
him	2. him	her	she	lady
wife	3. he	sir	wife	master
fellow	4. female	woman	fellow	girl
feminine	5. gentleman	husband	feminine	masculine
buck	6. cow	buck	doe	hen
sow	7. bull	boar	sow	stallion
ice	8. fire	ice	flame	boil
frost	9. spark	blaze	frost	smolder
simmer	10. frostbite	wintry	simmer	shiver
feeble	11. powerful	firm	strong	feeble
hardy	12. flabby	hardy	delicate	frail
thin	13. thick	outspread	broad	thin
wide	14. narrow	slim	wide	thin
rude	15. rude	respect	courtesy	polite
mannerly	16. uncivilized	mannerly	sarcastic	vulgar

The student reads each sentence and underlines the word in parentheses that cannot complete the sentence correctly.

Answers

tiny	1. A *huge* bear is a (big, tiny, large) animal.
him	2. A pronoun for *lady* is (she, her, him).
fellow	3. The *feminine* gender includes (woman, girl, fellow).
frost	4. *Heat* is related to (flame, blaze, frost).
simmer	5. The *wintry* air made the girl (shiver, cold, simmer).
surly	6. A *gentleman* is (respectful, courteous, surly) to a guest.
plod	7. John had to (scurry, plod, scamper) to get to class *on time*.
dry	8. The windows were *damp* because of the (humid, moist, dry) weather.
burlap	9. The slick surface of the rock was almost as *smooth* as (glass, burlap, silk).
descent	10. The hikers watched the mountain climbers' (descent, rise, ascent) to the top.

Recognizing Antonyms

Using words appropriate to the level of the class and subjects being studied, the teacher can present exercises in which the student gets practice in recognizing antonyms. In the following exercises, some of which are appropriate for high school students, the student concentrates on finding antonyms. The teacher will note that indirectly the exercises also give the student an opportunity to learn or recall appropriate synonyms.

The student reads each sentence and checks the word that best completes the sentence—the antonym of the italicized word.

Answers

courageous	1. A person who is *cowardly* is the opposite of a person who is courageous ___, timid ___, fearful ___.
traitorous	2. The king's *loyal* subject would not be traitorous ___, faithful ___, devoted ___.
prodigal	3. A *parsimonious* person may not be described as stingy ___, miserly ___, prodigal ___.
penury	4. Ancient *wealthy* chieftains did not live in opulence ___, penury ___, affluence ___.
humble	5. Conceited people are not humble ___, egotistic ___, vain ___.
indiscernible	6. If you can *see* an object, it is not indiscernible ___, manifest ___, perceptible ___.

Selecting Antonyms

Note that three of the words in line 1 below have a favorable connotation and one word does not. Three words in line 2 have an unfavorable connotation and one word does not. The words in 3 and 4 follow the same pattern but are more suitable for students at a higher level.

The student underlines the word that doesn't belong in each group.

Answers	Good and Bad			
corruption	1. goodness	decency	corruption	honesty
blameless	2. mischievous	blameless	wicked	bad
malignity	3. malignity	rectitude	respectability	modesty
integrity	4. baseness	integrity	profligacy	depravity

	Cowardly and Courageous			
cowardice	1. cowardice	boldness	bravery	courage
gallant	2. timid	bashful	fearful	gallant
timorous	3. intrepid	undaunted	timorous	dauntless
craven	4. craven	audacious	valorous	resolute

	Attractive and Unattractive			
homely	1. beautiful	handsome	homely	pretty
refined	2. refined	coarse	clumsy	awkward
uncouth	3. exquisite	fascinating	delicate	uncouth
polished	4. barbarous	polished	vulgar	boorish

	Thoughtful and Thoughtless			
foolish	1. careful	cautious	foolish	watchful
thoughtful	2. simple	thoughtful	silly	brainless
fatuous	3. fatuous	prudent	sagacious	sage
discreet	4. discreet	preposterous	imbecilic	irrational

	Dull and Clever			
dull	1. quick	dull	alert	sharp
active	2. slow	idle	active	lazy
indolent	3. diligent	industrious	indolent	sedulous
vigorous	4. slothful	vigorous	inert	quiescent

	Able and Unable			
idiocy	1. genius	idiocy	skill	ability
wisdom	2. silliness	foolishness	wisdom	folly
shallowness	3. faculty	perspicacity	shallowness	aptitude
capacity	4. incompetence	capacity	obtuseness	ineptness

	Truth and Falseness			
false	1. real	false	proven	true
actual	2. actual	questionable	mixed	clouded
deceptive	3. legitimate	authentic	unadulterated	deceptive
veritable	4. veritable	fallacious	spurious	counterfeit

Homonyms in Vocabulary Development

Homonyms are phonemically identical words — words identical in pronunciation but different in meaning and derivation. They are often a problem in spelling. Although homonyms are pronounced alike (*pear, pair*), contextual relationship generally indicates the meaning. When one woman tells another "There's a big sale on today," it's clear that she is not talking about a sailboat.

One of the chief problems in homonymy involves correctly transferring spoken meaning to print. Homonyms often can cause spelling difficulties such as those found in *there, their; to, too, two; principle, principal; whose, who's; new, knew; miner, minor; ascent, assent; cannon, canon; auger, augur.*

As with the study of synonyms and antonyms, the student needs much practice discriminating between one homonym and another. Students in the early grades can work with homonyms such as *no, know; bear, bare; fair, fare;* and *be, bee.* At the higher levels, students can deal with homonyms such as *colonel, kernel; ale, ail;* and *right, rite.* Some students might be challenged by *rye, wry; leaf, lief; hue, hew; freeze, frieze; brooch, broach; fold, foaled; fate, fete; metal, mettle; throws, throes; liken, lichen; sign, sine.*

Teachers can use written exercises to give the student an opportunity to discriminate between the spelling and meaning of homonyms. Most homonyms could be added to any list of spelling demons. Adequate practice with an ample number of examples can help the student become sensitive to the different spelling of two or three words that sound alike, such as *air, heir, ere.*

In the lessons that follow, we suggest several approaches for presenting homonyms. Exercises designed to emphasize the different spellings of homonyms may include merely arranging homonyms in pairs and asking students to note the difference in spelling and meaning between them. Students might practice with exercises in which they are given a word and asked to supply its homonym:

bear, __bare__ ; *fur,* __fir__ ; *grate,* __great__ ; *stare,* __stair__ ; *cite,* __sight__ .

Younger students can be given letter-space clues such as

grate, g r e a t; *hour,* o u r .

Older students may be asked to supply the homonym without the letter spaces. They can also be given definitions, descriptions, or related words and asked to match them with the proper homonym, for example:

a. justice __right__   b. ceremony __rite__

As a variation of this method, the teacher might supply definitions and ask the student to write the appropriate homonym to suit the definition. This procedure may also be reversed: the student supplies a definition for each homonym. Short practice periods of this kind can help the student fix the spelling and meaning of troublesome homonyms and can help him avoid errors such as *pane* for *pain, rein* for *reign,* and *vain* for *vein.*

Homonyms can be a source of ambiguity in speech: "He gave his (*all, awl*) for the cause." In general, the meaning of a word depends on its referent, which is defined by contextual relationship. Homonyms, like other words, are often metaphorized, and this extension of meaning, this duality, enables us to say, "A butcher can split hares without making subtle distinctions." (By the way, *hairbrained* is also spelled *hare-brained*.) Homonyms, then, are a source of puns and part of the fun in language.

Using a master list such as the one in this unit, the teacher can select pairs of words likely to be confusing to his students.

The process of merely presenting these word-pairs together (1) calls the student's attention to the homonymy involved and (2) focuses his attention on the differences in spelling. Thus, elementary students may be asked to distinguish between *tale* and *tail* and may practice with *see, sea; to, two, too; red, read; hear, here; their, there.*

The teacher might construct exercises in which the student chooses the correct homonym:

1. The engine's wheels are made of (steal, steel) .
2. They took an aerial picture of the golf (course, coarse) .
3. Play (fair, fare) .
4. They met on the (stairs, stares) .
5. The boys (peeked, peaked) through the fence.
6. (Meet, Meat) me at five.
7. The (capitol, capital) of Australia is Canberra.
8. The procession (past, passed) by the monument.
9. The two enemies made (piece, peace) .
10. The third baseman (through, threw) the ball away.
11. The German Porsche (lead, led) all the way.
12. They spent a (weak, week) together.
13. The cargo is iron (ore, oar) .
14. We stayed for the (hole, whole) game.
15. The (breaks, brakes) need relining.
16. The librarian's remark was ambiguous: No talking (aloud, allowed) .
17. His grades were below (sea, C) level. In short, he was sunk.
18. The magician said "Come (forth, fourth) ." The horse came fifth and lost the race.

Puns are not necessarily humorous. Ancient peoples first used the idea in pictograms in which, for example, a drawing of an eye might have stood for the pronoun "I." This kind of writing, called syllabic, is still used. For example, a puzzle might include a picture of a "walking log" (a travelog):

Therefore, syllabic writing (also known as *rebus* writing) is a system in which symbols may stand for one or more words or syllables. Thus a picture of a *bee* and the figure *4* might represent *before*.

Discriminating Between Homonyms

Learning to discriminate between words that sound alike but have different meanings increases a student's awareness of vocabulary. The student gets practice in spelling by filling in the letter spaces. These sentences may be written on the board, duplicated, or used with the overhead projector. The answer key on the left may be included on the student's copy if the teacher wishes to make the exercise self-corrective.

Answers

brake	1. It stops a car. It sounds like *break*. _ _ _ _ _
fir	2. It's wood. It sounds like *fur*. _ _ _
steel	3. It's hard. It sounds like *steal*. _ _ _ _ _
dyeing	4. It colors. It sounds like *dying*. _ _ _ _ _ _
stationery	5. It's paper. It sounds like *stationary*. _ _ _ _ _ _ _ _ _ _
heal	6. Wounds do it. It sounds like *heel*. _ _ _ _
fare	7. You pay it. It sounds like *fair*. _ _ _ _
flu	8. It makes you sick. It sounds like *flew*. _ _ _
pane	9. It's in a window. It sounds like *pain*. _ _ _ _
tacks	10. They're sharp. It sounds like *tax*. _ _ _ _ _
weak	11. It's the opposite of strong. It sounds like *week*. _ _ _ _
peal	12. It's the ring of a bell. It sounds like *peel*. _ _ _ _
peddle	13. It means sell. It sounds like *pedal*. _ _ _ _ _ _
wrap	14. It's done to presents at Christmas. It sounds like *rap*. _ _ _ _
haul	15. It means drag or carry. It sounds like *hall*. _ _ _ _
stakes	16. They're used for tents. They sound like *steaks*. _ _ _ _ _ _
pier	17. Boats stop here. It sounds like *peer*. _ _ _ _
aisle	18. You walk down it. It sounds like *isle*. _ _ _ _ _
sum	19. It's the answer to an addition problem. It sounds like *some*. _ _ _

Note: The following items might challenge more able students.

review	20. It means look over again. It sounds like *revue*. _ _ _ _ _ _
gambol	21. Sheep do it. It sounds like *gamble*. _ _ _ _ _ _
baron	22. It's a title. It sounds like *barren*. _ _ _ _ _
assent	23. It means agree. It sounds like *ascent*. _ _ _ _ _ _
bazaar	24. Things are sold here. It sounds like *bizarre*. _ _ _ _ _ _
augur	25. He's a fortune-teller. It sounds like *auger*. _ _ _ _ _

The teacher or a group in the class might take each of these homonyms and write a reverse exercise on it. For example:

1. It happens to an egg. It sounds like *brake*. _ _ _ _ _
2. It's an animal skin. It sounds like *fir*. _ _ _
3. It's taking what doesn't belong to you. It sounds like *steel*. _ _ _ _ _ _

The Relationship of Ideas in Words

Logical thinking is often based on the ability to understand the relationship of ideas represented by words. The following exercises give the student practice in seeing these conceptual relationships. The student

63

fills in the blanks with the related word. Exercises like these are often found in tests of mental ability.

1. *Hot* is to __cold__ as *fast* is to *slow*.
2. __Sweet__ is to *sour* as *good* is to *bad*.
3. *Up* is to *down* as __right__ is to *wrong*.
4. __Love__ is to *hate* as *weak* is to *strong*.
5. *Buy* is to *sell* as *stop* is to __go__.
6. __Old__ is to *new* as *ancient* is to *current*.
7. *Laugh* is to *cry* as __smile__ is to *frown*.
8. *Rich* is to __poor__ as *wealth* is to *poverty*.
9. __Happy__ is to *sad* as *joyful* is to *melancholy*.
10. __Heaven__ is to *earth* as *spiritual* is to *physical*.
11. __Male__ is to *female* as *bull* is to *cow*.
12. *Inch* is to *foot* as __month__ is to *year*.
13. __Cup__ is to *pint* as *pint* is to *quart*.
14. __Word__ is to *sentence* as *link* is to *chain*.
15. __Water__ is to *fish* as *air* is to *man*.
16. *Sand* is to *beach* as __water__ is to *ocean*.
17. *Coal* is to __black__ as *snow* is to *white*.
18. *Grass* is to __green__ as *cardinal* is to *red*.
19. *Fire* is to *hot* as *ice* is to __cold__.
20. *Branch* is to *trunk* as __finger__ is to *hand*.
21. *Thirst* is to *water* as __hunger__ is to *food*.
22. *Gosling* is to __goose__ as *kitten* is to *cat*.
23. __Star__ is to *constellation* as *sentence* is to *paragraph*.
24. __Soft__ is to *pillow* as *hard* is to *rock*.
25. *One* is to __two__ as *solo* is to *duo*.
26. *Hawk* is to __dove__ as *war* is to *peace*.

The teacher of literature might find exercises like this useful in helping students recall authors and their works. It might spark interest for review purposes or be used as a testing-teaching device.

Answers

Poe	1. P _ _ is to *raven* as *Shelley* is to *skylark*.
eagle	2. *Keats* is to *nightingale* as *Tennyson* is to e _ _ _ _.
daffodil	3. *Burns* is to *rose* as *Wordsworth* is to d _ _ _ _ _ _ _.
mouse	4. *Blake* is to *tiger* as *Burns* is to m _ _ _ _.
Puck	5. *The Tempest* is to *Ariel* as *A Midsummer Night's Dream* is to P _ _ _.
Huck	6. *Dickens* is to *Oliver* as *Mark Twain* is to H _ _ _.
Walden Pond	7. *Wordsworth* is to *Lake District* as *Thoreau* is to W _ _ _ _ _ P _ _ _.
Buck	8. *Lassie Come Home* is to *Lassie* as *Call of the Wild* is to B _ _ _.
Excalibur	9. *Prince Valiant* is to *The Singing Sword* as *King Arthur* is to E _ _ _ _ _ _ _ _.
Scrooge	10. *George Eliot* is to *Silas Marner* as *Charles Dickens* is to S _ _ _ _ _ _.
Alice	11. *Johanna Spyri* is to *Heidi* as *Lewis Carroll* is to A _ _ _ _.
Homer	12. *Aeneid* is to *Virgil* as *Iliad* is to H _ _ _ _.

Depending on the level of the students, the teacher might vary this exercise by including statements that are either true or false.

Answers

True 1. *Antony* is to *Cleopatra* as *Romeo* is to *Juliet*.
False 2. *David* is to *Delilah* as *Paris* is to *Helen*.
True 3. *Hemingway* is to *novel* as *Browning* is to *poem*.
False 4. *Hercules* is to *Goliath* as *Huck Finn* is to *Tom Sawyer*.
True 5. *David* is to *Absalom* as *Daedalus* is to *Icarus*.

Rhyming Opposites

An additional way of using synonyms and antonyms in relation to logical thinking is to present them in *rhyming* form as illustrated below. Elementary students may find this form more interesting. Students might also be encouraged to try making their own rhyming items. Note that connotative meanings need not be consistent, nor should there necessarily be a relationship between each set of opposites. It suffices that the students recognize that if one pair is antonymic then the other is also.

1. *Stop* is to *go* as *yes* is to _no_.
2. *Coldness* is to *heat* as *sour* is to _sweet_.
3. *Good* is to *bad* as *glad* is to _sad, mad_.
4. *Right* is to *wrong* as *weak* is to _strong_.
5. *Bottom* is to *top* as *start* is to _stop_.
6. *Early* is to *late* as *love* is to _hate_.
7. *Young* is to *old* as *hot* is to _cold_.
8. *Sickness* is to *health* as *poverty* is to _wealth_.
9. *Wet* is to *dry* as *laugh* is to _cry_.
10. *Up* is to *down* as *smile* is to _frown_.
11. *Sell* is to *buy* as *your* is to _my_.
12. *Low* is to *high* as *live* is to _die_.

More difficult words (both antonyms and synonyms) might be tested by the same form:

Answers

equestrian	1. *Foot* is to *pedestrian* as *horse* is to e _ _ _ _ _ _ _ _.
morose	2. *Near* is to *close* as *sanguine* is to mo _ _ _ _.
melancholy	3. *Foolishness* is to *folly* as *sad* is to me _ _ _ _ _ _ _ _.
concise	4. *Unpleasant* is to *nice* as *wordy* is to co _ _ _ _ _.
expire	5. *Despise* is to *admire* as *live* is to e _ _ _ _ _.
epilogue	6. *End* is to *prologue* as *beginning* is to e _ _ _ _ _ _.
titanic	7. *Gigas* is to *gigantic* as *Titan* is to t _ _ _ _ _ _.
macrocosm	8. *Aquarium* is to *microcosm* as *ocean* is to ma _ _ _ _ _ _ _.
morosity	9. *Sad* is to *ecstasy* as *blithe* is to mo _ _ _ _ _ _.
herculean	10. *Pygmy* is to *pygmean* as *Hercules* is to h _ _ _ _ _ _ _ _.
Sagittarius	11. *Water* is to *Aquarius* as *bow* is to S _ _ _ _ _ _ _ _ _.
Oxonian	12. *Boston* is to *Bostonian* as *Oxford* is to O _ _ _ _ _ _.

Spelling Homonyms

Students often need practice in relating meanings, definitions, and spellings of words that sound alike but have different meanings. In the following exercise the student draws a line from the word or phrase in column B that makes him think of the word in column A. The words in column B are not necessarily definitions. The first one is an example.

A	B		A	B
bear	uncovered		led	heavy
bare	furry		lead	guided
fair	taxi		steal	rail
fare	weather		steel	take
there	not here		red	robin
their	of them		read	studied
blew	wind		sow	wheat
blue	bird		sew	stitches
idol	lazy		isle	in water
idle	hero		aisle	in church
bow	ship		but	goat
bough	tree		butt	except
base	fiddle		bell	ring
bass	headquarters		belle	girl
birth	baby		be	hum
berth	pier		bee	exist
beat	strike		beach	tree
beet	vegetable		beech	sand

(In the example, "bear" is connected to "furry" and "bare" is connected to "uncovered" by crossing lines.)

Further Homonyms for Study

air	ate	bazaar	bow	bridal	cask
heir	eight	bizarre	beau	bridle	casque
ale	auger	bier	bowl	broach	cellar
ail	augur	beer	boll	brooch	seller
all	aye	bin	boy	bury	chews
awl	eye	been	buoy	berry	choose
altar	bail	bole	brake	by	choir
alter	bale	boll	break	buy	quire
ant	ball	bore	braze	cannon	clime
aunt	bawl	boar	braise	canon	climb
arc	baron	bored	breach	carrot	close
ark	barren	board	breech	carat	clothes
assent	bate	born	bred	caret	colonel
ascent	bait	borne	bread	karat	kernel

core	ferule	heart	lye	oar	racket
corps	ferrule	hart	lie	ore	racquet
				o'er	
course	fir	heel	maid		rain
coarse	fur	heal	made	one	rein
		he'll		won	reign
creek	flee		male		
creak	flea	here	mail	oral	raise
		hear		aural	raze
crews	flew		mane		
cruise	flue	him	main	pair	rap
	flu	hymn		pear	wrap
cue			marry	pare	
queue	flour	hoard	merry		read
	flower	horde		pale	reed
current			maul	pail	
currant	fold	holy	mall		real
	foaled	wholly		palate	reel
dam		holey	maze	pallet	
damn	fore		maize		reck
	four	horse		pane	wreck
dear		hoarse	meed	pain	
deer	foul		mead		right
	fowl	hour		patients	write
desert		our	meet	patience	
dessert	fourth		meat		rime
	forth	hue	mete	paws	rhyme
die		hew		pause	
dye	frieze		metal		ring
	frees	knows	mettle	peak	wring
do	freeze	nose		pique	
dew			mein		rock
	gamble	leaf	mean	pearl	roc
doe	gambol	lief		purl	
dough			might		rode
	gate	leak	mite	peddle	road
dun	gait	leek		pedal	
done			minor		roe
	gauge	lee	miner	peel	row
earn	gage	lea		peal	
urn			moat		roll
	gnu	lei	mote	piece	role
ewe	knew	lay		peace	
yew			morn		root
	great	lesson	mourn	pier	route
eyelet	grate	lessen		peer	
islet			muse		rows
	grown	liar	mews	plane	rose
faint	groan	lyre		plain	
feint			need		rude
	guild	liken	knead	plum	rood
faker	gild	lichen	kneed	plumb	
fakir					ruff
	guilt	lo	night	pole	rough
fate	gilt	low	knight	poll	
fete					rung
	hail	load	no	pray	wrung
feet	hale	lode	know	prey	
feat					rye
	hare	lone	none	rabbit	wry
feign	hair	loan	nun	rabbet	
fain					sale
	haul	loot	not	rack	sail
	hall	lute	knot	wrack	

seam	sight	son	sunny	the	waste
seem	site	sun	sonny	thee	waist
	cite				
sear		soul	surf	threw	wave
seer	sign	sole	serf	through	waive
sere	sine				
		stare	surge	throws	way
see	signet	stair	serge	throes	weigh
sea	cygnet				
		stationery	tale	time	we
seed	shoe	stationary	tail	thyme	wee
cede	shoo				
				toe	
seen	skull	steak	taught	tow	wear
scene	scull	stake	taut		ware
				two	
sell	slay	steal	tax	to	week
cell	sleigh	steel	tacks	too	weak
sense	slight	step	tea	vale	whole
cense	sleight	steppe	tee	veil	hole
sent				vein	
cent	so	stoup	team	vain	wood
scent	sew	stoop	teem	vane	would
serial	soar	strait	tear	wait	wreak
cereal	sore	straight	tare	weight	reek

Summary

It is useful to teach the concepts *synonym, antonym,* and *homonym* together, stressing the similar structure and the common root (*onym*) of these three words. The study of synonyms involves noting shades of difference in meanings. Synonyms can be used to define.

For example, *prodigious* may be defined as "huge," the easier word defining the harder. But synonyms can also be used to classify words in broad, general terms, as in a thesaurus.

Antonyms can be used to teach the concept of opposition in language. The student can learn that there is an implied relationship in apparently opposite ideas. We understand *dark* because we know *light.*

Antonyms can be used in word-analysis activities involving prefixes and suffixes: able, unable; active, inactive; bearded, beardless.

Homonyms can be used to sharpen semantic and spelling skills. Thus students learn to discriminate between words such as *sale, sail; there, their; principle, principal; colonel, kernel.*

The study of synonyms, antonyms, and homonyms enables the student to develop the range and depth of his concepts. He learns to see difference where he previously saw only similarity, and vice versa. Thus, as in all effective vocabulary study, the learner develops a web of relationships, learns new meanings, files them, and is able to recall them readily.

5

Word
Origins

Why should students study word origin? There are three main reasons: (1) The study of word history can help develop word-consciousness, (2) it can help the student develop an interest in word study, and (3) it can function as a memory device by providing additional context.

Visualizing a given word in a certain setting helps us remember the word. The student may more readily remember the word *fauna* (animal life in a certain period of time or a certain part of the world) if the teacher also teaches *flora* (plant life) and points out that in mythology, *Faunus* (god of animal life) was the brother of *Flora* (goddess of flowers and plants). Thus the phrase "fauna and flora."

The concept of association, seeing existing relationships between words, is central in effective vocabulary study. In studying the prefix *tri-* (three) the student may learn *trident* (a three-pronged fork). However, *trident* will have greater meaning for him when he reads a description or sees a picture of Neptune, the mythical god of the sea, holding a trident in his hand.

Given Names

Words, like persons, have a history; they came out of a need to communicate. Each person's name has a history. Thus the teacher might introduce the study of word origins by calling students' attention to the origins of their own names. He could begin by pointing out that the name *Bernard* means "bold bear," and *Rosabel* means "fair rose."

The teacher might make a list of common first names and their original meanings and can point out that some names come from flowers, birds, legend, mythology, and ancient history. Some names come from the Bible; *Abraham,* for example, means father, or leader of the people, in Hebrew.

As a beginning point, the origin of several first names can be discussed:

Flora: Latin "flower"
Florence: Latin "flowering" (related to *Flora*)
Amanda: Latin "worthy of love"
Angela: Greek "messenger," "angelic"
Annette: French "little Ann"
Annabel: Latin "beautiful Ann"
Dorothy: Greek "gift of God" (from *doron,* gift + *theos,* God)
Helen: Greek "bright as the dawn"
Eileen: Irish form of Helen
Alexander: Greek "aid to men" (from Greek *alexo,* aid + *aner,* man)
David: Hebrew "beloved"
Donald: Celtic "proud chief"
Charles: Teutonic "strong"
Frederick: Teutonic "peaceful ruler"
John: Hebrew "the Lord is gracious"
Ivan: Russian version of "John"

Some students may want to know where their last names come from. A boy may want to know why his name is *Smith* instead of *Brown*. Here the teacher might remind students that names, like other words, have meaning. Surnames (last names) sometimes come from the name of a town or a description of the place where the earliest members of the family lived. For example, the name *Douglas* comes from a section of Scotland near the Douglas River. The names of towns usually come from some physical characteristic or landmarks of the area where the town was built. For example, *Burton* (a town in England) means hill town. *Akron*, Ohio, is built on high ground (from Greek *akros*, highest). The name of the Acropolis (a city built on a hill) is derived from the same Greek word.

Hatfield means wooded field. The name *Lane* was used by a person who lived in a lane. And persons named *Wall* got their name because they lived near a wall.

A last name may be the result of a physical trait of a family: *Brown* (dark hair or complexion); *White* (light hair, fair complexion); *Black* (black or dark); and *Gray* (old, gray).

Other names are not so obvious. *Boyd* means yellow-haired; *Russell* means red-haired; *Lloyd* means gray or dark (similar to the names of Brown and Black).

The teacher might point out some of the more obvious occupational names such as *Baker, Carpenter, Smith, Tanner, Miller, Tinker* (mends pots and pans), *Cooper* (barrelmaker). Many other surnames are derived from occupations. Two of the most common are *Smith* and *Wright.* Both words mean "maker." A man named *Arkwright* was a maker of chests (from Latin *arca*, chest).

After students have learned the meaning of *Smith* and *Wright*, the teacher might ask them to guess the meaning of such names as *Arrowsmith* (maker of arrows), *Cartwright* (maker of carts), and *Wainwright* (maker of wagons). (A list of surnames and respective occupations is included in the lessons in this unit.)

The teacher might point out that parents often gave their children names they hoped their offspring would live up to. In early American times, girls were sometimes called *Faith, Hope, Charity, Purity, Patience, Humility,* and even *Silence.* Some girls are named after flowers or gems: *Daisy, Pansy, Lily, Pearl, Opal, Ruby. John* and *William* have long been the most popular names for boys; *Mary* for girls.

The teacher might find the following list helpful.

Some Common First Names

Boys

Albert: noble, bright
Alexander: aid to men
Andrew: manly
Arnold: eagle strength
Charles: strong
Christopher: Christ-bearer
Daniel: God is my judge

David: beloved
Donald: proud chief
Edgar: fair protector
Edward: guard of goods
Francis: free
George: farmer
Gregory: watchful

Guy: leader
Henry: home lord
Herman: army man
John: God is gracious
Joseph: he shall increase
Leo: lion
Louis: famous fighter
Martin: (of Mars) warlike
Matthew: gift of the Lord
Michael: Who is like God?
Patrick: noble

Paul: little
Peter: rock
Philip: lover of horses
Raymond: quiet protector
Richard: bold fighter
Roger: famous spear
Roy: king
Steven: fitly crowned
Thomas: twin
Timothy: one who honors the Lord
Victor: conqueror

Girls

Alice: noble
Amy: beloved
Ann: grace
Barbara: stranger
Bonny: little good one
Carol: joyful song
Clara: bright
Deborah: bee
Diana: goddess of the moon
  and the hunt
Dolores: sorrow
Donna: lady
Dorothy: gift of God
Elizabeth: oath of God
Eve: life, lively
Flora: flower
Frances: free
Gertrude: spear, strength
Gloria: glorious; song of praise to God

Grace: thanksgiving
Irene: peace; messenger of peace
Iris: rainbow
Judith: praised; Jewish woman
Kathleen: pure
Laura: laurel, victory
Margaret: pearl
Martha: lady, mistress
Mary: bitterness; wished-for child
Maureen: a form of Mary
Melissa: honeybee
Patricia: noble
Phyllis: a green leaf or bough
Regina: queen
Sophia: wisdom
Stella: star
Susan: lily
Vera: truth
Vivian: full of life

We often find famous surnames honored as given names: Washington Irving, Jefferson Davis, Lincoln Steffens, Franklin D. Roosevelt. The fictional character Robinson Crusoe got his first name from his mother's maiden name.

Nicknames have been popular since ancient times. *Plato,* meaning broad, is a nickname that stuck because of Plato's broad shoulders. Many nicknames are descriptive: *Shorty, Slim, Schnozzle, Red, Rusty.*

Initials often serve as names for famous political or literary figures: JFK (John Fitzgerald Kennedy), LBJ (Lyndon Baines Johnson), FDR (Franklin Delano Roosevelt), GBS (George Bernard Shaw). Often only the first two letters are used with the surname: P. T. Barnum, J. P. Morgan, A. A. Milne, H. G. Wells.

Combined names and initials may have humorous intent or results: Bob B. Good, Jack B. Quick, June First, Dewey Knight, Ima Hogg, Ima Wunder, U. R. Rong. Of course, names like these are puns, and the teacher may wish to use them as an introduction to the study of names in general. Students might collect odd double-meaning names found in newspapers and magazines.

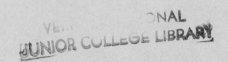

Surname Quiz

To point up the fact that surnames have meaning, the teacher might construct tests like the following, using a variety of appropriate surnames. (The key on the left may be covered and used later to check the answers, or it may be deleted and retained by the teacher.)

	A		B		
c	1. Taylor	a. woman baker		k. archer	
g	2. Wheelwright	b. barrelmaker		l. bailiff	
d	3. Butler	c. clothesmaker			
a	4. Baxter	d. bottlemaker			
b	5. Cooper	e. arrowmaker			
e	6. Fletcher	f. meat cutter			
f	7. Carver	g. wheel maker			
l	8. Bailey	h. knife sharpener			
k	9. Bowman	i. female brewer			
i	10. Brewster	j. shepherd			

Here is an additional test the students might try:

b	1. Ambler	a. woolworker	j. roofer
e	2. Cantor	b. horseman	k. potmaker
a	3. Carder	c. clerk	
f	4. Chandler	d. cowherd	
c	5. Clark	e. singer	
d	6. Crocker	f. candlemaker	
j	7. Decker	g. leather worker	
h	8. Hooker	h. fisherman	
i	9. Flesher	i. butcher	

Note: The teacher may wish to construct additional tests from the following list. If their own names are not found here, students may be interested in looking for them in a dictionary or encyclopedia.

Badger: peddler
Bannister: crossbowman
Boyer: oxherd
Chapman: tradesman
Coward: cowherd
Cowper: barrelmaker
Currier: leather worker
Day: laborer
Deemer: judge
Faber: smith
Farman: ferryman
Faulkner: hawk keeper
Flanner: cake maker
Foster: forester
Fowler: birdhunter
Fuller: cloth worker
Furber: polisher
Gaylor: jailer

Goddard: goatherd
Greer: herdsman
Grover: woodsman
Harrower: farmer
Hooker: fisherman
Inman: innkeeper
Joiner: carpenter
Kaufman: merchant
Keeler: barge tender
Kilner: furnace tender
Ladd: servant
Lambert: lambherd
Leech: physician
Lister: reader
Marner: seaman
Mellor: honey collector
Mercer: merchant
Milner: miller

Naylor: nailmaker
Norris: nurse
Osler: birdcatcher
Ostler: stableman
Packard: swineherd
Packman: peddler
Penner: pound keeper
Plumer: feather seller
Pointer: lacemaker
Porcher: swineherd
Pottinger: soup maker
Proctor: attorney
Sanger: singer
Sawyer: carpenter
Schawer: barber
Scherer: barber
Schneider: tailor
Schulze: magistrate
Sears: carpenter

Sellers: saddlemaker
Seward: swineherd
Stringer: bowstring maker
Sumner: summoner
Tiller: farmer
Tucker: cloth worker
Turner: woodworker
Tyler: tileworker
Wainwright: wagonmaker
Wakeman: watchman
Waller: mason
Ward: watchman
Wayman: hunter
Weber: weaver
Webster: female weaver
Wheeler: spinner
Woodward: forest warden
Wright: mechanic
Zimmerman: carpenter

Note: The purpose of this exercise is not to have students memorize the meanings of many names but to emphasize the fact that the derivation of a name is often apparent.

In the self-inventory quiz below, students may be asked to write the names suggested by the list of words on the left. After the students have completed as much of the exercise as they can, the teacher may wish to read aloud the correct answers and have students write in the missing names.

Word	Name
Rome	Romulus
Gargantuan	Gargantua
quixotic	Don Quixote
sandwich	Earl of Sandwich
ohm	Georg Ohm
ampere	André Ampère
watt	James Watt
galvanize	Luigi Galvani
derrick	Thomas Derrick
mesmerize	Franz Mesmer
volt	Alessandro Volta
pasteurize	Louis Pasteur
boycott	Capt. Charles Boycott
braille	Louis Braille
silhouette	Etienne de Silhouette
maverick	Samuel Maverick
diesel	Rudolf Diesel
Fahrenheit	Gabriel Fahrenheit
nicotine	Jean Nicot
Cincinnati	Cincinnatus
begonia	Michel Begon

74

bunsen (burner)	Robert Bunsen
colt (revolver)	Samuel Colt
bowie (knife)	James Bowie
cologne	Cologne, Germany
ferris (wheel)	Gale Ferris
forsythia	William Forsyth
gardenia	Alexander Garden
guillotine	Joseph Guillotin
lynch	Charles Lynch
poinsettia	Joel Poinsett
shrapnel	Henry H. Shrapnel
saxophone	Adolphe J. Sax

Note: The teacher may also wish to use some of the words and phrases listed below:

frankfurter: Frankfurt, Germany
hermetically sealed: Hermes, messenger of gods and chemical knowledge
hyacinth: Hyacinth, a Spartan youth changed by Apollo into the flower
iris: Iris, Greek messenger of gods, changed by Juno into a rainbow
laconic: Laconia, whose inhabitants were reputed to be terse
lavaliere: Louise de la Lavalière, a friend of Louis XIV of France
Leninism: Nikolai Lenin
Leyden jar: invented at Leyden, Holland
limousine: Limousin, an old French province
loganberry: J. H. Logan, a judge and gardener
mackinaw: Mackinac City, Michigan
mackintosh: Charles Macintosh, inventor of rainproof material
magnolia: Pierre Magnol, French botanist
malapropism: Mrs. Malaprop, in Sheridan's *The Rivals*
manila paper: Manila, Philippine capital
martinet: Jean Martinet, French army drillmaster
Marxism: Karl Marx
morris chair: designed by English artist, William Morris
Morse code: inventor Samuel Morse
odyssey: journey of Odysseus (Ulysses)
panama hat: Panama, Central America
panic: Pan, Greek forest god, who inspired fear in travelers
platonic: Plato, Greek philosopher
praline: Marshal du Plessis-Praslin, whose cook invented it
protean: Proteus, a god who kept changing his shape
pullman: George M. Pullman, inventor and railroad designer
rhinestone: River Rhine
Roquefort cheese: Roquefort, a French town
shanghai: Shanghai, Chinese seaport
Stalinism: Joseph Stalin, Russian political leader
stentorian: Stentor, a Trojan warrior famous for his loud voice
tabasco sauce: Tabasco, Mexico
tangerine: Tangier, Morocco
tobacco: *tabaco* (Spanish), large tube used by Indians for smoking
Winchester rifle: Oliver F. Winchester, American manufacturer
zeppelin: German Count von Zeppelin

The teacher might increase the students' interest in vocabulary by arousing an interest in the origins of words. For example, *hamburger* has nothing to do with *ham.* It is named after the way people prepared meat in Hamburg, Germany. Where did the word *cereal* come from? From *Ceres,* the Roman goddess of grain. Studying sources of words can help students become more word-conscious.

In the following lesson, the student is asked to check the correct answer.

1. The word *minister* once meant servant. Does this meaning remain?
   ___ Yes
   _X_ No

   (But *yes* in the sense of "ministering" to parishoners.)

2. *Sanctimonious* used to mean holy or sanctified. Now it means
   a. ___ very strange
   b. _X_ putting on airs of holiness
   c. ___ a truly religious person

3. *Spinster* used to mean a woman who spins wool. Today it means
   a. ___ a widower
   b. _X_ an unmarried woman
   c. ___ a knitter

4. *Cunning* once meant knowing. What does *cunning* imply today?
   a. ___ very sarcastic
   b. ___ inspecting things carefully
   c. _X_ a sly kind of knowledge

5. *Counterfeit* once meant only an imitation, a likeness, or a copy. Now it means
   a. ___ found guilty
   b. _X_ a copy meant to defraud
   c. ___ a sharp reply

6. *Uncouth* originally meant unknown or strange. Now it means
   a. ___ well-known
   b. _X_ without manners
   c. ___ refined

7. Is it an insult to call a person *couth?*
   ___ Yes
   _X_ No

   (Originally *couth* meant known or familiar. Now it means having polish and finesse. But it is not usually used except as a joke.)

Month Names

The teacher may wish to discuss with the class the origins of the names of the months of the year. The months and their origins are listed below:

January: from *Janus,* the god who had two faces, one on the front and one on the back of his head; he could see the old year go while he welcomed the new year

February: from *februa,* a Roman feast

March: from *Mars,* the god of war
April: from the Latin *aprilis,* opening (of the buds)
May: from the goddess *Maja*
June: from *Junius,* a Roman family name
July: from *Julius* Caesar
August: from *Augustus* Caesar
September: from *septem* (seven), the seventh month of the Roman calendar
October: from Latin *octo* (eight), the eighth month of the Roman calendar
November: from *novem* (nine), the ninth month of the Roman calendar
December: from *decem* (ten), the tenth month of the Roman calendar
Month: from Anglo-Saxon *mona* (moon)

Special Projects

Students may look up the origins of some of these words.

frankfurter: from Frankfurt, Germany
sandwich: from Lord Sandwich, who liked to play cards so well he had his
    servant bring his meat on bread so he didn't have to leave the game for meals
stew: from Middle English *stuwen,* to bathe, to steam
corral: from Spanish *corro,* a ring or a yard
mustang: from Spanish *mestengo,* untamed, wild
maverick: from Samuel Maverick, a Texan whose cattle were unbranded
    wanderers

Note: Teachers may have the students reserve a section of their note-
books for words with interesting histories. As a discussion question, you
might want to ask the students the meaning of "political maverick."

Days of the Week

Sunday: day of the sun
Monday: day of the moon
Tuesday: day of Tiu (Teutonic god of war)
Wednesday: day of Woden (Norse god)
Thursday: day of Thor (Norse god)
Friday: day of Fria (Woden's wife)
Saturday: day of Saturn (Roman god)

Names of Kinds of Cloth

Calico comes from *Calicut,* a city of India.
Cashmere comes from *Kashmir,* India.
Damask comes from *Damascus,* Syria.
Denim is derived from *serge de Nîmes* (fabric of Nîmes, a city in France)
Gauze comes from *Gaza,* Palestine.
Muslin comes from *Mosul,* Iraq.
Worsted wool came from the city of *Worsted* in England.
Chenille is French for *caterpillar.*
Linen is derived from Latin *linum* (flax).

History has given us some interesting words. The word *candidate* has its roots in ancient Rome, where a politician running for office wore a white toga as a sign of his pure and noble intentions. The Latin word for white is *candidus* and the office-seeker was called *candidatus.* A candidate, then, is a man with pure (purely) political intentions.

The Roman word for "old man" was *senex.* On the whole, old men (though not yet senile) filled the Roman *senate.* Although the U.S. Senate has a few young men, most of the members are older and, in the Roman sense, are rightly called *senators* (old ones).

No matter how we use words today it is difficult to escape from the fact that many had their beginnings in ancient Greece or Rome. For example, would you believe there is a connection between *dogs* and *canaries?* There is. Roman sailors who stopped at a group of islands off the west coast of Africa found large dogs on the islands. Since the Latin word for dog is *canis* (canine) the Romans called the islands the *Canarias.* Later on, birds from the Canary Islands were called *canaries.*

Some early Roman traders who couldn't read and write and who ran out of fingers, counted or *calculated* with pebbles. The Latin for "pebble" is *calculus.*

The Roman poet Horace tells us that when he was a boy his father used to take him down to the Forum to observe the citizens, politicians, and lawyers of the time. Horace might have heard that certain accused citizens had to appear before the courts *sub poena* (under the threat of punishment). The word we use today, *subpoena,* has the same meaning, and the same spelling, borrowed directly from Latin.

Other Latin phrases are used as legal terms:

habeas corpus (you may have the body): a writ for getting a prisoner out of jail;

rigor mortis (rigor of death): the stiffness of the corpse;

corpus delicti (the body of the crime): the fact necessary for proving that a crime has been committed. In a murder charge, this would be the body of the victim.

Lawyers, as well as defendants, have always been interested in an *alibi,* a Latin adverb meaning "somewhere else." A person with an alibi maintains that he was somewhere else when the crime was being committed. And a person on the wrong side of the law often uses an *alias,* an assumed name. *Alias* is short for the Latin phrase *alias dictus,* "otherwise called."

Greek is the basis for thousands of words we use today, and there's a good reason. The Greek language had over 92,000 words, all pure Greek, not borrowings from other languages. Many of the words used in city affairs today are derived from Greek. From Greek *polis* (city) we get the words *politics, politician, police,* and *cosmopolitan. Metropolis* comes from *meter* (mother) + *polis* (city), and thus means "mother city."

Athens is located in an ancient region of Greece called Attica, which was celebrated for its beautiful temples. The Attic style of architecture was characterized by gables, behind which were areas of empty space. Such a space in a house is now called the *attic.*

According to one of the Greek myths, Hercules fought a fierce group of women fighters called *Amazons*. The Amazon River was so named by a Spanish explorer whose party, while in the area, was attacked by Indians wearing grass skirts. The Indians reminded him of the female warriors, hence the name for the river.

The Greeks often buried their dead in a *sarcophagus*, a limestone coffin in which the dead body soon disintegrated. The word is descriptive of what happened: *sarkos* (flesh) + *phagein* (to eat). *Sarcasm* is also related to *sarcos* (flesh). It is derived from the Greek words *sarkazein* (to tear the flesh) and *sarkastikos* (biting, caustic). Sarcasm figuratively "tears the flesh" of its victim.

Science and medicine still rely on Greek and Latin terms to describe discoveries and inventions. When a patient thinks he needs a pill to quiet his nerves the doctor may give him a *placebo*, a pill which contains no active ingredients but satisfies the patient psychologically. *Placebo* is a Latin verb meaning "I shall please."

Students can learn to form vivid adjectives from proper nouns by adding suffixes such as *-ic, -ful, -ious, -al, -ian, -ine,* and *-like*. For example, *cosmic* is formed by adding *-ic* to the root of *cosmos*.

In the exercise below, the student is asked to write in the blank the adjective derived from the mythological name. A short explanation is included after each noun.

Name	Adjective
1. Vulcan: god of fire	vulcanized, volcanic
2. Mars: god of war	Martian, martial
3. Venus: goddess of love and beauty	venereal
4. Europa: first person brought to Crete, near Europe, by the king of the gods	European
5. Luna: moon goddess	lunar
6. Fata: the Three Fates, in charge of life and death	fatal
7. Morta: Death, one of the Three Fates	mortal
8. Flora: goddess of flowers, sister of Faunus, god of animals	floral
9. Olympus: mountain home of gods	Olympic
10. Sol: sun god	solar
11. Gigantes: giants, offspring of Gaea (earth) and Uranus (sky)	gigantic
12. Atlas: a Titan who held up the sky on his shoulders	Atlantic
13. Athena: Greek goddess of knowledge, in charge of Athens	Athenian
14. Graces: goddesses of feminine charms	graceful, gracious
15. Hygeia: Greek goddess of health	hygienic
16. Jove: Roman god, also called Jupiter; being born under the planet Jupiter supposedly made a person cheerful	jovial

Depending on the level of the students, the teacher may discuss some of these adjectives that relate to mythology:

Name	Adjective
1. Furies: three avenging Roman goddesses	furious
2. Homer: Greek epic poet	Homeric
3. Polyhymnia: muse of religious music	hymnal
4. Hypnos: Greek god of sleep	hypnotic
5. Somnus: Roman god of sleep	somnolent, insomnia
6. Juno: stately queen of the gods	Junoesque
7. Labyrinth: Built by the inventor Daedalus, this large building with winding passages like a maze was easy to get lost in.	labyrinthian
8. Icarus: Daedalus's son, who flew too close to the sun	Icarian (soaring too high for safety)
9. Leo: Latin word for lion; Leo is the fifth sign of the zodiac.	leonine
10. Lethe: river in Hades. Spirits of the dead drank its water for repose; they forgot the past. The Greek word *lethe* means forgetfulness.	lethal, lethargic
11. Mercury: messenger of the gods, known for his speed. The planet Mercury moves faster around the sun than do the other planets.	mercurial
12. Saturn: People born under this heavy, slow-moving planet were thought to be gloomy or grave.	saturnine
13. Narcissus: fell in love with his reflection in the water and remained there until he turned into the flower	narcissistic; Narcissus complex
14. Nox: goddess of night	nocturnal
15. Oceanus: a Titan, son of Earth and Sky, and god of the water	oceanic
16. Oracle: a spokesman for the gods who foretold future events	oracle, oracular
17. Phobos: god of fear, son of Mars	phobic; hydrophobic
18. Phosphorus: Greek word for "light-bearer," another name for the planet Venus	phosphorescent
19. Pluto: god of the underworld and of the metals of the earth — wealth	plutocratic
20. Proteus: Greek sea god who could change his shape at will	protean
21. Titan: offspring of giants or Gigantes	titanic
22. Cosmos: the name the Greeks gave to the universe; it means order or ornament	cosmetic, cosmopolitan

23. Terpsichore: Greek Muse of the dance	terpsichorean
24. Terra: Roman goddess of the earth	terrestrial
25. Gaea: Greek goddess of the earth	geological, geographic, geocentric
26. Amazons: a mythological race of tall, strong women warriors	Amazonian
27. ambrosia: food of the gods	ambrosial
28. nectar: the drink of the gods	nectarean, nectareous, nectarine
29. Eros: Greek god of love	erotic
30. Bacchus: god of wine and revelry	bacchanalian
31. Hercules: mythological superman who became a god	herculean
32. Cyclops: round-eyed. The mythological Cyclops were one-eyed giants.	cyclopean
33. Psyche: mythological princess loved by Cupid, who abandoned her. It is said she wandered about, like the soul or mind of man, seeking happiness. The Greek word *psyche* means soul.	psychic, psychological

The lesson below may be used to point up the meaning and origin of words which often carry rich associations. A high school literature class may be interested in the origin of "Achilles heel"; another class may be interested in "the Midas touch"; and another in "Atlas missile." Most of the phrases below are not well known even in the twelfth grade.

In the following exercise the student merely checks the phrases he has heard or seen. Students may be asked to explain the phrases they checked. (For the teacher's convenience, origins of the phrases are given at the end of the lesson.)

1. ___ Achilles heel		19. ___ Herculean labor
2. ___ Aeolian harp		20. ___ under the aegis of
3. ___ Alexandrine verse		21. ___ the Midas touch
4. ___ Amazonian stature		22. ___ Gordian knot
5. ___ Argus-eyed		23. ___ hydra-headed
6. ___ Atlas missile		24. ___ Stygian darkness
7. ___ Gemini mission		25. ___ laconic reply
8. ___ Saturn rocket		26. ___ Punic faith
9. ___ Titan rocket		27. ___ Lynx-eyed
10. ___ halcyon days		28. ___ Pandora's box
11. ___ hermetically sealed		29. ___ pile Pelion upon Ossa
12. ___ heroic age		30. ___ by Jiminy
13. ___ jovial mood		31. ___ the Pipes of Pan
14. ___ lunar month		32. ___ Procrustean bed
15. ___ Augean stables		33. ___ Promethean act
16. ___ bacchanalian revels		34. ___ Damascus blade
17. ___ Homeric laughter		35. ___ martial law
18. ___ by Jove		36. ___ iridescent glow

Phrase Origins

1. Achilles' heel: A weak spot. Achilles' mother thought that dipping him into the River Styx would make him invulnerable. It did, except for one place—the heel by which she held him. Achilles died after an arrow pierced his heel.

2. Aeolian harp: From Aeolus, Greek god of the winds. A box fitted with strings that produces a musical tone when the wind blows through them.

3. Alexandrine verse: Poetic line of six iambics, with a pause after the third foot. Used in old French poems about Alexander the Great.

4. Amazonian stature: The build of a strong, muscular woman. A mythical group of warrior women were called Amazons.

5. Argus-eyed: Describes someone who is always watchful. The giant Argus had a hundred eyes, some of which could watch while others closed in sleep.

6. Atlas missile: Named after Atlas, the Greek god who supported the heavens on his shoulders.

7. Gemini mission: Space project that sent two men together into space. From Latin *gemini* (twins).

8. Saturn rocket: Space vehicle named after the second largest planet and the Roman god Saturn.

9. Titan rocket: Rocket named after the Titans (giants).

10. halcyon days: Alcyone, daughter of Aeolus (god of wind) was turned into a sea bird, the kingfisher (or halcyon). According to Greek mythology, the halcyon bird nested at sea. At this time the seas were calm, thus "halcyon days" are calm, peaceful days.

11. hermetically sealed: From Hermes, messenger of the gods and Greek god of chemical knowledge. In early times drugs were often made airtight (hermetically sealed) as they are today.

12. heroic age: In Greek mythology, a person, one of whose parents was a god or goddess, who was greater than ordinary human beings, such as Achilles, was called a "hero." An age typified by great men or events is often called a "heroic age."

13. jovial mood: A person born under the sign of Jupiter, also called Jove, was supposed to be cheerful.

14. lunar month: From Luna, Roman moon goddess. The time it takes the moon to circle the earth.

15. Augean stables: Refers to something very dirty or corrupt. The Augean stables hadn't been cleaned for years. Hercules cleaned them as one of his "twelve labors."

16. bacchanalian revels: Celebrations in honor of Bacchus, Roman god of wine and revelry. Also called Dionysian revels, after Dionysus, the Greek name for Bacchus.

17. Homeric laughter: Long fits of unrestrained comic laughter. Homer tells about the gods sometimes having fits of uncontrollable laughter.

18. by Jove: An outdated expression using Jupiter's other name, Jove.

19. Herculean labor: From the Greek hero Hercules, who had great strength and performed extremely difficult tasks.

20. Under the aegis of: Under the protection or guidance of. Associated with the shield (*aegis*) of Athena and Zeus.

21. the Midas touch: Everything the mythical King Midas touched turned to gold. Today a person successful in business may be described as having "the Midas touch."

22. Gordian knot: An intricate problem. Derived from the knot tied by Gordus (Midas's father) that no one could untie.

23. hydra-headed: If one of the Hydra's nine heads was cut off, two others grew back. A *hydra-headed* problem gets worse with each attempt to solve it. In Greek mythology the Hydra was a water monster.

24. Stygian darkness: The vast darkness of the underworld. The River Styx was believed to encircle the darkness of Hades.

25. laconic reply: The Spartans, inhabitants of Laconia, were known for their military discipline and for their brevity of speech.

26. Punic faith: Treachery. The Romans spoke of their enemies in the Punic (Carthaginian) Wars as traitors.

27. Lynx-eyed: Derived from the mythical Lynceus, whose eyesight was so sharp he could see through rocks. The lynx is a species of wildcat.

28. Pandora's box: The mythical Pandora opened a box given her by Zeus and released all the evils into the world. Only Hope remained in the box.

29. pile Pelion upon Ossa: Two mythical giants attacking Olympus piled the mountain Pelion upon the mountain Ossa to get higher than Olympus. The phrase now refers to any superhuman feat.

30. by Jiminy: An outdated exclamation. At one time people swore by Gemini (twins), the third sign of the zodiac.

31. the pipes of Pan: A musical instrument made of hollow reeds played by Pan, Greek god of the woods.

32. Procrustean bed: The highwayman Procrustes made his victims fit his bed either by cutting off part of their legs or by stretching them. Today it refers to a preconceived idea being forced on someone.

33. Promethean act: A daring, creative act. Prometheus stole fire from the heavens and gave it to man.

34. Damascus blade: Originally a sword made of fine Damascus steel ornamented with wavy lines.

35. martial law: Enforcement of laws by the military, usually in times of danger or disaster (from Mars, Roman god of war).

36. iridescent glow: The rainbowlike movement of color in soap bubbles is called iridescence. The word is derived from the name of Iris who brought messages to earth from the gods, descending via the rainbow (*iris* is the Greek word for rainbow).

Even when men coin words they often rely on previously used words or word elements. Lewis Carroll, the mathematician who wrote *Alice in Wonderland* for amusement, coined the word *chortle,* a combination of *chuckle* and *snort.* Words formed from parts of other words are called portmanteau words. *Motel* is another example, formed from *motor* and *hotel.* Newspapermen, especially sportswriters, often coin such expressions as *twinight doubleheader,* a doubleheader that starts at twilight and goes on into the night.

Athletes, like sportswriters, often add new words (or new meanings of old words) to the language. Pitcher Carl Hubbell named his combination fast ball and curve *screwball,* a new twist on an old French word, *escroue.* Outfielders *shag* flies (catch and throw the ball back to the infield).

Note that today's *athlete* is the descendant of the ancient Greek athlete (Roman, *athleta*) who sought the *athlon* (prize).

Another term derived from mythology is *sub rosa.* Cupid bribed *Harpocrates,* god of silence, not to tell tales about Venus. For this, Cupid gave him a beautiful rose. Reportedly, in the confidential meeting rooms of Europe, a rose was hung from the ceiling (and later sculptured into the ceiling) as a symbol that what was to be discussed would be *sub rosa,* confidential.

The name of the Spanish *Armada,* which Philip II of Spain sent against England in 1588, was coined by the Spanish from the Latin *armata* (armed). Spanish explorers in America used another derivative of the Latin word *arma* (arms, weapons) in naming a little animal with a bony shell resembling an armored plate. They called the animal an *armadillo.*

Many of our words have a long and varied history. By digging up the past we often discover hidden curiosities that can make certain words come alive for us. The most important part of any word study is that it makes the students word-conscious. It frequently points up something about words that they perhaps have never noticed before. For example, the teacher might ask the students if they realized that the words *curfew* and *fire* were related. *Curfew* comes from the French *couvrir* (cover) + *feu* (fire). In olden days the curfew bell meant "cover up (put out) the fire and go to bed."

Astronomers have usually been sensitive to the mythology concerning the stars, and as they mapped the heavens, they took into account many of the legends of the ancient peoples. Thus, as they discovered new planets and other heavenly bodies, they gave them names according to their relative position or appearance in the sky. Often these heavenly bodies had already been named by generations preceding them. For example, the beautiful and brilliant planet Venus was named after the Roman goddess of love and beauty. Few persons ever notice the relationship between the goddess of love and *venereal* disease, but it's there. Phosphorus (Greek for "lightbearer") was another name for the planet Venus, the morning star seen in the east; and from this name we get the noun *phosphorus* and the adjective *phosphorescent.*

The science of astronomy grew out of an older study, astrology, the study of the influence of the planets and stars on the lives of men and women. The word *influenza* has its roots in the Latin verb *fluo,* meaning flow. In medieval times people believed that diseases such as flu emanated, or flowed, from the stars.

Astrologers and astronomers noticed that one planet whirled around the sun faster than the other planets did. They named this planet *Mercury,* after the messenger of the gods, known for his speed. From Mercury we get the adjective *mercurial.* They also thought that persons born under *Saturn,* a slow-moving planet, were gloomy or grave (the opposite of mercurial). Gloomy persons are often described as *saturnine.* Persons born under the planet Jupiter, another name for the god Jove, were supposedly cheerful or *jovial.*

Pluto is a planet named after the Greek god of wealth who controlled the precious metals hidden in the earth. Hence a wealthy person is sometimes called a *plutocrat.*

Our moon has also contributed words to the language. In mythology, Luna was the goddess of the moon. Thus the phrases "lunar probe" and "lunar orbit." People in medieval times thought that the moon (Luna) could affect people's minds, and referred to a "moonstruck" or crazy person as a "lunatic."

Phobos, one of the moons of Mars, is named after the mythological Phobos, the god of fear. He was the son of Mars, the god of war. Phobos attended Mars in war, just as fear generally accompanies war. And from Phobos we get *phobia,* a neurotic fear of something. *Francophobia* is a fear of (hence dislike for) France. Lazy people have *ergophobia,* from the Greek *ergon* (work).

Students need not learn all of the following *phobia* words, but if the words are brought to their attention, they will probably recognize them when they see them again in various contexts:

1. A person suffering from rabies becomes worse when he drinks water. Another name for rabies is *hydrophobia* (from *hydro,* water + *phobia*).

2. Persons who have a morbid fear of being enclosed suffer from *claustrophobia.* (A *closet,* a related word, may cause claustrophobia.)

3. A person who has a fear of open spaces has *agoraphobia* (from Greek *agora,* an open market place).

4. *Acrophobia* is fear of height (from *akros,* high). Think of an acrobat, who performs on a high wire.

5. Fear of too much sunlight is *heliophobia* (from Greek *helios,* sun). (A *heliograph* sends signals by reflected sunlight.)

6. Persons who are superstitious often suffer from *triskaidekaphobia,* fear of the number thirteen. Notice *tri* (three) and *deca* (ten).

Knowing some of these word origins can give the student a sense of the historic continuity of language and an understanding of association and classification in word study. Word history is often closely associated with the study of word families, a significant part of the mental filing system that can give vocabulary a boost.

Just as *Francophobia* (fear of France) led us into other *phobia* words, so *Francophile* (one who loves France) leads us into other *phil* words, such as *Anglophile* (one who loves England). These words come from the Greek root *phil* meaning love. A *philosopher* is a lover of wisdom (*sophos*). A *philanthropist* is a lover of mankind. A *philatelist* loves stamps. People who like harmony or good music may listen to a *phil-harmonic* orchestra. A certain plant that seems to like the shade is called a *philodendron* (from Greek *dendron*, tree). Why is *Philadelphia* called the "city of brotherly love"? It is from two Greek words, *phil* (love) and *adelphos* (brother).

The expression *OK* seems to have a variety of origins. Some people believe that it comes from the Indian word *okey*, meaning "it is so." Others believe that it started with General Andrew Jackson, who was a good soldier but not a good speller. It seems that in signing one of his documents he thought that "all correct" was written "oll korrect," which he abbreviated to OK. Another version: *OK* is from the initials of Old Kinderhook, a Democratic club that backed Martin Van Buren for a second term as president. It was called the Democratic O.K. Club.

What is the relationship between *wink* and *hood* in *hoodwink? Wink* once meant to have the eyes closed. During the Middle Ages persons often wore a hood. Robbers took advantage of this apparel by pulling the hood over their eyes or "hoodwinking" them. Thus a person who is hoodwinked has the wool pulled over his eyes, or is fooled.

Dandelion is the name of the flower that looks like a lion's tooth, from French *dent de lion*, originally from Latin *dens*, tooth + *leo*, lion.

The word *kerchief* is from two French words, *chef* (head) and *couvrir* (later corrupted to *ker*, cover). The *kerchief* carried in the hand soon became a *handkerchief*.

An *umpire*, related to the French *nomper* (from *non*, not + *per*, peer), is a third person called upon to settle an argument.

The original *eavesdropper* stood close to a house, under the eaves (from which the rain dripped), and listened at a door or window.

We see and use words daily without thinking about their background. For example, the word *barber* comes from the Latin word *barba* meaning beard. A barber shaves beards. Frederick I of Germany had a red beard. He was called Frederick *Barbarossa* (Redbeard).

Did you know *comb* was related to *unkempt?* These words are related to Anglo-Saxon *kemb* (to comb) and *kempt* (combed), and by extension have come to mean neat (well-kempt) or slovenly (unkempt).

Men wore *petticoats* at one time. The petticoat (literally "little coat") was an undergarment worn under a man's armor. Later on, women wore it as an undershirt and still later as an underskirt.

The following exercise gives the teacher further opportunity to check pupil understanding of certain words and to present interesting facts about word origins.

The student puts a check in the blank that best completes the meaning. He checks his answers later with the teacher. Answers and word origins are included with the exercise for the teacher's convenience.

1. The word *panic* is related to
   a. ___ bread
   b. ___ cooking utensil
   c. _X_ Greek god

(Note: This word has its origin in the name of *Pan,* a Greek god who inhabited the forest. Greeks walking through the forest at night often felt panic at his strange appearance.)

2. A *clipper ship* gets its meaning from
   a. ___ sail
   b. ___ float
   c. _X_ cut

(Note: Clipper ships had a sharp stem that "cut" through the waves. In a sense they "clipped off" nautical miles faster than other sailing ships.)

3. The *aster* is a
   a. ___ mark
   b. _X_ flower
   c. ___ fish

(Note: The *aster* is star-shaped. So is an *asterisk*.)

4. *Aster* gets its name from the
   a. ___ Greek word for "flower"
   b. _X_ Greek word for "star"
   c. ___ Greek word for "sky"

5. The word *tantalize* means
   a. ___ cheer up
   b. _X_ tease
   c. ___ hurt

(Note: The ancient king Tantalus was punished for giving away the secrets of the gods. He had to stand in a pool of water, but when he bent over to drink, the water receded. To further annoy him, fruit on a branch overhead continually eluded him. Thus we have the word *tantalize*, meaning to tease by keeping out of reach.)

6. The word *assassin* gets its name from
   a. _X_ a drug
   b. ___ a sword
   c. ___ a soldier

(Note: Murderers who were hired to kill often ate *hashish,* an Oriental drug, and were called *hashshashin*. In English it became *assassin*.)

7. The word *companion* is related to
   a. _X_ bread
   b. ___ a duel
   c. ___ suffering

(Note: Originally a companion was one with whom a person shared his food or "broke bread," a sign of friendship. The Latin word for bread is *panis*. So *com, cum* (with) + *panis* (bread) developed into the Latin *companio* and later into our word *companion*.)

8. The word *galaxy* is related to
   a. ___ blackness
   b. _X_ milk
   c. ___ cold

(Note: The Greek word for milk is *gala*. From the Greek word *galaxias* we get the word *galaxy*, or *Milky Way*.)

Words in Space

When the Russian moon rocket *Lunik II* and the United States lunar probe *Ranger IV* hit the moon, the Latin language, which had spread over much of the earth, had also gone to the moon. *Lunik* is from the Latin word for moon, *luna*. Printed on *Ranger IV,* from the Latin *unus* (one) + *sta* (stand) were the words *United States,* that is, "we stand as one."

The names of American rockets and spaceships are often deeply rooted in the mythology of the ancient Greeks and Romans, who also had a great interest in space and the heavenly bodies. The terms coined by the National Aeronautics and Space Administration (NASA) are usually borrowed from Greek and Roman mythology.

When American astronaut John Glenn orbited the earth in 1962, he did it in a Mercury *capsule. Capsula* is Latin for "little box." But why *Mercury?* The planet Mercury is closest to the sun and whirls around it faster than the other planets do. So the planet and John Glenn's capsule both get their name from the swift messenger of the gods, Mercury.

The Romans found it convenient to borrow a great deal from the Greeks and their gods. The Greek father of the heavens was Zeus, or *Zeus Pater,* which the Romans eventually corrupted to *Jupiter,* thus giving us the name of one of America's early missiles, the *Jupiter C.* Of course, *Juno,* Jupiter's jealous wife, was a great avenger in her day, and NASA scientists, presumably wary of her wrath, named a space rocket after her, *Juno II.*

The fourth letter of the Greek alphabet, the triangular-shaped letter Δ (*D*), is called *delta.* The three-stage launch rocket that hurled the American satellites *Telstar, Echo, Tiros,* and *Syncom* into orbit has a tailfin shaped like a triangle and is called the *Delta* launch vehicle. Other NASA rockets and spaceships with names related to ancient mythology include *Titan II, Atlas, Atlas-Centaur, Saturn V, Gemini,* and *Apollo.*

The *Mariner* spacecraft which went to Venus (the bright planet named for the goddess of love and beauty) and the *Ranger* probe that went to the moon were launched by the *Atlas-Agena* rocket. This powerful rocket is related to another, more powerful, rocket, the *Titan,* in somewhat the same fashion that the mythological Titans were related to the familiar character, Atlas. The *Titan* is named after the Titans, the offspring of the *Gigantes,* or giants, who supposedly first inhabited the earth. One of the offspring of the giants was Atlas, who held up the sky on his shoulders. Appropriately, *Atlas* is the name of one of our most powerful rockets.

Larger and more powerful than the Atlas rocket is the *Atlas-Centaur,* a combination rocket. This hybrid rocket is named after the *centaur,* a mythological creature having the head, arms, and chest of a man, and the body and legs of a horse.

Orbita is Latin for a course or track: a spaceship that stays on course is "in orbit." The relationship to *orbis* (circle) and the English word *orb* is clear.

Project *Gemini* was also rooted in mythology. The original twins, or *gemini,* Castor and Pollux, were interesting in their own right. Pollux was a champion boxer in his day, and Castor tamed wild horses.

Three American astronauts have orbited the moon in an *Apollo* Command Module, which gets its name from Apollo, the Greek god of the sun and the ideal of youthful manliness. The launch vehicle used to propel the module into its orbit is called the *Saturn V* rocket. This rocket is named after the Roman god for whom the second largest planet is named, *Saturn.*

The word *module* is used a great deal in the Apollo program. It comes from the Latin *modulus,* a diminutive of *modus* (a measure), and in space terminology it is "a small measure of," or a single part of, a spaceship, from which it can be separated for a lunar landing.

By orbiting the moon, man has become a *satellite* — a word much used in modern times but used also by the ancient Romans as *satelles* (an attendant). The phrase *moon probe* or *lunar probe* is also related to the language of the Romans (from Latin *probo,* prove, test, inspect).

The more scientists probe into the future, the more they seem to reach back into the past for words. For example, as a space scientist looks out from our planet, he is first aware of the air that surrounds the earth, or the *atmosphere* (from Greek *atmos,* vapor + *sphaira,* sphere).

Some space probes move out to the area between the earth and the moon. The space scientist calls this region *cislunar* (from Latin *cis,* on the side + *luna,* moon): on this side of the moon.

About a million miles beyond the moon, where combined gravity of the moon and the earth is still fairly strong, is an area called *translunar* space, from Latin *trans* (beyond): beyond, or on the other side of, the moon.

The space between the planets is called *interplanetary* space, from Latin *inter* (between, among) + *planetary,* from a Greek word meaning to wander (the planets seem to wander in their course through the heavens).

Beyond interplanetary space is *interstellar* space, from Latin *stella* (star): among the stars.

The star nearest our solar system (25 trillion miles distant) is *Proxima Centauri,* named from the word *centaur* and the Latin word for "nearest," *proxima.*

Man has also employed rockets and constructed his own satellites to serve his immediate purposes here on earth. Scientists have developed weather satellites, which they also call *meteorological* satellites, from the Greek *meteoron* (something in the air) and *logos* (word, or treatment of): the treatment of things in the air or atmosphere.

The first American meteorological satellites chosen to help study weather conditions were called *Tiros* satellites. *Tiros I* was among the first ones used for this purpose. It was given the name Tiros from the Latin word *tiro,* a novice. *Tiros VI,* no longer a novice, took weather photographs for the flight path of astronaut Wally Schirra, who orbited the earth six times in his space capsule, *Sigma 7* (another loan word from the Greek: the eighteenth letter of the Greek alphabet). Hurricanes have been tracked off the Florida coast by another weather satellite, *Nimbus I.* The word *nimbus* is Latin for "cloud" and figuratively refers to a tempest or a storm.

In 1960, the United States launched a "passive" satellite that reflects or *echos* signals back to earth. This satellite was called *Echo I. Echo* also stems from Greek mythology. The story is told of a nymph who was punished in such a way that she could not speak for herself but could only repeat what she heard. Her name was Echo. Thus the reflecting satellites *Echo I* and *Echo II* are appropriately named. The *Pegasus* satellite detects the number of meteoroids in space. As meteoroids hit its wings, Pegasus sends the information back by means of *telemetry* (from Greek *tele*, distant + *meter*, measure). The Pegasus satellite gets its name from a mythological flying horse named *Pegasus*. The outline of this winged horse is also seen in the sky in the constellation Pegasus.

Astronauts use electronic computers, gyroscopes, and sextants to aid them in navigation. These space-age instruments also have their origin in ancient languages:

Computer comes from the Latin *computare* meaning to reckon or calculate. The Greek words *gyros* (circle or ring) + *scopos* (a watcher) give the name to the spinning wheel used as a stabilizer on the spacecraft, the gyroscope. Astronauts and cosmonauts use another instrument, the sextant, presumably coined by the famous astronomer Tycho Brahe. With the sextant the space explorer can measure the altitude of the sun or a star to determine his position. A sextant, from the Latin word *sextans* (one sixth) has a graduated arc which is one sixth of a complete circle.

Successful *reentry* of spaceships depends on *retrorockets, ablation,* and *parachutes.*

The word *reentry* is from the Latin prefix *re* (again) and *intrare* (within) and means the act of entering again.

Retrorockets fire in the same direction in which the spacecraft is moving, thus slowing it down. *Retro* is a Latin prefix meaning backwards.

A spacecraft is protected in its reentry from the heat of friction by a heat shield. The melting and carrying away of heat by this shield is called *ablation* (from the Latin past participle *ablatus,* carried away).

The French word *parachute* has its origin in Latin *para* (protection against) and *chute* (a fall). Thus, a parachute is a protection against a fall resulting in the gentle landing of a spacecraft on the earth.

Scientists refer to future spaceships that will take space explorers on long journeys as ecological systems that will use body wastes to chemically produce air, food, or water. *Ecology* is a branch of biology dealing with the relationship of living things to their environment. In this case, the spacecraft will be the environment of the space travelers. *Ecology* is from Greek *oikos* (house) + *logy* (science of), a kind of biological housekeeping.

Space scientists are also concerned about radiation, such as that encountered in the Van Allen belt. Men in spaceships must be shielded from extended exposure to intense *radiation* (from Latin *radius,* a beam or ray).

Future space explorers who travel to the moon or the planets will naturally depend a great deal on navigation. Space navigation is called *astrogation,* navigation carried on by means of sighting the stars. *Astrogation* is a portmanteau word, or telescoped word, formed from *astro(navi)gation* (from Greek *astron,* star + Latin *navigare,* to sail). The word *astronaut* itself is a newly coined name from *astro* (star) + *nauta* (sailor). Astronauts are literally "sailors among the stars." In Russia they are sailors in the universe, or *cosmos: cosmonauts.*

6

Prefixes

Most students understand the importance of context—they know that words have meaning in relation to other words in a sentence. But not so many understand that words also derive meaning from their component parts. Two Greek elements serve as an example: *a* (not) + *tom* (cut) = *atom*, the smallest particle of matter, which scientists once thought could not be cut.

Students knowing the component parts of *atom* possess a potential for transfer: they can see the *tom*, for example, in *tonsillectomy, appendectomy,* and *anatomy* (literally "cutting up"). They can use their knowledge of the prefix *a-, an-* (not or without) to help them analyze other words, such as *amoral* (without a concern for morals), *anonymous* (not named), *atheist* (not believing in God).

They may learn that the prefix *pre-* (before) helps them remember the idea of "before" in *precede* (go before), *predict* (tell beforehand), *prefix* (put before the root or root word), *preheat, prejudge,* and *prelude.*

The following exercises offer students practice in the use of key prefixes. A master list of prefixes is included in the Appendix.

Negative Prefixes

The following lesson is divided into six parts. To maintain high interest, we suggest that the student complete only one part on a given day, although we do feel the lessons should be studied on consecutive days. In these exercises, the students use the prefixes *un-, in-, im-, il-, ir-* to form negative words. (Note: Dictionaries list these as different spellings of the same prefix, but for purposes of study here we are dealing with them as separate prefixes.) Answers are included.

Part One: The Prefix *Un-*

Answers

not; not	1. The word *unable* means _____ able. A person who is uncertain is _____ certain.
not	2. "He was unaware of the danger" means he was _____ aware of the danger.
not	3. The prefix *un-* means _____.
not	4. Unclean means _____ clean.
uncomfortable	5. A person who is not comfortable is _____.
not	6. An unconscious person is _____ conscious.
not; unemployed	7. A man out of work is _____ employed. He is _____.
not equal	8. Things that are unequal are _____ _____.
unhappy	9. A person who is not happy is _____.
unfair	10. The referee's decision was not fair. His decision was _____.

Students may continue the exercise by adding *un-* to other base words or roots selected by the teacher. Other words that might be included: *uneven, unfamiliar, unfavorable, unfinished, unfriendly, unfortunate, unbroken, unborn, unbalanced, undesirable, unconstitutional, unaffected.*

Part Two: The Prefix *In-*

Answers

not	1. An inactive person is _____ active.
not	2. An incurable disease can _____ be cured.
not	3. The prefix *in-* means _____.
inexpensive	4. Another way to say "not expensive" is _____.
indefinite	5. A person who is not definite is _____.
Indecent	6. _____ means not decent.
Independent	7. _____ means not dependent.
Indirect	8. _____ means not direct.
Incapable	9. _____ means not capable.
Ineligible	10. _____ means not eligible.

The teacher lists only those words suitable for his grade level. Other words that might be included: *incorrect, incomplete, inexact, inconsistent, ineffective, inexpert, inexpressible, inappropriate, inaccurate, inadequate, inattentive, inaudible.*

Additional Practice with *In-*

Have students fill in the blanks or put a check mark after the correct answer in the following exercises.

Answers

inactive	1. A boy who is not active is _____.
incomplete	2. A job that is not complete is _____.
incorrect	3. His answer was not correct. (It was _____.)
indecent	4. The opposite of decent is _____.
can't	5. The disease is incurable. It (can _____, can't _____) be cured.
insane	6. A person who is not sane is _____.
cannot	7. An invisible object (can _____, cannot _____) be seen.
not	8. In the word *indefinite*, the prefix *in-* means _____.
not	9. An indirect message is _____ direct.
not able	10. A newborn baby is incapable of walking. It is (able _____, not able _____) to walk.
does not	11. An inconsiderate person (does _____, does not _____) care about other people's feelings.
inexact	12. His measurements were not exact. They were _____.
were not	13. The students were inattentive. They (were _____, were not _____) paying close attention.

Answers

seldom	14. George's visits were infrequent. He (often _____, seldom _____) came to see us.
weak	15. An infirm patient is (strong _____, weak _____).
is not	16. A fancy dress is inappropriate for yardwork. It (is _____, is not _____) suitable.
didn't have	17. His check came back marked "insufficient funds." He (had _____, didn't have _____) enough money in the bank.
not enough	18. This small house is inadequate for a large family. There's (not enough _____, enough _____) room.
indefinite	19. His answer was not definite. It was _____.
independent	20. The United States is not a dependent country. It is _____.

Part Three: The Prefix *Im-*

The student fills in the blanks or puts a check mark by the correct answer.

Answers

not	1. Something that is impossible is _____ possible.
not	2. An immovable object can _____ be moved.
	3. Another word for *moving* is *mobile:*
not moving	An immobile object is (moving _____, not moving _____).
im	4. Not mature is the same as _____ mature.
impolite	5. Not polite = _____.
improper	6. Not proper = _____.
imperfect	7. Not perfect = _____.
impure	8. Not pure = _____.
improbable	9. Not probable = _____.
impractical	10. Not practical = _____.

At this point the teacher may wish to point out that *in-* becomes *im-* before a root beginning with *p: impossible, improbably, improper.* Linguists call this process assimilation.

The teacher may also show that this assimilation occurs with words beginning with *m* and *b*, as well as *p: impersonal, impatient, impartial, immortal, immodest, immoderate, imbalance, impassable, imperturbable.*

Part Four: The Prefix *Il-*

Note: Only a few familiar words begin with *il-* meaning "not."

Answers

	1. A person who can read is literate; a person who cannot read is
illiterate	_____.
illegal	2. Something that is not legal is _____.

illegible	3. Writing that cannot be read is _____.
illogical	4. An argument that is not logical is _____.
not	5. *Illegitimate* means _____ legitimate.
illiberal	6. The opposite of liberal is _____.
illicit	7. The opposite of *licit* is _____. (The word *illicit* is much more commonly used than *licit*.)

The teacher might discuss the use of a few other words by placing them on the chalkboard and noting, for example, that *illicit,* like *illegal,* also means not legal or unlawful. Variant forms of words in the exercise may be used for practice. For example, *illegality, illiteracy, illegibly, illogically.*

At this point the teacher might continue the discussion of assimilation, the process by which the final consonant of a prefix becomes the same as the first consonant of a root. To illustrate this process, write on the chalkboard *in + legal = inlegal.* Then point out that the correct word is *illegal.* The *n* has changed to *l* because *illegal* is easier to say than *inlegal.* Thus *inmaterial* becomes *immaterial; inmature* becomes *immature; inmodest* becomes *immodest.*

To further illustrate assimilation as a part of a systematic vocabulary study through word analysis and synthesis, the teacher might discuss with the class the following material on prefixes.

1. The prefix does not change to agree with the root.
com (with, together) + *pose* (put or place)

The combination *com + pose = compose* (which literally means to "put things together"). To *compose* a poem is to put the verses together. Note also the word *composition.*

2. The prefix changes to agree with the root.
ob (against, toward) + *pose*

The prefix *ob-* (toward, against) is not used with the root *pose,* as in *obpose* meaning "to place against." The *ob-* becomes *op-* because of the first letter of *pose,* and the word becomes *oppose.*

3. The prefix changes for easier pronunciation.
in (in, on) + *pose*

Through assimilation, *inpose* becomes *impose* (which is easier to say). *Im* (on) + *pose* (put) = *impose* (literally "to put on"). To impose a tax is to put a tax on something. (Note that the *n* sound gets along well with other sounds such as *s* and *k: incomplete, encircles, incision.*)

Part Five: The Prefix *Ir-*

Base words (roots) beginning with *r* usually use the prefix *ir-* to make them negative. For example, *not religious = irreligious.* We can also correctly say *unreligious,* but it is used less often then *irreligious.* The teacher should stress the double *r* in the spelling of these words: one *r* for the prefix, one *r* for the root. Note also that words beginning with *ir-* meaning "not" are comparatively difficult for students in the lower grades to spell correctly.

The teacher can continue the discussion of the prefix *ir-* by presenting the following exercise:

Answers

not	1. An irresponsible person is _____ responsible.
is not	2. An irregular verb (is _____, is not _____) regular.
not	3. The prefix *ir-* means _____.
irrational	4. Not rational = _____.
irredeemable	5. Not redeemable = _____.
irreplaceable	6. Not replaceable = _____.
irreclaimable	7. Not reclaimable = _____.
irreversible	8. Not reversible = _____.
irresistible	9. Not resistible = _____.
irreverent	10. Not reverent = _____.

Note: Nearly all words beginning with *ir-* mean "not," except *irrigate, irritable, irradiate.* The teacher might also wish to point out that the prefix *in-* is not always recognizable. For example, *in-* changes to *ig-* in the words *ignoble* (not noble) and *ignominy* ("shame"; literally "without a good name"). Note also that *in-* is not apparent to most of us in the word *ignore* (from *in* + *gnoscere* or *noscere,* not to know). The Latin word *ignoramus* (we don't know) is used in English to mean an ignorant person.

The Prefix *A-* or *An-*

There are some prefixes, roots, and suffixes that often are not recognized as such. Students should be taught to notice them as they can give clues to the meaning of words.

One of the often unnoticed prefixes is *a-* or *an-,* meaning "not" or "without." (Before a root beginning with a vowel or the letter *h, an-* is used instead of *a-*.) This prefix is usually associated with harder words. But some words beginning with *a-* or *an-* are common. For example: *a* (without) + *mnesia* (memory) = *amnesia* (without memory).

Notice the use of the prefix in each word below:

a + theism	not believing in God
an + esthesia	loss of feeling
a + centric	not on center
a + chromatic	having no color
an + emia	without good blood
a + typical	unlike the type
a + septic	free from bacteria (sepsis)
a + carpous	not bearing fruit
a + damant	can't be subdued (hard)
a + gamous	unmarried
a + gnostic	not knowing
a + graphia	not able to write
a + moral	without a concern for morals
a + morphous	shapeless, formless
an + onymity	without a name

a + symmetrical	not symmetrical, without proportion
a + synchronous	not happening simultaneously
a + branchial	without gills
a + byss	without bottom
a + clinic	without bending
a + kinesis	without movement
a + geusia	without taste
a + manous	without hands
an + hydrous	without water
an + ergy	loss of energy
an + omolous	irregular, deviating from the rule
a + pathetic	without feeling
a + phasia	loss of speech
a + phonic	loss of voice
a + photic	lightless
a + trophy	without nourishment
a + tom	uncut, indivisible (Scientists once believed the atom could not be split.)

Part Six: Review of Negative Prefixes

Students are to use the prefixes *in-*, *il-*, *im-*, *ir-*, and *un-* to make words with the "not" idea in them. Have them check their answers one at a time, place an **X** after any wrong words, and add up their final scores.

Answers

1. clear	unclear
2. happy	unhappy
3. formed	unformed
4. active	inactive (Did you put *un-?*)
5. exact	inexact
6. responsible	irresponsible (two *r*'s)
7. possible	impossible
8. legal	illegal
9. perfect	imperfect
10. active	inactive
11. proper	improper
12. covered	uncovered

Another Meaning of *In-*

As previously pointed out in this unit, the Latin prefix *in-* may mean "not," as in *insomnia* (not sleeping). However, *in-* may also mean "in" or "into," as in *inhale, inject, insert.*

In the following words the prefix *in-* means either "not" or "in." The student writes the correct meaning in the blanks.

1. in include
2. not indirect
3. in income

4. in infield
5. not indivisible
6. not informal

7. in indoors
8. in ingrown
9. not inartistic

10. _in_ inbred	23. _not_ inactive	36. _in_ indent
11. _not_ insane	24. _not_ inacceptable	37. _not_ inaccurate
12. _in_ inhabit	25. _in_ incision	38. _not_ invisible
13. _not_ inhuman	26. _in_ insect	39. _in_ inspect
14. _not_ inability	27. _not_ incapable	40. _in_ insert
15. _in_ involve	28. _not_ individual	41. _not_ inefficient
16. _in_ inhale	29. _in_ incorporate	42. _in_ inside
17. _not_ inexpensive	30. _not_ inhumane	43. _in_ infer
18. _in_ indebted	31. _not_ inadequate	44. _in_ instep
19. _not_ innocent	32. _in_ induct	45. _not_ inexact
20. _in_ inland	33. _not_ inappropriate	46. _in_ invade
21. _not_ insecure	34. _not_ incurable	47. _not_ inequality
22. _in_ input	35. _in_ insole	48. _in_ influx

The Prefix *Ex-*

Have the students read the explanatory sentences and fill in the blanks in the sentences that follow. (From the exercises below, the teacher can select those items appropriate to a particular grade level.)

1. To *export* goods is to send them out of the country.
2. The *exit* is the way out of a building.
3. To *expel* means to force out.
4. To *extract* a tooth is to pull it out.
5. An *exodus* occurs when a great many people go out of a country.
6. When you breathe in, you *inhale*. When you breathe out, you *exhale*.

The student now answers these questions based on the above.

1. What word is used in every sentence? _out_
2. What prefix is used in one word in every sentence? _ex_
3. The meaning of this prefix is _out_.

Other more difficult words are included here for advanced students.

1. To *exclude* someone is to shut him out of the group.
2. To *excavate* means to dig out.
3. To *exclaim* means to shout out.
4. To *expectorate* means to spit out.
5. An *expatriate* is a person who has been banished from or who has voluntarily left his country.
6. An *expeditionary* force is sent out of the country.
7. *External* organs are on the outside of the body.
8. When perspiration *exudes* from the body, it seeps out.
9. When a blackmailer *extorts* money from his victim, he "twists it out" of him.
10. To *expunge* is to erase or blot out.
11. When you *extricate* yourself from trouble, you get out of it.
12. An *expulsion* is a forcing out.
13. To *exhume* a body means to take it out of the grave.

The Prefixes *Ante-* and *Anti-*

The student covers the answer column on the left, completes the exercise, and checks his own answers. The teacher may wish to ask for volunteers to read and explain each answer.

Answers

before against	Do you confuse the prefixes *ante-* and *anti-?* *Antewar* means before the war. So the prefix *ante-* means _____. *Antiwar* means against war. So the prefix *anti-* means _____.

Notice the difference between these two prefixes as you work the exercises below. Fill in the blanks or put a check mark by the correct answer.

came before	1. The Revolutionary War *antedated* (came after _____, came before _____) the War of 1812.
against	2. An antiwar candidate gave many speeches. He was (for _____, against _____) war.
comes before	3. Read this sentence: Mary is the girl who called. *Who* refers to *girl*. *Girl* is called the *antecedent* of *who* because it (comes after _____, comes before _____) *who*.
is against	4. We have an *antislavery* law. This law (favors _____, is against _____) slavery.
before	5. The abbreviation A.M. stands for *ante meridiem*. *Ante meridiem* means (before _____, after _____) noon.
oppose	6. *Antitrust* laws (favor _____, oppose _____) the idea of a big company monopolizing an industry.
before	7. *Bellum* is Latin for *war*. *Antebellum* means (before _____, against _____) the war.
in front of (before)	8. An *anteroom* is a waiting room (behind _____, in front of _____) another room.
anti	9. *Septic* means rotten. To get rid of germs and keep things clean, hospitals use an _____ septic.
fights against	10. *Toxin* means poison. An *antitoxin* (fights against _____, helps spread _____) poison.
false	11. In World War II, Hitler was *antiwar*. (true _____, false _____)
opposes	12. An *antilabor* group (favors _____, opposes _____) labor unions.
doesn't like	13. An *anti-intellectual* (likes _____, doesn't like _____) intellectual people and ideas.
antisocial	14. A person who is against society could be called a <u>a</u> _ _ _ <u>s</u> _ _ _ _ <u>l</u>.
anti	15. An _____dote fights against the effect of poison.
ante	16. The room in front of a chamber could be called an _____chamber.
antihistamine	17. A medicine taken for a cold is an <u>a</u> _ _ _ <u>h</u> _ _ _ <u>a</u> _ _ <u>e</u>.

antiaircraft

18. To fight against air attack, soldiers use
a _ _ _ _ _ _ _ _ _ _ _ guns.

antifreeze

19. What do most automobile radiators need in a cold winter? _____.

opposite

20. Cold is the opposite of hot. Cold is an *antonym* of hot. The word *antonym* means o _ _ _ _ _ _ _ in meaning.

anti; against or opposite

21. *Antonym* comes from (*anti* _____, *ante* _____) meaning _____.

The teacher may duplicate the above procedure by using prefix words from the Appendix in sentences and then checking to see if the class can recognize the prefixes and their meanings. The words should be chosen according to the level of the students.

In constructing the sentences the teacher might note the exercises above and use some of their phraseology; for example:

Antisocial means _____.
To *antedate* is to _____.
External organs are _____.

(Some additional prefixes and words the teacher might use to construct exercises are found in the prefix inventory or review tests at the end of this unit.)

The Prefix *Sub-*

The student fills in the blanks or puts a check mark by the correct answer.

Answers

sub; under

1. A submarine goes under water. In the word *submarine,* the prefix is _____. It means _____.

underground

2. A subway train runs (overhead _____, underground _____).

under

3. *Terrain* means ground. A subterranean passage is an _____ground passage.

under

4. In a report, the subtopic would be (over _____, under _____) the main topic.

under

5. To be submerged in water is to be _____ water.

under/below

6. The subsoil is a layer of earth just _____ the topsoil.

below

7. Substandard food is (above _____, below _____) the standards set by the Federal Food and Drug Act.

below

8. A subnormal amount of rain is (above _____, below _____) the normal amount.

below

9. The science-fiction story was about subhuman creatures. Their development was (above _____, below _____) that of the human race.

under   10. The word *subscribe* literally means "to write _____."

11. Supersonic planes fly faster than, or over, the speed of

under   sound. Subsonic planes fly _____ the speed of sound.

Note: Students can learn the principle of *transfer* if they work with a like prefix in many different words. Once they learn that *sub-* in a word means under, below, or lower in rank, they possess a usable concept that offers them a consistent method of word analysis and a means of steady growth in vocabulary skills.

The Prefix *Super-*

A prefix with the opposite meaning of *sub-* is *super-*, meaning above, beyond, or over. A *supermarket* is an oversized grocery store. Notice the use of *super-* in the following sentences.

a. Hercules had *superhuman* power. It was above or beyond ordinary human power.
b. The TV commercial ended with the claim that "this sportscar will always give you *superb* performance, and its *superlative* finish will last for years."

Have the students fill in the blanks or put a check mark by the correct answer in the sentences below.

Answers

1. Superlative means of the highest quality—above or

beyond   b _ _ _ _ d all the rest.

2. Some cars have a device for forcing more than the normal amount of air and fuel into the cylinders. This

super   device is called a s _ _ _ _charger.

3. The magician seemed to have supernatural powers.

above; beyond   Supernatural powers are a _ _ _ _ or b _ _ _ _ d natural powers.

above   4. The actor gave a superb performance. It was a _ _ _ _ the ordinary.

5. A man who oversees or directs the workers on a job may

super   be called a s _ _ _ _intendent.

super   6. Extra-fine sugar is sometimes called _ _ _ _ _ fine.

7. Using a transparent sheet, the artist superimposed the main rivers on a map of the United States. He put the

over   sheet (over _____, under _____) the map.

8. A writer who uses superfluous words uses (fewer

more   _____, more _____) words than are needed.

9. An abundance of rain is a great supply. A *super-*

greater   *abundance* of rain is a (smaller _____, greater _____) amount than is needed.

above   10. A superior brand of paint is (above _____, below _____) average.

Number Prefixes

When a student learns that words can be put into logical groupings based on roots, prefixes, and suffixes, he is on the road to building an effective vocabulary. One such logical grouping is that of number.

Some key number prefixes are *mono-* and *uni-* (one); *bi-* and *di-* (two); *tri-* (three). Notice that from *mono-* we get *monocle, monoplane, monogram, monorail,* and *monotonous.* From *bi-* we get *bicycle, binocular, bisect, bigamy.*

As an exercise, the teacher might use the chalkboard or overhead projector to display the following prefixes: *uni-* (one), *mono-* (one), *bi-* (two), *tri-* (three), *quad-* (four), *pent-* (five), *sex-* (six), *sept-* (seven), *oct-* (eight), *novem-* (nine), *dec-* (ten), *cent-* (hundred). He can then ask the students to form as many words as they can, using these prefixes.

Using the master prefix list in the appendix, the teacher can also supplement the number list and show the great range of words in this category.

Another exercise of this type is to select roots and use number prefixes to change their meanings. For example, the root *gamy* means marriage. Thus we form *monogamy, bigamy, trigamy,* etc. Some of these words are difficult, but the harder words may be used to challenge abler students.

Students in the lower grades might work with words such as *uni + cycle; bi + cycle, bi + weekly, bi + monthly, bi + yearly; tri + cycle, tri + weekly, tri + monthly, tri + angle.*

Additional words formed from number prefixes are:

biannual:
  twice a year

bicorn:
  two-horned animal

bicuspid:
  two-pointed tooth

bifocal:
  having two focuses

bifoliate:
  having two leaves

bipolar:
  having two poles

bisect:
  to cut in two

bivalve:
  two-shelled animal

centenarian:
  person who is a hundred years old

centennial:
  one-hundredth anniversary

centipede:
  hundred-legged

century
  one hundred years

decade:
  ten years

decathlon:
  ten contests

December:
  Roman tenth month

decimal:
  one tenth

dioxide:
  has two oxygen atoms

diphthong:
  two vowels with one sound

duet:
  two singers

duplicate:
  two copies

monarch:
  one ruler

monk:
  one who lives alone

monotheism:
  belief in one God

monotone:
  one tone

monoxide:
  has one oxygen atom

November:
  Roman ninth month

octet:
  group of eight

octopus:
  eight-footed

quadrangle:
  having four angles

quadrilateral:
  four-sided

quadruped:
  four-legged

quart:
  one fourth of a gallon

quarter:
  one fourth

quartet:
  group of four

quintet:
  group of five

sextet:
  group of six

trident:
  three-pronged fork

trifocal:
  having three focuses

trio:
  group of three

triple:
  three-base hit

triplets:
  three of the same age

triplicate:
  three copies

tripod:
  three-legged

unicorn:
  one-horned animal

unifoliate:
  having one leaf

unique:
  only one of its kind

unison:
  agreement in pitch; same sound

unite:
  become one

Using Number Prefixes in Context

Number prefixes can be used in a variety of ways to help students generalize their meaning. For example, the student might be asked to write short paragraphs using the number prefixes, in order, from one to ten. Here is one approach:

During the summer months this *uni*que (1) musical group performs as *du*ets (2), *tri*os (3), *quar*tets (4), and *quin*tets (5). The *sex*tets (6) perform in *Septem*ber (7), *Octo*ber (8), *Novem*ber (9), and *Decem*ber (10).

Here is another example:

A *mon*k (1) wearing *bi*focals (2) wrote a *tri*logy (3) related to the Medieval *quadr*ium (4)—arithmetic, geometry, astronomy, and music. He described his *quinqu*agenarian (5) teacher, who had taught him that a *penta*gon (5) has five angles, and from whom he learned to write dactylic *hexa*meter (6) verse with which he wrote a *sept*ennial (7) celebration poem—an *octa*ve (8), celebrating the *hept*archy (7) of seven ancient rulers, which he recited on a feast day at noon (9) and which remained popular for several decades (10).

The student might also use the number prefixes in whatever order he prefers, for example:

Early in September (7), a university (1) group visited Washington. Some had never been to the Capitol, others hadn't been there for a decade (10). But all were united (1) in their desire to see as much as possible in a short time. They had no uniform (1) plan for travel. Some hired taxis, some rented bicycles (2) and others hired cabs drawn by quadrupeds (4).

After visiting the Pentagon (5), I looked through my binoculars (2) and saw the huge monolith (1), the Washington Monument ...

Students might continue with the story or begin others. The stories can then be read aloud in class and discussed.

Sentences and passages from textbooks can also be analyzed in terms of the meanings of the prefixes in words. Teachers of science and of mathematics can illustrate and discuss such words as biceps, monoxide, binomial, triangle, trifoliate, unipod, bipod, octopus, etc.

One prefix might be used in several words in a paragraph. One example, tri (3), is given below. To save time the teacher might refer to the list of number prefixes included in this unit. Students might write short paragraphs such as the following:

Trivia

Mrs. Brown, who is trilingual, wears trifocals and talks about trivial things. She often brags about her talented sons, who are triplets.

Bob is a triple-threat quarterback. He also lifts weights to develop his triceps. Bill plays the triangle in the school orchestra, and Don sings with a trio. In school plays, Don played Neptune carrying a trident and Ben Franklin wearing a tricorn hat.

Bill, who is good with his hands, made his mother a trivet, built a tripod for his telescope, constructed a model of a Roman trireme, and repaired his sister's tricycle. All three boys are studying trigonometry. Mrs. Brown keeps their pictures on the mantel — in a triptych.

Master List of Number-Prefixed Words

Mono- (one)

monandry	monk	monochromatic	monocular
monarch	monocellular	monocle	monocycle
monastery	monocentric	monocline	monody
monastic	monocephalous	monocotyledon	monogamy
monaural	monochloride	monocracy	monogeny

monogram	monometallic	monophobia	monotheism
monograph	monometer	monophonic	monotone
monogyny	monomial	monophthong	monotonous
monolingual	monomineral	monoplane	monotype
monolith	monomorphic	monopoly	monovular
monolog	mononuclear	monopropellant	monoxide
monologist	mononucleosis	monorail	
monomania	monoparental	monosyllable	

Uni- (one)

uniaxial	unifoliate	uniparental	unitary
unicameral	uniform	uniparous	unite
unicellular	unify	uniped	unitization
unicentric	unilateral	unipod	unity
unicolor	unilinear	unipolar	univalve
unicorn	unilingual	unique	universal
unicuspid	unimanual	unisexual	universe
unicycle	unimolecular	unison	university
unification	union	unit	
uniflorous	unioval	Unitarian	

Bi- (two)

biangular	biennium	bimillennium	biplane
biannual	bifacial	bimolecular	bipod
biaxial	bifocal	bimonthly	bipolar
bicameral	bifoliate	binary	biquarterly
bicellular	biforked	binaural	biracial
bicentenary	biform	binocular	bireme
bicentennial	bifurcate	binomial	bisect
biceps	bigamy	binuclear	biserrate
bicolor	bilabial	biovular	bisexual
biconcave	bilateral	biparasitic	bitheism
biconvex	bilinear	biparental	bivalent
bicorn	bilingual	biparous	bivalve
bicuspid	billion	bipartisan	biventral
bicycle	bimanual	bipartite	biweekly
bidimensional	bimester	biped	biyearly
biennial	bimetallic	biphonemic	bizonal

Di- (two)

diambic	dihedral	dioxide	disyllable
dichotomy	dilemma	diphthong	dyad
dichromatic	dimeter	diploma	
digram	dimorphic	diplomacy	
digraph	diode	diptych	

Duo-, Dua- (two)

| dual | duality | duet | duologue |
| dualism | duarchy | duo | duopoly |

duotone duplex duplicate duplicity
duotype duplexity duplicator duumvirate

Tri- (three)

triad triennium trimonthly tripolar
triangle trifocal trimotor triptych
triannual trifoliate trinity trireme
triarchy triform trinomial trisect
triaxial trifurcate trinuclear triskaideka-
triceps trigamy trio   phobia
trichotomy trigon tripartisan trisyllable
trichromatic trigonal tripartite tritheism
tricipital trigonometry tripetalous triumvir
tri-city trigraph triphibian triumvirate
tricolor trilateral triphthong trivalve
tricorn trilingual triple trivet
tricuspid trillion triplet trivia
tricycle trilogy triplex trivial
trident trimester triplicate triweekly
tridimensional trimeter triply trizonal
triennial trimolecular tripod

Quad-, Quat-, Quart- (four, fourth)

quadragenarian quadriceps quadrumvirate quartersaw
quadragesima quadricycle quadruped quartet
quadrangle quadriform quadruple quarto
quadrant quadrilateral quadruplicate quatercentenary
quadratic quadrilingual quart quatrain
quadrennial quadrille quarter quatrefoil
quadrennium quadrillion quarterback
quadricentennial quadrivium quarterly

Tetra-, Tetr- (four)

tetrachromatic tetrahedron tetranuclear tetrarchy
tetragonal tetralogy tetrapod tetratheism
tetragram tetrameter tetrapolar tetraxial
tetragraph tetramorphic tetrapterous

Quinque-, Quinqu-, Quint- (five)

quinary quinquagesima quintet quintuplicate
quinate quinquefoliate quintillion
quincentennial quinquennial quintuple
quinquagenarian quintessence quintuplet

Penta-, Pent- (five)

pentacle pentahedral pentarchy pentatomic
pentagon pentalogy pentasyllable pentatonic

Sex- (six)

sexagenarian	sexcentenary	sextet	sextuplet
sexagesima	sexennial	sextile	sextuplicate
sexagonal	sextain	sextillion	
sexangular	sextant	sextuple	

Hexa-, Hex- (six)

hexagon	hexahedron	hexapod	hexatomic
hexagram	hexameter	hexasyllable	hexoxide

Sept- (seven)

September	septet	septuagenarian	septuplicate
septemvirate	septicentennial	septuagesima	
septennial	septillion	septuple	
septennium	septisyllable	septuplet	

Hepta-, Hept- (seven)

heptad	heptameter	heptasyllable	heptatonic
heptagon	heptarchy	heptatomic	

Octa-, Octo- (eight)

octachord	octangular	octet	octopus
octad	octant	October	octoroon
octagon	octarchy	octodont	octosyllable
octahedron	octave	octofoil	octuple
octameter	octavo	octogenarian	octuplet
octane	octennial	octopod	octuplicate

Novem-, Non- (nine)

nonagon	nonagesimal	November	novenary
nonagenarian	nones	novena	

Dec-, Deca- (ten)

decade	Decameron	decathlon	decibel
decagon	decamerous	December	decigram
decagram	decameter	decennary	decimal
decahedron	decapod	decennial	decimate
decaliter	decasyllable	decennium	decuplet

Cent-, Centi- (hundred)

cent	centesimo	centime	centuplicate
centenarian	centigrade	centimeter	centurial
centenary	centigram	centipede	centurion
centennial	centillion	centumvir	century

Prefixes Showing Quantity or Size

Prefix	Meaning	Example Words
ambi-	both, either	ambivalent, ambidextrous, ambilateral
amph-	both	amphitheater, amphibious, amphibian
bi-	two, twice	bimonthly, biweekly, biennial
cent-	one hundred	century, centipede, centigram
dec-	tenth	decimal, decimate, decade
demi-, hemi-, semi-	half, partly	demigod, hemisphere, semiconscious, hemidemisemiquaver
deuter-	second	deuter, deuteron, deuterium, Deuteronomy
di-, du-, dy-	two, doubly	dichotomy, duplex, duplicate, dyad
en-, em-	in	enclose, encircle, embrace, embalm
heca-, hect-	one hundred	hecatomb, hectogram, hectometer
hept-, sept-	seven	heptagon, septennial, September
hex-	six	hexagon, hexagonal, hexagram, hexapod
holo-	whole	holomorphic, holocaust, holograph
hyper-	over, excessive	hyperthyroid, hyperactive, hypersensitive
hypo-	under, too little	hypodermic, hypothyroid, hyposensitive
iso-	equal, same	isobar, isometric, isosceles
kilo-	one thousand	kilowatt, kilometer, kilocycle
long-	long	longboat, longevity, longitude
macro-	long, large	macrocosm, macroscopic, macron
mega-	large	megalopolis, megalomania, megaphone
micro-	small	microscope, micrometer, microfilm
milli-	one thousandth	milligram, millimeter, milliampere
mono-	one	monocle, monorail, monarch
multi-	many	multitude, multimillionaire, multiply
myriad-	ten thousand	myriad, myriapod, myriadfold
nona, novem-	nine, ninth	nonagon, nonagenarian, November
oct-	eight	octogenarian, octagon, octagonal, octuple
olig-	few	oligarch, oligarchy, oligocarpous
omni-	all	omnivorous, omnipresent, omniscient
over-	above, beyond	overwork, overestimate, overlearn
pan-	all	pandemonium, pan-American; panoply
pent-	five	pentameter, pentagon, pentecost
poly-	many	polygon, polygamy, polysyllable
prim-	first	primer, primary, primitive, primogeniture
proto-	first	protozoa, prototype, protoplasm
quad-, quatr-, quart-	fourth	quadruple, quatrain, quadrangle, quarter
quin-	five, fifth	quintet, quintuplet, quinquennial, quintain
sesqui-	one and a half	sesquilateral, sesquicentennial, sesquipedalian
sex-, sext-	six	sextet, sextant, sexagonal
sol-	alone, only	solitary, solo, desolate
sub-, sup-	under, below	submarine, substandard, support, supplant

super-, supr-	over	supersede, supernatural, supreme, supranational
ter-	third	tertiary, tercentenary, *tertium quid*
tetra-	four	tetrameter, tetrarch, tetrarchy, tetrad
tri-	three	triangle, trigonometry, triple, triad
uni-	one, single	unified, unit, unity, unicorn, unilateral
vigint-, vicen-	twenty	vigintennial, vicennial, vigesimal

The Prefixes *Over-* and *Under-*

The prefixes *over-* and *under-* are often used to form a word or to accentuate the meaning of a word. For example, *overrated, overpaid, overacted;* or *underrated, underpaid, underacted.*

The prefix *over-* has four main meanings, as illustrated below.

1. He overate. (*too much*)
2. We overslept. (*too long*)
3. They played overtime. (*extra*)
4. The stream overflowed its banks. (*over*)

The prefix *under-* has six main meanings.

1. Romans wearing togas also wore short tunics as undergarments. (*beneath*)
2. Underlined words will be italicized. (*below*)
3. The underside of the ship must be scraped. (*lower*)
4. Our steaks were tough because they were undercooked. (*not enough*)
5. She was an understudy to a famous actress. (*lower in rank*)
6. A dwarf is undersized. (*below normal*)

Using the prefixes *over-* and *under-,* the teacher might point out that although we can often use *over-* and *under-* with the same word to express opposite meanings (*overpass* and *underpass*), other opposites are not always so logically formed. Thus we can "undermine a plot," but we cannot "overmine a plot." We can get "underway" but not "overway."
 The teacher might point out how *over-* and *under-* are used in these expressions:

1. *underlying* themes, but not *overlying* themes
2. *overwhelming* ideas, but not *underwhelming*
3. *undermining* one's health, but not *overmining*
4. *overstaying* our welcome, but not *understaying*
5. *overstepped* the bounds of propriety, but not *understepped*
6. *undernourished,* but not *overnourished*
7. guilty of an *oversight,* but not an *undersight*
8. works *overtime,* but not *undertime*
9. an *undersecretary,* but no *oversecretary*
10. an *undersheriff* (deputy), but no *oversheriff*
11. *underbrush,* but no *overbrush*
12. *underpinnings,* but no *overpinnings*
13. the *undersigned,* but not the *oversigned*
14. an *understudy,* but no *overstudy* (as a noun)
15. we *overburden,* but don't *underburden*

The following might also be noted:

a. A person can be *overwrought* (wearied, or worked up to a high pitch), and also *underwrought* (underworked).
(*Underwrought* is not often used, but it is listed in some dictionaries as an adjective. *Wrought* is a past participle of *work*. It was used in the first telegraph message, "What hath God wrought!")
b. *Overwriting* something is not the opposite of *underwriting* it.
c. *Overtaker* is not the opposite of *undertaker*.

Prefix Inventory or Review Test

The teacher may present the following exercise on prefixes as either a diagnostic or a review lesson. The same format may be used to test knowledge of roots or suffixes.

The teacher might explain that the students should know these key prefixes because they combine with roots to form thousands of words.

In this exercise, the student studies the meaning of each prefix, notices the sample word it forms, and using the same prefix writes two additional words beside each sample word. Students should discuss their words.

Prefix	Sample Words	Student's Words
ab- (away from)	abduct	
ad- (to)	adhere	
ante- (before)	antecedent	
anti- (against)	antislavery	
auto- (self)	autograph	
bene- (well, good)	benefit	
bi- (two, twice)	bimonthly	
cent- (hundred)	centimeter	
circu- (around)	circular	
col- (together, with)	collaborate	
com- (together, with)	combine	

contra- (against)	contradict	_____
counter- (against)	counteract	_____
de- (away)	detract	_____
de- (down)	descend	_____
dia- (through, between)	diagonal	_____
dis- (apart from)	dislocate	_____
dis- (not)	disobey	_____
dis- (opposite)	disorganize	_____
dys- (bad)	dysentery	_____
eu- (well, good)	eulogy	_____
extra- (outside, beyond)	extradite	_____
fore- (in front)	foreground	_____
il- (not)	illegible	_____
im- (not)	immaculate	_____
in- (not)	inactive	_____
inter- (between, among)	intermission	_____
ir- (not)	irrational	_____
macro- (large)	macroscopic	_____
magni- (great, large)	magnitude	_____
mal- (bad)	malaria	_____
medi- (middle)	median	_____
mega- (large)	megaphone	_____
meta- (beyond)	metapsychosis	_____
micro- (small)	microfilm	_____

Prefix	Sample Words	Student's Words
mid- (middle)	midship	_____ _____
mis- (wrong)	misdeed	_____ _____
mono- (one)	monocle	_____ _____
multi- (many)	multicolored	_____ _____
neo- (new, modern)	neolithic	_____ _____
omni- (all)	omnipotent	_____ _____
per- (through)	permeate	_____ _____
peri- (above, near)	pericranium	_____ _____
peri- (around)	perimeter	_____ _____
poly- (many)	polygon	_____ _____
post- (after)	postdate	_____ _____
pre- (before)	predict	_____ _____
pro- (before, in front)	proseminar	_____ _____
pro- (forward)	project	_____ _____
proto- (first)	prototype	_____ _____
pseudo- (false)	pseudonym	_____ _____
quasi- (seemingly)	quasihistorical	_____ _____
re- (again)	rediscover	_____ _____
re- (back)	repay	_____ _____
retro- (back)	retroactive	_____ _____
sub- (under, below)	submerge	_____ _____
super- (over)	superhuman	_____ _____
supra- (beyond)	supraorbital	_____ _____

sym- (together, with)	symmetry	_____ _____
syn- (together, with)	synopsis	_____ _____
trans- (cross, over)	transmit	_____ _____
ultra- (beyond)	ultramodern	_____

Inventory or Review Tests on Common Prefixes

The teacher can use the following matching tests to diagnose or evaluate the student's ability to recognize common prefixes.

The tests are arranged in two main groups: (1) Lower Level, for prefixes often met in reading material used in elementary and junior high grades, and (2) Higher Level, for prefixes found in the reading material of the higher grades.

Our studies indicate that many common prefixes classified here as Lower Level are actually not known by many high school seniors. In addition, the authors have worked with college-level students who do not recognize common prefixes such as *tele-* (distant) or *dec-* (ten). The tests marked Lower Level might therefore be used to advantage at all levels.

Test instructions: The student matches the prefix in Column 1 with the correct definition in Column 2 by writing the appropriate number in the blank. For the teacher's convenience in checking the students' answers, the correct numbers are given. Answers may be used more than once.

Lower Level

Section A

Column 1		Column 2
3	re-	1. far away
4	im-	2. eight
1	tele-	3. back
2	oct-	4. not
7	counter-	5. near
8	bene-	6. below
12	homo-	7. against
10	col-	8. well, good
13	ante-	9. across
9	trans-	10. together with
		11. beside
		12. same
		13. before

Section B

Column 1		Column 2
3	non-	1. back
4	bi-	2. in
1	retro-	3. not
2	en-	4. two
7	co-	5. above
9	mid-	6. wrong
12	circum-	7. together with
11	ab-	8. apart from
8	dis-	9. middle
3	ir-	10. all
		11. from
		12. around

Section C

Column 1

3	in-
4	fore-
1	super-
2	vice-
7	con-
13	dia-
11	cent-
10	auto-
12	uni-
9	de-

Column 2

1. over
2. in place of
3. into
4. in front of
5. behind
6. around
7. together with
8. near
9. away from
10. self
11. hundred
12. one
13. through, between

Section D

Column 1

2	il-
4	ex-
6	circu-
1	intra-
8	over-
5	de-
9	com-
13	post-
10	pro-
12	dec-

Column 2

1. within
2. not
3. all
4. out of
5. down
6. around
7. below
8. above, beyond
9. together with
10. in favor of
11. distant
12. ten
13. behind, after

Higher Level

Section A

Column 1

3	a-
5	per-
1	neo-
2	tetra-
7	preter-
9	dys-
11	quasi-
13	penta-
12	demi-
8	eu-
15	hetero-
14	amphi-

Column 2

1. new
2. four
3. on
4. except
5. through
6. among
7. beyond
8. good
9. bad
10. near
11. seeming
12. half
13. five
14. both
15. different

Section B

Column 1

4	hex-
5	cata-
1	para-
2	pseudo-
8	macro-
9	meta-
11	iso-
7	hyper-
10	epi-
12	hept-
15	apo-
14	hypo-

Column 2

1. beside
2. false
3. around
4. six
5. down
6. within
7. over
8. large
9. change
10. upon
11. equal, same
12. seven
13. many
14. under
15. away from

7

Suffixes

Many teachers consider it unwise to teach vocabulary by asking students to master unknown prefixes, suffixes, and roots. We agree completely. We believe that prefixes, suffixes, and roots should be learned from the study of known words. In short, we move from the known to the unknown. The student learns best by discovery. He should be encouraged to make his own generalizations through intelligent inference.

For example, we want him to generalize the fact that *ed* at the end of a verb indicates the past tense. We want him to generalize, from dozens of words which he already knows, that *tele* means distant or far away, as in *television, telemeter, telephone, telegraph,* and *telepathy.*

We believe that attention must be given to separate parts in order that they may be integrated into larger units. We start with a familiar word, break it into meaningful parts, and then transfer the meaning of these parts to new words. We are always working from known to unknown words by a process of generalization.

We ask the teacher to put before the student a series of selected words, such as *automobile, autograph, autobiography, automatic,* and then show him that if he learns the meaning of *auto* (self) in these words, he can apply this concept to other words, such as *automation, autonomy,* and *autopsy.* He should be able to infer the meaning of an unfamiliar word if he knows the meaning of a prefix or root used to form the word.

Our aim is to move by easy steps from some knowledge (*automobile*) to increased knowledge (*autonomous*). It is not to move from zero knowledge to increased knowledge.

Many teachers say, "Students will learn these roots in the words they read." There is some merit in this approach. However, as was pointed out earlier, such learning often turns out to be accidental. Actually, if students really did learn these roots "as they came up," they would already know *tele, graph, son, phon,* because they know many words in which these word elements appear. But they don't know the word parts. Many people do not know the meaning of *dys, dec, itis, proto,* or *pseudo,* although they have seen them in hundreds of words.

Our studies show clearly that many children do not know common roots, prefixes, and suffixes. This is not because teachers really think it unwise to teach them but because many teachers have not shown the student that he already has the raw material for this learning.

Grouping Words

One way to learn and remember words is to classify them according to families. For example, if you look closely at the following words you will notice that they are related: *local, locally, locate, location, locality, localize, dislocate, locus.* These words all come from the Latin word *locus,* meaning place. The root of all these words is *loc.*

Other words may belong to a family group having the same prefix. For example, *ex,* meaning "out of," produces words such as *exit, export, exodus, exhale,* and *expel.*

Furthermore, the meanings of the words within these families can be broadened by the addition of suffixes. For example, *export* (to ship out goods) can be changed to *exporter* (*one who* ships out goods).

In presenting the exercises in this unit, the teacher may use the chalkboard, duplicated sheets, or the overhead projector. The answers are provided here for the teacher's convenience and may be included on the student's worksheet if the teacher wishes to make the lessons self-corrective. The exercises are not prepared for specific grades. Teachers should select the exercises or those parts of the exercise that best fit their grade level. Less able students may do the easiest parts of a lesson. More able students will be challenged by the harder concepts presented in a lesson.

Word Association

By using various exercises and models the teacher can create in the student a sensitivity to word association, the relationship existing between word parts that make up key words. Students can be taught early that suffixes have meaning, that their meaning can be transferred from one word to another. For example, a student who knows the word *hatless* can transfer the suffix *-less* from *hatless* to other words of negation: *homeless, shoeless, fearless,* etc. Other easily transferred suffixes are *-er* (more), as in *greater, stronger, higher, larger, wider;* and *-fy* (make), as in *simplify, purify, magnify, beautify, pacify*. Merely seeing words of like endings together is a key factor in vocabulary development, and teachers should list them for study.

Suffixes and Word Parts

The following exercises in suffixes show the relationship of one word to another through their component parts. They may serve as models which the teacher can use to construct additional exercises suitable for various classes.

The teacher may illustrate the following concepts on the chalkboard or overhead transparency. He might explain that one way to learn more about words is to analyze them, since many words are made up of parts. For example, the word *unselfishness*.

Take the basic word	*self*
Add an ending	self + *ish*
Add another ending	self + ish + *ness*
Now add a beginning	*un* + self + ish + ness

Or he might display these words: *enter* (go in), *entered* (went in). He would make sure that the students understood that the ending *-ed* changed the meaning of the word *enter* from present time to past time and help them draw the inference that the endings of words have special meanings. He would then show them that in the word *guns* the *s* means "more than one."

Instead of saying "He is a person who raises crops or cattle on a farm," we just say "He is a farmer." The first sentence has twelve words; the second sentence has only four. The difference is in the *-er* ending in the word *farmer*.

The exercise below helps the student learn the meaning of words from their parts.

Answers

farms	1. A farmer is a person who _ _ _ _ <u>s</u>.
calls	2. A caller is a person who _ _ _ _ <u>s</u>.
teaches	3. A teacher is a person who _ _ _ _ _ _ <u>s</u>.
person who	4. A listener is a <u>p</u> _ _ _ _ _ _ _ _ listens.
person who	5. The ending *-er* means "a _____ _____ does something."
act	6. Write the word *act* here: _____
actor	7. Write the word *actor* here: _____
or	8. The difference between *act* and *actor* is _____.
actor	9. A *person who acts* is an _____.
sailor	10. A *person who sails* is a <u>s a i l</u> _ _.
person who	11. A preacher is a _____ _____ preaches.
person who	12. The endings *-er* and *-or* mean "a _____ _____ does something."
baker	13. A *person who bakes* is a _____.
rower	14. A person who rows is a _____.
walker	15. A person who walks is a _____.
leader	16. A person who leads is a _____.
runner	17. A person who runs is a _____.
swimmer	18. A person who swims is a _____.

The endings of words have meaning. By putting an ending on a word we can change the <u>meaning</u> of that word. Such endings are called suffixes. In the words *writer* and *author, healer* and *doctor, worker* and *operator, speaker* and *orator*, the suffixes are <u>er</u> and <u>or</u>. In the word *actor, -or* is a <u>suffix</u>. The part of a word after the root is called the <u>suffix</u>.

The Suffix *-less*

The student needs to know that a suffix can change the meaning or the function of a word. In the following self-instructional exercise the student gets practice in generalizing about the meaning and use of a suffix. The student reads the sentences and fills in or checks the blanks. If you provide answers, he can cover the answer column on the left and check his answers as he completes each item.

Answers

fear	1. A fearless man is a man without _____.
beard	2. A beardless man is a man without a _____.
home	3. A homeless person is a person without a _____.
without	4. A windowless room is a room _____ windows.
without	5. In the word *hopeless*, the suffix *-less* means _____.
clean	6. A spotless table is (clean _____, dirty _____). It
has no	(has _____, has no _____) spots on it.
not to blame	7. The judge said the prisoner was guiltless. The prisoner was (to blame _____, not to blame _____).
without	8. Some scientists believe space is infinite, or endless. (It is _____ end.)

Note: The teacher may present additional nouns being studied to which the students might add the suffix *-less*.

Suffixes and Spelling: Part I

Some trouble spots in spelling can be eliminated by grouping words according to their similarity of construction. For example, one group would consist of words that have one vowel and end with a single consonant:

fan   run   hot

Here are some others:

swim   run   spin   wrap

We can change the meaning of these words by adding the suffix *-er:*

swim—swimmer   run—runner
spin—spinner   wrap—wrapper

But notice what happened. We doubled the final consonant before adding *er*. Here are some exercises to try:

Answers	Word	Adding *er*
planner	1. plan	plan _ _ _
dipper	2. dip	d i _ _ _ _
stopper	3. stop	s _ _ _ _ _
batter	4. bat	_ _ _ _ _ _

What did you do before you added *er* to these words?
(doubled the last letter of the word)

119

When a word has only one vowel and ends in a single consonant, the consonant is doubled before adding a suffix beginning with a vowel. Examples:

swim   swimmer (double the *m*)
run   runner (double the *n*)

But notice these words:

cup   cupful
hat   hatful

The rule doesn't work here. Why? Compare the suffix *-ful* and the suffix *-er*. One begins with a vowel, the other begins with a consonant. (Since *ful* does *not* begin with a vowel, you don't double the *p* in *cupful* or the *t* in *hatful*.)
Now look at these words:

sit   sitter (double the *t*)
hat   hatful (don't double the *t*)

Before you add a suffix beginning with a vowel you double the final consonant. Using the rule, add *ing* to the following words to make other words. Remember, *ing* begins with a vowel.

Answers

batting   1. bat _ _ _ _ _ _ _
pinning   2. pin _ _ _ _ _ _ _
winning   3. win _ _ _ _ _ _ _

Add *ed* to these words (*ed* begins with a vowel):

matted   1. mat _ _ _ _ _ _
jammed   2. jam _ _ _ _ _ _
petted   3. pet _ _ _ _ _ _

Add *en* to these words (*en* begins with a vowel):

fatten   1. fat _ _ _ _ _ _
gotten   2. got _ _ _ _ _ _
rotten   3. rot _ _ _ _ _ _

The suffixes *-er, -ed, -ing, -en* begin with a vowel.

For further practice, add *ing* to these words:

dabbing	1. dab	_ _ _ _ _ _ _	nagging	11. nag	_ _ _ _ _ _ _
gabbing	2. gab	_ _ _ _ _ _ _	sagging	12. sag	_ _ _ _ _ _ _
jabbing	3. jab	_ _ _ _ _ _ _	snagging	13. snag	_ _ _ _ _ _ _ _
padding	4. pad	_ _ _ _ _ _ _	tagging	14. tag	_ _ _ _ _ _ _
bagging	5. bag	_ _ _ _ _ _ _	wagging	15. wag	_ _ _ _ _ _ _
bragging	6. brag	_ _ _ _ _ _ _ _	fanning	16. fan	_ _ _ _ _ _ _
dragging	7. drag	_ _ _ _ _ _ _ _	tanning	17. tan	_ _ _ _ _ _ _
flagging	8. flag	_ _ _ _ _ _ _ _	banning	18. ban	_ _ _ _ _ _ _
gagging	9. gag	_ _ _ _ _ _ _	spanning	19. span	_ _ _ _ _ _ _ _
lagging	10. lag	_ _ _ _ _ _ _	scanning	20. scan	_ _ _ _ _ _ _ _

Suffixes and Spelling: Part II

Another group of words might be formed of those having two vowels and ending with a single consonant:

boat   beat   lead

When we add *er,* we have:

boater   beater   leader

Add *er* to these words to make other words:

Answers

feeler	1. feel	f e e l _ _
peeler	2. peel	p _ _ _ _ _
sealer	3. seal	s _ _ _ _ _
healer	4. heal	_ _ _ _ _ _
stealer	5. steal	_ _ _ _ _ _ _

Look at this word: *steep* (Note the *two* vowels.)

Add *er:*   *steeper*

Look at this word: *step*

Add *er:*   *stepper*

What's the rule? When a word has one vowel and ends with a single consonant, the final letter is doubled before adding a suffix beginning with a vowel (such as *er*).
Look at these words:

peep	peeper	creep	creeper
keep	keeper	sleep	sleeper
reap	reaper		

What's the rule? In a word containing two vowels and ending in a single consonant, the final consonant is not doubled when a vowel suffix is added.

Now try out the above rule with the following words. Add *ing* (suffix beginning with a vowel) to these words:

Answers

reaping	1. reap	_ _ _ _ _ _ _
weeping	2. weep	_ _ _ _ _ _ _
seeping	3. seep	_ _ _ _ _ _ _
leaping	4. leap	_ _ _ _ _ _ _
heaping	5. heap	_ _ _ _ _ _ _

Check one: You (do ___, do not _X_) double the final consonant in these words.

121

Now add *ing* (suffix beginning with a vowel) to the following words:

napping	1. nap	_ _ _ _ _ _ _
mapping	2. map	_ _ _ _ _ _ _
rapping	3. rap	_ _ _ _ _ _ _
tapping	4. tap	_ _ _ _ _ _ _
clapping	5. clap	_ _ _ _ _ _ _ _
trapping	6. trap	_ _ _ _ _ _ _ _
snapping	7. snap	_ _ _ _ _ _ _ _
slapping	8. slap	_ _ _ _ _ _ _ _

Check one: You (do _X_, do not ___) double the final consonant in these words.

Using the rules you've learned, add *er* (suffix beginning with a vowel) to these words:

Answers

flapper	1. flap	_____
sleeper	2. sleep	_____
steeper	3. steep	_____
scrapper	4. scrap	_____
clearer	5. clear	_____
sweeper	6. sweep	_____
loader	7. load	_____
steamer	8. steam	_____
nearer	9. near	_____
setter	10. set	_____
neater	11. neat	_____
blotter	12. blot	_____
floater	13. float	_____
trotter	14. trot	_____
dreamer	15. dream	_____
speaker	16. speak	_____
kidder	17. kid	_____
skidder	18. skid	_____
header	19. head	_____
threader	20. thread	_____

Can you write the rules you've learned above? Try it.

_____
_____

Suffixes and Word Associations

The student needs practice in constructing the variant forms of familiar words so that he will readily see the relationship between such words as *care* and *carefulness, change* and *changeable,* or more difficult words such as *credit* and *creditable; sign, signify,* and *signification.* He will learn to associate certain words if he can recognize parts of speech by their inflectional endings (*-fy, -er, -or, -able, -ful, -less, -ness,* etc.). The teacher may introduce the following exercises on the chalkboard, a slide, or an overhead transparency.

1. Nouns name things or ideas. *Bread, butter, air, love, hate, goodness,* and *honesty* are nouns. Adjectives describe nouns. *Hot, cold, blue, pretty, reckless,* and *careful* are **adjectives**.
2. The adjective *careful* becomes a noun when you change it to *carefulness.* By adding the suffix *-ness* to an adjective you can make a **n o u n**.
3. *Careful* is an **adjective**.
4. *Carefulness* is a **noun**.

Below are nouns formed by adding the suffix *-ness* to adjectives:

fair*ness*   kind*ness*
idle*ness*   sad*ness*
rough*ness*   smooth*ness*

Note: If the teacher wishes to make this exercise self-corrective, he may duplicate it and include the answer key.
The student makes nouns from the following adjectives.

Answers

dimness	1. dim _____
stillness	2. still _____
quickness	3. quick _____
brightness	4. bright _____
fondness	5. fond _____
greatness	6. great _____
tenderness	7. tender _____
nearness	8. near _____
sickness	9. sick _____

A variation of this exercise is given below. Students are to write the correct answer in the blank.

Answers

sweetness	1. The opposite of sourness is (a) sweetness, (b) sweet, (c) sweetly. _____
goodness	2. The opposite of badness is (a) good, (b) goodness, (c) goodly. _____
thickness	3. The opposite of thinness is (a) thick, (b) thicker, (c) thickness. _____
slowness	4. The opposite of quickness is (a) slowness, (b) slow, (c) slowly. _____
weakness	5. The opposite of strength is (a) weak, (b) weakly, (c) weakness. _____
darkness	6. In the daytime we have light. At night we have d _ _ _ n _ _ _.

Call the students' attention to the fact that some words ending in *y* change the *y* to *i* before adding *ness*.

silly   sill*i*ness   nasty   nast*i*ness

They may try it with these words:

Answers

hastiness	1. hasty	_____
prettiness	2. pretty	_____
loveliness	3. lovely	_____
healthiness	4. healthy	_____
homeliness	5. homely	_____
naughtiness	6. naughty	_____
haughtiness	7. haughty	_____
craftiness	8. crafty	_____

Point out also that there are some words that do not change the *y* to *i*, for example:

dry   dryness   shy   shyness   sly   slyness

Review

The students add *ness* to the following words. The teacher might remind them about changing *y* to *i* and doubling consonants. Note the exception to the rule with *shyness*.

1. worthy	worthiness	9. damp	_____
2. green	_____	10. brown	_____
3. prepared	_____	11. stout	_____
4. sturdy	_____	12. worldly	_____
5. tight	_____	13. haughty	_____
6. kindly	_____	14. rough	_____
7. happy	_____	15. sick	_____
8. manly		16. shy	

Here is another approach to grouping words of similar construction as an aid to spelling. If a word has a single vowel and ends with two consonants, such as *nd* in *band, sand,* and *land,* we can add suffixes without doubling the final letter: *banded, sander, landing.*
Here are some others:

hand, handed   grand, grander
brand, branding   strand, stranded

Add *ing* to these words.		Add *ed* to these.		Add *er* to these.	
1. bank	banking	1. grant	granted	1. mark	marker
2. crank	cranking	2. chant	chanted	2. bark	barker
3. flank	flanking	3. pant	panted	3. dark	darker
4. spank	spanking	4. plant	planted	4. park	parker
5. thank	thanking	5. slant	slanted	5. spark	sparker

124

Before you add a suffix to a word ending with two consonants, you (double ___, do not double <u>X</u>) the final letter of the word.

Suffixes and Parts of Speech

The Suffix -ment

The suffix -ment (the state of) is used to form nouns.

Example:

content   <u>contentment</u>
enjoy   <u>enjoyment</u>
arrange   <u>arrangement</u>
treat   <u>treatment</u>

Note: Students can check their spelling in the dictionary, or they may exchange papers.

move — movement
refresh — refreshment
pave — pavement
improve — improvement
entertain — entertainment
state — statement
advertise — advertisement
announce — announcement

assort — assortment
establish — establishment
contain — containment
induce — inducement
commence — commencement
arrange — arrangement
require — requirement
engage — engagement

Words ending in e are often misspelled when a suffix like -ment is added. From exercises like this, students should be able to formulate the general rule that a final e is retained before adding ment (or any other suffix that begins with a consonant).

Some words ending in y preceded by a vowel add ment without changing the root:

pay — payment
enjoy — enjoyment

repay — repayment
employ — employment

But note that some words ending in y change the y to i before adding ment.

merry — merriment
embody — embodiment

accompany — accompaniment
disembody — disembodiment

The Suffix -ish

The suffix -ish can mean like, somewhat, belonging to, tending to, near to. The following exercise shows how the suffix -ish can be used to form adjectives from nouns. The student checks the words he knows. Difficult words should be discussed in class.

1. ___ reddish	21. ___ sheepish
2. ___ Swedish	22. ___ Micawberish
3. ___ childish	23. ___ feverish
4. ___ oafish	24. ___ impoverish
5. ___ raffish	25. ___ Irish
6. ___ selfish	26. ___ boorish
7. ___ wolfish	27. ___ Moorish
8. ___ piggish	28. ___ amateurish
9. ___ freakish	29. ___ British
10. ___ bookish	30. ___ coquettish
11. ___ English	31. ___ Scottish
12. ___ devilish	32. ___ loutish
13. ___ foolish	33. ___ bluish
14. ___ girlish	34. ___ slavish
15. ___ boyish	35. ___ shrewish
16. ___ stylish	36. ___ knavish
17. ___ Danish	37. ___ Jewish
18. ___ Spanish	38. ___ thirtyish
19. ___ Rhenish	39. ___ mannish
20. ___ snobbish	40. ___ Finnish

The Suffix -logy

Words ending in *logy* may at first look more difficult to the student than they really are. However, if the student learns that *logy* means "the study of," he can then concentrate on the base word or root of words ending in *logy*.

Thus *musicology*, which may look hard, means simply the study of music. *Mineralogy* is the study of minerals. The student knows what glaciers are. He may therefore easily infer that glaciology is the study of glaciers.

Many names of the sciences are *logy* words. The class may study the roots in Section A, noting that *logy* can be added to each of them to form the name of a science. After learning the combining forms, the students can test themselves on Section B. (Answers are provided.)

Section A

zoo
   (animal)

astro
   (star, planet)

anthropo
   (man)

archaeo
   (ancient, primitive)

meteoro
   (high atmosphere)

ornitho
   (bird)

pharmaco
   (drug)

bio
   (life)

geo
   (earth)

psycho
   (soul, mind)

entomo
   (insect)

etymo
   (origin of a word)

herpeto
   (reptile)

Section B

The student puts the letter of the correct definition in the blank:

The Science   **The Definition** (The study of:)

- <u>g</u>   1. biology   a. the origins of words
- <u>i</u>   2. geology   b. man's mind
- <u>h</u>   3. anthropology   c. insects
- <u>b</u>   4. psychology   d. birds
- <u>j</u>   5. archaeology   e. reptiles and amphibians
- <u>c</u>   6. entomology   f. drugs
- <u>k</u>   7. meteorology   g. life
- <u>a</u>   8. etymology   h. man
- <u>d</u>   9. ornithology   i. earth's history and life
- <u>e</u>   10. herpetology   j. material remains of early human life
- <u>f</u>   11. pharmacology   k. the atmosphere, especially weather
- <u>m</u>   12. zoology   l. the influence of the stars and planets on human affairs
- <u>l</u>   13. astrology   m. animals

Note: The student obviously should not be asked to learn all the words presented here. The exercise merely shows how the suffix -*logy* can be used with various roots to create new words.

Follow-up Exercise

The following list of *logy* words might be duplicated and the student asked to check the words he thinks he knows. Meanings of selected words should be discussed. Some students may be interested in tracing the etymology of certain *logy* words in the list. For example, *seismology* (the study of earthquakes) from Greek *seismos* (earthquake) and *seiein* (to shake).

Words Ending in -*logy* (Study of)

agrology	cosmology	ethnology	hydrology
algology	craniology	etiology	hypnology
anthropology	criminology	etymology	ideology
apiology	crustaceology	gastrology	laryngology
arachnology	cryptology	genealogy	lexicology
archaeology	cytology	geology	lithology
astrology	demonology	geratology	liturgiology
audiology	dendrology	gerontology	metapsychology
bacteriology	dermatology	glaciology	meteorology
bibliology	ecclesiology	graphology	methodology
biology	ecology	gynecology	metrology
biopsychology	Egyptology	heliology	microbiology
cardiology	embryology	herpetology	microclimatology
carpology	enterology	hierology	micrology
chronology	entomology	hippology	micromineralogy
cosmetology	epistemology	histology	mineralogy

morphology	orology	pharyngology	symbology
musicology	osteology	phonology	technology
mythology	paleoanthropology	physiology	terminology
nasology	paleology	piscatology	theology
nematology	paleontology	pteridology	topology
neurology	parapsychology	psychology	toxicology
numerology	parasitology	radiology	typology
	pathology	radiobiology	zoology
oceanology	patrology	seismology	
odontology	pedology	sexology	
ontology	penology	sitology	
oology	pharmacology	sociology	

The Suffix *-itis*

The Greek suffix *-itis,* referring to diseases, means inflammation. When we combine it with other word elements such as the Greek root *arthr* (a joint) we get the word *arthritis,* a disease characterized by swelling or inflammation of the joints. A person suffering from this disease may be described as *arthritic* (from the Greek adjective *arthritikos*).

It should be noted that *itis* words are often humorously coined to express a sort of mania. For example, a group of sports enthusiasts may be described as having *footballitis* (and a team may have *fumbleitis*), or high interest in an election may be referred to as *electionitis.* Nervous tension characteristic of American hurry and drive has been called *Americanitis.*

In the list below, students may check the words they know or have heard, and later discuss their meaning or origin with the teacher. The words are not meant to be memorized, but their compound parts should be noted. A teacher's key to the root meanings of these medical terms is listed below.

___ adenoiditis	___ encephalitis	___ neuritis
___ appendicitis	___ enteritis	___ osteomyelitis
___ arthritis	___ gastritis	___ peritonitis
___ bronchitis	___ laryngitis	___ phlebitis
___ bursitis	___ mastoiditis	___ pharyngitis
___ carditis	___ meningitis	___ sinusitis
___ conjunctivitis	___ myelitis	___ splenitis
___ dermatitis	___ nephritis	___ tonsillitis

Root Meanings

adenoiditis (Greek *aden,* gland + *eidos,* form + *-itis*): inflammation of the adenoids

appendicitis (Latin *append,* hang on + *-itis*): inflammation of the appendix. (*Appendix* is a Latin word meaning "that which hangs." It "hangs onto" the large intestine.)

arthritis (Greek *arthr,* joint + *-itis*): inflammation of a joint

bronchitis (Greek *bronchos*, windpipe + *-itis*): inflammation of the bronchial tubes

(Note: The Greek *bronchos*, windpipe, and Latin *branchia*, gills, are cognates. Cognates are words that come from the same root. Latin *pater*, German *Vater*, and English *father* are cognates.)

bursitis (Greek *byrsa* and Latin *bursa*, bag, purse + *-itis*): inflammation of a bursa (a sac with lubricating fluid) near the shoulder or hip joints

carditis (Greek *kardia*, heart + *-itis*): inflammation of any part of the heart

conjunctivitis (Latin *conjunctus*, joined together + *-itis*): inflammation of the conjunctiva, a connecting membrane covering the front of the eyeball and the eyelid's inner surface

dermatitis (Greek *derma*, skin + *-itis*): inflammation of the skin. (Note such words as *dermatology*, study of the skin and its diseases; *hypodermic*, needle under the skin; and *pachyderm*, "thick-skinned" elephant, hippopotamus, or rhinoceros.)

encephalitis (Greek *enkephalos*, brain + *-itis*): inflammation of the brain

enteritis (Greek *enteron*, intestine + *-itis*): inflammation of the intestines. (Note also *dysentery*, "bad intestines.")

gastritis (Greek *gastros*, stomach + *-itis*): inflammation of the stomach

laryngitis (Greek *larynx*, upper windpipe + *-itis*): inflammation of the larynx

mastoiditis (Greek *mastos*, breast + *eidos*, form + *-itis*): infection or inflammation of the mastoid. (The mastoid bone is shaped like a breast or nipple.)

meningitis (Greek *meningos*, membrane + *-itis*): inflammation of membranes surrounding the brain or spinal cord

myelitis (Greek *myelos*, marrow + *-itis*): inflammation of the bone marrow or the spinal cord

nephritis (Greek *nephros*, kidney + *-itis*): inflammation of the kidneys

neuritis (Greek *neuron*, nerve + *-itis*): inflammation of a nerve or nerves (Note also *neurosis, neuralgia, neurology, neurosurgeon*.)

osteomyelitis (Greek *osteon*, bone + *myelos*, marrow + *-itis*): an inflammation of the bone marrow

peritonitis (Greek *peritonaion*, stretched over + *-itis*): inflammation of the peritoneum, a membrane lining the abdominal cavity and its organs

phlebitis (Greek *phlebos*, vein + *-itis*): inflammation of a vein

pharyngitis (Greek *pharynx*, windpipe, throat + *-itis*): inflammation of the mucous membrane of the pharynx

sinusitis (Latin *sinus*, bend, curve + *itis*): inflammation of the sinuses, the curved air cavities in the skull

splenitis (Greek *splen*, spleen + *-itis*): inflammation of the spleen, a gland near the stomach

tonsillitis (Latin *tonsillae*, tonsils + *-itis*): inflammation of the tonsils

Forming Diminutives

The exercises below are designed to show the student how the suffixes *-et, -ette, -cule, -ule, -le, -icle, -ling,* and *-let* can be used to express the concept of smallness. The teacher should select words from the exercises that will be suitable to the level of his class.

Part One

The student fills in the blanks.

If an *owlet* is a small owl, then
1. an eaglet is a _small_ _eagle_.
2. a piglet is a _small_ _pig_.
3. a small ring is a _ringlet_.
4. the suffix *-let* means _small_.

Part Two

Students are to match the definitions on the right with the words on the left.

Section A

1. _j_ leaflet
2. _g_ starlet
3. _h_ booklet
4. _k_ corpuscle
5. _b_ minuscule
6. _c_ globule
7. _e_ molecule
8. _a_ kitchenette
9. _l_ dinette
10. _f_ rivulet
11. _d_ cygnet
12. _i_ particle

a. small kitchen
b. adjective meaning very small
c. tiny drop or small ball
d. a young swan
e. a particle in an atom
f. a small stream
g. little star, young actress
h. little, thin book
i. a tiny bit, a speck
j. small or young leaf
k. small body, or blood cell
l. small dining room

Section B

1. _d_ canticle
2. _a_ fledgling
3. _j_ icicle
4. _h_ cubicle
5. _f_ yearling
6. _k_ piglet
7. _c_ gosling
8. _i_ sonnet
9. _l_ islet
10. _e_ duckling
11. _g_ bassinet
12. _b_ suckling

a. a young bird
b. an unweaned animal
c. a young goose
d. a short hymn or chant
e. a young duck
f. one that is a year old; a young animal
g. a little basin
h. a little room or compartment
i. a little sound or song
j. a little piece of ice
k. a little pig
l. a small isle, or island

130

Note: The teacher may wish to construct additional exercises on suffixes meaning "little." Therefore we have included in the Appendix a supplemental list of these words and some information on the origin of certain words. They may interest abler students who may not have noticed why these words are related to the concept of smallness.

Students should be aware that the suffix -ette has also taken on the meaning of "feminine" (usherette, majorette) or "substitute for" (leatherette, flannelette, satinet or satinette).

The Suffixes -fy, -able, and -ible

Many words can be formed from the suffix -fy (Latin facere, to make or cause something to happen). Another form of the same suffix is -ify. Beautify means to make beautiful. Let's look at some others: pacify means to make peaceful; magnify means to make larger.

Students are to read the sentences and fill in the blanks.

Answers

	1. What does a magnifying glass do? It makes things appear
larger	l _ _ _ _ r.
purify	2. To make something pure is to p u r i _ _ it.
simplify	3. To make something simple is to s i m p l i _ _ it.
make	4. A fort is a stronghold. To fortify something is to _ _ _ _ it strong.
make	5. To clarify something is to _ _ _ _ it clear.

Note: The suffix -fy may also mean "cause to be," or "become." These sentences illustrate:

1. To make glorious is to glorify.

2. Actresses are often glorified (made to appear more beautiful or glamorous than they really are).

3. When water solidifies it becomes ice (becomes solid).

4. The pitcher intensified his efforts to develop a slider. (His efforts became more intense.)

5. To liquefy something is to change it into a liquid.

6. To humidify is to make humid or damp. A humidifier makes air more humid.

7. The leader unified the three groups (made them into one).

8. She signified her approval by raising her hand (made her feelings known by a sign or signal).

9. To terrify someone is to make him frightened (terrified).

10. Inhumane acts shock us or horrify us (cause us to feel horror).

11. Most auto manufacturers modify (make slight changes) in their cars each year.

12. Magicians often depend on mystifying their audience (making their feats seem mysterious).

13. In "L'Allegro," Milton *personified* mountains and clouds (made them like persons) by saying:

Mountains on whose barren breast
The laboring clouds do often rest.

The teacher can combine the study of the suffix *-fy* with root study by pointing out that *-fy* is often affixed to Greek and Latin roots, as illustrated in the following sentences:

1. In the *petrified* forest in Arizona the trees have become stone. From Greek *petra,* stone + *facere* (-fy), to make or become.

2. To *gratify* someone is to cause him pleasure or satisfaction. From Latin *gratus* (pleasing).

3. To *sanctify* a thing is to make it holy. From Latin *sanctus* (holy).

4. In a play we often *identify* with a character. From Latin *idem* (same).

5. To *notify* is to inform (make known). From Latin *notus* (known).

6. The milk *satisfied* the baby. From Latin *satis* (enough).

7. They *nullified* the agreement (made it not binding). From Latin *nullus* (not any, none, no).

8. Monticello was *dignified* (made noble) by the presence of Jefferson. From Latin *dignus* (worthy).

The suffix *-able* (or *-ible*) means "can be," "worthy of," or "deserving of." A dependable person can be depended on. A lovable person is worthy of love.

A reliable boy can be relied on.
A portable radio can be carried.

Mark the best phrase:

1. The rocket is *visible.*
   a. ___ It cannot be heard.
   b. _X_ It can be seen.
   c. ___ It is out of sight.

2. A *transportable* cargo
   a. ___ stays where it is.
   b. ___ cannot be moved.
   c. _X_ can be moved.

3. The airplane has *detachable* wings. The wings
   a. _X_ can be taken off.
   b. ___ are not removable.
   c. ___ stay on the plane.

4. Do you remember?
   The suffix *-able* (or *-ible*) may mean can be .
   Remember also that *-able* or *-ible* may mean worthy of .
   Blamable means deserving of blame.
   An *admirable* painting is worthy of your admiration.
   Contempt means lack of respect. A *contemptible* person is deserving of contempt (not worthy of respect).

Suffixes of Gender

Gender is often shown by words such as *father, mother; brother, sister; uncle, aunt; he, she; gander, goose.* Gender can also be shown by compound words: *billygoat, nannygoat; Englishman, Englishwoman; grandfather, grandmother; landlord, landlady; peacock, peahen.*

Gender is also indicated by inflectional endings, such as the feminine suffix *-ess* (from the Latin suffix *-issa* and the French *-esse*). A familiar example is *god, goddess.*

Words designating profession are rarely used today in the feminine form (*authoress, poetess, instructress,* etc.), but the suffix *-ess* is used in other words such as those listed below.

Students might be asked to indicate the gender in the blank next to each of the following words by writing *M* (masculine) or *F* (feminine):

1. ___ heir	___ heiress		10. ___ prophet	___ prophetess
2. ___ giant	___ giantess		11. ___ prince	___ princess
3. ___ baron	___ baroness		12. ___ tiger	___ tigress
4. ___ deacon	___ deaconess		13. ___ sculptor	___ sculptress
5. ___ prior	___ prioress		14. ___ benefactor	___ benefactress
6. ___ host	___ hostess		15. ___ waiter	___ waitress
7. ___ shepherd	___ shepherdess		16. ___ enchanter	___ enchantress
8. ___ priest	___ priestess		17. ___ idolater	___ idolatress
9. ___ patron	___ patroness		18. ___ conductor	___ conductress

The suffix *-er*, meaning one who (from Anglo-Saxon *-ere*), once indicated masculine gender but is now used for both sexes: *talk, talker; read, reader; walk, walker.* In forming the feminine gender we drop *er* (or *or*) before adding *ess:*

murderer–murderess
sorcerer–sorceress
adventurer–adventuress
governor–governess

The formation of the feminine gender can vary more extensively:

master–mistress
duke–duchess
marquis–marchioness
lad–lass
lord–lady
abbot–abbess

Other suffixes indicating the feminine gender are *-trix, -a, -ine, -etta, -enne,* and *-ette:*

aviator–aviatrix
  (pilot)
testator–testatrix
  (one who makes a will)
executor–executrix
  (one who carries out the details)
hero–heroine
Joseph–Josephine
Paul–Pauline
Don–Donna

sultan–sultana
administrator–administratrix
Julius–Julia
Cornelius–Cornelia
Henry–Henrietta
comedian–comedienne
tragedian–tragedienne
equestrian–equestrienne
usher–usherette
czar–czarina

Prefix and Suffix Review

Students can gain word-analysis and word-structure skills by learning to manipulate word parts. The words in the middle column have both prefixes and suffixes. The student writes the prefix in the blank on the left and the suffix in the blank on the right.

Prefix		Suffix
1. in	inspector	or
2. ex	exporter	er
3. sub	subscription	tion
4. in	inhabitable	able
5. pre	prescriber	er
6. de	deportment	ment
7. in	inaudible	ible
8. trans	transporter	er
9. in	informal	al
10. re	rearmament	ment
11. un	unavailable	able
12. re	reproducing	ing
13. under	understatement	ment
14. com	compartment	ment
15. ex	expendable	able
16. dis	distrustful	ful
17. de	dejected	ed
18. inter	international	al
19. col	collection	tion
20. in	investment	ment
21. pro	procession	ion
22. en	enrollment	ment
23. re	resistance	ance
24. ex	exactness	ness
25. a	atomic	ic

Note: The teacher will find a master list of suffixes, meanings, and example words in the Appendix.

8

Roots

A teacher said to a colleague, "My students don't need instruction in vocabulary. What they need is to learn to speak, read, and write better." Obviously this is the purpose of all vocabulary study. This teacher assumed that vocabulary meant the dull, uninviting, repetitious task of memorizing words out of context. He said further, "We teach words when they come up in class." But this approach contains a fallacy. New words that students learn may come up outside the classroom. The student needs a system for receiving, storing, and retrieving words at any time.

Everyone has had the experience of looking up an unknown word and finding it popping up again in his reading or listening. An eleventh-grade pupil complained to her father that she had to learn the "silly word" *vertigo*. "I'll never use it," she said. But that very night she saw it on television as the title of a movie. "Why should I learn the word *acrophobia*?" asked a high school student. He saw it the next day in a magazine article on why some people are afraid of height.

But in this book we do not recommend teaching single words out of context or without relating words to cognates (words formed from the same root). For example, we teach *phobia* as a root meaning fear, and show that it appears in several words such as *hydrophobia, acrophobia, claustrophobia, agoraphobia,* and *xenophobia.* Indeed, we suggest that students might "coin" some of their own *phobia* words, such as *bookphobia* (fear of books), *microphobia* (fear of small things), *phono-phobia* (fear of sounds).

The teacher might use this approach with students: "To be a good reader, writer, speaker, and listener, you have to know and like words. To be successful with words you have to be curious about words and the roots of words. You must notice how words are used in sentences and how words themselves are made up, what their parts are.

"How closely do you look at words? Have you noticed the root *disc* in *discus*? the *vision* in *television*? the *sign* in *signature*? Knowing how words are related can help you build a large, useful vocabulary.

"Have you noticed that many words belong to one family, such as *paragraph, telegraph, autograph, biography*? Did you know all these *graph* words refer to writing?

"Have you noticed the words that belong to the *phon* family? *Earphone, headphone, microphone, phonograph, saxophone,* and *symphony* all refer to sound.

"*Graph* and *phon* are Greek roots used in English. Learning the roots of words is a shortcut to learning hundreds of words. Knowing the root *port* (carry) helps you figure out or remember the words *import, export, porter, portable, transport,* and *portage.*

"Why be content with learning one word at a time if you can learn two, three, or four? For example, if you're going to learn the word *insect*, you might as well learn *section, intersection, sector, bisect, dissect, sect, sectional,* and, if you like, even harder words such as *vivisection* (Latin roots *viv,* living + *sect,* cut) meaning the dissection of living organisms in scientific experiments.

"You will notice that all these *sect* words belong to one family, and as members of the same family they look somewhat alike. They are all made from the same root, *sect,* meaning cut. (If you look closely at an *insect* you will notice that it looks 'cut in two.' Its body is divided into separate parts.)"

Words and Word Parts

Word parts have meanings of their own. A word part by itself may be a symbol for an object, an idea, or a concept. Two or more word parts may combine to give us a combination of ideas. For example, in the word *contradict* the root *dict* means say or speak, and the prefix *contra-* means against. Thus *contra + dict = contradict,* a combination of two ideas that results in several new concepts: to voice an opposite point of view, to deny, to declare untrue—in short, to "speak against."

Students with some knowledge of word elements have less difficulty unlocking the meaning of big words. Students of medicine, biology, and botany who know word parts easily transform polysyllabic terms into simple phrases that describe the shape, color, action, and operation indicated by the various parts of the word to be defined. For example, *multiflorous* (*multi*, many + *flor*, flower) merely means many-flowered. A grasshopper places eggs in the ground with its *ovipositor* (*ov*, egg + *posit*, put, place). *Pneumectomy* (*pneum*, lung + *ec*, out + *tom*, cut) means cutting out a lung.

We feel that mastering the root-meaning of words through a systematic study of word parts is as necessary for the elementary and secondary student as it is for the college student.

A student adequately instructed in the process of dividing words will quickly learn how words are formed and will acquire the habit of automatically analyzing unfamiliar words whose meanings he can often infer from the sum of their parts.

Prefixes and Roots

Presenting prefixes and roots is one way to illustrate word formation. The following section helps illustrate the generative quality of key prefixes and roots in forming words. A suggested recall-test form is included at the end of this section.

The Roots *Ject* and *Pel* (*Puls*)

Here are two roots: *ject* and *pel* (or *puls*). Notice how many words can be formed by combining these roots with prefixes.

The root *ject* means hurl, cast, or throw.

When a rifle is fired, the cartridge is *ejected* from the chamber. (It's thrown out.) The prefix *e-* or *ex-* means out.

A movie *projector projects* an image on the screen. *Pro* means forward. (The image is "thrown forward.")

A *projectile* is something thrown or hurled forward. A stone hurled by a sling is a *projectile*.

Even the word *jet* is a *ject* word with the *c* omitted. A jet plane is hurled forward because the engine "throws" or forces back streams of air and exhaust gases.

If a ship is caught in a storm, sometimes the cargo is *jettisoned* (thrown overboard) to make the ship lighter.

Other *ject* words include *inject, injection, rejection, objection,* and *trajectory.* Note also the verb *subject* (force under) and the adjective *abject* (cast away).

A *dejected* person is downcast (low in spirits). *De* means down. (To *descend* is to go down.)

Two other *ject* words are the names of parts of speech: *interjection* and *adjective.*

We get many other words from the root *pel* (or *puls*) meaning push, drive, or force. Many airplanes are *propelled* by jet engines. Jet *propulsion* enables some planes to fly faster than the speed of sound.

Notice that all the words below have something to do with pushing, driving, or forcing:

repel (*re*, back): force back
repulse (*re*, back): drive back
propel (*pro*, forward): drive forward
propeller: a device that pushes a ship or plane forward
expel (*ex*, out of): force out
expulsion: a forcing out
dispel (*dis*, apart): drive away
Propellants are used to drive rocket engines.
Insect *repellent* "drives back" mosquitoes.
Something that is *repulsive* is unattractive; it "drives you back."

Recall Test

Using the roots *ject, pel,* and *puls,* have the student write an appropriate word opposite each prefix listed below. If he can, he should list additional words at the end of the exercise. (He may use the same prefix more than once.)

1. e- (out)	eject (etc.) _____
2. ex- (out)	_____
3. in- (in, into)	_____
4. inter- (into)	_____
5. re- (back)	_____
6. de- (down)	_____
7. pro- (forward)	_____
8. ob- (against)	_____
9. sub- (under)	_____
10. tra-, trans- (across, over)	_____
11. dis- (apart, away)	_____

Additional Words:

_____   _____
_____   _____
_____   _____
_____   _____

Forming Words from Roots

The student completes the following sentences by filling the blanks with a word containing the root in parentheses. Answers provided are for the teacher's convenience.

1. The car stopped at the (*sect*) to let the children cross.
   intersection

2. I was eager to hear the voice of this famous (*voc*).
   vocalist

3. I glanced at the (*meter*) to see how fast the car was going.
   speedometer

4. A well-known musician will (*duct*) the orchestra.
   conduct

5. The actor wrote his name in my (*graph*) book.
   autograph

6. In geography class we measured the (*circum*) of the globe.
   circumference

7. The airplane is a fast means of (*port*).
   transportation

8. In a shoe factory the workers (*fact*) shoes.
   manufacture

9. He will (*dict*) a letter to his secretary.
   dictate

Note: Although the student may be able to write the word suggested by the roots provided, he may not know the meaning of the roots themselves. The following exercise deals with the specific meaning of the roots *voc, duct, graph, port, volv* in words that are familiar though not fully understood. In short, by this method the roots can be "discovered," generalized, and related to other words of the same family. *This approach is a significant part of the general method of structural analysis in learning vocabulary.*

Teachers should avoid using a list of roots that will be very hard for a class, or, on the other hand, so easy that no challenge is presented. The student's ability to recognize and use word parts will grow as planned vocabulary instruction becomes a regular part of the language development program.

The student matches columns A and B:

A		B	
a. _4_ voc		1. cut through	6. lead, guide
b. _6_ duct		2. carry	7. write, record
c. _7_ graph		3. roll, turn	
d. _2_ port		4. call, voice	
e. _3_ volv		5. remain, stay	

139

Note: The teacher can use these additional roots to form words:

aud (hear) — auditorium
auto (self) — autobiography
ject (throw) — projector
meter (measure) — thermometer
phon (sound) — phonics
scope (watch) — microscope

script (write) — inscription
spect (look) — spectator
vid (see) — video
vis (see) — visual
vit (life) — vitality
viv (life) — vivid

Discovering Roots in Words

Students can discover the meaning of a given root by analyzing a series of words derived from that root.

Example:
The root *port* (carry) is found in *transport, export, import, portable.*
The root *spect* (look) forms *inspect, spectator, spectacles, aspect.*

Step 1: The student is presented with a list of words derived from a common root, such as:

credit	discreditable	accredit	incredible
credible	incredulous	creditably	credibility
discredit	credence	incredibility	credulous
incredulity	creditable	creed	incredibly
credo	discreditably	credentials	
credibly	creditor	credulity	

Step 2: The teacher pronounces the words and the students repeat them. The teacher writes a few prepared sentences on the board using words from the list. (The sentences may also be prepared for use with the overhead projector.) For example: The speed of a spaceship in orbit is *incredible* (unbelievable). His story is *credible* (believable).

Step 3: To check his understanding, the student is asked to check the correct blank in the following multiple choice item:

The words *credible, incredible, credibly,* and *incredibly* all have something to do with love ___, hope ___, belief _X_, friendship ___).

Step 4: To see if he has noticed the root *cred,* the student is asked to fill in the blanks in the following exercise:

The words *credible, incredible, credibly, incredibly* have a common suffix (___, root _X_, prefix ___). The root of all these words is (*dit* ___, *ceed* ___, *ibly* ___, *cred* _X_). The root *cred* has something to do with (listening ___, believing _X_, hoping ___, moving ___).

Step 5: The student goes back to the list in Step 1 and underlines the root in each word (*cred*). The student should note that the words are all formed from the root *cred* and have something to do with believing. Note the following additional roots:

aud (hear)	vol, volv (roll)
phon (sound)	voc (call)
graph (write, record)	viv, vit (life)
spect (look)	duc, duct (lead)
port (carry)	vid, vis (see)
dic, dict (say)	cycle (wheel)
astro, aster (star)	mit, miss (send)
ject (throw)	annu, enni (year)
equ (equal)	pel, puls (push)

Note: The teacher might also have students use the dictionary to make short lists of familiar words from the roots given above. These lists can be edited and duplicated as a master list of words derived from common roots, such as the sample classified list, Roots and Words, below.

Roots and Words They Generate

A list of roots and the words derived from them, in easy-to-hard order, are presented below. The roots might be discussed in terms of the original meanings of the words and their extended meanings within other words. This list is a small part of a more extensive list that we have prepared for the teacher's use at various levels. (See *List of Common Roots and Derived Words* in the Appendix.)

The teacher can teach many key words and emphasize the principle of generalization: filing, classifying, and making associations between words formed from common, generative roots.

Roots and Words (First Level)

form (shape)	color (color)	dent (tooth)	mari (sea)
uniform	discolor	dentist	marine
reform	colorful	dental	submarine
formation	colorless	dentifrice	mariner
deform	Colorado	indent	maritime
transform	coloration	trident	aquamarine

circ (ring)	cycl (ring, circle)	div (separate)	phon (sound)
circle	bicycle	divide	earphone
circus	tricycle	division	microphone
circular	cycle	indivisible	saxophone
circuitous	cyclone	divisional	symphony
circumspect	cyclist	divisor	phonics

vis (see)	geo (earth)	cand (glow, white)	min (small)
television	geography	candle	minute
vision	geology	candidate	miniature
visual	geometry	candid	minor
visa	geophysical	candelabra	minimize
visage	geopolitics	incandescent	minuscule

gram (letter)	hos(p) (host)	cin (ashes)	villa (farmhouse)
telegram	hospital	cinders	village
diagram	hostess	Cinderella	villager
grammar	hospitable	incinerator	villain
monogram	hostelry	cinerator	villainy
pictogram	hospice	cinerarium	villa

graph (write)	vaca (empty)	merc (trade)	vin (wine)
phonograph	vacation	merchant	vine
autograph	vacant	merchandise	vinegar
biography	vacate	commerce	vineyard
paragraph	vacationist	mercenary	vintage
graphic	vacancy	mercantile	vintner

cap (head)	cav (hollow)	mov (move)	face (countenance)
captain	cave	move	face
cape (headland)	cavern	movement	surface
capital	cavity	remove	facial
capitol	excavate	movable	deface
decapitate	cavernous	immovable	efface

Roots and Words (Second Level)

fort (strong)	enni (year)	journ (daily)	crim (judge, accuse)
fort	biennial	journey	crime
fortify	centennial	journal	criminal
fortitude	perennial	journalism	criminality
fortification	bicentennial	journalist	incriminate
forte	millennium	journeyman	discriminate

duc (lead)	equ (equal, fair)	civ (citizen)	cult (cultivate, worship)
conduct	equality	civic	agriculture
educate	equator	civilization	cultivate
abduct	equation	civil	culture
aqueduct	equilateral	civilized	floriculture
induce	equivocal	civics	cult

dict (say)	multi (many)	grat (please, thank)	mand (order)
contradict	multiply	congratulate	command
verdict	multiplicand	grateful	demand
prediction	multimillionaire	gratitude	remand
dictate	multitude	gratify	mandate
dictaphone	multiple	gratuitous	countermand

man (hand)	vict (conquer)	flam (flame)	mort (death)
manual	victory	flame	mortal
manuscript	convict	inflammable	mortality
manipulate	evict	flamboyance	immortal
manufacture	victor	flammable	mortician
manacle	Victorian	flambeau	post-mortem

milit (soldier)	meter (measure)	fer (bring, bear)	mod (manner, measure)
military	diameter	transfer	mode
militia	barometer	fertile	model
militarism	perimeter	refer	modern
demilitarize	centimeter	infer	moderate
militant	hexameter	confer	modulate

mob (move)	micro (small)	flor (flower)	veh (carry)
automobile	microphone	florist	vehicle
mobile	microfilm	floral	convey
mobility	micrometer	florid	vehicular
mobilize	microbe	flora	conveyance
immobilize	micron	floriculture	vehemence

Word Families

The Roots *Nov* and *Serv*

Students can learn words by grouping them in word families. For example, the following exercise is on some of the words that refer to "newness." The student fills in the blanks.

Answers

new
newer
novelette

1. The Latin word *novus* means new. A novel way of serving a dish is a _____ way.
2. The novel is a _____er form of writing than the ballad.
3. A little novel is a _____ette.

143

new	4. People were attracted by the novelty of the horseless carriage. The auto was something _____.
new	5. A novice driver is a beginner. He's _____ at it.
new	6. A nova is a _____ star that shines with a sudden burst of light.
New	7. Nova Scotia is another name for _____ Scotland.
new	8. An innovator likes to change things and to try something _____.
new	9. Innovations in men's styles are not so frequent as in women's. Men don't have as many _____ styles in clothes.
newly	10. The French phrase *nouveau riche* describes a person who has just recently become rich. He is _____ly rich.

The following exercise deals with the root *serv* and words formed from it.

preserve	1. The root *serve* means keep or save. We tend to keep or pre_____e memories of happy times.
preserves	2. Fruits cooked with sugar and sealed from the air so they will keep are called p_____s.
conservatory	3. Some parks have large greenhouses where plants are kept. Another name for this greenhouse is con_____atory.
conserve save	4. The channel swimmer floated on his back to _____ his strength. (He wanted to s_____ his energy.)
preserver	5. Persons who ride in boats should always wear a life p_____, or life "saver."
conservation	6. Saving forests from fires is an important part of con_____n.
reserved	7. When you buy a ticket on a plane the airline saves or keeps a seat for you. (Your seat is re_____.)
reservation	8. If you expect to take a plane, you make a r_____n.
conservative	9. In politics, a person who likes to keep things the way they are is often called a con_____.
preservative	10. To keep bread from spoiling, a pre_____ative is added.
kept	11. A subservient person is easily "k_____ under thumb."

The Root *Prim*

Instructions: The student fills in the blanks and checks his own work.

first	1. Students learn to read from a primer in the f_____ grade.
first	2. Preprimer materials are used before the _____ grade.

before	3. The prefix *pre-* probably means _____.
	4. In driving a car, safety is of primary importance. Safety
first	is our f_____ concern.
	5. The prime object of the safety director is to reduce auto
first	accidents. That is his _____ goal.
	6. "Primitive Indian culture" refers to the culture of the
first	f_____ Indians in America.
	7. The first or earliest men who lived in caves were
primitive	p_____e.
first	8. Primates, the highest, or _____ order of mammals,
	include humans, apes, and monkeys.
	9. Primaries are held before a general election. They are
first	held _____.
first	10. The primer is the _____ coat of paint.
	11. Longfellow's poem *Evangeline* begins: "This is the forest
	primeval. The murmuring pines and the hemlocks...."
	He was writing about an ancient forest, one belonging to
first	the _____ ages.
	12. The prime meridian passes through Greenwich, England.
	It is the first, or main, meridian (line) from which longitude
	is measured. To measure longitude you start at the
prime	p_____ meridian.

Roots as Words and Parts of Words

Some roots form complete words (*break*); others seldom do (*fract*). Notice we use *fract* with a prefix or a suffix or both. For example, to *fracture* means to break. This is illustrated in the short exercise below.

Answers

word	1. A root may be a w_____.
word; root	2. *Break* is both a w_____ and a r_____.
part; word	3. A root may also be a p_____ of a w_____.
root	4. *Fract* is a r_____.
break	5. The root *fract* means b_____.
	6. Instead of saying "He broke his arm," you could say "He
fractured	f_____d his arm."
	7. Our best player was removed from the game because of a rule
broke	infraction. (He b_____ one of the rules.)

The Root *Fract*

When you study *fractions*, you break whole numbers into parts $(1 = \frac{4}{4} = \frac{3}{4} + \frac{1}{4})$. One fourth can be called a fractional part. Ask students to underline the root in these words: *fraction, fractional, infraction.*

Note: Students who are interested in telescopes might want to look in a dictionary or an encyclopedia to find out the difference between a *reflecting* telescope and a *refracting* telescope. (The refracting telescope turns, bends, "breaks" the light rays.)

Depending on the level of the students, the teacher might discuss additional words containing the root *fract* or *frag* (from *frangere*, to break).

1. The nagging pain made the patient very fractious (irritable).

2. A fracto-cumulus cloud is low, ragged (broken), and rounded; a fracto-stratus cloud is low, ragged (broken), and elongated.

3. A fragment is a broken piece.

4. The instructor was referring to the disconnected sentences in my term paper when he commented about my "fragmentary writing."

5. Three soldiers were wounded by the fragmentation (the breaking into bits) of the exploding grenade.

6. In science class we learned that water refracts (bends) rays of light.

7. The thin water glasses were fragile (easily broken).

Note: The teacher might also point out that the word *frail*, coming from French, is a doublet of *fragile*. (A doublet is one of two words derived from the same origin but coming into the language by different routes.)

The Root *Migr*

The teacher might use the following self-instructive lesson to introduce the study of the root *migr* (move). Notice that if the student knows just one of the words in the lesson he can learn the others easily because they all have the same root. The student underlines the root (*migr*) in each of the words in the list.

migrate	immigrate	emigration	migratory
migration	immigration	emigrant	migrancy
emigrate	immigrant		

The students can now try the following sentences:

Answers

moved

1. Many Europeans have immigrated to the United States. (They have m_____d to this country.)

movement
(Did you
keep the *e*?)

2. In the 1500's a great migration took place. (There was a great m_____ment of people.)

move

out

3. The prefix *e-* means "out of." People who emigrate _____ out of their own country.

4. An emigration is a moving _____.

migr

5. The root of *emigration* is _____.

6. The suffix *-ant* means "a person who (does something)."

person who

Therefore, an emigrant is a _____ _____ moves out of his own country.

146

into	7. The prefix *im-* means into. An immigrant moves _____ a country.
immigrate (Did you use two *m*'s?)	8. Many people will probably move into a new country next year. (They will _____.)
root	9. Why do we need two *m*'s in *immigrate*? One *m* is for the prefix *im-*, and one *m* is for the ʳ_____, *migr*.
into	10. Immigration is moving (up ___, into _X_, out of ___, down ___).
into	11. An immigrant moves (out of ___, into _X_) a country.
out	12. An emigrant moves (in ___, out _X_).
fly south in the winter	13. Migratory birds (never move far from their nests ___; spend both the summer and winter in the North ___; fly south in the winter _X_).
	14. What would you guess to be the meaning of *émigré*?
emigrant	_____

Notice the use of *migr* in these sentences:

1. *Migrant* farm workers move from one part of the country to another to help with harvests.

2. John Steinbeck's *The Grapes of Wrath* describes the "Okie" *migration* to California.

3. *Migratory* locusts move in swarms and destroy crops.

4. The death of Atilla in 453 ended the *migration* of the Huns into Europe.

5. When the Roman Empire weakened, nomads *migrated* into Spain and Gaul.

6. During the French Revolution, royalist refugees from France were called *émigrés*.

7. People who *remigrate* move back to their former home or country (*re,* back or again).

8. The aphid is an insect that returns to the plant which was the original host of a previous generation of aphids. These insects are called *remigrants*.

9. Persons passing through one country on their way to another are *transmigrants* (*trans,* across, over, through). When the Helvetians *migrated* from their land, they asked Caesar if they could *transmigrate* through the Roman Province.

The Generative Quality of Roots: A Programmed Approach

We suggest two approaches that the teacher might follow in teaching a series of words formed from one root, in this case the root *bio* (life). In the first approach (A), the paragraph is self-explanatory; by the process of reading, the student assimilates the material. In B, the student must work with the material, in programmed steps, before he can complete his analysis of the key word.

Approach A. Presentation of the Root *Bio* Through Reading or Discussion

One of the best-known autobiographies is the *Autobiography of Benjamin Franklin* in which he describes his own life. The word *autobiography* has three main parts: *graph* (write), *auto* (self), and *bio* (life) — a writing about one's own life.

Approach B. Presentation of the Root *Bio* Through Programmed Steps

Answers

life	1. The root *bio* means life. The root *graph* means write. The word *biography* refers to writing about someone's _ _ _ _.
writes	2. A biographer _ _ _ _ _ _ about a person's life.
autobiography	3. *Auto* means self. The story of a person's life written by himself is called an _ _ _ _ b i o g r a p h y.
himself	4. *The Autobiography of Benjamin Franklin* was written by Franklin h i m _ _ _ _.
biography	5. The story of a person's life is a _ _ _ _ _ _ _ _ _.
autobiography	6. The story of a person's life written by the person himself is an _ _ _ _ _ _ _ _ _ _ _ _ _.
biographer	7. A person who writes the story of another person's life is a _ _ _ _ _ _ _ _ _ _ _.

The following sections (using Approach A above) illustrate the generative quality of productive roots. Some of them can be put in programmed form so that the student can work through the material at his own speed, correcting his own work. Words suitable for the level of the student should be chosen for presentation.

The Root *Graph* (Write)

1. A Greek schoolboy called his pencil a *graphion*. The substance now used in what are often called "lead" pencils is actually *graphite* — a material used for writing. Note also that a *grapheme* is the smallest unit of an alphabet — a letter.

2. Ancient peoples wrote on papyrus (from the papyrus plant). The Greeks called the bark of the papyrus *biblos,* and the Greek word *biblion* (book) combined with *graph* (write) gives us the word bibliography — a list (a writing) of book titles.

3. A *bibliographer* (*er,* one who) is one who compiles *bibliographies.*

4. *Biblio* also gives us the word *Bible.*

5. A person who worships *idols* is an *idolater* (from Greek *latreia,* worship). A person who interprets each word in the Bible as a literal fact is called a *bibliolater.* Another meaning for *bibliolater* is *worshiper* of books. A person with a craze for collecting books is called a *bibliomaniac* (from *mania,* madness).

6. When a *stenographer* takes a letter, she usually writes in shorthand. If we analyze the word *stenographer* in reverse, we get:

er (one who)
graph (write)
steno (short)

Thus the basic meaning of the word *stenographer* is "one who writes in shorthand."
Note: The meaning of the root *graph* (write) is extended to include an instrument that *draws, records, describes,* but the root still retains the idea of writing, as in sending a written message by *telegraph.*

7. An earthquake is recorded by a *seismograph,* an instrument that "writes" a line on paper, showing how severe a quake is. We get the word from the Greek word for earthquake, *seismos* (from the Greek verb *seiein,* to shake).

8. The flashes of the mirror on a *heliograph* represent the dots and dashes of the Morse code. The message is carried by flashing beams of sunlight. The Greek word for sun is *helios.*

9. The sunflower, which turns to follow the sun, is called a *heliotrope* (from Greek *tropos,* turning).

10. A *heliocentric* universe is one in which the sun is the center.

11. *Choreo* comes from Greek and means dance. (A Greek chorus danced, sang, and spoke on stage.) A *choreographer* designs a dance. Our word *chorus* is Latin for "choir" and comes from the Greek *choros,* band of dancers. Today, chorus girls are often both dancers and singers. Note that *choir* and *chorus* are doublets.

12. Secret messages written in code are called *cryptographs* (from *cryptos,* hidden or secret). A *cryptic* statement has a hidden meaning. And a *crypt* is a "hidden" underground room or vault.

13. Modern man uses Greek and Latin elements to name his inventions. For example, he uses a *barograph* to record atmospheric pressure. *Baros* is Greek for "weight." Note also *barometer* (*baros,* weight + *meter,* measure), which measures the atmospheric pressure. We get the word *baritone,* a heavy, deep voice, from the Greek *barytonos,* deep-sounding (from *barys,* heavy, deep + *tonos,* tone).

14. Doctors use an instrument that records the movements of the heart — a *cardiograph. Cardio* comes from the Greek *kardia,* heart. A *cardiac* muscle is a heart muscle. *Carditis* is an inflammation of the heart (from *itis,* inflammation).

15. *Cardialgia* (from Greek *algos,* pain) is pain in the heart region. Note also that *algia* gives us the word *nostalgia,* a painful yearning for another place or time, a homesickness.

The Root *Phon* (Sound)

The *phoneme* is one of a group of distinct sounds that form words. *Phonetics* is the study of speech sounds. *Phone* is the Greek word for sound.

149

1. A *microphone* (from Greek *micros*, small) magnifies and transmits "small sounds."

2. A cheerleader uses a *megaphone* (from Greek *megas*, great, large) to make his voice louder. It increases the sound of his voice. Note also that a stone of great size is a *megalith*. A *megalomaniac* is a person with great delusions of power. A *megalopolis* (*polis*, city) is a city of great size and power.

3. Antoine Sax, a Belgian, invented the saxhorn, now called the *saxophone*. Another musical instrument with a name formed from *phone* is the *xylophone* (from Greek *xylon*, wood).

4. A brass instrument somewhat like a tuba is called a *euphonium* (*eu*, well, good). A *euphonium* is often heard in a symphony orchestra. The word *symphony* (from *sym*, together) means harmony of sounds.

5. The opposite of *euphony* is *cacophony* (from Greek *kakos*, bad). A *cacophonist* composes music with harsh or discordant sounds. *Cacophonic* music might also be *cacorhythmic* (having irregular rhythm). *Orthodox* (*doxa*, opinion) means having generally accepted opinions. *Cacodoxy* describes a false or wrong opinion. *Cacography* is bad handwriting. Good handwriting is *calligraphy* (from *kallos*, beauty). Note also *Calliope* (Muse of eloquence), *calisthenics* (exercise that makes the figure attractive), and *kaleidoscope* (an instrument that forms beautiful colors).

The Root *Gon* (Angle)

1. *Trigonometry* (from Greek *trigonon*, triangle) is the study of triangles. The word *trigonometry* has three main parts: *tri* (three), *gon* (angle), *metr* (measure). A *trigon* (triangle) has three corners, or angles.

2. *Bigonial* (*bi*, two) means having two angles; *tetragonal* (*tetra*, four) means having four angles.

3. The *Pentagon* building in Washington, D.C., has five angles (from *penta*, five).

4. A *hexagon* (*hex*, six) is a figure with six angles.
   A *heptagon* (*hepta*, seven) has seven angles.
   An *octagon* (*octo*, eight) has eight angles.
   A *nonagon* (*nonus*, ninth) has nine angles.
   A *decagon* (*deca*, ten) has ten angles.
   An *undecagon* (*undecim*, eleven; from *unus*, one + *dec*, ten) has eleven angles.
   A *duodecagon* (*duo*, two + *dec*, ten), or *dodekagon*, has twelve angles.

5. The word *agonic* (Greek *a*, not, without + *gonia*, angle) means not forming an angle or without an angle.

6. The angle of the jaw has a name—the *gonion*, where the lower and rear parts meet at an angle.

7. A direction-finder for aircraft is called a *radiogoniometer*, or *goniometer*. It measures angles. A goniometer also measures solid angles of crystals.

8. Figures having three or more angles are often called *polygons,* from the Greek *polys* (many). *Polygonometry* is the mathematical study and measurement of polygons. *Polygonaceous* plants include knotgrass and jointweed (they have many joints or angles).

The Root *Ambul* (Walk, Go, Move)

1. An *amble* is the easy, slow pace of a horse; but a person can also amble. An ambler is a slow, leisurely walker.

2. An *ambulance* is so called from its original role as an ambulatory (movable, moving) hospital. Ambulances are *ambulatory* because they move about.

3. To *circumambulate* (*circum,* around) is to walk around. A *circumambulator* is a person who walks around, but he may also be a person who "wanders around" the point of a discussion.

4. A person who walks through a garden and examines the flowers is *perambulatory* (*per,* through). A *perambulator* (*ator,* one who) is a baby carriage pushed by a person walking around. The British shorten the word to *pram.*

5. *Ambulacra* include radial parts of the starfish that move or "walk" by means of organs that protrude and withdraw.

6. The *Preamble* (*pre,* before) to the Constitution of the United States goes before Article I.

7. *Somnambulism* (from Latin *somnus,* sleep) is sleepwalking. A *somnambulist* (*ist,* one who) is one who walks in his sleep. A person who has *insomnia* (*in,* not) cannot sleep. He is called an *insomniac.* A *somnolent* person is drowsy or sleepy. A *somniferous* (from *fer,* bring, carry) drug brings on sleep.

The Root *Anthrop* (Man)

1. *Anthropology* (from Greek *anthropos,* man + *logy,* study of) is the study of the origin, development, and races of man.

2. *Anthropogeography* is "human geography," which deals with the various environments of man.

3. *Anthropography* describes the distribution of man throughout the world.

4. *Anthropogenesis* (Latin *genesis,* birth, creation) deals with the origin and evolution of mankind. *Genesis,* the first book of the Bible, deals with the Creation.

5. The *anthropoid* ape, which has no tail, is the ape that most nearly resembles man. The suffix *-oid* (form, shape, likeness), as in *spheroid,* shape of a sphere, comes from Greek *eidos,* form.

6. *Anthropomorphous* (from Greek *morphe,* form) describes whatever has the form of a man. The Greeks and Romans had an *anthropomorphic* religion—their gods were given human characteristics.

151

7. *Anthropocentric* people view man as the central factor in the universe. Those who worship man as a divine being are *anthropolatric* (from Greek *latreia*, worship). Note also *idolatry*, *bibliolatry* (previously discussed with *graph* derivatives), and *anthropolatry*.

8. *Anthropometry* deals with measurements of the human body (measure of man).

9. *Anthropozoic* (from Greek *zoion*, animal, and *zoe*, life) means relating to the time of man's existence on earth.

10. *Misanthropy* (from Greek *misein*, to hate) is hatred or distrust of one's fellowman. A *misanthrope* is a hater of mankind. A *misogynist* (from Greek *gyne*, woman) is a woman-hater. A *gynecologist* is a specialist in the functions and diseases of women. A *misogamist* (from Greek *gamos*, marriage) is a person who hates marriage. A *bigamist* (*bi*, two) has two wives or husbands at the same time. A *trigamist* has *three* (*tri*).

11. *Anthropophagy* (from Greek *phagein*, to eat) is another word for cannibalism. Note also *esophagus*, the passage from the pharynx to the stomach. Shakespeare combines the two roots *anthrop* and *phag* when Othello says:

> And of the Cannibals that each other eat,
> The *Anthropophagi* and men whose heads
> Do grow beneath their shoulders. This to hear
> Would Desdemona seriously incline.

12. A *philanthropist* (from *philos*, loving) loves his fellowman. He shows kindness or is charitable to mankind. The root *phil* also gives us words such as *Philadelphia* (city of brotherly love), *philately* (love of collecting stamps), *philharmonic* (loving harmony), *philhellenic* (friendly to Greece). The *philodendron* (*dendron*, tree) clings to trees. *Philologists* (now often called *linguists*) love words. They are skilled in *philology*, the study of words (*logos*) and other aspects of language. Some philologists are *philobiblic* or *bibliophiles* (lovers of books). A *philosopher* (from Greek *sophos*, wise) is a lover of wisdom. (A *philanderer* is a flirt—from the character *Philander*, a trifling lover in ancient romantic poetry.)

The Root *Meter* (Measure)

1. A *speedometer* (*meter*, measure) measures the speed of a vehicle.

2. *Geometry* comes from the Greek word *geometrein* (to measure land). *Geo* (earth) is found in other words such as *geography*, *geology*, *geocentric*, *geodetic*, *geophysical*, and *geopolitical*. A *geophagist* (from the root *phag*, eat) is a person who eats earth.

3. A *diameter* is a straight line passing through the center of a circle and joining two points on the circumference. *Dia* means through or across.

4. *Trigonometry* deals with the measurement of and relationship between the sides and angles of triangles.

5. The *thermometer*, invented by Galileo, measures temperature (from Greek *thermos*, heat). Note also *thermonuclear*, *thermodynamics*.

152

6. A *micrometer* (from Greek *mikros*, small) measures very small angles and distances.

7. An *altimeter* (from Latin *altus*, high) measures how high an airplane is flying.

8. An *anemometer* (from Greek *anemos*, wind) measures the speed or pressure of the wind.

9. An *optometrist* (from Greek *optikos*, belonging to the sight) measures the range of a person's vision. Note that the *optic* nerve is the nerve of sight.

10. A *pedometer* (from Latin *pedis*, of the foot) measures the number of steps you take (the distance you walk). Note also *pedestrian, pedal, pedestal* (base or foot on which a statue or bust stands). A *pedicurist* (*curo*, care) treats or takes care of the feet. The *curator* of a museum is in charge (takes care) of the museum. An *accurate* measurement is a careful, precise measurement. *Manicure* (from Latin *manus*, hand) means hand care.

11. A *barometer* (from Greek *baros*, weight) measures atmospheric pressure, indicating probable changes in the weather.

12. The *perimeter* is the distance around an area. The Greek prefix *peri-* (around) also appears in *periphery* and *peritonitis*. Note also *periodic* (from Greek *hodos*, a going), which has the meaning of "going around" (occurring again and again).

The *peripatetics* belonged to the school of Aristotle, who taught while walking around. A *peristyle* is a row of columns surrounding a building. A *periscope* (*scope*, look) lets a person look around. *Periphrasis* (sometimes described as circumlocution) is a roundabout way of speaking, for example:

The king did join the plot against the son of his brother.
  instead of
The king joined the plot against his nephew.

Note: *Periphrase*, to express in lengthy phrases, should not be confused with *paraphrase* (from Greek *para*, alongside of + *phrazein*, to speak), stating the meaning of a sentence, a passage, or a poem in other words.

The Root *Scrib, Script* (Write)

1. When an author *describes* a scene he writes it down (from Latin *de*, down + *scrib*, write).

2. When an engraver makes an *inscription* on a monument, he writes letters and numbers on a stone (from Latin *in*, on + *scriptus*, written).

3. A radio *script* is written to be read, a movie *script* is written for an actor to memorize. A certain style of handwriting is called *script.*

4. *Scrip* (a written receipt) was paper money used during the Civil War.

5. The Bible is sometimes called Holy *Scripture.*

6. *Scribes* were men who in early times took dictation and wrote letters for people. Sportswriters today are sometimes humorously called scribes.

7. A *postscript* is the "PS" often found at the end of a letter (from Latin *postscriptum*, written after).

8. A *prescription* (directions for the use of medicine) comes from the Latin verb *praescribere*, to write beforehand.

9. *Circumscribe* has the meaning of "writing" or drawing a line *around* (*circum*). The Magna Carta *circumscribed* (limited) the powers of King John.

10. Men were *conscripted* into the armed forces during World War II (from Latin *conscribere*, to write down together, to enroll).

11. A *manuscript* is a written or typed composition (from Latin *manuscriptum*, written by hand). *Manual* labor is work done by hand. A Boy Scout *manual* is a handbook. *Manu* also gives us *manipulate, maneuver,* and *maniple* (a vestment worn on the wrist by a priest). Note also that a *maniple* in the Roman army was a "handful" of men (sometimes sixty men), a subdivision of a legion (from *manus*, hand + *plenus*, full).

The Root *Spect* (Look, See)

1. The root *spect* comes from the Latin verb *spectare*, to look at. An *inspector* examines or looks into things (from Latin *in*, into).

2. A *spectator* who sees the Olympic Games is looking at a *spectacle.*

3. *Spectacles*, or glasses, help people see better.

4. *Expect* is to wait for (from Latin *exspectare*). *Expectant* means looking forward with hope or confidence.

5. A person with a sober *aspect* looks serious. A person's look is his *aspect*. A different *aspect* is a different point of view, a way of looking at something.

6. The *spectrum* is the image formed when rays of light are broken up into a band of colors such as the colors seen in the rainbow. *Spectrum* is both a Latin word and an English word. The plural can be spelled *spectra* or *spectrums*. We study the *spectrum* with two instruments, the *spectrograph* and the *spectroscope.*

7. An *introspective* person looks into his own thoughts, or looks within himself (from Latin *intro*, within, into).

8. A *circumspect* person is careful, cautious, watchful on all sides (always looking over his shoulder; looking around).

9. Synonyms for *ghost* include phantom, spirit, apparition, vision, and *specter* (something seen).

The Root *Aud* (Hear)

1. *Audible* sounds can be heard. *Inaudible* sounds cannot be heard (from Latin *audire*, to hear).

2. *Audiovisual* materials are those that can be both seen and heard (from *aud*, hear + *vis*, see).

3. The *auditory* canal leads to the middle ear. The *auditory* (hearing) nerve carries messages to the brain.

4. An *auditor* is one who *audits,* or listens to, a classroom lecture. An *audition* is a hearing.

5. An *audiphone* was an early instrument used to help the deaf hear sounds (from *aud,* hear + *phone,* sound).

6. *Auditorium* is a Latin word meaning lecture room (from *aud + orium,* a place for). Thus an auditorium is a room where an audience hears, or listens to, a concert, play, or speech.

The suffix *-arium* also means a place for. Thus, an *aquarium* is a place for fish and other water animals (from Latin *aqua,* water). Sometimes sick persons convalesce in a *sanitarium,* a place for getting well (from Latin *sanus,* healthy). A *natatorium* is a place for swimming (from Latin *natare,* to swim). A *planetarium* is a building (place for) containing an apparatus for showing the movements of the planets and stars. A *crematorium* is a place for cremating the dead. An *insectarium* is a place for keeping and breeding insects. A *serpentarium* is a place for keeping and observing snakes. A *solarium* is a room or porch where a person can sun himself (from *sol,* sun).

The Root *Aster, Astro* (Star)

1. *Astronomy* is the science of observing the celestial bodies (from Greek *astron,* star + *nemien,* to arrange, or state the laws of). Thus, an *astronomer* is one who studies the arrangement (position and movement) of the stars.

2. *Astronomical* figures are enormous, like the large numbers used to describe the distances between stars.

3. *Astronauts* are literally sailors in starry space (from Greek *astron,* star + *nauta,* sailor).

4. *Astrology* is the attempt to relate the movements of the planets and stars to man's affairs on earth. In early days, astrology and astronomy were closely connected. In fact, astrology was the beginning of the science of astronomy.

5. *Influenza* and *influence* are doublets (two words having the same origin but coming to us by different routes). The words *flu* and *influenza* are so called because of man's early belief that the disease was *influenced* by the heavenly bodies (from Italian *influenza,* related to the Latin verb *fluo,* flow). Note also that the supposed effect of the heavenly bodies or stars on man gave us the word *disaster* (from *dis,* opposite, against + *aster,* star) — opposed to or "against" the stars. Thus a flood or an earthquake came to be called a disaster.

6. *Asteroids* are starlike forms of matter orbiting between Jupiter and Mars (from *aster + oid,* in the form of, like).

7. An *asterisk* (*), often used to call attention to a footnote, is shaped like a star (from Greek *asteriskos,* little star).

8. The *aster's* petals have a star-shaped appearance.

The Root *Annu, Enni* (Year)

1. The Latin word *anniversarius* means returning yearly (from *annus, anni*, year + *versus*, turn). A person has only one birthday but many anniversaries of his birthdate.

2. *Annualis* is Latin for "yearly." The World Series is an annual event (it happens yearly).

3. The growth on a tree is called an *annual* ring. A book or journal published once a year is an *annual*.

4. The prefix *semi-* means half. A semicircle is half a circle. A semiannual event lasts half a year or occurs twice a year. (Note *biannual* in item 5 below).

5. *Biannual* and *biennial* are often confused. A *biannual* journal is published twice a year. A *biennial* (or sometimes, loosely, *biannual*) convention meets every two years (from *bi*, two, twice). Note also that *biweekly* means happening every two weeks, and *bimonthly* means happening every two months; but *semiweekly* means occurring twice a week, and *semimonthly*, twice a month.

6. A *centennial* celebration is held to commemorate the hundredth anniversary of an event. (*Cent* means hundred, as in *percent*. There are one hundred cents in a dollar.)

7. A city celebrating its *sesquicentennial* is 150 years old (from *sesqui*, one and a half).

8. An *annuity* is a sum of money paid out yearly through an insurance policy.

9. The *annals* of a country are written accounts of events year by year.

10. *Perennial* flowers live through the years (from *per*, through).

The Root *Arch* (Rule, Chief)

1. A *monarch* rules alone (from *monos*, alone, one + *archein*, to rule).

2. In a *patriarchal* society or family, the father rules; mothers rule in a *matriarchal* society or family (from *pater*, father; *mater*, mother).

3. A government ruled by a woman would be a *gynarchy* (*gyn*, woman).

4. Pompey, Caesar, and Crassus formed the First *Triumvirate*, a group of three men (from *tri*, three + *vir*, man). This coalition might be called a *triarchy*, a government ruled by three persons.

5. A government ruled by a few is an *oligarchy* (*olig*, few).

6. A country without a government (without rule) is in a state of *anarchy* (*a* or *an*, without).

7. An *architect* is a "chief builder" (*arch*, chief + *tect*, builder).

8. The building where *archives* (government records) are kept was once the seat of the government (where the ruler lived) (from *arche*, government).

9. In architecture, an *architrave* (from Latin *trabis* or *trav*, beam) is the chief beam on a column. It supports the frieze and cornice.

10. An *archipelago* (*archi* + *pelagos*, sea) is a sea with many islands in it. The Greek name for the Aegean Sea, the chief sea of the Greeks, is *Archipelago*.

Unseen Roots

The root of a word, like the root of a plant, is often unseen. The following paragraphs contain underlined words whose roots are not always easily apparent:

1. The albumen of an egg is the white part—from *alb* (white) as in *albino, alb, albescent, album.*

2. Merchants advertise a product to turn the customer's attention to it—from *vert* (turn) as in *divert, revert, invert, convert, vertigo* (dizziness).

3. A terrier catches animals that burrow in the earth—from *terra* (earth, land) as in *territory, terrain, subterranean* (underground), *terra cotta, terra firma, Terre Haute* (high land), *Mediterranean* (sea in the middle of the land), *pied-à-terre* (temporary lodging, literally "a foot on the ground").

4. A rebel wants to fight again (make war again)—from *bellum* (war) as in *belligerent, bellicose, ante bellum, post bellum.*

5. An anachronism (*ana*, not + *chron*, time) is the placing of an event or action in time where it doesn't belong. For example, the clock in Shakespeare's *Julius Caesar* is an anachronism: clocks hadn't been invented when Caesar lived. Note also *chronicle, chronic, chronology, synchronize, synchroflash.*

6. When we make a decision about a problem we cut off further argument—from *cis* (cut) as in *incision, excision, concise, incisor* (tooth), *scissors.*

7. North and south are antipodes: two places on directly opposite sides of the earth. Australia and New Zealand are called antipodes because they are directly opposite most of the English-speaking peoples—from *anti* (against, opposite) + *pod* (foot). Thus, *antipodes* also refers to people who live on opposite sides of the earth (their feet are directly opposite each other). Note also *bipod, tripod, chiropodist, apode* (an animal without feet), *gastropod* (a shellfish that uses its stomach like feet to move from place to place).

8. A corner has a sharp edge or point somewhat like a horn—from *cornu* (horn) as in *cornet, unicorn, bicorn, cornucopia* (horn of plenty), *cornea* (transparent or hornlike substance coating the eyeball).

9. A sarcophagus (from *phag*, eat) is a stone coffin. The ancient Greeks used limestone coffins in which the flesh of dead bodies would be consumed quickly. Note also *esophagus, anthropophagous* (cannibal-

istic, man-eating), *ichthyophagous* (fish-eating), *hippophagous* (horse-eating). A *xylophagous* insect feeds on wood (*xylo*). A person with *dysphagia* (*dys*, bad + *phag*, eat) has difficulty in swallowing.

11. In early times a coroner represented the king. He investigated untimely deaths in the name of the crown — from *coron* (crown) as in *coronet* (small crown), *coroneted* (adorned with a crown), *coronation* (crowning ceremony), *coroniform* (crown-shaped), *corona* (crown or halo of the sun), *coronagraph* (instrument used to observe the sun's corona).

12. Would you guess that the word cosmetics comes from a word meaning universe? *Cosmetic* comes from *kosmos*, the Greek word for order, arrangement, or universe; the opposite of *chaos*, no order. *Cosmetics*, dealing with arranging, adorning, beautifying, comes from the Greek *kosmetikos* (skilled in arranging). Other words from *cosm* include *cosmic*, *cosmography* (description of the cosmos), *cosmonaut* ("sailor" of the cosmos), *cosmopolis* (a center for the arts, crafts, and ideas of the world). A *cosmopolite*, or a *cosmopolitan* person, feels at home in any city of the world (from *polis*, city).
Microcosm (*micro*, little) means little world.
Macrocosm (*macro*, great) means the great universe.

13. The pendulum on a clock hangs from a fixed point and swings freely (from *pend*, hang). An *appendix* "hangs" from the large intestine. Some other *pend* words are *impending* (hanging over threateningly), *pendant* (hanging ornament, for example, a locket), *appendage* (something attached, hung on), *appendicitis*, *pendulous*, *suspend*, *perpendicular*.

14. Amphibious animals live both in water and on land (from *bio*, life and *amphi*, both). *Bio* also gives us *biography*, *autobiography*, *biology*, *biochemistry*, *microbiology*, *macrobiotic* ("long-lived," from *macro*, long or large), *biometry* (the measuring of life expectancy), *biopsy*, the removing of tissue from a living body to examine it (from Greek *opsis*, a viewing). Note also *autopsy*, a medical examination to see for oneself what caused a death (from *auto*, self).

Significant Word Parts

The following material is useful to illustrate the relationship between various words and word parts. It may be presented in a variety of ways — by using lesson forms previously illustrated or by furnishing additional words.

The Root *Crat* (*Cracy*)

People in high social position are known as the *aristocracy*, a ruling body of nobles (from *crat* or *cracy*, rule, power, government + *aristos*, best), "rule of the best."

Theos means God or a god; a *theocracy* is "a government ruled by God," that is, one in which God is considered as both civil and religious leader.

In a *plutocracy*, wealthy men rule (from *ploutos*, wealth). Pluto was the god of the underworld, which contained minerals, metals, and other sources of wealth.

An *autocrat* has absolute power. He rules by himself (from *autos*, self).

Crat and *cracy* also combine in English words, such as *bureaucrat* (from French *bureau*, desk), *mobocracy*, "mob rule," and *Dixiecrat* (from Dixie, a name for the Southern states).

The Root *Dem*

Democracy (from *demos*, people) is rule or government by the people. Note also *demagogue*, a "leader" of the people who appeals to their emotions and prejudices (from *agog*, leader), as in *pedagog* (from *paedos*, boy, child), teacher or leader of a child. Note *pediatrician*.

Other words formed from *dem:*

demography:	the study of births, deaths, diseases of people
epidemic:	rapid spread of disease among the people (from *epi*, upon + *dem*, people)
endemic:	regularly found in a certain population. For example, a disease peculiar to a region is called an endemic disease (from *en*, in + *dem*, people).
demotic:	having to do with the common people. For example, the speedier, simplified writing the ancient Egyptian people developed in place of hieroglyphics is called *demotic*.

The Roots *Lys* and *Thesis*

Breaking up words into meaningful parts is called word *analysis* (from Greek *ana*, up + *lyein*, loosen), a "breaking up." Word *synthesis* means putting parts together to form whole words (from Greek *syn*, together + *tithenai*, to place). The root of the word *synthesis* is the Greek word *thesis* (a *setting* down, a *placing*).

Evil is the *antithesis* (the direct opposite) of good (from *anti*, against + *tithenai*, to set), to set opposite or against.

Authors often use antithesis for effect—to emphasize a contrast. For example, Pope in his "Essay on Criticism" says:

Be not the first by whom the new are tried,
Nor yet the last to lay the old aside.

In the same poem Pope wrote:

To err is human, to forgive divine.

Macaulay used antithesis in his *Life of Samuel Johnson:* "But though his pen was now idle, his tongue was active."

Qualifying words inserted within a sentence (literally "set beside" the main thought) are called parenthetical expressions and are often put in *parentheses* (from *para*, beside + *en*, in + *thesis*, a setting).

Hypothesis (*hypo*, under) literally means "a placing under," an assumption or theory supporting and explaining certain related facts.

The Root *Derm*

A *hypodermic* needle goes under the skin (*derma*). *Dermatology* deals with the skin and skin diseases. The derma is the sensitive layer of skin under the *epidermis* (from *epi*, upon), the outer layer of skin.

A *pachyderm*, such as the elephant, has thick skin (from *pachys*, thick). A *taxidermist* stuffs and arranges the skins of animals for display.

Roots and Word Meanings

The Latin *costa* (side, rib) gives us the word *coast*, the side of a country bordering the sea.

Rectangle (from Latin *rectus*, right, straight) literally means right angle. A person who stands *erect* stands up straight.

A *crescent* moon keeps getting bigger—it grows (from Latin *crescere*, to grow, increase). A *crescendo* is a gradual increase in loudness.

The name *Christopher* means the one who carries Christ (from Greek *pherein*, to carry).

The root *pher* also gives us *paraphernalia* (equipment, personal belongings). At one time paraphernalia referred particularly to a woman's personal belongings (in addition to her dowry), which she could carry with her, or beside her (from *para*, beside).

A *philtre* or *philter* is a magic drink supposed to make a person fall in love (from *phil*, love). The name *Philip* means lover of horses (from *ip* or *hippo*, horse, as in *hippopotamus*, river horse).

A person getting paid for a position that requires little or no work has a *sinecure* (from Latin *sine*, without + *curo*, care), without care. He who can put care aside is *secure* (from Latin *se*, aside + *curo*, care).

When you care, you have *sympathy* (from *path*, suffer, feel + *sym*, together, with). *Apathy* means without feeling (*a*, not, without + *path*).

Charlie Chaplin comedies combine fun with *pathos* (they arouse a feeling of pity for "the little tramp.")

In Greek mythology, *Cyclops* was a giant with a round eye in the middle of his forehead (from Greek *kyklos*, circle, ring + *ops*, eye). Note *cycle* also in *monocycle*, *bicycle*, *tricycle*, etc. A *cyclone* is a circling, spiraling windstorm.

Off the coast of Greece lie many small islands arranged in a circle— the *Cyclades*. They seemingly form a protective ring around the sacred island of Delos, the smallest of the islands, and center of the worship of Apollo.

A person who *deviates* turns aside from a planned route, or way. A person may also *deviate* from the truth (from Latin *de*, away from, aside + *via* way, road). *Trivial* matters were originally those discussed at the crossroads—where three roads met (from *tri*, three + *via*, road).

The Romans used a *sundial* to tell the time of day (from Latin *dies*, day). In a *diary* a person records daily happenings.

Moths are *nocturnal* insects, active at night (*nox*). Butterflies are *diurnal* insects, active during the day (*dies*).

At midday the sun reaches the *meridian*, its highest point (from Latin *medius dies*, middle of the day).

The abbreviations A.M. and P.M. stand for *ante meridiem*, before noon, and *post meridiem*, after noon.

When a legislative body adjourns *sine die* (Latin *sine*, without + *dies*, day), the members set no returning date. Note also that the word *adjourn* (from French *a jorn*, to a given day) is ultimately traced back to Latin *ad* (to) + *diurnus* (daily), from *dies* (day).

Mono means one or single. A *monarch* rules alone (*arch*, rule).

A *monolog* is a talk by one person (*log*, speak).

A single company with exclusive control of a product has a *monopoly* on it (from the Greek verb *polein*, to bargain, sell).

A *monotonous* voice is wearisome because it seems to continue in the same, unvarying tone (from Greek *tonos*, something stretched + *monos*, one).

Like hermits, some *monks* live solitary lives, they live alone (from Greek *monos*, one, single).

Each of the single stones at Stonehenge in England is a *monolith* (*lith*, stone).

Matrimony usually results in motherhood (from Latin *mater, matr*, mother). A *matron* often looks motherly.

A *metropolis* such as Chicago or London is the most important city in a region or country and is a source of wealth, power, and influence. Many ancient Greek colonies were controlled by a parent state, or *metropolis* (mother city), from *metr* (mother) + *polis* (city).

Killing one's mother is *matricide*, from (*cide*, kill), as in *suicide* (killing oneself), from *sui* (self). Note also:

fratricide (killing a brother)—from *frater* (brother)

sororicide (killing a sister)—from *soror* (sister)

infanticide (killing an infant)—from *infans* (infant)

genocide (systematic extermination of a race)—from Greek *genos* (race)

filicide (killing one's child)—from Latin *filius* (son) and *filia* (daughter)

homicide (killing a person, literally "killing a *man*")—from *homo* (man)

parricide (killing one's parent or parents or someone equally revered)—from Latin *parricidium* (relative-killer).

Some more killers:

Insecticides kill insects.

Pesticides kill pests such as insects.

Fungicides kill fungi.

Bactericides destroy bacteria.

Rodenticide is a poison for rats, mice, and other rodents (from Latin *rodere*, to gnaw).

Avicide is the killing of birds—from Latin *avis* (bird). Note also *aviator* and *rara avis,* literally "a rare bird"—a person or thing seldom seen anymore, e.g., a wheelwright.

The above words dealing with killing are formed from the English suffix *-cide,* from the Latin verb *caedere* meaning to *cut, kill, slay.* (In ancient times, *cutting* with knife, sword, or spear was a typical way of killing.)

A brown-eyed father and a blue-eyed mother are likely to have a child with brown eyes, as the gene for brown eyes is *dominant*—that is, it is more powerful than the gene for blue eyes (the recessive gene). The word *dominant* comes from Latin *dominus,* meaning master, lord, chief of the house (*domus*).

The Romans *dominated* (mastered) the tribes of Gaul.

Fjords are the *predominant* (chief) feature of Norway's landscape.

A *domain* is the territory ruled by a master.

The English language *predominates* in North America.

The abbreviation A.D. (*Anno Domini*) means "in the year of our Lord."

An *immense* area is very big or vast. We get the word *immense* from Latin *im* (not) + *mensus* (measured). *Immense* literally means "cannot be measured."

The root *mens* also gives us *dimension,* from *di* (*dis*) meaning "apart" + *mens.* Therefore, the basic meaning of *dimension* is "measuring apart," that is, in different directions—width, breadth, length.

The *dormouse* sleeps most of the winter—from Latin *dormire* (to sleep) + *mouse* (one *m* has been dropped).

In winter, tulip bulbs are *dormant,* or inactive (sleeping).

A *dormitory* is a building with sleeping rooms.

A *dormer* is a sleeping-room window projecting from a roof.

Persons in marshy, swampy areas often catch *malaria,* transmitted by the bite of the anopheles mosquito. *Malaria* literally means "bad air" (from Italian *mala aria* and Latin *malus,* bad).

A *malefactor* is an evildoer (from Latin *facere,* to do).

A *malediction* is a curse, speaking evil to or of another (from *mal,* evil + *dict,* speak).

A *malevolent* person wants evil to happen to others (from *mal* + *volens,* wanting, wishing), wishing evil.

Note that from *vol* we get the word *volunteer* (one who wants to do it, that is, will do it of his own *volition*).

In grammar the *volitive* subjunctive expresses a wish, for example:
I wish that I were there.
Would that he were here.

An *eloquent* speaker "speaks out" effectively (from *e,* out + *loquor,* speak). A *loquacious* person talks a lot.

In the *soliloquy* "To be, or not to be . . ." Hamlet is alone, speaking to himself (from *solus,* alone + *loqu,* speak). A *colloquy* is a conversation, a speaking together (the prefix *col-* or *con-* comes from *cum,* meaning together, with).

A *ventriloquist,* who makes his voice appear to come from somewhere else, or speaks without apparent movement of the lips, "speaks from his belly" (from Latin *venter,* belly + *loqu*).

Note: A master list of roots, meanings, and examples can be found in the Appendix.

9

Pronunciation and Spelling

This unit does not try to set up a basic program of spelling. We assume that such a program is always going forward in the schools. Our purpose is to show how pronunciation and spelling are related to vocabulary development. Earlier we noted that word development is concept development and that concept development involves noting similarities and differences. This often means being sensitively aware of the sounds and spellings of words. If a student commonly mispronounces a word, he is likely to misspell it.

The student mistakes *effect* for *affect* partly because he does not distinguish the *e* from the *a*. Perhaps he doesn't hear the difference, or perhaps his parents and teachers do not give enough attention to early oral language development. Often, spelling errors occur when words sound the same: *principle, principal*. Here the syllables *-pal* and *-ple* have the same sound. Hence, one must often depend on the context to know how a word is to be spelled.

Pronunciation is important in vocabulary development because it involves discrimination between sounds that combine to form words and concepts. Thus, students must make distinctions between the sounds of words such as *wear* and *where, ever* and *every, while* and *wile*. Likewise, students must learn to make discriminations in spelling, distinguishing between *stake* and *steak, pain* and *pane, flew* and *flu*.

We have assumed that in the typical school, accurate spelling is considered important. Actually, nearly all words that children and young people write are correctly spelled, but our standards are high and we object to the misspelling of two or three words on a list of 150. Bad spelling, if nothing else, is annoying to the reader. Moreover, it requires a large amount of a teacher's time to mark misspelled words and then try to reteach them.

We know that spelling ability ranges widely. Possibly there is a sharp difference in the innate ability of persons to visualize the arrangement of word parts and letters. However, most students can sharply improve their spelling skills by (1) developing a spelling conscience, (2) noticing word structures, and (3) being aware that certain words are commonly misspelled and need to be doublechecked until they are well known. Since the number of words that are commonly misspelled is relatively small, students who are alerted to their own personal "demons" should show rapid improvement.

Communicating Clearly

The chief reason for discriminating between sounds is to communicate clearly. There are other reasons. For example, the relationship between the pronunciation of words and social acceptance is important. We refer here to accepted standards of schools, professions, business, and industry, where correct pronunciation may be of prime concern; where it is important, for example, not to pronounce *our* like *are*, or *for* like *fur*, especially if mispronunciation not only is unacceptable but leads to misunderstanding as well.

Pronunciation and spelling are means by which we send and receive words and exchange ideas. Students need to be reminded that poor enunciation, mispronunciation, and incorrect spelling distract the listener or the reader and cause static in the communication system.

The teacher can help students become more aware of pronunciation by having the class listen to recordings of speeches by both Americans and Britons. Students might then note the differences between American and British pronunciations. (In England, *laboratory* is pronounced *laboratory*, *schedule* becomes *shedule*, *garage* is *garage*.

Practicing Pronunciation

We sometimes mispronounce words because we spell them incorrectly, though more often the reverse is true. Students are nevertheless embarrassed when they mispronounce words that others know well. Obviously, then, it is best to create a situation in which students' pronunciation can be corrected in the spirit of constructive criticism.

Students should be encouraged to take note of mispronunciations they hear and discuss them in class. Common mispronunciations might include *ashfalt* for *asphalt*, *chimley* for *chimney*, *athalete* for *athlete*, *attackted* for *attacked*, *ast* for *asked*, *excape* for *escape*.

Such key words can be spelled aloud or written on the chalkboard. Members of the class can repeat each one to themselves until the correct pronunciation is firmly implanted. The teacher might also prepare tapes that spell out key words, allow intervals for the student to pronounce each one, then present the "accepted" pronunciation in each case.

Students may be at the stage where they are aware of errors in pronunciation or usage on television and radio. One distinguished commentator talked about something as being "the penultimate of success." He meant "the last word." *Penultimate* (from Latin *paene*, almost, and *ultima*, last) means next to the ultimate, almost last—it does not mean the highest achievement. Words heard mispronounced over the air include *fortay* for *forte* (fort), *skism* for *schism* (sizzem).

The teacher might record voices of the class members so they can listen to themselves talk. This can be done during regular class discussion periods. This experience helps students note and correct their own pronunciation errors, as well as enjoy a new experience.

Variety in Pronunciation

Few words are limited to one pronunciation. Words that change the accented syllable when they change from noun to verb or adjective are common. We "*refuse* to be laughed at" but we "empty the wastebasket into the _refuse_ container." Other words, while not changing their general meaning, shift from one part of speech to another:

a. He wrote an _abstract_ of the article.
b. He _abstracted_ the material from the article.

Some words are pronounced more than one way though their meaning or part of speech does not change. You may say "advert_ize_ment" and the television announcer says "advert_is_ment"; but the word _is_ the same, and both pronunciations are acceptable. Actually, our pronunciation is influenced by where we live, what we have been taught, or what our friends and family say.

In dealing with pronunciation, differences in regional dialect must be considered. Therefore, we do not suggest a preference for one pronunciation over another. As previously suggested, the main reason for "careful" pronunciation is to communicate clearly and avoid ambiguity or confusion. Therefore, the teacher need not stress one, exclusive pronunciation of a word, since family background, regional traditions, experience, travel, and preference all influence the pronunciation of words and the changing of pronunciations.

Spelling Problems

Teachers might remind students that while the pronunciations of many English words slowly but constantly change, their spelling became static centuries ago. For example, when Chaucer wrote "The Knight's Tale," the word _knight_ was pronounced _k-nicht_ (the _ch_ having the Greek _chi_ sound). It is now pronounced _nite_ but still retains the original spelling, _knight_. The word _night_ has gone through the same process: the pronunciation has changed but the spelling has not. Another example is the variation of pronunciation of _gh_ words, in which the _gh_ is silent or stands for the same sound as _f:_

light, bright; furlough, plough; rough, enough

Other silent letters are found in _knee_ and _knife_. The _k_ was once pronounced, as was the _g_ in _gnash_ and _gnarled_. The _e_ and _a_ in _sea, break, wealth,_ etc., were once separate sounds. The _w_ in _two,_ now silent in English, is pronounced in the Scottish word for two—_twa_ (pronounced _twah_). The _w_ in _answer_ was once pronounced (_answear_), and the _w_ is still pronounced in a word related to _answer—swear_.

Unlike students in ancient Rome, our students have a fairly difficult time learning to spell. Roman students learning Latin knew that each consonant had only one sound and that each vowel had only two sounds, long and short. Italian children today learning their hightly phonemic language have little difficulty with spelling because of the high degree of one-to-one correspondence of phoneme and grapheme, in which one letter stands for one sound. To gain such ideal correspondence it would be necessary to follow the advice of George Bernard Shaw, who recommended a completely new system of English spelling. To illustrate the inconsistency of present spelling, he pointed out that *ghoti* could be pronounced *fish:*

> *gh* in *laugh* = f
> *o* in *women* = i
> *ti* in *nation* = sh

Aside from phonemically irregular words, one of the chief causes of poor spelling is careless pronunciation. *Government* is often mispronounced and therefore spelled *goverment, quantity* becomes *quanity, probably* becomes *probly, bronchial* becomes *bronichal, vanilla* becomes *vanella,* and *arctic* becomes *artic.* (Actually, the latter pronunciation of *arctic* is now acceptable though the spelling is not.

Spelling and Vocabulary Study

Vocabulary acquisition precedes reading skill, since students must already know words in order to read (*decode* written symbols). However, if the student is to go beyond decoding to *encoding* (writing), he must gain skill in letter discrimination. He must *spell* (place the graphemes of a word in conventional order) before he can write, or encode with skill. While the decoder (the reader) recognizes the word *descend,* the encoder (the writer) has to reproduce the grapheme relationships that make up the word *descend.* Therefore, the skillful encoder (the student who spells words correctly) is in a better position to recognize *descend* in reading and in addition is likely to learn more easily the related words *descending, descendant, descendants, ascend,* and *ascendant.* Students who can spell (encode) can easily read (decode) and are likely to have less difficulty with writing skills.

The most effective spelling program works simultaneously with vocabulary study. Since over 80 percent of English words are phonemically regular, we may be neglecting a ready-made method of learning words and how to spell them: encoding language patterns and word patterns.

The language code, which we must decode to read and encode to write, has order; otherwise we could make no generalizations about the language. This order is quite clear. For example, the *ou* sound is peculiar to different words such as *house, louse, couch, grouch, slouch.* From them the student can generalize about the *ou* pattern and the sound it represents. Exceptions to this generalization are easily learned later.

From recognizing meaningful syllables, the student can proceed to a study of the parts of words (roots and affixes). The spelling of words should include encoding sounds, symbols, syllables, and meaningful syllables or elements such as *ab* (from), *ad* (to), *ante* (before).

In addition to making generalizations about regular patterns of graphemes that make up sounds, symbols, and syllables, the student needs practice in making discriminations. He should note that variations in word meanings are often distinguishable by the arrangement of similar letters or even by the addition or omission of a letter: *rat, rate; hat, hate; bat, bait, bate; singing, singeing; dying dyeing*.

The lack of a solid relationship between spelling and vocabulary skills is apparent when students spell *bare* as *bear*, *there* as *their*, *fete* as *fate*. The significance of choosing the correct letter in spelling is easily seen in words such as *homily* and *homely*, *blackhead* and *blockhead*, *mallet* and *mullet*, *winch* and *wench*, *cook* and *kook*. Anagrammatic words result from the transposition of letters. The position of a letter makes a big difference in words such as *lair* and *liar*, *dairy* and *diary*, *lie* and *lei*, *complaint* and *compliant*, *trial* and *trail*, *causal* and *casual*.

It is clear, therefore, that the study of spelling is important for these reasons, to name a few:

1. Incorrect spelling can cause the reader to misunderstand the meaning of a word: *set* for *sit*, *red* for *rid*, *loath* for *loathe*, *ingenious* for *ingenuous*.

2. Correct spelling is needed to make discriminations in meaning: *import* or *export*, *antiwar* or *antewar*, *dissect* or *bisect*, *immigrate* or *emigrate*, *hypertension* or *hypotension*.

3. The student who knows how to spell a word can obviously find it faster in a dictionary.

4. Knowing how to spell is a social matter. Ability, education, and literacy are attributes often associated with spelling skill.

5. Poor spelling wastes the time of both teacher and pupils.

6. Spelling and pronunciation are related. Linguists recognize the relationship between pronunciation and spelling skills. Students who spell a word correctly usually pronounce it correctly.

7. Poor spellers may avoid using words they know in their written work. They thus deprive themselves of the means to express their thoughts as fully as they might.

We have pointed out the relationship between spelling and vocabulary, noting that spelling enables the decoder (the reader) to encode (to write). Encoding gives the student practice in discriminating regular letter patterns that form meaningful syllables—roots and affixes that are generative of many words.

Knowing how to spell correctly is a combination of remembering letter patterns that represent sounds (*sleek, slick; angel, angle*) and recognizing letter discriminations that distinguish between the meaning of one word and that of another (*heir, air*).

Organizing Words for Spelling Study

As we have previously pointed out, in teaching spelling as a part of word study, the teacher supplies a *context* that is missing in many spelling programs. Combining spelling and word study makes the learning of spelling a more relevant activity; it integrates it with a study of the written language. Effective word study helps the student make associations, form patterns, relate one concept to another. An effective spelling program organizes materials in terms of word-attack skills, learning whole words and their meanings, learning word parts and their meanings, analyzing elements, and rebuilding whole words by synthesizing elements.

Just as the teacher helps the student generalize about word formation, so he can help the student make generalizations about spelling. The teacher can arrange words to be learned and spelled in groups that help the student make visual and aural associations. For example, the student can readily see patterns in the following sets of words:

multiply	omit	multitude
multiplicand	permit	altitude
multiplier	admit	aptitude
multiple	commit	attitude
multiplication	submit	fortitude
multitude	remit	beatitude

Such arrangements visually and aurally reinforce the learning of letter patterns that the student must know to be a good speller.

Spelling and Word Analysis

English is in some respects phonemically irregular. The *f* sound in *photo* is not spelled like the *f* sound in *first.* The *f* sound and the *u* sound in *muff* are found in words like *enough* and *rough.* Note the *shun* sound in *carnation,* the *a* sound in *they.* These few examples indicate that irregularities exist in the grapheme-phoneme relationships in English; and because of this irregularity many words are difficult to spell.

But, linguists have pointed out that there is a great deal of regularity in English sounds and corresponding symbols. This means that many prefixes, roots, and suffixes (actually syllables and compounds of syllables) appear in predictable positions in respect to phoneme-grapheme correspondence. This becomes increasingly important as the pupil develops greater sophistication in his approach to his spelling problems.

We know that speech comes before writing and that syllabication helps the student pronounce a word. For example, dictionaries give the pronunciation-syllabication of words such as *fanatic* (fa·nat'ic) and *fanciful* (fan'ci·ful). This type of entry is an aid to the student in pronouncing the words, but it should be pointed out that syllabication does not always help the student see the meaningful parts of words; it does not help him decide whether *fa, fan,* or *fanat* are meaningful word parts. In short, the student gets no hint about how to classify meaningful parts as a way of remembering the spelling of a word. The teacher must supply this help.

Let's consider the word *telegram*. Dictionaries give the syllabication of *telegram* as *tel'e·gram*. An approach to spelling emphasizing meaningful part combinations would stress not *tel* but *tele,* meaning distant. Such an approach would tie in directly with a systematic study of key prefixes in the early grades. Thus the teaching of *tele,* for example, as a meaningful entity, offers an effective way of attacking the spelling of this word. Students learning *tele* as a unit meaning distant would be unlikely to spell *telegram* as *telagram, telegraph* as *telagraph,* and *telephone* as *telaphone*—all common spelling errors.

Likewise, students who know that the prefix *im-* means "not" are less likely to forget to use two *m*'s (one for the prefix and one for the root) in the word *immortal.*

Therefore, in addition to learning phonetic syllabication in spelling activities, the student needs to be aware that word elements with meaning also exist, that the phonetic syllabication of *atom* (found in the dictionary as (*at'om*) tends to prevent his learning that the word *atom* is made up of two meaningful parts, *a* and *tom,* from *a* (not) + *tom* (cut), referring to the early notion that an atom was the smallest particle of matter and could not be cut.

This does not mean that students are to disregard the syllabic sounds of words found in phonetic keys. Rather, we suggest that, in addition to phonetic aids, greater emphasis be placed on the meaningful word elements as an aid to spelling and reading, and as a word-building device. For example, the dictionary listing of *biology* as *bi·ol'o·gy* helps with pronunciation, but the student should also know that this syllabic arrangement does not have meaning. A meaningful formation is *bio* (life) + *logy* (study of).

Classifying Words as an Aid to Spelling

Through the systematic teaching of prefixes, roots, and suffixes (meaningful word parts), and by analyzing words, the teacher can give the student spelling help, as illustrated in the few words listed below.

Prefixes

ab sent	*re* fund	*mis* spell	*sym* phony
ab duct	*re* play	*mis* state	*sym* pathy
ad verb	*cent* ennial	*trans* plant	*peri* scope
ad here	*cent* imeter	*trans* fer	*peri* phery
mono plane	*tri* cycle	*super* natural	*syn* thesis
mono rail	*tri* vial	*super* structure	*syn* tax
bi cycle	*contra* dict	*fore* head	*anti* toxin
bi sect	*contra* ry	*fore* most	*anti* venom
anti social	*uni* lateral	*inter* national	*di* urnal
anti septic	*uni* form	*inter* val	*di* chotomy

Roots

tele *graph*	*aud* ition	*vis* ible	*tract* or
steno *graph* er	in *aud* ible	super *vis* e	sub *tract* ion
un *arm* ed	*tele* vision	bi *cycl* e	un *equ* al
arm y	*tele* phone	en *cycl* opedia	*equ* ator
neur *alg* ia	trans *port* ation	dis *miss* al	in *volv* e
nost *alg* ia	*port* able	*miss* ionary	re *volv* er
micro *phon* e	uni *form*	*grad* uate	*voc* ation
sym *phon* y	re *form*	de *grad* e	con *voc* ation
de *script* ion	pre *dict* ion	con *junct* ion	sur *viv* or
pre *script* ion	*dict* ionary	*junct* ure	re *viv* e
in *spect* or	dis *aster*	*manu* facture	e *duc* ate
spect ator	*aster* isk	*manu* al	ab *duc* t
bell igerent	pro *ject*	*anima* l	*para* sol
re *bell* ion	re *ject*	in *anima* te	*para* chute

Suffixes

psycho *logy*	tonsill *itis*	induc *tion*	civil *ize*
mytho *logy*	appendic *itis*	dic *tion*	crystal *ize*
depend *able*	part *icle*	real *ist*	material *ism*
avail *able*	cut *icle*	art *ist*	social *ism*
invent *ive*	book *let*	conservat *ory*	audit *orium*
extens *ive*	ring *let*	observat *ory*	natat *orium*
assist *ance*	friend *ship*	din *ette*	mole *cule*
resist *ance*	penman *ship*	kitchen *ette*	minus *cule*
ill *ness*	brother *hood*	inspect *or*	free *dom*
ful *ness*	neighbor *hood*	act *or*	king *dom*

Spelling and Context

Vocabulary instruction aimed at helping the student understand how language develops can contribute to his spelling skills. Linguists divide the study of language structure into three areas: (1) *phonology*, the system of sounds used in a language (Latin *phon*, sound), (2) *syntax*, the arrangement of words to form sentences (Greek *syn*, together + *taxis*, arrangement), and (3) *morphology*, the forms of words brought about by inflection and derivation (Greek *morphe*, form + *logy*, study of).

Recent studies indicate the following:

1. Spelling is a more consistent symbolic representation of speech than was formerly believed. Eighty percent of the time, a phoneme is consistently represented by a grapheme.

171

2. The arrangement of phonological (sound) elements is consistent in consonant-vowel, vowel-consonant, and consonant-vowel-consonant positions. The speller does not have an unlimited choice of position for placing letters.

3. These consonant-vowel, vowel-consonant patterns are readily learned through the teaching of meaningful syllables and word elements (morphological elements): prefixes, roots, and suffixes.

Too often students are asked to learn the spelling of each word as a discrete act, a separate task unrelated to former learning. For effective learning the student must see the word *jumping* as an inflected form (morphological change) of *jump*. He must note the morphological aspects of language: compounds, prefixes, suffixes, roots, and derivatives that point up the relationships between words. He must get the idea that every word he spells is not a new experience.

The student can learn to generalize about spelling as he generalizes about words and derivatives. He can learn that words such as *mate, fate, rate* (having the long *a* sound) generally have a final silent *e*. The same is true of other vowels in words with a long *i: kite, site, rite*. Exceptions such as *bade* (pronounced *bad*) and *forebade* (short *a* with silent *e*) can be discussed after the concept is learned.

Additional generalizations and rules that can help students spell correctly are offered in the lessons that follow. We believe, however, that organizing spelling lessons to coincide with the study of morphology gives the student a contextual structure for the study of spelling.

It is often thought that presenting spelling words in the context of sentences is of great help to the student. It may help him relate one word to another, one idea to another. However, it offers no structure for learning to spell, no principles he can follow, no way to help him organize his formerly learned knowledge to apply to newly learned knowledge about spelling.

Students who relate spelling practice to word study, who are taught to recognize certain syllables as meaningful units, readily recognize these units when they turn up in new words (the *anti* in *antifreeze* is spelled the same as the *anti* in *antidote*). If the student knows how to spell *bicycle*, he can be shown that he already knows how to spell one part of *bisect*. If he can spell *circus*, and is taught to recognize *circu* (around) as a unit, it is a short step to the spelling of harder words—*circuit, circuitous*, etc. If he has been taught *epi* (upon) in *epitaph*, the words *epilogue, epidemic*, and *epithet* will be easier to spell.

Spelling Rules

Spelling rules are possible only because there is predictable structure in words. In prefixes such as *pre-, pro-, eu-, dys-*, and many others, the letter patterns are stable and can therefore be easily learned once they are observed.

Roots have regular letter patterns that help the speller who is aware of the roots. It is easy for students to recognize the spelling of recurring roots such as *vis* in *vision, television, visionary, televise,* and *visor* if they are alerted to these roots.

A student who knows the root *labor* (work) is unlikely to misspell the word *laboratory* as *labratory* (leaving out the *o*). A student who knows the root *rupt* (break) and the prefix *inter-* (between) will be less likely to misspell *interrupt* as *interupt* (with one *r*).

Since letter patterns form meaningful units that make up words, it is possible to form generalizations about them, in the form of spelling rules. For example,

Use *i* before *e*
except after *c*
or when sounded like *a*
as in neighbor or weigh.

The rhyme is good to remember when spelling words such as *relieve* and *deceive,* or *believe* and *receive,* although there are some weaknesses in the rule (discussed later in the lesson). Note that we might make up a related rule about verbs, using *e* after *c:* If the noun form contains *cep, c* will be followed by *ei.*

reception   receive
perception   perceive
deception   deceive
conception   conceive

Existing spelling rules are often helpful, and at the appropriate time the teacher may wish to discuss and review some of the following rules and spelling hints. We include here only a few examples illustrating each principle. Students might be encouraged to gather additional illustrative examples and discuss them in class.

Spelling Hints

1. We make most singular words plural by adding *s* (*book, books; magazine, magazines; puzzle, puzzles*).

2. We make singular words ending in *s, ss, sh, ch, x,* and *z* plural by adding *es* (*bus, buses; glass, glasses; wish, wishes; church, churches; box, boxes; topaz, topazes*).

3. Some plural spellings do not follow rules; rather, there are internal changes to indicate plural (*man, men; woman, women; child, children; mouse, mice; goose, geese; tooth, teeth*). Some plurals are the same as the singular nouns (*deer, deer; sheep, sheep*).

4. We add only *s* or *es* (not *'s*) to make names plural (*Bill,* two *Bills; Mary,* two *Marys;* Mr. and Mrs. *Brown,* or the *Browns;* the *Joneses*).

5. For nouns ending in *y* preceded by a consonant, change the *y* to *i* and add *es* (*army, armies; baby, babies; city, cities; berry, berries*).

6. For nouns ending in *y* preceded by a vowel, merely add *s* (*monkey, monkeys; play, plays; valley, valleys; turkey, turkeys*).

7. In general, we drop the final *e* of a root word before adding a suffix beginning with a vowel (*-ing, -er, -ed, -ent, -ence, -er, -able, -ible*). Examples: *love, loving; care, caring; circle, circling; range, ranging; love, lovable.*

8. In general, we keep the final *e* of the root word before adding a suffix beginning with a consonant (*-ment, -ness, -less, -ful*). Examples: *arrange, arrangement; care, careless; spite, spiteful; humane, humaneness.*

9. A word ending with a consonant preceded by a single vowel usually doubles the consonant before adding a vowel suffix. Examples: *skip, skipping; scan, scanning.*

10. A word of more than one syllable ending in a single consonant preceded by a single vowel, and with the accent on the final syllable, doubles the consonant before adding a vowel suffix. Examples:

begin	beginning
compel	compelled
prefer	preferring
refer	referring
control	controlling
commit	committed
forgot	forgotten

But if the accent is not on the final syllable, we do not double the consonant.

cancel	canceled
counsel	counseled
benefit	benefited
bigot	bigoted

Note: The rule works most of the time, but *canceled, traveler*, and *kidnaper* are sometimes spelled (mostly in Britain) *cancelled, traveller*, and *kidnapper.*

11. To retain the soft sound of the *c* (*s* sound) and of the *g* (*j* sound) in words ending in *ce* and *ge*, we keep the final *e* (*peace, peaceable; replace, replaceable; arrange, arrangement; advantage, advantageous; notice, noticeable; change, changeable*).

12. Words ending in two vowels (a vowel + final *e*) retain the final vowel (*e*) before adding a suffix. Examples: *see, seeable; shoe, shoeing; canoe, canoeing.*

13. Check the dictionary for nouns ending in *o* before adding *es* for the plural. Although there are about a dozen common *o* words whose plurals end in *es* (*vetoes, mosquitoes, potatoes, tomatoes, heroes, volcanoes, echoes, embargoes, torpedoes, Negroes, buffaloes*), some of those words may add only *s* to form the plural (*buffalos, volcanos*). Other words that add only *s* are *silos, cameos, radios*, and *dynamos.*

14. In general, we add *s* to the main word of a compound (*brothers*-in-law, *sisters*-in-law, *attorneys*-at-law). We add *s* to compound words ending in *ful* (*teaspoonfuls, tablespoonfuls, cupfuls, mouthfuls, basketfuls*). (But note *manservant, menservants.*)

15. Loan words from Greek and Latin often cause difficulty. English plurals are often used with these words. Either the Greek and Latin plurals or the English plurals are acceptable.

Greek or Latin Singular	Greek or Latin Plural	English Plural
alumnus	alumni (*masculine*)	
alumna	alumnae (*feminine*)	
medium	media	mediums
datum	data	
radius	radii	radiuses
spectrum	spectra	spectrums
stadium	stadia	stadiums
fungus	fungi	funguses
criterion	criteria	criterions
phenomenon	phonemena	phenomenons
locus	loci	
dictum	dicta	dictums
crisis	crises	
oasis	oases	
thesis	theses	
formula	formulae	formulas
forum	fora	forums
fulcrum	fulcra	fulcrums
gladiolus	gladioli	gladioluses
index	indices	indexes
memorandum	memoranda	memorandums

16. A contraction is two words joined with an apostrophe to show the omission of a letter or letters: *we'll* (we will), *haven't* (have not), *they've* (they have), *who's* (who is, who has). The word *apostrophe* comes from Greek *apostrophos* (from *apo*, away + *strephein*, to turn).

   In addition to its use in contractions, the apostrophe is used to show ownership (*boy, boy's; dog, dog's; man's* best friend, *man's* inhumanity to man). To singular nouns we usually add *'s* (*girl, girl's*). To plural nouns not ending in *s* we add *'s* (*men, men's*). To plural nouns ending in *s*, we add just an apostrophe (*girls'* bikes). If a singular noun ends in *s* or an *s* sound, we add just an apostrophe (*Illinois'* population; his *conscience'* sake.) If a noun of one syllable ends in *s*, we add *'s* (*Tess's* book).

17. We form the plural of numbers, signs, letters, and words used as words by adding *'s* (*a's; 9's; &'s; p's* and *q's*. You used too many *said's*).

Predicting Spelling Difficulties

Students need to be reminded that certain words are often misspelled, and thus be alerted to check these words after spelling them. But spelling not only involves the ability to put letters together in the correct form, it also requires the attitude or concern to see that it is done. We need, in other words, a spelling conscience. We must care whether we spell correctly or not.

Sometimes we can use memory devices such as rules, but they do not always work. And even if we improve our spelling by learning certain principles and by using memory devices such as noting roots and affixes, we will still misspell words unless we are able to predict and doublecheck the words which we might misspell, and then learn them thoroughly.

We have included here a list with a number of words often misspelled, although they are not, on the whole, difficult words such as those included in the usual lists of "spelling demons." In developing this list of words we have made use of Arthur I. Gates's *Spelling Difficulties in 3,876 Words*[1] and Harry A. Greene's *The New Iowa Spelling Scale*,[2] listing only those words scored below 50 percent on the Iowa Spelling Scale at the eighth-grade level. The student would first be asked to check the words in the list that he thinks he might misspell. The words he checks are probably the ones he needs to look up when he is writing.

Word (% Correct)	Most Common Misspelling	Word (% Correct)	Most Common Misspelling
abandon (49%)		approximately (21%)	
absolutely (41%)	absolutly	artificial (38%)	artifical
abundant (47%)	abundent	association (47%)	
acceptable (48%)		attorney (40%)	
acceptance (44%)	acceptence	authority (45%)	
accepting (49%)		available (41%)	
accommodate (24%)	accomodate	bankruptcy (19%)	
accompanied (42%)		bearing (46%)	
accordance (49%)	accordence	benefit (39%)	benifit
accustomed (30%)		bicycle (45%)	
achievement (36%)		bough (36%)	
acknowledgment (25%)		boundary (49%)	boundry
acquaint (28%)		bouquet (45%)	
acquire (35%)	aquire	boys' (39%)	
adequate (22%)		bulletin (38%)	bullitin
adjourned (43%)		bureau (32%)	
administration (45%)	addministration	campaign (28%)	campain
advertisement (46%)	advertisment	cancellation (30%)	
affidavit (15%)		candidate (41%)	
agricultural (40%)		capacity (44%)	
all right (41%)		ceased (40%)	
altar (34%)		challenge (49%)	
amendment (43%)	ammendment	characteristic (28%)	
analysis (22%)		children's (45%)	
annual (43%)	anual	chocolate (48%)	
anticipate (27%)	antisipate	chorus (44%)	
anxiety (21%)		Christian (49%)	Christain
appetite (36%)	appitite	circuit (27%)	
applicant (43%)		circumstance (45%)	curcumstance
appreciated (48%)		civilization (42%)	civilazation

[1]Arthur I. Gates, *Spelling Difficulties in 3,876 Words* (New York: Columbia University, 1937).
[2]Harry A. Greene, *The New Iowa Spelling Scale* (Iowa City: State University of Iowa, 1954).

Word (% Correct)	Most Common Misspelling	Word (% Correct)	Most Common Misspelling
cocoon (45%)		economy (42%)	
collateral (12%)		edition (47%)	
colonel (31%)		efficiency (13%)	
columns (40%)		efficient (25%)	
commencement (42%)	commencment	elapsed (46%)	
commercial (49%)		eligible (31%)	
commission (45%)	commision	eliminate (36%)	
committed (37%)		embroidery (34%)	
committee (34%)		employees (42%)	
communicate (48%)		enclosure (47%)	
communication (48%)	comunication	encouraging (38%)	
compel (43%)		enthusiastic (41%)	
competition (39%)		epistle (18%)	
compliment (39%)	complement	equipped (24%)	equiped
conceive (39%)		exceptionally (37%)	
condemn (33%)	condem	excessive (37%)	
congratulations (41%)		execute (42%)	
conscience (24%)	concience	executive (31%)	
conscious (13%)		exercise (49%)	
consequence (33%)		exhaust (42%)	
continuous (25%)		exhibition (29%)	exibition
controversy (27%)		existence (23%)	
convenience (23%)		experienced (46%)	
correspond (42%)		extension (49%)	extention
correspondence (34%)		extraordinary (33%)	
council (40%)		extremely (43%)	
counsel (17%)		facilities (31%)	
courteous (34%)	courtious	faculty (48%)	
courtesy (41%)	curtesy	familiar (40%)	
crisis (31%)		fascinating (20%)	
criticism (12%)		February (47%)	Febuary
curiosity (35%)	curiousity	financial (34%)	
cylinder (25%)		flu (41%)	
day's (46%)		foliage (26%)	
debtor (38%)		foreign (48%)	
deceive (49%)		fortunately (36%)	
definite (38%)		fraternity (35%)	
definitely (21%)		gratitude (40%)	graditude
definition (40%)		grieve (47%)	
delegate (41%)		guarantee (16%)	
deny (48%)		guardian (47%)	gaurdian
descend (29%)	decend	ignorance (47%)	ignorence
despair (35%)		Halloween (49%)	
discipline (14%)		handkerchiefs (49%)	
discussed (49%)		heir (48%)	
distinguish (36%)		hygiene (31%)	
distribution (49%)		icicles (31%)	
doctrine (36%)		illustration (44%)	
dormitory (24%)		imagination (46%)	
earnestly (48%)		immediately (33%)	

Word (% Correct)	Most Common Misspelling	Word (% Correct)	Most Common Misspelling
immense (28%)		offense (39%)	
immortal (44%)	imortal	official (46%)	offical
incident (46%)		opportunities (34%)	
incidentally (12%)		oppose (49%)	
inconvenience (33%)		ordinarily (29%)	
indefinitely (10%)		originally (37%)	
individual (41%)		ornaments (47%)	
inevitable (24%)		pamphlet (29%)	pamflet
initial (35%)		pamphlets (32%)	
initiation (23%)		paradise (46%)	
innocent (43%)	inocent	parliament (16%)	parliment
inquiry (46%)		partial (29%)	
inspiration (45%)		particularly (47%)	
installation (33%)		patience (44%)	
instinct (44%)		patronage (42%)	
institutions (46%)		peasant (47%)	
intellectual (22%)		peculiar (36%)	pecular
intelligence (37%)		perceive (28%)	
interrupt (43%)	interupt	peril (27%)	
interval (49%)		permanent (46%)	
intimate (33%)		petition (35%)	
jealous (48%)		philosophy (21%)	
laboratory (38%)	labratory	physical (47%)	
legislation (48%)		physician (38%)	
legislature (44%)		pigeon (45%)	
leisure (43%)		pilgrims (41%)	
liability (46%)		politician (21%)	
license (31%)		positively (44%)	positivly
lieutenant (18%)		possess (31%)	
liquor (43%)		possibility (45%)	posibility
loyalty (48%)		practically (36%)	
luxury (43%)		precious (48%)	
magnificent (49%)	magnificient	precisely (23%)	
manufacturer (37%)		preference (43%)	
materially (44%)		preferred (42%)	
mathematics (35%)		presence (46%)	presense
maturity (46%)		principle (39%)	principal
mechanical (44%)		prior (38%)	
merchandise (45%)	merchandize	privilege (22%)	
merely (49%)		probability (45%)	
minimum (38%)		professional (46%)	
mortgage (16%)	morgage	psychology (7%)	
mountains (44%)		pursuit (33%)	
multiplication (41%)		quantities (45%)	
murmur (38%)	murmer	receipt (33%)	
mutual (41%)		receiving (45%)	recieving
necessarily (22%)		recognized (45%)	
niece (47%)	neice	recommend (30%)	
occasionally (32%)		recommended (31%)	
occurred (28%)	occured	references (41%)	

Word (% Correct)	Most Common Misspelling	Word (% Correct)	Most Common Misspelling
referred (48%)		sufficient (22%)	sufficiant
refrigerator (44%)		sufficiently (29%)	
regretting (41%)		supplement (34%)	
reign (35%)		survey (42%)	
remembrance (36%)	rememberance	suspicion (22%)	
remittance (41%)		sympathy (45%)	
representative (36%)	representitive	temporarily (20%)	
requisition (14%)		temporary (41%)	temperary
responsibility (40%)		tendency (42%)	
restaurant (21%)	resturant	they're (40%)	
reverence (49%)		thorough (24%)	
scarcely (43%)		thoroughly (22%)	
schedule (37%)		tongue (48%)	
scheme (43%)		tournament (39%)	
scholarship (46%)		tradition (47%)	
scissors (40%)		tragedy (30%)	
sensible (49%)		transferred (37%)	transfered
separate (41%)		unanimous (25%)	
separately (37%)		undoubtedly (25%)	
shepherd (39%)		unfortunately (40%)	
similar (43%)	similiar	universal (49%)	
sincerely (49%)	sincerly	unnecessary (25%)	unecessary
skiing (43%)		urgent (43%)	
skis (29%)		utilize (37%)	
solemn (30%)		vacancies (39%)	
sorority (18%)		vague (37%)	
specific (35%)		variety (42%)	
squirrel (41%)		veil (38%)	
statistics (35%)		vein (43%)	
statues (28%)		vicinity (45%)	
straightened (45%)		whether (49%)	
substitute (49%)	subsitute	wholly (46%)	
succeeded (42%)	succeded	woman's (46%)	
successfully (46%)		wretched (25%)	
succession (42%)		wrought (33%)	

The list has implications for other grades also. The word *bicycle*, with a spelling score of 45 percent at the eighth-grade level, will be difficult for students below this level. The word *counsel* (17 percent at the eighth-grade level) will still be difficult for students beyond the eighth-grade level.

After the student has used this master spelling list, which he should keep in his notebook, the teacher might give a series of spelling tests on a number of words taken from it. After each test the student can check himself against the master list to see whether he can spell the words he predicted he knew how to spell, or whether those words are in reality his personal spelling "demons." (The list can be expanded periodically.)

By using this table the teacher will be prewarned about the spelling-difficulty level of certain words. Foreseeing his students' probable spelling problems, he can then plan ways of eliminating them.

Of course, the teacher can tell how hard these words are by consulting Greene's book. One advantage of the table, however, lies in Gates's listing of the most common misspellings of certain words, as it enables the teacher to alert the student to the most probable source of his misspelling. It shows, for example, that the most common misspelling of *absolutely* is *absolutly* (not retaining the final *e* of *absolute*), or that the most common misspelling of *bulletin* is *bullitin*.

The Role of Accent in Words

The development of oral and written language skills requires extensive practice in auditory discrimination. The teacher may point up the importance of pronunciation in changing the meaning of words by showing the student that the meaning of certain words depends on accent (special stress or force given a syllable), for example, conVICT (verb) and CONvict (noun)

The following lesson emphasizes the role of accent in words and points out that words spelled alike often change their meaning or part of speech according to where the accent falls. A verb may become a noun, or vice versa; a noun may become an adjective. The student needs to know that the way he pronounces a word, the way he accents a syllable, often gives a certain meaning to the word or influences the listener's comprehension of the meaning intended.

The student may use the following list of words to practice pronunciation. The teacher may use the list with the overhead projector to illustrate that words spelled alike are not necessarily pronounced alike, and that accent often changes the meaning of a word.

ABsent	abSENT	CONverse	conVERSE
ABstract	abSTRACT	CONvert	conVERT
ADdress	adDRESS	CONvict	conVICT
ALly	alLY	DEfense	deFENSE
COLlect	colLECT	DIgest	diGEST
COMpact	comPACT	EScort	esCORT
COMplex	comPLEX	ESsay	esSAY
COMpound	comPOUND	EXport	exPORT
COMpress	comPRESS	EXtract	exTRACT
CONcave	conCAVE	FREquent	freQUENT
CONcert	conCERT	IMport	imPORT
CONcrete	conCRETE	IMpress	imPRESS
CONduct	conDUCT	INcense	inCENSE
CONfine	conFINE	INcline	inCLINE
CONflict	conFLICT	INcrease	inCREASE
CONserve	conSERVE	INsert	inSERT
CONsole	conSOLE	INside	inSIDE
CONtent	conTENT	INsult	inSULT
CONtest	conTEST	INtern	inTERN
CONtrast	conTRAST	INvalid	inVALID

INvert	inVERT	RElay	reLAY
OBject	obJECT	REprint	rePRINT
OFFset	offSET	RErun	reRUN
OUTlay	outLAY	REset	reSET
OUTreach	outREACH	REsole	reSOLE
PERmit	perMIT	REsurvey	reSURVEY
PREsage	preSAGE	REtail	reTAIL
PROceeds	proCEEDS	REtake	reTAKE
PROGress	proGRESS	REtread	reTREAD
PROJect	proJECT	REwrite	reWRITE
PROtest	proTEST	RUNdown	runDOWN
REcess	reCESS	SUBject	subJECT
RECord	reCORD	SUFfix	sufFIX
REdress	reDRESS	SURvey	surVEY
REfuse	reFUSE	SUSpect	susPECT
REgress	reGRESS	TRANSfer	transFER
REject	reJECT	TRANSplant	transPLANT
RElapse	reLAPSE	TRANSport	transPORT

Note: Certain words do not necessarily change their meaning because of shift of accent. Furthermore, people in certain parts of the country may pronounce some of the above listed words in different ways. For example, as a noun, *address* may be pronounced either "*add*ress" or "add*ress*." Debatable points can often be settled by consulting the dictionary.

Pronunciation Demons

Many students hesitate to use words they know simply because they are unsure of how to pronounce them. The words listed below (many of which are hard to spell) are often mispronounced. Careful attention to many of them should help the average upper-grade student. Note that some words may be pronounced two ways:

abdomen: *ab* domen (ab *do* men)
abstemious: ab *stee* mious
affluence: *aff* luence
alias: *ale* ius
altimeter: al *tim* eter
anathema: a *nath* ama
antipodes: an *tip* o *dees*
apropos: appro *poe*
archetype: *ark* etype
bade: bad
bayou: *by* oo
bestial: *best* yal
cerulean: se *rule* ian
chiropodist: ki *ropp* edist

chiropractor: *ky* ra *prak* ter
comparable: *com* parable
condolence: con *do* lence
covert: *co* vert (*cuv* vert)
crevasse: cre *vass*
dais: *day* uss (*dye* uss)
decadent: *dek* a dent (de *kay* dent)
demoniacal: demon *eye* ical
despicable: des *pick* able
 (*des* pick able)
desultory: *dess* ultory
devotee: devva *tee*
diphtheria: dif *theer* ia
disheveled: di *shev* eled

dour: *dow* er (also as in *doer*)
effete: eh *feet*
efficacy: *eff* icasy
endemic: en *dem* ic
ephemeral: eh *fem* eral
exacerbate: ex *ass* erbate
exquisite: *ex* kwizit (ex *kwiz* it)
facade: feh *sahd*
finis: *fin* is
flaccid: *flak* sid
formidable: *form* idable
forte: fort (what one does well)
forte: for *tay* (played loudly)
genuine: *jen* you in
gondola: *gon* dola (gon *doe* la)
halcyon: *hal* see on
haphazard: *hap* hazard
harbinger: *har* bin jer
hedonism: *heed* onism
height: *hite*
heinous: *hay* nous
hospitable: *hos* pitable (hos *pit* able)
impious: *imp* ious
impotent: *imp* otent
incognito: in cog *neat* o (in *cog* nito)
incomparable: in *com* parable
incongruous: in *kong* gruous
indefatigable: inde *fat* igable
indict: in *dite*
indigent: *in* dijent
infinite: *in* finite
infrared: *in* fra *red*
ingenuous: in *jen* uous
interdict: *in* ter dict (n.), inter *dict* (v.)
intricacy: *in* tricasy
irremediable: irre *meed* iable
irreparable: ir *rep* erable
irrevocable: ir *rev* ocable
lamentable: *lam* entable
  (la *ment* able)
lichen: *like* n

machinations: *mack* in *na* tions
  (*mash* i *na* tions)
maintenance: *main* tenance
maniacal: man *eye* acal
metonymy: me *ton* ome
minuscule: *min* us kyool (min *us* kyool)
mischievous: *mis* che vus
naive: na *eve*
obdurate: *obb* durate
obese: oh *beese*
onerous: *on* erous (*own* erous)
onus: *own* us
ophthalmologist: *off* thal *moll* ogist
plebeian: ple *bee* an
plethora: *pleth* ora
podiatrist: poe *dy* atrist
posthumous: *pos* chumous
preferable: *pref* erable
prelate: *prell* ate
pseudo: *sue* doe
qualm: kwawm (kwom)
quay: *key* (kway)
quietus: kwy *eet* us
redolent: *red* olent
respite: *ress* pit
ribald: *rib* ald (*rye* bald)
scabrous: *sca* brus (*skay* brus)
schism: *sizz* im
scion: *sigh* un
secretive: *seek* retive (se *cree* tive)
solace: *soll* iss
specious: *spee* shuss
splenetic: sple *net* ic
succinct: suck *sinkt*
taciturn: *tass* iturn
telemeter: te *lem* eter
travail: tra *vale* (*trav* el)
typography: ty *pog* raphy
ultimatum: ulti *mate* um
vagary: *vague* ary (va *gary*)
valet: *val* it (va *lay*)

Inflections in Language

Students often have difficulty learning words because they don't relate
an unfamiliar word to any known word. Many English words are formed
merely by inflectional change, so spelling a "new" word may merely
involve adding a syllable or changing a letter of a known word.

Students can benefit from the transfer involved in forming new words from words already known. For example, *exemplify* will not appear so hard if it is associated with *example*.

The following list provides pairs of related words with their grade-level scores as found in the Dale nationwide study, *The Words We Know—A National Inventory*. Note that *example* is known on the fourth-grade level, but *exemplify* (an inflectional form of *example*) is not known before the tenth-grade level. *Exemplify* could be learned earlier and more easily if the student were shown that it is merely another form of the word *example*. (Actual percentage scores above grade 12 are included.)

Selected List from Dale's *The Words We Know*

active (4)—activate (12)
adaptable (8)—adaptability (12)
break (4)—breakage (10)
captive (6)—captivate (13–88%)
catechism (8)—catechize (13–58%)
clarification (6)—clarify (10)
college (4)—collegiate (12)
competing (6)—competitive (10)
decision (6)—decisive (12)
decorate (6)—decor (12)
demolish (6)—demolition (10)
deprive (6)—deprivation (10)
elephant (4)—elephantine (12)
emblem (6)—emblematic (12)
erase (4)—erasure (8)
error (6)—erroneous (12)
erupt (6)—eruptive (10)
escape (4)—escapade (10)
evacuate (6)—evacuation (12)
example (4)—exemplify (10)
ferocious (8)—ferocity (12)
flirt (6)—flirtation (10)
globe (4)—globular (8)
habit (4)—habitual (10)
herb (8)—herbivorous (12)
infant (6)—infancy (10)
information (6)—informant (10)
injury (4)—injurious (8)
migrate (6)—migratory (10)
nice (4)—nicety (10)
nominate (4)—nominee (8)

note (4)—notation (10)
opinion (6)—opine (16–42%)
opportunity (6)—opportune (12)
oval (8)—ova (13–83%)
pacify (8)—pacifist (12)
part (6)—partition (12)
penalty (6)—penal (12)
persuade (6)—persuasive (10)
pharmacist (8)—pharmaceutical (12)
pilgrim (4)—pilgrimage (10)
plural (4)—plurality (10)
pollen (6)—pollinate (10)
population (6)—populace (12)
portrait (6)—portray (10)
pretend (4)—pretense (12)
quiet (4)—quietude (10)
real (4)—reality (8)
recommend (6)—recommendation (10)
remedy (6)—remedial (13–53%)
resolution (8)—resolute (12)
response (6)—responsive (12)
result (6)—resultant (12)
revel (6)—revelry (10)
savage (6)—savagery (10)
simple (4)—simplify (8)
slavery (4)—slavish (16–63%)
sober (6)—sobriety (12–63%)
true (8)—truism (13–74%)
type (4)—typical (10)
unanimous (8)—unanimity (13–66%)
vein (6)—venous (12–33%)

Note: It is apparent from glancing at the few words listed above that students, in general, are not making connections between related words. It is true that a student may have no need of certain words before he is a junior or senior in high school (for example, *cognizance*), but if the word *infant* is known by 78 percent of sixth-graders, *infancy* could be taught earlier. It is now known by only 70 percent of the students in the tenth grade.

The teacher will note that many of the word pairs listed above are separated by as much as an eight-year span. If the spelling program emphasized the relationship of words formed from common roots, if the inflections of words were stressed to show that many words are slightly changed forms of words the student already knows, an appreciable gain could be made in spelling ability and in word knowledge.

Confused Pairs

The exercise below indicates one way to alert students to words often confused because of pronunciation or spelling similarities. The difficulty of the word pairs ranges from easy to hard, thus elementary teachers or teachers at the higher levels can select appropriate word pairs for their students.

As noted earlier, through faulty pronunciation or bad spelling habits students often confuse one word for another. This sometimes results in humorous situations or *malapropisms* (misused words).

Instructions: The student draws a line to the word or phrase in column B that makes him think of the word in column A.

Example:

their————here
there————cat

A	B	A	B
slick	seal	sink	a metal
sleek	ice	zinc	in the kitchen
popular	girl	tired	weary
poplar	tree	tried	attempted
mole	on bread	inspire	put life into
mold	on body	expire	die
famine	hunger	quiet	very
feminine	woman	quite	not noisy
angle	wings	ever	always
angel	corner	every	all
champagne	politics	saucer	magician
campaign	drink	sorcerer	plate
palm	leaf	anecdote	remedy
psalm	song	antidote	funny story
decal	sticker	umpire	British
ducal	duke	empire	referee
allusion	indirect reference	trial	test
illusion	not real	trail	path

A	B	A	B
scow	frown	ellipse	sun
scowl	boat	eclipse	oval
squaw	storm	diagram	a sketch
squall	Indian	diaphragm	membrane
curtsy	manners	respectively	with politeness
courtesy	to bow	respectfully	in this order
gamble	romp	canary	preserving food
gambol	dice	cannery	yellow feathers
narrow	thin	apostle	letter
marrow	bone	epistle	disciple
which	choice	specter	watcher
witch	magic	spectator	ghost
alleys	partners	morbid	about to die
allies	narrow streets	moribund	gruesome
surplus	garment	gaunt	thin and bony
surplice	extra	jaunt	travel

Note: The teacher may wish to construct additional items from the following list, choosing pairs that are suitable for the level of the students.

loath	formally	pastor	perspicuity
loathe	formerly	pasture	perspicacity
baron	putrefy	emulate	affect
barren	petrify	immolate	effect
illegible	canon	precedents	inimitable
ineligible	cannon	precedence	illimitable
eminent	respiration	loping	batten
imminent	perspiration	lopping	baton
missile	latitude	apprehension	dissect
missive	lassitude	comprehension	bisect
augur	irreverent	revolution	interment
auger	irrelevant	evolution	internment
persuade	weather	confident	flaunt
dissuade	whether	confidant	flout
venal	borne	bland	except
venial	born	blend	accept
immigrate	creditable	presence	ascent
emigrate	credible	prescience	assent
wander	cunning	euphemism	commiserate
wonder	conning	euphuism	commensurate
antewar	immorality	ingenious	bauble
antiwar	immortality	ingenuous	bubble

blazer	bedlam	caribou	indigent
blazon	beldam	carabao	indigenous
presence	below	presentment	interpellate
presents	bellow	presentiment	interpolate
amoral	exceptional	eerie	incredible
immoral	exceptionable	aerie	incredulous
continuous	decry	ibex	noisy
continual	descry	ibis	noisome
introspective	acronym	filet	squid
retrospective	acrostic	fillet	squib
faker	paladin	fictitious	selvage
fakir	palanquin	facetious	salvage
hallow	gallon	refractory	relic
hollow	galleon	refectory	relict
cavernous	squab	oscillate	advantageous
carnivorous	squad	osculate	adventitious

Visualizing Word Pairs

Sometimes it helps children in the lower grades to have confusions within word pairs presented visually. From the list above, here are some illustrations that the teacher might use for display:

angel   angle   hare   hair

fir   fur   pear   pair

Malapropisms

Malapropisms (named after Mrs. Malaprop in Sheridan's play *The Rivals*) involve the misuse and mispronunciation of words. For example, *enervating* might be used when *energizing* is intended.

The following malapropisms have been taken from the play and set in contemporary usage. Students are to fill in the blanks with the correct word for the misused italicized word.

Answers

alligators

1. In Florida swamps we saw many *allegories*.
   The right word should be a _ _ _ _ _ _ _ _.

phraseology

2. His grammatical *physiognomy* is perfect.
   Right word: p _ _ _ _ _ _ _ _ _

obliterate

3. An atom bomb would *illiterate* the whole city.
   Right word: o _ _ _ _ _ _ _ _

injunction

4. The management requested a *conjunction* against the union. Right word: i _ _ _ _ _ _ _ _

influence

5. The Senator has much *affluence* with these men.
   Right word: i _ _ _ _ _ _ _

intuition

6. For judging people she relies too much on her *tuition*.
   Right word: i _ _ _ _ _ _ _

desisted

7. She *persisted* from talking any longer.
   Right word: d _ _ _ _ _ _ _

allusions

8. His *delusions* to classical antiquity were lost on us.
   Right word: a _ _ _ _ _ _ _

affection

9. I'm happy to be the recipient of her *infection*.
   Right word: a _ _ _ _ _ _ _

cogitation

10. The process of deep thought is known as *agitation*.
    Right word: c _ _ _ _ _ _ _ _

approached

11. The gallery around the green was hushed as the golfer *reproached* the ball. Right word: a _ _ _ _ _ _ _ _

enveloped

12. Soon the mountain darkness *developed* us.
    Right word: e _ _ _ _ _ _ _

impression

13. The mayor's speech made a great *oppression* on him.
    Right word: i _ _ _ _ _ _ _ _

commiseration

14. The prisoner at the bar hoped for some *commensuration* from the judge. Right word: c _ _ _ _ _ _ _ _ _ _ _

fragrant

15. We were attracted by the sweet, *flagrant* odor of the flowers. Right word: f _ _ _ _ _ _ _

sects

16. The group was made up of different religious *sex*.
    Right word: s _ _ _ _

refuge

17. She thought of her aunt's house as a *refuse* from her troubles. Right word: r _ _ _ _ _

reference

18. The student looked through the *reverence* book for more facts. Right word: r _ _ _ _ _ _ _ _

prescribed

19. She took the medicine that the doctor had *subscribed*.
    Right word: p _ _ _ _ _ _ _ _ _

repository

20. The mind is a *suppository* for facts and experiences.
    Right word: r _ _ _ _ _ _ _ _ _

persecution

21. *Ben Hur* describes the Roman *prosecution* of the Christians. Right word: p _ _ _ _ _ _ _ _ _ _

conception

22. He has a good *inception* of his role in the project.
    Right word: c _ _ _ _ _ _ _ _

infection

23. Bill was laid up with a leg *inflection*.
    Right word: i _ _ _ _ _ _ _

187

Answers

angles	24. We were able to study the problem from several *angels*. Right word: a _ _ _ _ _
pulmonary	25. Mr. Brown's breathing difficulty results from a *pre-liminary* disease. Right word: p _ _ _ _ _ _ _ _
prodigy	26. The pianist was a child *progeny*. Right word: p _ _ _ _ _ _
superficial	27. Despite the bad accident, the boy suffered only *super-cilious* cuts. Right word: s _ _ _ _ _ _ _ _ _ _
geography, contiguous	28. In Sheridan's play *The Rivals* (Act I, Scene 2), Mrs. Malaprop, speaking of her daughter, says, "I would have her study *geometry* so she'd know about *contagious* countries." She meant: g _ _ _ _ _ _ _ _ and c _ _ _ _ _ _ _ _ _

Note: The teacher may present this lesson in other forms. One way is suggested in item 29 below, with the choices supplied.

apprehended reprehended	29. The policeman _ _ _ _ _ _ _ _ _ _ _ _ the speeder and the judge _ _ _ _ _ _ _ _ _ _ _ him.

(reprehended, apprehended)

Phonemically Irregular Words

Words with phonemically irregular letters (e.g., words in which e and ei have the sound of a, as in they and sleigh) often present spelling problems. Notice the following:

The a in *snake* has the sound of the e in *they*.
The a in *take* = the ei in *eight*.
The a in *care* = the e in *there*.
The a in *stare* = the ei in *heir*.

The exercise below presents additional illustrations of words in which some letters have the same sound as others. Example:
The e in *she* = the i in machine.

Answers

poli*c*eman	1. The e in *he* = the i in pol ceman.
says	2. The e in *set* = the a in s ys.
said	3. The e in *wet* = the ai in s d.
many	4. The e in *penny* = the a in m ny.
rhyme	5. The i in *ice* = the y in rh me.

hymn	6. The i in *him* = the y in h___mn.
busy	7. The i in *slim* = the u in b___sy.
women	8. The i in *skim* = the o in w___men.
sew	9. The o in *show* = the e in s___w.
wand	10. The o in *pond* = the a in w___nd.
son	11. The u in *up* = the o in s___n.
done	12. The u in *cup* = the o in d___ne.
come	13. The u in *pup* = the o in c___me.
wool	14. The o in *wolf* = the oo in w_____l.
enough	15. The f in *fur* = the gh in enou_____.
phonics	16. The f in *fun* = the ph in _____onics.
touch	17. The u in *sun* = the ou in t_____ch.
catastrophe	18. The k in *kill* = the c in _____atastrophe.
antique	19. The k in *kick* = the q in anti___ue.
chorus	20. The k in *kiss* = the ch in _____orus.
cent	21. The s in *space* = the c in _____ent.
fixed	22. The t in *sit* = the ed in fix_____.
of	23. The v in *violin* = the f in o___.
queen	24. The w in *win* = the u in q___een.
was	25. The z in *whiz* = the s in wa___.
nation	26. The sh in *sheen* = the ti in na_____on.
social	27. The sh in *shield* = the ci in so_____al.
thank	28. The ng in *going* = the n in tha___k.

Note: This exercise can be varied as follows:

    The e in *she* = the ___ in *machine*.

A Self-Test on Words Often Misspelled

Instructions: Some of the following words are correct as they are. Some have a letter or letters left out. Some blanks will not be filled, while some will need *one or more* letters. If the word is correct, leave it alone. Cover the answers until you have completed the item.

Answers

hypocrisy	1. h_pocr_sy
gauge	2. g__ge (measuring instrument)
Cincinnati	3. Cin_ci__at_i
liaison	4. lia_son
It's correct.	5. excel_
It's correct.	6. an_oint
privilege	7. priv_l_ge

sacrilegious	8. sacr_l_g_ous
exhilarating	9. ex_il_rating
accommodate	10. ac_om__date
consensus	11. con_en_us (agreement)
embarrassed	12. embar_as_ed
mischievous	13. misch__v_ous
hemorrhage	14. hemor__age
occurrence	15. oc_ur__nce
paraphernalia	16. paraph__nalia
questionnaire	17. questio__air_
liquefy	18. liqu_fy
inferred	19. infe_red
silhouette	20. sil_ouet__

More about *ie* and *ei* Words

The old rule "*i* before *e* except after *c* or when sounded like *a* as in *neighbor* or *weigh*" is helpful to the student only in a limited sense. While it is true that when a long *a* sound is represented the spelling is always *ei* (*eight, feint*), the rule does not apply to many words having the long *e* sound. Here, for example, are some *ei* words that do not fit the "*i* before *e* except after *c*" rule. In these words the *ei* sounds like long *e*.

caffeine (*also* caffein)	leisure	sheik
either	protein	codeine (*or* codein)
neither	seize	

Some proper nouns that don't follow the rule are:

Neil	Leila	Cassiopeia
Keith	Sheila	Pleiades

Notice, also, that close interpretation of the rule would cause us to spell *conscience* as *consceince*, and that the rule does not apply to words like *science, nescience, omniscient, species,* and *financier,* which have *i* before *e* after *c*.

In the following exercise, the student checks his spelling skill by writing *ei* or *ie* in the blanks to complete the words. The correct spellings are given on the left.

either	1. __ther	achieve	9. ach__ve
frieze	2. fr__ze	receive	10. rec__ve
mischievous	3. misch__vous	receipt	11. rec__pt
weigh	4. w__gh	shriek	12. shr__k
aggrieve	5. aggr__ve	seize	13. s__ze
feint	6. f__nt	height	14. h__ght
reign	7. r__gn	piece	15. p__ce
fiend	8. f__nd	siege	16. s__ge

relief	17. rel__f	countries	39. countr__s
mischief	18. misch__f	conceit	40. conc__t
lieutenant	19. l__utenant	either	41. __ther
conceit	20. conc__t	handkerchief	42. handkerch__f
foreign	21. for__gn	eighth	43. __ghth
brief	22. br__f	niece	44. n__ce
rein	23. r__n	feign	45. f__gn
friend	24. fr__nd	seizure	46. s__zure
chief	25. ch__f	seine	47. s__ne
perceive	26. perc__ve	relieve	48. rel__ve
ceiling	27. c__ling	quiet	49. qu__t
thief	28. th__f	deceit	50. dec__t
their	29. th__r	alienation	51. al__nation
neighbor	30. n__ghbor	besiege	52. bes__ge
neither	31. n__ther	armies	53. arm__s
leisure	32. l__sure	beige	54. b__ge
achievement	33. ach__vement	believable	55. bel__vable
alien	34. al__n	deign	56. d__gn
inveigle	35. inv__gle	weird	57. w__rd
allies	36. all__s	chow mein	58. chow m__n
belief	37. bel__f	hygiene	59. hyg__ne
biennial	38. b__nnial	freight	60. fr__ght

Spelling Compound Words

Many English words are made by compounding simple words (*suit + case = suitcase*). The practice of making compounds out of simple words is a good way for elementary students to learn one of the principles of language: many words are formed through combining words which retain their original spellings and original meanings.

Simple Words	Compounds		
grand + daughter	_ _ _ _ _ _ _ _ _ _ _ _ _	over + reach	_ _ _ _ _ _ _ _ _
bath + house	_ _ _ _ _ _ _ _ _	wash + house	_ _ _ _ _ _ _ _ _
can + not	_ _ _ _ _ _	grand + dad	_ _ _ _ _ _ _ _
shirt + tail	_ _ _ _ _ _ _ _ _	room + mate	_ _ _ _ _ _ _ _
book + keeping	_ _ _ _ _ _ _ _ _ _ _	dumb + bell	_ _ _ _ _ _ _ _
rough + house	_ _ _ _ _ _ _ _ _	with + hold	_ _ _ _ _ _ _ _
under + rated	_ _ _ _ _ _ _ _ _	dog + gone	_ _ _ _ _ _ _
over + run	_ _ _ _ _ _	over + rated	_ _ _ _ _ _ _ _ _
out + trick	_ _ _ _ _ _ _ _	fish + hook	_ _ _ _ _ _ _ _
beach + head	_ _ _ _ _ _ _ _ _	night + time	_ _ _ _ _ _ _ _ _
cut + throat	_ _ _ _ _ _ _ _ _	cat + tail	_ _ _ _ _ _
out + talk	_ _ _ _ _ _	over + rule	_ _ _ _ _ _ _ _
high + handed	_ _ _ _ _ _ _ _ _ _	metal + like	_ _ _ _ _ _ _ _ _
head + dress	_ _ _ _ _ _ _ _ _	over + ride	_ _ _ _ _ _ _ _
out + think	_ _ _ _ _ _ _ _	yellow + wood	_ _ _ _ _ _ _ _ _ _ _
red + dogging	_ _ _ _ _ _ _ _ _ _	out + last	_ _ _ _ _ _ _
house + coat	_ _ _ _ _ _ _ _ _	mid + day	_ _ _ _ _ _
step + parent	_ _ _ _ _ _ _ _ _ _	sand + box	_ _ _ _ _ _

Krazy Kompounds

The elementary teacher can emphasize the use of compounds in word formation by simple drawings. Students might enjoy making some of these illustrations. Some may be puns.

birddog   catfish

Prefixes and Spelling

This lesson emphasizes the importance of recognizing prefixes in spelling words. Using the following forms, the teacher may present key prefixes in words that are often misspelled because of the failure to notice these prefixes.

Part One

Look carefully at these words. They are separated into prefix and root. Write the whole word in the blank:

Prefix and Root   Whole Word

mis + spell   _____

mis + spend   _____

mis + state   _____

mis + step   _____

mis + treat   _____

mis + use   _____

mis + understand _____

mis + take   _____

mis + read   _____

mis + place   _____

mis + shapen   _____

Notice that if the root begins with *s* you must have *two* *s*'s in the word.

Part Two

Here is a list of words that could add the prefix *dis-* to form new words. In each blank put (2) if you think the new word should have a double *s*, and (1) if you think the word should have only one *s*.

1. _1_ ease
2. _2_ solve
3. _2_ similar
4. _1_ appear
5. _2_ service

6. _2_ satisfied
7. _1_ regard
8. _1_ able
9. _1_ appoint
10. _1_ advantage

Now write out each new word in the spaces below.

1. _____
2. _____
3. _____
4. _____
5. _____

6. _____
7. _____
8. _____
9. _____
10. _____

Sesquipedalian Words

Students sometimes like the challenge of learning to spell a *sesquipedalian* word—a big word (from Latin *sesqui,* one and one half + *ped,* foot)—literally, a word a foot and a half long. Many students have heard the word *antidisestablishmentarianism.* This word describes a doctrine (*ism*) that is against (*anti*) the idea of opposing (*dis*) the establishment— or the doctrine that an established national church (as the Church of England) should be maintained.

But the longest word in the dictionary is not a nonsense word. In one word, what name would you give a *miner's disease of the lungs* caused by the constant inhalation of irritant mineral particles such as superfine silicate or quartz dust?

Here it is: *pneumonoultramicroscopicsilicovolcanoconiosis*

It has forty-five letters—the longest word in *Webster's Third New International Dictionary.* Long as it is, you can learn to spell it and analyze its meaning if you look at its component parts (a mixture of Greek, Latin, and English).

pneumono / ultra / micro / scopic / silico / volcano / con / iosis
   pneumono: related to the lung (as in *pneumonia*)
   ultra: beyond, exceedingly, super
   micro: very small
   scopic: related to sight
   (*ultramicroscopic:* exceedingly small to the sight)
   silico: related to hard stone or quartz, a mineral
   volcano: related to volcanic dust; very fine particles of rock powder
   con: dust (from Greek *konis*)
   iosis: disease

Now put it back together: a lung disease caused by inhaling superfine silicate dust is

pneumono / ultra / micro / scopic / silico / volcano / con / iosis

A town in Wales has a name with fifty-eight letters:
Llanfairpwllgwyngyllgogerychwyrndrobwllllandysiliogogogoch.

Spelling Pointers

The following information on some of the characteristics of English spelling might be used as discussion points or review items.

1. When the final letter of a prefix and the first letter of a base word or root are the same, both letters must be written. For example:

dis + similar = dissimilar

under + rate = underrate

2. When the last letter of a baseword and the first letter of a suffix are the same, both letters must be written, for example:

tail + less = tailless

soul + less = soulless

3. Using the overhead projector or the chalkboard the teacher might list the following words and ask the students to make a generalization about their spelling: quintuplet, quick, quilt, quibble, acquire, quit, quite, quotation, eloquent, acquit, tranquility, quantity, quality, quiet. Spelling hint: The letter *q* is followed by *u.*

4. In some words *k* is added to *c* to make sure we give *c* the hard sound (*k*) rather than the soft sound (*s*). For example:

A politician (*c* has a soft sound) was politicking (*c* has a hard sound). Without the *k, politicking* might be pronounced as *politissing* or *politiseing.*

Here are some other *ck* words:

a. Shellac the chair. *But:* I shellacked the chair.
b. The crowd was in a state of panic. *But:* The crowd became panicky— they panicked.
c. Yesterday we went on a picnic. *But:* We were picnicking yesterday.
d. Children often frolic on the lawn. *But:* The children frolicked on the lawn.
e. A mime is an actor who mimics. *But:* The clown mimicked the ring-master.

Note, however, that this spelling (adding *k* to *c*) applies only to certain words. Mimicry, for example, does not add a *k*. The point of this and other exercises in this unit is to alert students to the characteristics of English spelling, to point up the regularities that exist, and to emphasize the need to consult the dictionary for help with irregular spellings.

10

Semantics

Semantics is the study of meanings. It deals with symbols or signs that denote meaning, their relationships with one another, and their influence on man and society. Semantics, therefore, involves word meanings, their development and change. Aptly named, the word *semantics* is originally derived from the Greek *semantickos* (significant), and from *semainein* (to signify, or show), and ultimately from *sema* (sign), as in the word *semaphore.*

Semantics has to do with the meanings of words and the meanings people get out of words. Meaning may refer to the etymology of words. For example, the word *dismal* comes from Latin *dies* (day) + *malus* (bad): literally "a bad day." Meaning may also refer to the denotative and connotative meanings as found in the dictionary. The denotation of a word is its exact literal meaning. For example, *blue* denotes a particular color. However, the connotation of the word *blue* might be "sad" or "gloomy." The word *cool* literally means "moderately cold." But when someone describes a movie as *cool,* he usually means to imply that it is excellent.

Semantics and Vocabulary

What is the relationship of semantics to the teaching of vocabulary? For one thing, the study of semantics suggests to the teacher the importance of experience in word interpretation. Tennyson's Ulysses says, "I am a part of all that I have met." Experience influences both perception and conception.

Students interpret words in the light of their past experiences. The student with a rich background of experience brings more to the words he meets, decodes the symbols in terms of what he already knows. He interprets the abstract symbol and then reapplies it in usable, concrete terms.

The teacher can help the student grow in semantic skill by helping him associate his present knowledge with what he is learning. The best approach in teaching vocabulary is to get the student to classify new words and to make finer discriminations about words he already knows.

For example, some critics have attacked the long definition of *door* in *Webster's Third International Dictionary.* Surely everybody knows what a door is, so why the long explanation? The reason is that we must make sure our definition includes anything that in fact *is* a door and excludes what clearly *is not* a door. What about metaphorical extensions: "His curt remark closed the door on our negotiations"; "He strove to keep scandal from his door"? These must also be included in the definition of a word.

In short, semantics can be the basis for discussion with students about the *what* and the *why* of words. Why, for example, can we say "bask in the sun" but not "bask in the shade"? Can we get "long shrift" as well as "short shrift"? Why can we use the verb *temper* to mean both soften and harden? Why does *cleave* mean to split as well as to stick or cling to? It is apparent that certain usage becomes standard because it satisfies a particular meaning. If we vary the usage, the meaning is lost.

Ambiguity

Much ambiguity is caused by poor sentence structure. What is ambiguous about these sentences?

1. A man was wanted by the detective who had committed a crime.
2. A red boy's sweater was found in the hall.
3. Hanging from the ceiling I noticed a gigantic chandelier.
4. Driving in the mountains several deer were seen.
5. I scrubbed the garage with my brother.
6. My father shot an elephant in his pajamas.

Ambiguity also occurs when we accept one term to describe a number of concepts. Note the use of *run* in the following sentences.

1. The athlete took a *run* around the track.
2. The train makes a *run* from here to New York.
3. She had a *run* in her stocking.
4. That salesman is always on the *run.*
5. We like to *run* around the lake in our boat.
6. The price of gold *runs* high.
7. The vines *run* up the wall.
8. He needs to *run* over his notes before class.
9. A wall *runs* around the garden.
10. The color will *run.*
11. There was a *run* on the bank.
12. *My Fair Lady* had a long *run.*

We are able to use a word such as *run* in so many ways because we are willing to assign one symbol to a variety of meanings. In a sense, we encourage ambiguity by overloading symbols. Thus we must rely heavily on context clues.

Ambiguity, however, is part of the joy of language. Multiple meanings are desired by poets and welcomed by punsters. The poet may wish to avoid the careful categories and neat niches of the botanist. The punster may want to say that a Westerner with five grown boys called his cattle ranch "Focus" because that is where the sons raise meat (sun's rays meet).

Gaining Semantic Skill

We can best help the student gain skill in semantics by enriching his experiences. This can be done in a variety of ways: conducting adequate oral language activities, promoting stimulating conversation both in and out of the classroom, and encouraging students to listen critically to their own recorded conversations and to those of others on television, radio, films, filmstrips, and other audiovisual media.

Success in semantic skill is often related to enjoyment. Students should play more with language, get involved with puns, riddles, jokes, rhymes, puzzles, and other word games (see Unit 14). Students should be encouraged to manipulate and combine word parts, to "create" words.

Class discussion helps in semantic study. The teacher can encourage discussions about the meanings of words in context, their origin, their change, and their general or particular use. Discussion about word meanings helps build concepts. It stimulates students to observe likenesses and differences, to generalize and discriminate, to weigh words and their meanings. In short, we can help build interest in vocabulary by talking about what we say, and about how and why we say it.

In the following lessons, the student gets an opportunity to examine the meanings of words in terms of their likenesses and differences, their relationship to context (see Unit 3), their origin and structure, their tendency to change and to take on new meanings.

Shortened Word Forms

We are constantly looking for shorter ways of saying what we want to say. Thus we drop superfluous words and letters from various expressions until they roll easily off the tongue—or pen. In the lessons that follow, students can gain some insight into word meaning, origin, and change through a study of these shortened forms.

Contractions

Jonathan Swift in No. 230 of the *Tatler* was worried about the "corruption of the English tongue." He was against the practice of using contractions such as *he'd, he's,* and *I'd.* But such contractions typify the tendency of speakers and writers to shorten the forms of the words they use. The following list illustrates this point. Some of these contractions are seldom used except in stories to illustrate a given dialect or period of time. Some are used only in verse. Others are used regularly.

The list might be used to check the student's knowledge of contractions. He might be asked to write in the blank the meaning of each contraction, or check those he doesn't know.

Note: The difference between *its* and *it's* should be clarified: *its* is the possessive; *it's* is the contraction. Students may be surprised to find that some contractions have more than one meaning, for example, *one's* means either *one is* or *one has.*

List of Contractions

ain't	am/is/are/have/has not	aren't	are not
can't	cannot	could've	could have
daren't	dare not	didn't	did not
doesn't	does not	don't	do not
e'en	even	e'er	ever

198

hadn't	had not	Halloween	all hallow even
hasn't	has not	haven't	have not
he'd	he had/would	he'll	he will
he's	he is/has	I'd	I had/would
I'll	I will/shall	I'm	I am
isn't	is not	it'd	it had/would
it'll	it will	it's	it has/is
I've	I have	let's	let us
mightn't	might not	might've	might have

Additional Contractions

mustn't	those'll	you're	this'll
o'clock	'twasn't	needn't	'tis
one'll	'twill	o'er	'twas
shan't	wasn't	one's	'twon't
she'll	we'll	she'd	we'd
shouldn't	weren't	she's	we're
'tain't	what'd	should've	we've
that'll	what's	that'd	what'll
there'd	who'd	that's	what've
there's	who're	there'll	who'll
these'll	who've	there've	who's
they'll	wouldn't	they'd	won't
they've	you'd	they're	would've

Contracted Forms

After presenting the contractions in the previous lesson, the teacher might point out to the class that the principle of contraction has always been at work in the development of the language.

The law of parsimony (the least possible expenditure of energy) is perhaps the biggest force at work in shortening long words. Polysyllabic words contain both syllables that are accented and those that are unaccented. As a result, unstressed sounds often drop out and so do their corresponding letters.

For example, words such as *king* and *lady* were longer in their Old English forms: *cyning* and *hlaefdige* (literally "loaf kneader"). Note also that *lord,* discussed later in this unit (See *Amelioration*), is an example of a contracted word. In Old English, *lord* was spelled *hlaford* (literally a "loaf ward, or guard").

Here are some other clipped forms:

Sham is a shortened form of *shame.*

Curio is a clipped form of *curiosity; tend* came from *attend,* and *mend* from *amend.*

God be with you has become *goodbye.* From *St. Audrey* comes *tawdry. Fence* is a variant of *defense.*

Fall refers to the "fall of the leaf" in autumn. *Private* comes from "private soldier." A *lyric* is a "lyric poem."

Canter is from *Canterbury gallop.* (Pilgrims going to Thomas à Becket's shrine in Canterbury rode at this easy gait.)

Alarm is a contracted form of *all' arme,* an old Italian phrase meaning "to arms."

Contracted words are often a part of slang. When first used, those words may be considered by some to be unrefined, unworthy of the language. But in time many of these clipped forms persisted and were soon recognized as bona fide words. For example, *perk* is used as often as *percolate* to describe a way of making coffee.

Pop is used to mean popular music. *TV* in the United States and *telly* in Britain are used as often as the word *television.*

Middies are *midshipmen. Miss* is short for *Mistress. Hack* is used for *hackney.* And *loony* means *lunatic.*

Latin phrases are often clipped: *mob* is short for *mobile vulgus* (the fickle, common people). *Confab* comes from Latin *confabulari* (to tell tales or fables). Although the latest dictionaries indicate that the origin of *nincompoop* is unknown, some scholars believe that *nincompoop* is a corrupted form of *non compos mentis* (not of sound mind).

Coon is a short form of *raccoon; rickshaw* is short for *ginrickshaw;* a *non-com* is a *non-commissioned officer; cycle* may mean *bicycle* or *motorcycle;* in Britain, *public house* was shortened to *pub.*

Using the overhead projector, the teacher can present the shortened form of each word below and then reveal the longer, original version of the word. The teacher might also duplicate the short form of the words and ask the student to write in a blank what he thinks is the longer form.

Short Form	Longer Form		
varsity	university	fan	fanatic
cute	acute	bust	burst
piano	pianoforte	clerk	cleric
pram	perambulator	pants	pantaloons
gas	gasoline	fortnight	fourteen nights
auto	automobile	mum	chrysanthemum
bronc	bronco	cab	cabriolet
coed	coeducational	zoo	zoological
flu	influenza	trump	triumph
con	convict	vandal	the Vandals
Yank	Yankee	gab	gabble
cop	copper	van	caravan
gat	Gatling gun	togs	togas
Halloween	all hallow even (evening)	cent	centum (100)
(cotton) gin	engine	sport	disport
isle	island	movie	moving picture
scram	scramble	petrol	petroleum
pep	pepper	knickers	knickerbockers
bus	omnibus	lube	lubricating oil
chemist	alchemist	mart	market
cello	violincello	wig	periwig
metro	metropolitan	still	distill
cop	copper ("catcher")	cafe	cafeteria

Acronyms

The word *radar* comes from *ra*dio *d*etecting *a*nd *r*anging. What is a *scuba* diver? He's a deep-sea diver. Why *scuba*? It comes from *s*elf-*c*ontained *u*nderwater *b*reathing *a*pparatus.

Radar and *scuba* are acronyms. The word *acronym* comes from the Greek *akros* (highest) + *onyma* (name). In English, *acro* is seen in words like *acrobat* (sometimes a high-wire artist). People with *acrophobia* have fear of being high up.

If you look again at *ra*dio *d*etecting *a*nd *r*anging, you'll notice that the initial letter or letters of the words spell *radar*. So an acronym is generally formed from the first letters or syllables of a compound term.

Submarines are detected by *sonar* (*so*und *na*vigation *r*anging).

An important word at Cape Kennedy is *lox*. It's the rocket fuel *l*iquid *ox*ygen.

Scientists often talk about *l*ight *a*mplification by *s*timulated *e*mission of *r*adiation. It's commonly called *laser,* a thin, intense beam of light that can burn a hole in a diamond.

Zip Code is used to speed up mail delivery. It means *z*oning *i*mprovement *p*lan.

An acronym often becomes an accepted word. In fact, the acronym is often known when the words for which it stands are not.

For example, many students will know the general purpose of the organization called *Care* but they may not know what the letters stand for (Cooperative for American Relief for Everyone). Many persons will recognize *LEM* as the Apollo lunar module but may not know that this acronym stands for *Lunar Excursion Module*.

In the lesson below, the student takes an inventory of his knowledge of popular acronyms by writing their meanings in the blanks. (Answers are provided.)

1.	Gestapo	Geheime Staats Polizei (Secret State Police)
2.	laser	light amplification by stimulated emission of radiation
3.	LEM	Lunar Excursion Module
4.	lox	liquid oxygen (rocket fuel)
5.	maser	microwave amplification by stimulated emission of radiation
6.	NASA	National Aeronautics and Space Administration
7.	NATO	North Atlantic Treaty Organizaion
8.	radar	radio detecting and ranging
9.	scuba	self-contained underwater breathing apparatus
10.	sonar	sound navigation ranging
11.	UNESCO	United Nations Educational, Scientific, and Cultural Organization
12.	UNICEF	United Nations International Children's Emergency Fund
13.	VISTA	Volunteers in Service to America
14.	WAC	Women's Army Corps
15.	WHO	World Health Organization
16.	Zip	Zoning Improvement Plan (Postal Department)
17.	HEW	Health, Education, and Welfare
18.	SOS	Save Our Ship

Portmanteau Words

Other language shortcuts are found in portmanteau words. A *portmanteau* is a folding traveling bag. Some words "fold" or "blend" together like a portmanteau to form new words.

1. We blend *smoke* and *fog* to get *smog.*
2. *Chuckle* and *snort* become *chortle* (coined by Lewis Carroll).
3. *Gallop* and *triumph* telescope to form *galumph* (also coined by Carroll).
4. *Brunch* comes from *breakfast* and *lunch.*
5. A *twinight* baseball game is played during the hours of *twilight* and *night.*
6. We blend *motor* and *hotel* to get *motel.*

Multiple Meanings

As we have pointed out, semantics deals with meaning. But meaning is sometimes unclear because we often use the same word for different objects, acts, or ideas. Thus a pipe may *leak* and let water out, a boat may *leak* and let water *in,* or a government agency may *leak* a story to the press. Thus, context controls meaning.

But the listener or reader also helps create the meaning of words. He hears or mishears, reads or misreads, interprets or misinterprets, according to his background of experience and beliefs. To the liberal, a *conservative* statement may sound *reactionary.* The other person is *tightfisted* but you are *thrifty.* You are *bold* but your opponent is *reckless.* In dealing with semantics, therefore, we are dealing not only with the origin, structure, and context but with the use of words changed by time and by the experiences of people.

Using the following lesson, the teacher may present multiple-meaning words in groups to emphasize their variant meanings in idiomatic expressions. For example, the word *lean* has several meanings and can be used in several ways: to lean on the desk, to lean on (rely on) someone, to lean toward a political party, lean pork chops, a lean harvest, a lean fuel mixture in the carburetor.

The teacher may wish to write some of the following sentences on the board or have them duplicated. Students might explain the italicized word and discuss its use in the illustrated phrase or sentence. These italicized words may also be classified according to their part of speech.

Same Word, Different Meaning

Instructions: The student reads each sentence and writes in the blank a meaning for each underlined word. (There may be a variety of acceptable answers.)

Air

sky (noun)	1. There are birds in the <u>air</u>.	s _____
ventilate (verb)	2. Open the door and <u>air</u> the room.	v _____ te
speak (verb)	3. <u>Air</u> your opinion.	s ____ k _____
song	4. He sang an old <u>air</u>.	s ____ g _____
way (noun)	5. He has a strange <u>air</u> about him.	w _____

Note: Students may be encouraged to think of and discuss other uses of the word *air*, such as "putting on airs," "hot air," "on the air," and others.

Below is additional material, part of which the teacher may wish to write on the chalkboard or have duplicated like the above exercises. The class may discuss the context clues which help create the intended meaning of the words. Spelling clues may be given as above, or the teacher may lead the class in an oral lesson.

Back

1. He turned his *back*.
2. He went *back* again.
3. They will *back* his project.
4. He can *back* the car well.
5. He is *back* in his studies.
6. He is *back* in uniform.
7. She read a *back* issue.
8. Pay him *back*.
9. It was discovered some years *back*.

Bar

1. A candy *bar*.
2. A *bar* of soap.
3. *Bar* the door.
4. Let down the *bar*.
5. To *bar* one's progress.
6. She played one *bar* of the song.
7. The lawyer approached the *bar*.
8. He passed his *bar* exams.
9. A sand *bar*.

Bare

1. *Bare* facts.
2. *Bare* hands.
3. The hill is *bare*.
4. The room was *bare* of furniture.
5. Earn a *bare* living.
6. He laid *bare* his secrets.

Base

1. The *base* of the statue.
2. He stole third *base*.
3. At the naval *base*.
4. A *base* coward.
5. Iron is a *base* metal.
6. The serf was *base*born.

Bat

1. The baseball *bat*.
2. *Bat* the ball.
3. He's up to *bat*.
4. *Bat* an eyelash.
5. Can he *bat* .300?
6. I *bat* flies.
7. The *bat* flies.

Block

1. A *block* of wood.
2. To *block* the way.
3. We *block* hats.
4. A *block* of buildings.
5. He walked a *block*.
6. *Block* and tackle.
7. Don't *block* out the view.

Beat

1. He *beat* the drum.
2. He *beat* the horse.
3. She *beat* the eggs.
4. They *beat* the woods for game.
5. The attacker *beat* him.
6. We *beat* the other team.
7. They *beat* a path to his store.
8. The birds *beat* their wings.
9. A heart*beat*.
10. The dancer missed a *beat*.
11. The policeman's *beat*.
12. *Beat* around the bush.
13. *Beat* a retreat.
14. Rock music has a strong *beat*.

Bay

1. The *bay* extends inland.
2. A *bay* window.
3. The hounds *bay*.
4. The deer stood at *bay*.
5. A *bay* horse.

Blind

1. He's *blind*.
2. *Blind* justice.
3. A *blind* alley.
4. A window *blind*.
5. A *blind* stitch.

Word Discrimination Within a Sentence

The following lesson gives the student practice in discriminating between the various uses of multiple-meaning words within a single sentence. The teacher may ask the student to note and explain the differences in the meaning of the sets of words in these sentences.

a. After^1 they robbed the bank the police were after^2 them.

   1. Subsequent to the time
   2. chasing

b. From my angle,^{1} he seems to have an angle.^{2}

   1. point of view
   2. selfish reason

c. Sometime back^1 a wealthy man promised to back^2 our college back^3 if he would pay him back.^{4}

   1. in the past
   2. support financially
   3. football player
   4. in return

d. The baying^1 hounds chased the bay^2 horse along the shore of the bay^3 into a grove of bay^4 trees where the dogs held it at bay.^{5}

   1. howling
   2. reddish brown
   3. sheltered water area
   4. kind of tree
   5. the point of being almost caught

204

e. His arch[1] rival made arch[2] remarks about him.

    1. chief
    2. sly

f. A hunter went out to bag[1] squirrels; he put them into a bag[2], and the game warden checked the bag[3].

    1. catch or kill
    2. sack
    3. number killed

g. Tipped off about[1] the robbery, the police were all about[2] the house; but after wandering about[3] for about[4] five minutes, they all turned about[5] and left.

    1. concerning
    2. on every side
    3. from place to place
    4. approximately
    5. around

h. You can bank[1] on his banking[2] at the bank[3] on the west bank[4] of the river.

    1. rely
    2. making financial transactions
    3. place where money is kept
    4. border

i. The city council's act[1] of passing an act[2] banning certain lines from the play's third act[3] may act[4] only to increase the play's popularity.

    1. behavior
    2. law
    3. division
    4. have the effect of

j. Things looked bad[1] for the exconvict in bad[2] health, whom the parole officer described as a bad[3] risk after he tried to pass a bad[4] check.

    1. serious
    2. poor
    3. not good
    4. worthless

k. The role was only a bit[1] part in which the actor bit[2] into a stale doughnut, tossed the sandwich and two bits[3] onto the counter, and walked off a bit[4] unhappy.

    1. small
    2. took a bite
    3. a quarter (one bit is 12½ cents)
    4. little

Word Formation

One of the characteristics of semantic change and variation in the language is found in the process of compounding. The following lesson points up the tendency of the language to form different compounds from the same word. We thus easily form new words from known words.

Many words are formed from a single compound term. The word *head* might be used as an example. In the exercise below, the student checks the words he knows. Then the class can discuss their meanings.

___ arrowhead	___ hothead
___ baldhead	___ letterhead
___ beachhead	___ loggerhead
___ blackhead	___ lunkhead
___ blockhead	___ masthead
___ bridgehead	___ overhead
___ bulkhead	___ pighead
___ bullhead	___ pinhead
___ cabbagehead	___ puddinghead
___ chowderhead	___ redhead
___ copperhead	___ roundhead
___ dunderhead	___ sleepyhead
___ egghead	___ softhead
___ fathead	___ sorehead
___ forehead	___ spearhead
___ hammerhead	___ squarehead
___ hardhead	___ subhead
___ hogshead	___ thunderhead

Compound Adjectival Forms

Further illustration of semantic change is emphasized in the following lesson, which illustrates how words formed from compound terms combine with suffixes to form adjectives. Students can be reminded that a word such as *head* (used in the previous lesson) can be used as a part of a compound term which, with the addition of the suffix *-ed*, becomes an adjective: *head, headed, hardheaded*.

In addition to adding *ed* to form an adjective, some compounds also take *ing* or *er*. For example, *slow-moving, money-lending, laborsaving;* a *six-footer*, a *doubleheader*, a *forty-niner*, a *three-master* (schooner).

Using the list below, the student writes in the blank any noun described by the hyphenated term, for example, ivory-headed <u>**cane**</u>. There are no "right" answers. The purpose is to complete each phrase and later discuss what each means.

Face

bold-face	_____	freckle-faced	_____
straight-faced	_____	pale-faced	_____

Voice

full-voiced	_____	soft-voiced	_____
deep-voiced	_____	shrill-voiced	_____

Hand

one-handed	_____	right-handed	_____
empty-handed	_____	heavy-handed	_____

Blood

hot-blooded	_____	cold-blooded	_____
warm-blooded	_____	pure-blooded	_____

Choosing the Right Word

Choosing the right word is essential in gaining semantic skill. It provides practice in making discriminations between words that may look or sound alike but which will cause confusion if they are used incorrectly. The teacher can use the following exercise as a quick check on the vocabulary skill of the students. He might note those students who score high and be ready to prepare additional, more challenging work for them.

Using the same form, but less difficult words, the elementary teacher might present appropriate key words for the class. The lesson can be used to emphasize word recognition, meaning, and letter discrimination (spelling).

Choosing from the three words under each sentence, the student writes the most appropriate word in the blank.

Answers

philatelist   1. A conscientious _____ really prizes his stamps.
philosopher, philatelist, philanthropist

censure   2. The committee voted to _____ the senator's behavior.
censor, censure, sensor

empathy   3. A person who feels another's misfortune has _____.
antipathy, apathy, empathy

baccalaureate   4. The dean spoke at the _____.
bacchanalia, baccalaureate, bacillary

imminent   5. An eruption from the live volcano above the village is
_____.
imminent, immanent, eminent

facade	6. The _____ of a Grecian temple often tells a story. faces, facade, facet
bucolic	7. Poetry dealing with shepherds and fields is often called _____ poetry. bucolic, cholic, melancholic
indolent	8. An _____ person usually avoids work. indigent, indolent, indigenous
efflorescent	9. In May the fields are _____. efficacious, effervescent, efflorescent
supercilious	10. The pompous lady gave us a _____ look. superfluous, superficial, supercilious

Discriminate and Classify

The teacher can emphasize the principle of general likeness or difference in words by using the following exercises. The student needs practice in recognizing synonyms and antonyms, but he should also be challenged to recognize minor but semantically important differences in words related to general meaning, for example: *hurry, speed, streak, skitter, pace.*

In the following lesson, the student (1) underlines the misfit, and (2) states in his own words the meaning of the other three words. His answers should have the same general meaning as those provided.

Answers	Underline the misfit.
stroll hurrying	1. stroll, spurt, scamper, scurry The other words refer to _____.
extinguish burning	2. blaze, glow, extinguish, kindle The other words refer to _____.
rare many, a lot	3. numerous, frequent, rare, abundant The other words refer to _____.
obscure fame	4. renowned, glorious, celebrated, obscure The other words refer to _____.
minute bigness, largeness	5. huge, bulky, massive, minute The other words refer to _____.
contentment anger, being upset	6. temper, wrath, contentment, rage The other words refer to _____.
prohibited legality, lawfulness	7. legitimate, authorized, prohibited, just The other words refer to _____.

jousting joking, jesting	8. joking, jousting, jovial, jocose The other three words refer to _____.
saturnine animal nature	9. canine, feline, saturnine, bovine The other words refer to _____.
tepid courage, fearlessness	10. valiant, tepid, intrepid, audacious The other words refer to _____.
immaculate dirtiness	11. squalid, putrid, maculate, immaculate The other words refer to _____.
trivial importance, significance	12. cardinal, paramount, salient, trivial The other words refer to _____.

Note: The teacher may reverse the procedure used above and ask the student to underline the three words in each item below that are synonymous in a general sense. They may also be asked to define the misfit. The student may check his answers with those provided here or use the dictionary to check the accuracy of his definitions. There may be several correct answers.

Definition of Misfit

1. joking, joust, jovial, jocose

   joust: a combat (with lances) between two mounted knights (from French *jouster*, and Latin *juxtare*, to be next to)

2. canine, feline, saturnine, bovine

   saturnine: gloomy (People born under the sign of Saturn were thought to be grave or sad.)

3. valiant, tepid, intrepid, audacious

   tepid: lukewarm, moderately warm (The tepidarium was a warm room in the Roman baths.)

4. squalid, putrid, maculate, immaculate

   immaculate: without spot or stain; opposite of *maculate* (from Latin *im*, not + *macula*, spot)

5. cardinal, paramount, salient, bagatelle

   bagatelle: a mere trifle, something of little importance (from Italian *baga*, berry, and Latin *bacca*, berry).

Additional Sets

spark	flimsy	sleek	*calm*
smolder	flabby	sheen	crash
simmer	flexible	satinet	clatter
shiver	*flinty*	serrate	clang
hateful	feeble	glare	dim
harmony	frail	gleam	*day*
hostility	*firm*	*gloom*	dusk
hotspur	flimsy	glimmer	dawn
ridged	sinewed	plentiful	scarcity
ruffled	*spent*	plenary	*swarm*
refined	stoutness	*paucity*	scant
rumpled	stamina	plenitude	sparse

Semantic Change

Both words and their meanings change with the changing times. Semantic change often accompanies social change brought about by wars, migrations, technological advances, and other factors.

To maintain student interest in word study, the teacher might discuss with the class four of the main forms of semantic change: (1) specialization, (2) generalization, (3) amelioration, and (4) pejoration.

1. Specialization

Specialization (restriction) refers to the process by which the meaning of a word becomes more limited in its application. A given word at one time may be applied to a general class and may later become restricted or specialized in its meaning. For example, the word *hound* (from Old English *hund*) once referred to any dog. Now the word is used for a certain hunting breed with drooping ears.

Note the following examples of specialization.

City at one time referred only to a fortified place, but now refers to any urban area.

Maid used to mean any girl. Now, except in poetry, a maid is a domestic employee in the home or in a hotel.

Century, originally any group of 100, now means 100 years.

Cattle, once any group of quadrupeds, now refers only to bovines.

Success, originally any kind of outcome, now generally means a favorable one.

Corn was originally the name for grain or cereal in general. Now, in the United States, corn is the name of a particular grain.

Typewriter once meant either the machine or the typist; but now it refers only to the machine.

Corpse is a doublet of corps (body) and once meant any body at all; but now *corpse* refers only to the body of a deceased person. (Doublets are different words derived from the same source.)

College used to mean company, assemblage, or crowd; but now it usually refers to a university.

Popular used to mean public or gregarious. (Julius Caesar belonged to the *Popular* Party, the party of the common people in Rome.) The narrowing process has given *popular* the meaning of "has the acceptance of the public," or "liked by one's associates."

Deer, like *cattle,* changed its meaning from any four-legged animal to a certain species.

Note the old meaning from Edgar's lines in *King Lear:*

But mice and rats and such small *deer,*
Have been Tom's food for seven long year.

2. Generalization

Changes in meaning also take place through the process of *generalization,* the opposite of specialization. Through generalization, or expansion, a word loses its specialized or restricted meaning and becomes the symbol for a general class of objects. For example, *boycott* once had a specialized meaning relating to the obstruction of an Irish land agent, Captain Boycott. It is now applied worldwide and has a more generalized meaning: combining against or refusing to do business with a firm or a nation.

Note the following examples of generalization:

Graphic has expanded from its specialized meaning in three stages: from "written" to "depicted" to "colorfully concrete."

Lady once referred only to the wife of a lord, and then later to any woman who behaved like the former. The term later came to include almost all women.

Coke was once short only for Coca-Cola; *cola* now (whether authorized or not) generally refers to all soft drinks with a cola base.

In the early days of the record player, the brand name Victrola became synonymous with the phonograph itself.

Vaseline is a trade name that is widely substituted for the generic name of the product petroleum jelly.

Manuscript has now been extended from "handwritten" to include typed material as well.

Kleenex, like Victrola and Vaseline, is another example of a specific trade name that became the term used for a general class of products.

Ghetto, which in former times was the part of a city set aside for Jewish people, is coming to mean a place to which any particular group is restricted.

Realm, once restricted to meaning "kingdom," has taken on more vague dimensions. For example, in Shakespeare's *Richard II,* John of Gaunt uses *realm* in the restrictive sense:

This blessed plot, this earth, this *realm,* this England.

But *realm* has an extended meaning in Bryant's "Thanatopsis":

The innumerable caravan, which moves
To that mysterious *realm,* where each shall take
His chamber in the silent halls of death.

3. Amelioration

The meaning of a word is often changed through *amelioration* (making better, from Latin *melior,* better). Ameliorative change refers to the elevation of a word in meaning. For example, *knight* (Old English *cniht*) at one time meant boy or youth, but by extension came to mean a follower or servant who moved up the social ladder from page to squire to *knight,* a servant of a lord or a king.

Queen (from Old English *cwen*) didn't always refer to royalty.

Originally *queen* merely meant woman. Later it came to mean the "woman of the country," that is, the king's wife, or the female monarch.

Lord used to be literally a "bread keeper." Old English *hlaf* (loaf) and *weard* (keeper, ward) contracted to form the word *lord*.

Mansion is now a large, stately residence; but originally it referred to a farm house or to a modest dwelling or building. Note Goldsmith's lines in "The Deserted Village":

There, where a few torn shrubs the place disclose,
The village preachers modest *mansion* rose.

There, in his noisy *mansion,* skilled to rule,
The village master taught his little school.

Holmes, in "The Chambered Nautilaus," illustrates the ameliorative quality of *mansion:*

Built thee more stately mansions, O my soul,

In the world of women's fashion, the *chemise* has been upgraded and now has fancier connotations than its original French meaning, a shirt. *Lingerie* also now connotes more than its original meaning, a linen garment (from Latin *linum,* flax).

At one time, the word *chiffon* meant not the light, silky fabric of today, but merely a rag. And before *chiffonier* came to refer to a high chest of drawers, it meant ragpicker.

Many words have gained more dignity with age.

Country *squire* now indicates more dignity than did the original *squire,* which meant servant or shield-carrier.

At one time a *marshal* (now an officer) merely groomed horses (from Old High German *marah,* horse + *scalc,* servant).

Angel in its religious sense now occupies a loftier position than it did formerly. It used to mean merely a messenger.

4. Pejoration

We have already described three main forms of semantic change: (1) *specialization,* in which a word takes on a limited use; (2) *generalization,* in which a word loses its limited meaning and signifies a general class; and (3) *amelioration,* in which a word becomes elevated, or more favorable in its meaning.

The fourth form of semantic change is *pejoration* (making worse, from Latin *pejor,* worse). Pejoration (or degeneration) refers to the lowering in esteem of a word's meaning. For example, *knave* once meant merely boy (from German *knabe,* boy), but now means a rogue or a rascal. Thus through time the meaning of a particular word often degenerates, takes on less favorable meaning.

Here are some examples of pejoration:

Persecute once meant to follow persistently. Now it means to follow persistently with an evil purpose, or to treat badly or oppress.

Temper, once simply a state of mind, now when used as a noun without an adjective often means an angry state of mind.

Stench originally meant any kind of smell, but now its meaning has degenerated to "a bad smell."

Problem (from Greek *proballein,* to propose or put forth, from *pro,* forward + *ballein,* to throw) originally referred merely to a proposal, but now generally refers to a troublesome question, one that causes difficulty.

Silly once meant blessed (from Old English *saelig,* happy), but now it refers to childish or immature behavior.

Rash didn't always mean too hasty or reckless. *Rash* (Middle English *rasch*) at one time merely meant quick.

Comedy, once a drama with a happy ending, now generally means a funny play.

Dame, except when specifically used as a title (feminine counterpart of *knight*), is now slang for woman.

Bourgeois once represented the new middle class (merchants or businessmen below aristocrats but wealthier than the proletariat), but now often connotes commonness, lack of dignity or refinement.

Villain once meant farmer (from Latin *villanus,* farmhand; originally from *villa,* farmhouse), but *villain* now has degenerated to mean a wicked person or a scoundrel.

Cunning (from Old English *cunnung,* knowing how) once meant clever but now means clever in deceiving.

Sly, which once meant skilled or wise, now means tricky, cunning, or acting secretly.

Collaborate (to work together) took on a pejorative or unfavorable meaning during World War II, when *collaborators* were traitorous cooperators with the Nazi regime. The meaning of the word is now probably losing its tinge of treason.

Pious (from Latin *pius,* dutiful) may still refer to a bona fide goodness or religious motive, but it may also connote a pretended goodness.

Propaganda is a Latin form meaning "must be propagated" (the ending *-nda* is also found in words such as *agenda,* "must be done"). Basically, *propaganda* meant a systematic effort to spread an opinion or belief; but propaganda has also taken on the unfavorable connotation of swaying public opinion by spreading slanted or incomplete information.

Idiot (from Greek *idios,* one's own; and *idiotes,* layman) originally meant a private person, apart from the state. Latin *idiota* meant an inexperienced or uneducated person. Later on in English literature we find the now-obsolete use of *idiot* meaning fool or jester. For example, in 1711, Joseph Addison, in Paper No. 47 of *The Spectator,* wrote:

Everyone laughs at somebody that is in an inferior state of folly to himself. It was formerly the custom for every great house in England to keep a tame fool dressed in petticoats, that the heir of the family might have an opportunity of joking upon him and diverting himself with his absurdities. For the same reason, *idiots* are still in request in most of the courts of Germany...where there is not a prince of any great magnificence who has not two or three dressed, distinguished, undisputed fools in his retinue. The Dutch...hang up in several of their streets what they call the sign of the Gaper, that is, the head of an *idiot* dressed in cap and bells....

Another example of pejoration is *counterfeit,* now meaning a copy made to deceive, a forgery, but which once meant merely a copy, an image, or a likeness. Thus we find Hamlet comparing his father's and uncle's portraits:

Look here, upon this picture, and on this,
The *counterfeit* presentment of two brothers.

And in *The Merchant of Venice,* Bassanio opens the leaden casket to find a picture of Portia:

What find I here?
Fair Portia's *counterfeit!*

We noted earlier that the word *popular* has become narrower or more restricted in its meaning. However, in Shakespeare's *King Henry V,* Pistol uses *popular* in a general but also pejorative sense:

Discuss unto me; art thou officer?
Or art thou base, common, and *popular?*

The teacher might use the following lesson as a basis for discussion. It will help the student become aware of the tendency of certain words to change their meanings over the years. Many of the following words now have a different meaning from what they had three centuries ago.

The teacher could ask for a current definition of each word below and then explain to the class the earlier meaning of the word. Some etymological information has been included to show the relationship between meanings.

Word	Then	Now
painful	painstaking, careful	hurting
amuse	to cause to muse (think), to occupy one's mind with	to make one smile or laugh
wretched	wicked (from Anglo-Saxon *wrecca,* outcast)	miserable
hobby	small walking horse (from Middle English *hobyn,* small horse)	favorite pastime
awkward	heading in the wrong direction (from Middle English *awk,* contrary)	clumsy
usury	money paid for using something	charging very high interest
brave	showy, excellent	courageous
palliate	to cover with a cloak (from Latin *pallium,* cloak)	to ease but not cure
adamant	very hard rocks (from Old French *adamaunt,* the hardest metal or stone, such as a diamond)	unyielding, firm
pallbearer	a pall-holder, one who held up the edges of the pall, or cloth, carried over a coffin	one who helps carry a coffin
snob	a commoner	a stuck-up person

214

bachelor	a young knight (from Latin *baccalarius*, originally a farm helper or tenant)	unmarried man
gossip	friend, godparent (from Old English *godsibb*, godparent, from *god* + *sibb*, relative)	idle talk or talker
havoc	a battle cry. In *Julius Caesar*, Antony says, "Cry 'Havoc,' and let slip the dogs of war."	great destruction
iconoclast	an image-breaker (from Greek *eikon*, image + *klas*, break)	one who attacks cherished or traditional ideas or institutions
sinister	left, on the left hand (from Latin *sinister*, left). Omens appearing on the left side were considered ominous	threatening, evil
sloth	slowness (from Old English *slawth*, and *slaw*, slow)	laziness; an animal
craven	vanquished, defeated	cowardly
farce	stuffing for fowl or roast (from Old French *farce*, comic intermission in a mystery play)	comical play
urbane	to live in the city (from Latin *urbs*, city)	civilized, refined
carriage	whatever was carried; a burden or load	a conveyance
unkind	unnatural (from Old English *gecynde*, natural)	lacking in kindness
censure	opinion (from Latin *censere*, to think, judge)	to express disapproval
uncouth	unknown (from Old English *un* + *cuth*, known)	crude
pencil	artist's small brush (from Latin *penicillus*, painter's brush)	writing tool
clumsy	stiff from the cold (from Middle English *clumsen*, numb with cold)	awkward
quaint	skillful (from Old French *queinte*, clever; originally from Latin *cognitus*, known). In *The Tempest*, Prospero refers to Ariel disguised as a water nymph: "Fine apparition! My *quaint* Ariel."	strange, odd
tuition	guardianship, custody (from Latin *tuitio*, protection, and *tueri*, to watch over)	instruction, or the charge paid for it
conceit	thought; wit; concept	too much pride
trivial	commonplace, ordinary (from Latin *trivia*, where three roads meet, *tri*, three, and *via*, road)	trifling, not important

Word	Then	Now
tarpaulin	sailor (from *tar* + *pall* + *ing,* a combination meaning tar-covered, as a sailor's tarred canvas suit). *Tarpaulin* was later shortened to *tar,* which even now refers to a sailor.	waterproofed canvas
danger	jurisdiction; having power over. In *The Merchant of Venice,* Portia asks Antonio, "You stand within his *danger,* do you not?"	chance of harm
perspective	an optical glass instrument, such as a magnifying glass (from Latin *per,* through + *specere,* to look)	the view from a distance; the appearance of distance; an outlook
disease	discomfort, trouble (from Old French *desaise: des,* away from + *aise,* ease)	sickness
starve	to die	to suffer or die from hunger
novelist	an innovator, one who likes *novelty*	writer of novels
spices	kinds (from Latin *species,* kind, sort). *Spices* is a doublet of the English word *species;* that is, both words came from the same root by different routes. *Species* is direct from Latin; *spices* came through French.	flavorings, seasonings
duke	military leader (from Latin *dux,* leader)	nobleman
fond	foolish (from Middle English *fonned,* foolish)	having strong affection
plausible	worthy of applause (from Latin *plaudere,* to applaud)	appears reasonable or fair
explode	to drive an actor from the stage, to hoot off by clapping the hands (from *explodere,* to clap the hands). *Explode* was the opposite of *applaud* (from *plaudere,* to clap hands in approval).	to blow up, burst
generous	high-born of noble lineage (from Latin *genus,* race)	unselfish
polite	polished (from Latin *politus,* refined, and *polire,* to polish)	having good manners
handsome	apt, easy to handle, skilled with the *hands*	good-looking
pomp	a procession (from Latin *pompa,* procession, display)	splendor

peevish	obstinate	cross, complaining
harbinger	person sent ahead to secure a *harbor* (lodging) for royalty	forerunner, announcer
insolent	unusual (from Latin *in*, not + *solere*, to be used to)	boldly rude
nephew, niece	grandchildren (from Latin *nepos*, grandson, and *neptis*, granddaughter). Note also *nepotism*, hiring relatives.	children of one's brother or sister
miscreant	unbelieving (from *mis*, wrongly + Latin *creant*, believing, from *credere*, to believe)	base, depraved
miser	wretched person (from Latin *miser*, wretched, miserable)	stores up money
prevent	go before (from Latin *pre*, before + *venire*, to come)	to keep from
heathen	one who lives on a *heath*, outside the society (from Old English *haethen*, heath dweller)	a pagan, unenlightened
punctual	careful about details, about small points (from Latin *punctum*, point)	on time
preposterous	to put the last first (from Latin *pre*, before + *post*, after)	absurd, contrary to

Spoonerisms (Metathesis)

Speech boners resulting from the accidental transposition of sounds (usually the initial sounds of two words) are often called *spoonerisms,* after the Reverend William A. Spooner, who was noted for such mistakes. For him, "a well-oiled bicycle" came out "a well-boiled icicle," and "our dear old queen" became "our queer old dean."

We call such transpositions spoonerisms; but the Greeks also had a word for it—*metathesis,* the transposition of sounds, syllables, or letters in a word. Metathesis comes from Greek *metatithenai* (to transpose), which comes from *meta* (across) + *tithenai* (to put).

Metathesis does not always have a humorous effect. The transposition of letters may merely result in a spelling change. For example:

Old English *bridd* became *bird.*
Icelandic *hross* became *horse.*
Middle English *drit* became *dirt.*

But metathesis often results in unexpected humor. A well-known radio announcer once excitedly introduced President Herbert Hoover as "Hoobert Heever." Other bloopers include those of two radio commentators who used the following metathetical phrases:

"A twenty-one sun galoot"
"The Duck and Doochess of Windsor"

217

The Variability of Language

The teacher can stress the variability of language by pointing out that many common objects have different names. In Maine, if you ask for a milk shake, you get it without ice cream. If you want ice cream in it, you ask for a *frappe*.

Some people sit in the *living room;* others in the *front room*. Some sit on a *sofa;* others on a *couch*. A *chest of drawers* may also be a *bureau* or a *dresser*. Some fry in a *skillet;* others use a *frying pan;* while still others use a *spider*. One person uses a *saltshaker;* another a *saltcellar*. Some people eat *dinner;* others call the same meal *supper*. Some grocers put groceries in a *poke;* others put them in a *bag* or a *sack*. The following lesson emphasizes the use of synonymous expressions.

In the following lesson the student writes an appropriate noun in each blank.

Answers

cellar	1. Another name for *basement* is c_____.
carpet	2. Another name for *rug* is c_____.
lamp	3. You can turn on a *light* or a l_____.
faucet	4. You can turn off a *spigot* or a f_____.
nails	5. Carpenters often use *brads* or small n_____.
abdomen	6. Another word for *belly* is a_____.
limb	7. Another word for *leg* is l_____.
snakes	8. *Adders* and *asps* are also called s_____.
pail	9. A *bucket* is also known as a p_____.
bureau	10. A *chest of drawers* may be called a b_____.
divan	11. A *couch* is sometimes called a d_____.
drumstick	12. A *cooked turkey leg* is called a d_____.
fee	13. The *charge* for a service is a f_____.
fiancé	14. An *engaged man* is a f_____.
fiancée	15. An *engaged woman* is a f_____.
gift, tip	16. A *gratuity* is a g_____, or t_____.
hamlet	17. He lived in a *small village,* or h_____.
hide	18. An animal's *skin* is called h_____.
image	19. An *icon* is an i_____.
tax	20. An *impost* is more often called a t_____.
informer	21. *Stool pigeon* is slang for i_____.
kennel	22. A *doghouse* is a k_____.
	23. In Greek mythology, the architect Daedalus built a building with confusing passages to imprison a monster, the Minotaur.
Labyrinth	This *maze* was called the L_____.
dictionary	24. A *lexicographer* is a d_____-maker.
	25. The *colorful language* of sportswriters is often called
lingo	l_____.
cassette	26. The film was in a *cartridge* or c_____.

11

Figures
of
Speech

Effective speakers and writers make much use of figures of speech to get their ideas across. This ancient rhetorical device was used by Cicero and by Suetonius, the Roman novelist who used *figura* to mean a hint or an allusion. A figure of speech is picturesque, imaginative language used to heighten effect by comparing or identifying a particular thing with another, more familiar thing. Notice how the use of figurative language changes connotation, as in the two sentences below:

a. That fullback is much bigger than the halfback.
b. That fullback was a giant beside the halfback.

In sentence *a* the comparison is *literal* (made between nouns in the same class—men or boys who are football players). But in sentence *b* the comparison is *figurative*—the fullback is made to appear like something else. By comparing the fullback to a giant, the size of the fullback is exaggerated for effect (this special figure of speech is called *hyperbole,* discussed later in this unit).

In this unit we will discuss the following figures of speech:

Personification:
"Caesar said to me, 'Darest thou, Cassius, now leap in with me into this *angry* flood?' "
(Shakespeare gives the flood personal qualities.)

Simile:
"But pleasures are *like* poppies spread—You seize the flow'r, its bloom is shed"
(Burns makes a *direct* comparison.)

Metaphor:
"Robed in the long *night* [darkness] of her deep hair"
(Tennyson makes an *implied* comparison.)

Hyperbole:
"Bowed by the *weight of centuries* he leans upon his hoe and gazes on the ground"
(Markham exaggerates.)

Metonymy:
The laundryman brought back her *linen*.
(*Linen* stands for several things: tablecloths, sheets, shirts, handkerchiefs, etc., whether made of linen or not.)

Synecdoche:
The retiring sprinter hung up his *spikes*.
(Here, a part is used to represent the whole shoe.)

Litotes:
It's *no easy feat* to walk a tightrope.
(It's hard to walk a tightrope. This is making a statement by denying the reverse of it; understatement.)

Allegory:
A story, such as *Pilgrim's Progress* or *Gulliver's Travels,* in which the events and characters have meanings other than the ones they seem to have is an *allegory*.

Euphemism:
> We regret to inform you of *your termination of employment.*

> (You're fired. This is a device to avoid saying something disagreeable or unpleasant.)

Note: While *personification, simile, metaphor,* and *hyperbole* are the most common figures of speech, the others listed here occur frequently enough to require their recognition by the student.

Personification

Personification is from Latin *persona* (person, actor, or mask worn in a drama) + *fic* (make). Hence when we use personification we give human or personal qualities to inanimate things or ideas. Thus a ship is referred to as *she.* Its foghorn *moans.* The waves *lap* at the side of the ship.

We often personify the forces of life, nature, and civilization. The sun is masculine: Old Sol sends down *his* rays. The moon is feminine: The moon travels "in *her* circled orb." In addition, we speak of *Father* Time and *Mother* Earth. We speak of the *mother* country and *Miss* Liberty. Justice is represented as a blindfolded woman holding a balance scale: Justice is *blind.*

Personification may run through a whole poem, as in Shelley's "The Cloud" in which the personified cloud speaks:

> I bring fresh showers for the thirsting flowers...
> I sift the snow on the mountains below...
> I am the daughter of Earth and Water,
> And the nursling of the Sky.

Carl Sandburg personifies Chicago as

> Hog Butcher for the World...
> City of the Big Shoulders

In "Barter," Sara Teasdale says,

> Life has loveliness to sell—

Benjamin Franklin says, in *Poor Richard's Almanac,*

> Experience keeps a dear school, but a fool will learn in no other.

In "Thanatopsis," Bryant says,

> To him who in the love of Nature holds
> Communion with her visible forms, she speaks
> A various language

In *Romeo and Juliet,* Friar Lawrence says,

> The gray-eyed morn smiles on the frowning night

Longfellow says,

> The green trees whispered low and mild.

In *Measure for Measure,* Lorenzo says to Jessica,

> How sweet the moonlight sleeps upon this bank.

In *The First Snowfall,* Lowell says,
Every pine and fir and hemlock
Wore ermine too dear for an earl.

In "Ode to Duty," Wordsworth combines personification with apostrophe (addressing an imaginary person or object):
Stern Daughter of the Voice of God!
O Duty!

In "Ode to the West Wind," Shelley addresses the wind as if it were a person:

O, Wind,
If Winter comes, can Spring be far behind?

Simile

Another example of figurative language is *simile.* Simile (from Latin *similis,* meaning "like") is a direct comparison between things, often using the clue words *as, like, than, as . . . as,* or *so . . . as.* Notice the simile in "He fought like a tiger." His fighting is likened to that of a tiger.

Similes are useful and easy to use. They help us illustrate our thoughts and ideas with references to external things: persons, objects, nature. Thus a heavy man may be said to be "as big as a house." Another man may be "as sly as a fox."

In *Romeo and Juliet,* a sword wound is described:
'tis not *so* deep *as* a well, nor *so* wide *as* a churchdoor

Simile is a favorite device of the poet. Notice the following examples:
She walks in beauty *like* the night.
—Byron

And what is *so* rare *as* a day in June?
—Lowell

Apollo came *like* the night.
—Homer

O my love is *like* a red, red rose.
—Burns

Love deep *as* the sea *as* a rose must wither.
—Swinburne

Homer describes Ulysses' manner of speaking:
His words fell soft, *like* snow upon the ground.

Describing the knight, Chaucer says:
And in his bearing modest *as* a maid.

Mark Twain uses this simile:
Nothing *so* needs reforming *as* other people's habits.
—Pudd'nhead Wilson's Calendar

Speaking of government theorists who had a variety of plans for modifying the Mississippi River, Mark Twain says in *Life on the Mississippi:*

the moment you rub against any one of those theorists, make up your mind that it is time to hang out your yellow flag . . . for he is *like* your family physician, who comes and cures the mumps, and leaves the scarlet fever behind.

Lady Macbeth says to Macbeth:

Your face, my thane, is *as* a book where men
May read strange matters.

Describing a summer storm, Huck Finn uses simile:

dark *as* sin again in a second, and now you'd hear the thunder . . . go tumbling down the sky . . . *like* rolling barrels down-stairs
— *The Adventures of Huckleberry Finn*

William Blake in "Night" combines personification and simile in the following lines:

The moon *like* a flower
In heaven's high bower,
With silent *delight*
Sits and *smiles* on the night.

Wilbur Schramm's short story "Windwagon Smith" contains a variety of concrete figures:

Personification:

Westport shrank and Kansas City grew and after a while Kansas City swallowed Westport. . . .

. . . grit chewed off your soles and left you barefoot.

Simile:

Punch Dunkelberger's hound dog woke up bristling like a hairbrush.

The Pawnees were peeking from behind trees, eyes bulging like hard-boiled eggs.

His voice . . . clipped the consonants like axbites in an oak tree.

Cliché Similes

Before the student can use similes effectively in his speaking and writing, he must first be able to recognize them. One approach is to work with similes that are clichés, well-known phrases that the student may have heard but hasn't associated with similes.

The lesson below gives the student practice in recognizing the use of comparison as a means of making ideas clear.

The student completes each simile below by filling in the blank:

Answers

pie	1. as easy as p_____
shootin'	2. as sure as s_____
breeze	3. as free as the br_____
wink	4. as quick as a w_____
molasses in January	5. as slow as m_____

Answers

snow	6.	as white as s_____
night	7.	as black as n_____
day	8.	as plain as d_____
picture	9.	as pretty as a p_____
rain	10.	as right as r_____
fox	11.	as sly as a f_____
honey	12.	as sweet as h_____
bee	13.	as busy as a b_____
button	14.	as cute as a b_____
ox	15.	as clumsy as an o_____
whip	16.	as smart as a w_____

Metaphor

A figure of speech often adds punch to a sentence. *Metaphor,* for example, can help a speaker or writer paint a clear picture through comparison or contrast. *Metaphor* comes from Greek *metaphora* meaning "transfer," from *meta,* over + *pherein,* to carry. A metaphor draws a comparison between two things to create a vivid mental image, although it is not introduced by the *like* or *as* of the simile. For example, Shakespeare says, "All the world's a stage"; and Santayana says, "Words are weapons."

In the *Idylls of the King,* Tennyson describes old Sir Bedivere:

when the man was *no more than a voice*
In the white winter of his age

John Donne says,

No man is *an island,* entire to itself;
Every man is *a piece of the continent,*
a part of the main.

Alexander Pope says,

True wit is *nature to advantage dressed,*
What often was thought, but ne'er so well expressed.

Carlyle metaphorizes history by saying:

History is a mighty *drama,* enacted upon the *theater* of time

Note the following metaphors (implied comparisons):

In *King Richard II,* John of Gaunt compares England to a gem:

This *precious stone* set in the silver sea

Horace says,

Anger is a short *madness*

Samuel Johnson said,

Language is the *dress* of thought

224

Greenough and Kittredge point out that our language is "constantly subjected to what may be called mechanical processes of growth."[1] These processes include roots, affixes, derivations, inflections, and compounds.

One of the main contributors to this process of language growth is the *metaphor*. Metaphor is the expression of the poetic sense in man, his ability to combine the literal and the emotional senses. Thus Antony can say, "Caesar were no lion were not the Romans hinds [deer]"; and Polonius can say, "Borrowing dulls the edge of husbandry [thrift, wise management]."

Metaphorization is an attempt to say something in a fresh, new way. It keeps the language lively, hence alive. Some metaphors, like slang, are tried and either accepted or rejected. Students should be encouraged to learn what metaphor is and should be encouraged to write their own metaphors. (Exercises on metaphors are included later in this unit.)

Metaphors may cluster around a given concept like heat, for example. People often *roast* each other at meetings. A person may be *burned up* by a *searing* attack or a *blistering* remark, and later *simmer* down.

Fruits and vegetables (tomato, cabbage, plum, berries, etc.) have been metaphorized as slang. G. K. Chesterton in *A Defense of Slang* says, "All slang is metaphor and all metaphor is poetry." Slang is a way of experimenting with the language. She's a peach. It's a lemon. A rhubarb developed on the diamond. He's the top banana. A fellow may have enough lettuce to buy a new suit or he may be low on bread. The word *pippin* (an apple, and also a slang expression meaning someone or something really attractive) has, in general, lost its extended meaning as slang and its original meaning of "seed."

Metaphorical Extent

People often make the mistake of assuming that metaphors are rare. On the contrary, metaphors are so abundant and we use them so frequently that it is often hard to judge whether a word is really a metaphor or not. Almost every word we use is metaphorized to some extent. For example, the word *fall* ranges in meaning from "dropping down from a higher place" to the metaphorical meaning of the Fall of Man as used by Milton. A variety of other meanings *fall* in between: his eyes *fell;* he *fell* into sin; he has *fallen* from high estate.

In addition, a city may *fall* to the enemy; a soldier may *fell* his enemy; one may *fall* asleep or *fall* in love or *fall* into a bad habit. In the word *fallen,* the accent *falls* on the first syllable. Longfellow says, "The shades of night are *falling* fast." These phrases, like the *fall* (autumn) of the year, are metaphorical extensions of the original concept of *fall:* to drop down.

When a politician promises to *eradicate* corruption from city government he means get rid of it entirely, eliminate it. But he is metaphorizing the original sense of the word, which is taken from Latin *eradico* (pull out by the roots), from *e,* out + *radix*, root.

A person who says he is *astonished* means he is amazed or surprised. The original sense of astonished was "thunderstruck," from Latin *ad* + *tonare,* thunder.

[1]James B. Greenough and George L. Kittredge, *Words and Their Ways in English Speech* (New York: The Macmillan Company, 1961), p. 9.

225

When we say that the word *boy's* is an <u>inflected</u> form of *boy,* we don't consciously note that the *inflection* is literally a "bending" away from the usual form of the word *boy* and has its origin in Latin *inflexio,* bend.

We metaphorize when we use the expression "*neuter* gender" or "*neutral* country." The Latin word *neuter* merely means "neither." People who order *espresso* coffee don't think about the original sense of the word—squeezing the juice out of the bean—from Latin *expressus,* squeezed or pressed out.

The *cardinal* or pivotal point of a proposal is that on which it *hinges,* from Latin *cardo,* hinge, pivot.

We become so accustomed to metaphorized expressions that we do not recognize them as such. In general, we mean more than we say. If a boy *falls* into trouble with the law, his parents get into a *stew* and try to get to the *bottom* of things. What is the *bottom* here, literally? Literally, it doesn't exist. We are using it metaphorically.

The expression "getting to the bottom of things" implies such images as searching for, uncovering, or discovering the *fundamental* (from Latin *fundus,* bottom) reasons for a given problem—perhaps getting at the *root* of the problem (another metaphor). Thus the parents *rack* their brains to set the boy's thinking *straight* and get him on the *right* road. And so we reinforce metaphorical phrases with more metaphorical phrases. We make unknown things clear by making analogies to known things.

It might be argued that while metaphor is applicable to literature, sociology, and art, when dealing with the cold, clear logic of a science, you must choose accurate terms. Consider the subject of magnetism, for example: Like poles *repel* each other; unlike poles *attract* each other. *Repel* and *attract* are used metaphorically.

Gravity is often described metaphorically as the force that pulls an object toward the earth. Newton said in his law of gravitation that "all objects *attract* each other." *Attract* is also metaphorical, from *trahere,* to draw or pull.

Parts of the eye have been metaphorized: the eyelid, the retina (a "network" of thin rods and nerves, from the Latin *rete,* net) and the lens (from the Latin *lens,* lentil, whose seeds are shaped like biconvex lenses). The iris of the eye, which controls the amount of light entering the pupil and contains the eye's color, is ultimately related to the light and color of the rainbow (*Iris* was the goddess of the rainbow). The pupil of the eye reflects a small image, said to be related to Latin *pupilla,* little doll.

When we hear sounds our *eardrums* vibrate. When sounds are not loud enough to be heard the scientist says these sounds are below the *threshold* of audibility. Other parts of the ear are also metaphorized: *stirrup, anvil, hammer.* Scientists speak of sound *waves,* or vibrating objects that *compress* the surrounding air.

Parts of the Body as Metaphors

Part One

The following lesson gives the student practice in recognizing metaphors that refer to various parts of the body. Students often hear or read these metaphors in idiomatic expressions like "He put his foot in it."

In the exercise below, the student is asked to write in each blank what he thinks each of the metaphors, or metaphorical expressions, literally means. There may be a variety of answers.

1. Keep a stiff upper lip.
_____

2. Chin up.
_____

3. Heads up.
_____

4. Don't stick your neck out.
_____

5. Lend an ear.
_____

6. Don't split hairs.
_____

7. Put your nose to the grindstone.
_____

8. He got an earful.
_____

9. You said a mouthful.
_____

10. None of your lip.
_____

11. The magician showed us how to palm a card.
_____

12. She has a finger in every pie.
_____

13. Don't browbeat him.
_____

Note: Additional expressions may be supplied by the teacher or the students. These might include:

a highbrow	harebrained scheme
won by a nose	to wink at his faults
nosey	your foot in your mouth
a handout	a legman
to get it off your chest	belly laugh
the skin of your teeth	to put the finger on him
elbow grease	to see eye to eye
to face the music	thumbs down
won by a hair	a tongue-lashing
shoulder the burden	under his thumb
knuckle under	Don't lose your head.
a pain in the neck	Put your back into it.
He's spineless.	He's back on his feet again.

Part Two

The teacher might point out that some metaphors have become so common that their original meaning has been lost. The student has probably used some of the phrases below many times without realizing that he was using metaphors.

In the exercises below, the student chooses the phrase that best defines the metaphorical expression.

Answers

a   1. "To stick your neck out" means (a) to take a chance, (b) to brag, (c) to stare at someone.

c   2. When you "foot the bill," you (a) leave without paying, (b) kick something, (c) pay it.

c   3. "To split hairs" is to (a) tell a lie, (b) accuse unfairly, (c) be overly exact.

b   4. "Putting your nose to the grindstone" means to (a) be punished, (b) work hard, (c) have a nose operation.

c   5. People with a "finger in every pie" (a) are big eaters, (b) are selfish, (c) are involved in many activities.

b   6. "To get something off your chest" means (a) to take off your coat, (b) to tell something, (c) to realize a goal.

b   7. "To face the music" means (a) to learn to dance, (b) to meet trouble boldly, (c) to deny the truth.

c   8. "None of your lip!" means (a) don't kiss me, (b) don't give advice, (c) no backtalk.

a   9. "Thumbs down" means (a) to disapprove, (b) to approve, (c) to consider.

Metaphors as Adjectives

We can metaphorize a word by making it an adjective. Put the word *serpentine* on the board and underline the suffix *-ine*. Note that the word means "like a serpent." The class may suggest others, such as *elephantine*. Point out that *ermine* means "like a weasel." *Canine* (doglike) is from the Latin *canis* (dog); *feline* (catlike) is from the Latin *felis* (cat). Write the word *giraffine* on the board. Although this is not a lexical word, students should be able to arrive at a meaning through analysis of its parts. Using exercises with the suffix *-ine* offers students an excellent opportunity to create or metaphorize.

There are a number of harder *-ine* words that students can learn, like *hominine* (manlike), for example. The teacher may list the following words on the chalkboard or an overhead transparency by number (without the meanings) and ask the students to write the number (1, 2, 5, etc.) of those words they know. Or he may duplicate the material and have students check the words they know and discuss the list or look up the origins of certain words.

This list should not be required learning. Rather, the purpose is to show the student that we can metaphorize many animal-like characteristics by using the suffix *-ine*.

Suggested Word List

	Metaphor	Meaning			Metaphor	Meaning
1.	anopheline	like a mosquito		14.	leonine	lion
2.	anserine	like a goose		15.	leopardine	leopard
3.	aquiline	eagle		16.	lupine	wolf
4.	asinine	donkey, ass		17.	ovine	sheep
5.	bovine	cow		18.	piscine	fish
6.	canine	dog		19.	porcine	pig
7.	cervine	deer		20.	ranine	frog
8.	elephantine	elephant		21.	salamandrine	salamander
9.	equine	horse		22.	sealine	seal
10.	ermine	weasel		23.	serpentine	serpent
11.	feline	cat		24.	taurine	bull
12.	hircine	goat		25.	tigrine	tiger
13.	hominine	man		26.	ursine	bear

Note: To check the student's recall, the teacher might present some of the above *ine* words in test form. The student writes the adjective ending with *ine*.

1. With a __bovine__ expression on her face.
2. The __aquiline__ features of the nobleman.
3. With __feline__ stealth, he crept forward.
4. Attacked by a __lupine__ pack.
5. With sharp __canine__ teeth.
6. A hulking, __elephantine__ figure.
7. The vet majored in __equine__ medicine.
8. Spotted a __sealine__ herd.
9. With __leopardine__ spots.
10. A creeping __serpentine__ vine.

Simple drawings often teach the concept of metaphorization. For example, the expression "she's catty" can be illustrated as

cat   catty

Students can be given selected words from the Suggested Word List and asked to supply illustrations that metaphorize each. In the lower grades, students can be supplied with illustrations and asked to identify the metaphors they represent.

Color Metaphors

The following lesson emphasizes color metaphors often associated with familiar phrases. Children learn the names for colors early. Therefore reference to color is an easy and fruitful way of teaching students to recognize metaphors. For example, well-known sayings or overused phrases (clichés) are often associated with color, and can be used to introduce the concept of metaphor in language. Exercises using such phrases can be used to encourage the student to create his own metaphors.

In the following exercise, the student writes the appropriate color in each phrase below and checks his own answers (with those on the left) as he goes through the lesson. Before duplicating the material, the teacher may wish to delete the answers on students' copies and use them as a basis for class discussion about the meaning of some of these phrases.

Answers

green	1.	g_____ with envy
purple	2.	p_____ with rage
blue	3.	in a b_____ mood
red	4.	a r_____-letter day
pink	5.	in the p_____ of condition
blue	6.	once in a b_____ moon
purple	7.	a book with p_____ passages
black	8.	a b_____ sheep
brown	9.	a b_____ study
yellow	10.	y_____ journalism
white	11.	w_____ as a sheet
black	12.	b_____ as coal
red	13.	in the r_____
yellow	14.	y_____-bellied
yellow	15.	y_____ with age
silver	16.	s_____-tongued orator
golden	17.	g_____ tresses
black	18.	b_____ as night
gold	19.	good as g_____

The Metaphor as Cliché

Although many metaphorical expressions are clichés, the teacher might want to point out that phrases such as "right as rain" are clichés only to those who know them, who have heard them often. To the inexperienced reader, a cliché may have much meaning.

The teacher might present the following tongue-in-cheek essay to the students and ask them to underline or point out the phrases that are trite (overworn, stale), from the Latin *tritus,* rubbed off, worn out. Later he may wish to ask the students how clichés are sometimes helpful. The clichés, not all of which are metaphoric, are listed at the end of the essay.

Clichés and Conversation

Far be it from me to find fault with clichés. As bread is the staff of life, so the cliché is one of the mainstays of language. You couldn't begin to hold a conversation without clichés. For example, how would you start without using trite expressions such as "How are you?" "Is it hot enough for you?" and last but not least, "What do you know?"

When you deal with trite phrases, hackneyed quotations, and expressions along this line, the evil they do has to be weighed with the good. The anthropologist Malinowski calls this type of communication *phatic communion.* It is used to open the door. It's a way of telling the other person that the barriers are down, that you're ready and eager to have a chat with him. It seems to me that life would be a little on the dull side without these friendly little reminders. These phrases let you know that you can feel free to talk with this person, and that silence won't reign supreme, as far as he's concerned.

It would be sheer madness to presume that every time you opened your mouth you had to weigh your words, that no phrases would bear repeating, that instead of saying "Good morning," you would have to rack your brain to think up a new greeting such as "It looks like the beginning of a pleasant day," "The matutinal sun is bright today," "It certainly was a dark night," etc. You wouldn't dare say, "A new day is dawning," — that's a cliché.

Actually, there's little need to talk of Mother Nature's handiwork in brand spanking new terms, because in the long run you only use the weather and the climate to break the ice when you don't know where to start, for example, when you sit down at the festive board with a complete stranger, or when you trip the light fantastic with a member of the fair sex with whom you are not yet on friendly terms.

It is my opinion that the hackneyed phrase or the cliché is an important factor in communication. It's like a conversation piece. It's a cog in the wheel that gets things rolling.

Therefore, trite expressions are, in a sense, the backbone of social life. They are tried and true expressions that need no further explanation. An expression such as "How's everything?" does not mean that the interrogator *really* wants to know how everything is, it's a social amenity, another way of putting out the welcome mat to promote an exchange of ideas, a sharing of thoughts.

Since man is a social animal, he is inclined to seek the company of other men. As far as speech is concerned, he tends to take the easy way out by using language filled with easily recognizable phrases that are really none the worse for wear. Thus he usually begins his conversations with a few well-chosen words and carries on from there. These phrases are not meant to be earthshaking. They merely get across the idea that whether he has anything to say or not he wants to communicate.

List of Clichés

far be it from me
bread is the staff of life
one of the mainstays
you couldn't begin to
last but not least
along this line
the evil . . . has to be weighed
  with the good
open the door
the barriers are down
ready and eager
have a chat with
a little on the dull side
friendly little reminders
feel free to talk
silence won't reign supreme
as far as he's concerned
sheer madness to presume
every time you opened your mouth
weigh your words
bear repeating
rack your brain
Mother Nature's handiwork
brand spanking new
in the long run

break the ice
festive board
trip the light fantastic
a member of the fair sex
on friendly terms
it is my opinion
an important factor
conversation piece
cog in the wheel
gets things rolling
the backbone of
tried and true
need no further explanation
putting out the welcome mat
exchange of ideas
sharing of thoughts
man is a social animal
seek the company of
as far as speech is concerned
take the easy way out
none the worse for wear
a few well-chosen words
carries on from there
earthshaking
get across the idea

Metaphors of Measure

The sentences below use metaphors of measure. Students should be able to identify them (they are underlined here) and to discuss their meaning.

1. He is narrow-minded about politics.
2. She is broad-minded.
3. He has a narrow point of view.
4. He stuck with me through thick and thin.
5. Tom is deep in thought.
6. Mary is a shallow thinker.
7. It's as broad as it is long.
8. The title of the film was *Wide Horizons*.
9. Everyone had high hopes.
10. His wife was in low spirits.
11. He has a high income and low aspirations.
12. The Greeks liked high tragedy and low comedy.
13. He certainly is a thick-headed person.
14. The team has only a slim chance of winning.
15. The sea captain told a tall tale.
16. These poor people are in narrow straits.
17. The long-faced boy took home a bad report card.
18. She is short-sighted about money matters.

Hyperbole

Hyperbole is a Greek word meaning extravagance, from *hyper,* beyond + *ballein,* to throw—note *ballistic* missile. Hyperbole is an exaggeration for effect, a figure of speech in which truth is stretched. Some examples of hyperbole are:

I haven't seen him in a million years.

He hits the ball a mile.

He's as fast as greased lightning.

The waves were as high as mountains.

She waited an eternity for him.

I was scared to death.

He laughed his head off.

An old song goes "Gee, but I'd give the world to see that old gang of mine."

Movie advertisers use hyperbolic expressions: colossal, super-colossal, magnificent, breathtaking, spectacular, star-studded, etc.

We tend to use hyperbole in ordinary conversation:

I could've just died!

She cried her heart out.

He is up to his neck in work.

He is dead tired.

Hyperbole in Literature

Writers from early to modern times have used hyperbole. Joseph Conrad in his short novel *Typhoon* describes the storm:

> It was something formidable and swift like the sudden smashing of a vial. It seemed to explode all around the ship with an overpowering concussion. . . .

Tennyson in "Lancelot and Elaine" describes the shock of two armies meeting in battle:

> . . . a man far off might well perceive . . .
> The hard earth shake, and a low thunder of arms.

In *Julius Caesar,* Antony says,

> . . . let me not stir you up
> To such a sudden flood of mutiny.

In *Henry IV, Part I,* Prince Hal describes Falstaff:

> . . . Falstaff sweats to death,
> And lards the lean earth as he walks along:

233

In *The Pit and the Pendulum* Poe mixes hyperbole with horror:

I was sick—sick unto death . . . I felt every fibre in my frame thrill . . . all sensations appeared swallowed up in a mad rushing descent as of the soul from Hades . . . perspiration burst from every pore . . . my eyes straining from their sockets . . .

In *Romeo and Juliet,* Shakespeare uses hyperbole:

JULIET: At what o'clock tomorrow
              Shall I send to thee?
ROMEO: At the hour of nine.
JULIET: I will not fail: 'tis twenty years till then.

In "The Legend of Sleepy Hollow," Irving describes Ichabod Crane as having "hands that dangled a mile out of his sleeves."

Burns uses hyperbole when he says in "A Red. Red Rose":

And I will luve thee still, my dear,
Till a' the seas gang dry . . .
And the rocks melt wi' the sun!

Hamlet says that if one of the strolling players, speaking with tears in his eyes, had as much cause to weep as Hamlet has "He would drown the stage with tears."

Julius Caesar uses both simile and hyperbole when he says to Cassius: "But I am constant as the northern star."

Metonymy

Metonymy, from the Greek *meta*. change + *onym*, name, is the use of the name of one thing for that of another which it suggests. In metonymy one thing is said but another thing is meant. "I like to read Poe" means "I like to read Poe's works." The Crown might mean the king. The White House may mean the president or the president and his staff.

Like metaphor, we often use metonymy (name-changing) without realizing it. Note the following uses of metonymy:

He fell in battle means he was killed in battle.

In "Richelieu," Bulwer-Lytton says.

The pen [literature] is mightier than the sword [physical force].

Whittier in "Maud Muller," instead of saying "words spoken" and "words written," says

For of all sad words of tongue or pen,
The saddest are these: "It might have been!"

Metonymy is so commonly used it is often unrecognized as such. "Put on your glasses" means "Put on your spectacles" (a word seldom used now). Here metonymy allows us to use the name of the material (glass) to represent the object made from the material (spectacles).

"I'll take a glass of milk" means "I'll take a drinking glass full of milk."

When we use metonyms we don't, in effect, call a spade a spade:
She's my own flesh and blood (my daughter).

In the poem "Winter" in *Love's Labor Lost,* Shakespeare says,

When icicles hang by the wall,
And Dick the shepherd blows his nail

"Blows his nail" really means blows his hands to warm them up.

When a camp counselor "counts noses," he is counting people.

A prisoner in irons is manacled or in chains.

"The world is shocked" means "the people of the world are shocked."

A car salesman may say, "This car has good rubber (tires)."

"Take heart" means "Have courage, be brave."

Some angry citizens demanded action from City Hall (they wanted action from the mayor and his administration).

"We have that dish quite often" means that we eat that kind of food a lot.

Metonymy often involves the using of one word for another closely related to it. For example, *scepter* can mean sovereignty; *labor,* the workers; and *capital,* management or employer. A business may be in the *black* (ink for credits) or in the *red* (ink for debits).

"United States meets Britain at Wimbledon" means players representing U.S. and British tennis teams are going to play against one another. We don't turn on a light, we flip a switch that completes an electric circuit resulting in light. When a smoker asks for a light, he really means the fire produced by a match or a lighter.

When we pledge allegiance to the flag we really mean to the country which the flag symbolizes.

When a ballplayer plays to the grandstand, he shows off to get the attention of the fans in the grandstand.

The press can mean newspaper reporters and magazine writers.

The court can refer to the judge and jury.

Redcoats stood for the British soldiers who wore them.

A patient going under the knife is in surgery.

A teenager with a set of wheels has a car.

One type of metonymy relates the container to the thing contained. For example, "A watched pot never boils" actually refers to the water in the pot.

Other examples include:

The last jar had a better flavor than the first.

My cup runneth over.

The fruit dealer said that whole crate was spoiled.

Students might be asked to contribute additional examples. They can get practice working with metonymic expressions in lessons like the one below.

Recognizing Metonymy

In the following lesson the student gets practice reading between the lines, looking for the implication. Most of the material is easy to understand and may be used to check the student's understanding of the use of an important and often-used figure of speech—metonymy. The teacher will note that the name of the figure is not important but the concept is—that we often imply more than we say.

Answers

milk
1. "The baby finished her <u>bottle</u>" means she finished her _____.

water
2. "The <u>pot</u> is boiling" means the _____ is boiling.

chairman
3. "He addressed the <u>chair</u>" means he spoke to the _____.

soup
4. After finishing the soup, Jack said, "I think I'll have another <u>bowl</u>." He meant another bowl of _____.

works, essays
5. "Have you read <u>Emerson</u>?" means "Have you read Emerson's _____?"

the people of Chicago
6. "<u>Chicago</u> felt the impact of the cold Canadian air" means _____.

ships
7. "Ten <u>sail</u> came into view" means ten _____.

king, queen
8. The new ambassador represented the <u>Crown</u>. _____

bullets
9. In a Western movie a lot of <u>lead</u> flies. _____

smoking, pipe tobacco
10. Grandfather enjoys his <u>pipe</u>. _____

food
11. "Give us this day our daily <u>bread</u>." _____

judge, judges
12. "Will the prisoner face the <u>bench</u>?" means face the _____ on the bench.

workers and management
13. <u>Labor</u> and <u>capital</u> never seem to agree. _____ and _____

people
14. The <u>city</u> went to work. _____

water
15. "His <u>radiator</u> boiled over" actually refers to the _____.

Synecdoche

Synecdoche (si·nek′de·kē), from the Greek *synekdechesthai* (*syn*, with + *ex*, out + *dechesthai*, to take, receive), literally means to supply something to what's been said. For example, if someone says, "India has too many mouths to feed," you must supply the rest: whole bodies, human beings, Indians. Synecdoche is a figure of speech in which a part is used for the whole.

Actually, synecdoche is a kind of metonymy, but it is sufficiently different to be classified as a separate figure of speech. In reality, the teacher should not insist on the student making a neat distinction between metonymy and synecdoche, although an explanation might, on occasion, be necessary. An easy way to remember the distinction is to keep in mind the *sailing* figure of speech noted previously:

Metonymy: Let out more <u>canvas</u>. (Actually refers to the <u>sail</u>, which is <u>made of canvas</u>.)

Synecdoche: They saw a hundred <u>sail</u> on the horizon. (The <u>sail</u> is a <u>part of the whole ship</u>.)

236

Additional examples of synecdoche are:

All hands on deck (all sailors on deck).

Great minds of history (great men of history).

Keep an eye on this (pay attention to this).

Two hundred head of cattle (two hundred animals).

"Lend me your ears" (give me your attention).

The foreman hired ten new hands (workers).

The British Museum houses the Elgin Marbles (Greek marble statues).

Note: *antonomasia* is a form of synecdoche that applies the specific to the general, or attributes traits of a specific person to a general kind of trait in other persons:

He is a regular Don Juan (lady's man).

He is a second Napoleon (egomaniac, conqueror).

He is a veritable Solomon (wise, like the wise biblical king).

She is another Cassandra (always warning people—Cassandra warned the Trojans not to keep Helen, but they wouldn't listen).

She's a regular Xanthippe (shrewish, like Socrates' wife).

He's truly a Job (patient, like the biblical character).

A very rich man may be called a Croesus (ancient wealthy king of Lydia).

A strong man may be referred to as Samson.

A hunter is now often humorously described as a Nimrod (a biblical king who was a great hunter).

Litotes

The opposite of hyperbole is *litotes* (līt'ə·tēz'), from the Greek *litos*, plain, simple. Litotes is a figure of speech that makes an assertion about something by denying its opposite. For example, "London is no mean city" means "London is a great city."

Since we often tend to overlook or discount hyperbolic claims such as those of advertising agencies (*the greatest, superb, outstanding, exquisite, gigantic proportions,* etc.), we may use litotes to catch attention, or to emphasize a point by stating it negatively.

Other examples of litotes or understatement are:

Winston Churchill was a figure of no little importance.

This exotic flower has a not unpleasant scent.

Thurber was a writer of no little ability.

She is no clinging vine.

I've just read *Kon-Tiki*. Crossing the Pacific Ocean on a forty-foot raft is <u>no small achievement</u>.

Leo Durocher <u>wasn't a bad ballplayer</u> when he was young.

Joe Louis was <u>no second-rate fighter</u>.

Mary is <u>not unhappy</u> with her new job.

Litotes is often effective because of what it leaves unsaid. In a speech to the Canadian Parliament in 1941, Churchill indicated that the French generals had told their cabinet ministers that "in three weeks England will have her neck wrung like a chicken." Churchill's reply was litotes or understatement: "Some chicken! Some neck!"

Allegory

The word *allegory* is from the Greek *allegorein,* to speak figuratively, from *allos,* other + *agoreuein,* to speak. (Note *agora,* the market place where Greeks met to speak.)

An allegory is a story told in symbols. It is an extended, continuing metaphor in which objects or ideas are symbolized. Allegories often deal with the moral or spiritual nature of man. They are usually long, complicated stories with an underlying meaning.

Longfellow's long poem "The Ship of State" is an allegory. On the surface, it deals with the building of a great ship. The union in marriage of the ship architect's daughter and a young craftsman gives the ship its name, *Union,* which in turn symbolizes the union of our country.

Using *apostrophe,* speaking to the country as if it were the Ship of State, Longfellow says near the end of the poem,

Thou, too, sail on, O Ship of State!
Sail on, O Union, strong and great!

Two long classic allegories are Edmund Spenser's *The Faerie Queene* and John Bunyan's *Pilgrim's Progress. The Faerie Queene,* which deals with the chivalrous deeds in King Arthur's day, personifies virtues and vices in allegorical form. Bunyan's allegory is said to be the greatest in the English language. It is told as if it were a dream in which the hero, Christian, leaves the City of Destruction and travels (in spite of great difficulties such as the Slough of Despond) to the Celestial City. The characters and problems he meets are comparable to those met in real life. His companion Pliable and others, including Mr. Worldly Wiseman, Atheist, Ignorance, Helpful, Faithful, and Lord Hategood, have names descriptive of the qualities of their characters in the story.

Allegories may be written in prose (Bunyan's *Pilgrim's Progress*) or poetry (Spenser's *The Faerie Queene,* Dante's *Divine Comedy*). In allegory the writer uses a variety of style devices, a combination of figures of speech, such as personification, simile, metaphor, hyperbole, metonymy, and others.

In allegory the chief elements represent something unmentioned. For example, Swift skillfully uses satire in his political allegory *Gulliver's Travels.* Ironically, the allegory of this brilliant satirist is usually undetected by surface readers; it is considered a juvenile book by many who make no connection between the pretensions of the Lilliputian court and those of the English royal court, or who do not see that the character of England's Lord of the Treasury, Sir Robert Walpole, is represented by the Lilliputian Flimnap.

Fables and *parables* are short allegories. A fable is an allegory in which animals speak and behave like people. In *Aesop's Fables,* for example, the fox, unable to reach the grapes, rationalizes: "They were probably sour anyway."

A parable (a biblical story) is also a short allegory that teaches a moral lesson or truth. A parable is an extended metaphor (a comparison). The word *parable* is indirectly related to *compare,* from the Latin *parabola* (proverb, parable), and is originally from the Greek *ballein,* to throw, and *para,* beside, to compare. Thus a parable invites the listener or reader to compare a specific or general situation in his own life with the situation described in the story, as in the parables of "The Sower," "The Laborer in the Vineyard," "The Prodigal Son."

Euphemism

While figures of speech such as personification, simile, and metaphor are based on similarity, *euphemism* is based on contrast. We use euphemism to express a disagreeable or unpleasant fact indirectly. Death, for example, is described in a variety of ways: "gone to the happy hunting ground," "passed away," "passed on."

The word *euphemism* itself is from the Greek *euphemizein,* to speak with fair words, from *eu,* good, + *phanai,* speak. The Romans, especially in regard to omens and sacrifices to the gods, had a phrase that parallels euphemism: *favete linguis,* an imperative phrase literally meaning "favor with tongues" (speak well). The Greeks used euphemism to placate the Erinyes (the Furies), three females who avenged unpunished crimes. Afraid to call them by their original, older name, Erinyes, the Greeks called them *Euminides,* a euphemism which means "the well-meaning," "the soothed goddesses," hoping to avoid unpleasantness by saying something pleasant.

Because of its unpleasant aspects, we often invent euphemistic terms for death or for a dead person (the "deceased"). We speak of the "departed one's demise." We say that he

has fallen asleep,

is in the bosom of Abraham,

has returned to the Father, or

is at rest.

239

Instead of dying, a person <u>expires</u>, <u>perishes</u>, <u>is taken</u>, <u>ends his days</u> or his <u>earthly career</u>, <u>breathes his last</u>, or <u>goes the way of all flesh</u>.

Less reverently, a man may

<u>give up the ghost</u>,

<u>croak</u>,

<u>head for Davy Jones' locker</u> or <u>the last roundup</u>,

<u>kick the bucket</u>, or

<u>cash in his chips</u>.

The poet Southey euphemizes death in "The Widow":

"There did the traveler find her in the morning;
God has <u>released</u> her."

We use many euphemisms for circumstances related to death. *Funeral director* or *mortician* is used for *undertaker; cemetery* is used more often than *graveyard; casket* is preferred to *coffin;* and *laid to rest* stands for *buried.*

Euphemisms are also used to soften profanity. *Gee* is really an exclamation or a mild oath for *Jesus; gosh, gosh darn* and *darn it* are milder expressions standing for *God* and *damn. Goodness* as an exclamation is a euphemism for *God.* The archaic exclamation *zounds* is a euphemism for *God's wounds*—(God)'s (w)ounds. Speaking to Tybalt, who has baited him, Mercutio draws his sword and says

... here's my fiddlestick; here's that shall make you dance. 'Zounds ...
—*Romeo and Juliet*, Act III, Scene I

We use euphemisms for every occasion. We have a tooth *extracted,* not *pulled; withdrawal* is used instead of *retreat;* we *perspire* rather than *sweat;* a *boarder* is a *paying guest;* a *beautician* is a *hairdresser;* an *alcoholic* may be a *drunkard;* we *make the truth elastic* instead of *tell a lie.*

Practice in Recognizing Euphemisms

The following lesson gives the student practice in recognizing euphemisms. The student reads the related sentences in sections A and B then puts a check in the blank beside the sentence containing a euphemism. (Correct items are marked on this form.)

	A	B
1.	A thousand men were killed in that battle. ___	A thousand men were presumed lost in that conflict. _X_
2.	He got into trouble with the police. ___	He ran afoul of the law. _X_
3.	He's unemployed. _X_	He's out of work. ___
4.	I bought a reconditioned car. _X_	I bought a used car. ___
5.	His accounts were short. _X_	He was an embezzler. ___

A	B
6. She's a guest at the motel. **X**	She's a customer at the motel. ___
7. He beat me. ___	He emerged victorious over me. **X**
8. He was detained by the police overnight. **X**	He was jailed overnight. ___
9. I'm an employee in a big department store. ___	I'm associated with a big department store. **X**
10. The Mob threatened to "take care of" him. **X**	The Mob threatened to rub him out. ___
11. Mr. Jones is the janitor. ___	Mr. Jones is the building custodian. **X**
12. That's not quite true, I'm afraid. **X**	You're lying. ___
13. Where shall I take my dirty clothes? ___	Where shall I take my laundry? **X**
14. That hat doesn't seem to bring out your good points. **X**	You look terrible in that hat. ___
15. It might be a good idea to... **X**	Do it! ___
16. He's as game a fighter as they come. **X**	I beat the bum every round. ___
17. He's been put away. **X**	He's been put into prison (or some other institution). ___
18. I sweat a lot. ___	I perspire heavily. **X**
19. Don't spit on the sidewalk. ___	Don't expectorate on the walk. **X**
20. I don't imbibe. **X**	I don't drink. ___
21. He's a press agent. ___	He's a public relations man. **X**
22. She is untidy. **X**	She is messy. ___
23. He was arrested for drunkenness. ___	He was arrested for intoxication. **X**
24. His condition has deteriorated. **X**	He's dying. ___
25. Insanity is a big problem. ___	Mental disorders are a big problem. **X**
26. He's a slow learner. **X**	He's not very bright. ___
27. Don't call us, we'll call you. **X**	We don't want you bothering us anymore. ___

Summary

We have pointed out four common figures of speech: (1) *personification,* giving inanimate objects lifelike qualities (*Old Man* Winter, the *breath* of Spring); (2) *simile,* making a direct comparison between two things, often using *like* or *as* (a vacation is *like* a tonic); (3) *metaphor,* an implied comparison between two unlike things (a vacation *is* a tonic); (4) *hyperbole,* exaggeration for effect (this bag *weighs a ton*). We also discussed metonymy and synecdoche.

All figures of speech are forms of *rhetoric* (using words in speaking or writing to persuade or affect others). *Rhetoric,* from Greek *rhetor,* orator, was an important part of an education in ancient times, and the various figures of speech were well known to the Greeks and Romans who named these various arts of persuasion.

12

Literature

What is the relationship between literature and vocabulary development? Reading literature and building a vocabulary go hand in hand. One is dependent on the other. Reading is probably the single greatest contributing factor to the building of an extensive vocabulary.

Of course, we do not read literature to build a vocabulary, but we need an adequate vocabulary to appreciate and learn from literature. An acquaintance with literature broadens the student's understanding of the world and his knowledge of human nature. The teacher can advantageously use literature to show the importance of words, their varied meanings, and the importance of style in getting ideas across.

Much of the pleasure of reading escapes the student with a meager vocabulary. Any student may get some pleasure from the jingle of a stanza of poetry because he feels the rhythm or hears the rhyme, but his enjoyment and understanding increase when he also recognizes the poet's meaning, use of metaphor, imagery, allegory as an integral part of the versification.

The most important factor in building a vocabulary is rich experience. Our vocabulary is the residue of our experiences. But in addition to firsthand experiences, much is gained from vicarious experience through listening, observing, and reading. Literature provides important vicarious experiences. The reader may relive the exciting adventures of Jim Hawkins in *Treasure Island* or of David Balfour in *Kidnapped*. A student might sense the warm relationship between human and animal in stories such as Jack London's *The Call of the Wild* or Marjorie K. Rawlings' *The Yearling*.

Uncle Tom's Cabin has historical and social significance, as do *Oliver Twist* and *David Copperfield*. These books present the student with word-pictures that help him understand another person's feelings, thoughts, and actions. He sees the world over the shoulder of a variety of characters, shares in their decisions, experiences their happiness and sorrow.

Adventure stories of war and of great deeds may range from Homer's *Iliad* to Quentin Reynolds' *Custer's Last Stand;* love stories, from Shakespeare's *Romeo and Juliet* to Maureen Daly's *Seventeenth Summer* (both stories of a girl's first love); fantasy, from *A Midsummer Night's Dream* to A. A. Milne's *Winnie-the-Pooh* and Kenneth Grahame's *The Wind in the Willows*. Stories depicting human nature, the happiness and sadness of life, may range from Louisa M. Alcott's *Little Women* to Taro Yashima's *Crow Boy;* animal stories, from *Aesop's Fables* and Kipling's *The Jungle Books* to Kate Seredy's *The White Stag* and the boy-dog relationship of Fred Gipson's *Old Yeller*.

Children's Literature and Vocabulary

Children's literature once dealt predominantly with religion and conduct but now covers a wide variety of subjects. Children's literature includes standard books such as *Tales of Mother Goose* by Charles Perrault, *Tales From Shakespeare* by Charles and Mary Lamb, *Grimm's Fairy*

Tales collected by the linguist Jacob Grimm, and *The Adventures of Tom Sawyer* by Mark Twain. And there are a great many more appropriate, exciting, well-written, and well-illustrated books aimed at children's tastes and reading levels.

The list of books written especially for children continues to grow. By reading these books, elementary students gain pleasurable experience in reading and vocabulary skills. They learn to "read" pictures, to weigh words, to think critically. They get some understanding of human nature.

Sensitive and skillful teaching of children's literature can create in students an interest in words and a lasting enjoyment in reading that will remain with them throughout high school and beyond.

The planned reading of literature can help young people get a better understanding of their schoolmates regardless of differences in race or in background. For example, a child who reads *Crow Boy* sees a reason for accepting persons who are "different." Crow Boy's problems become the reader's problems. Through reading literature children may learn the need to stand by one's values in the face of great odds.

In general, children's literature reflects life. It presents words spoken by a variety of characters in a variety of situations, and, most important, it presents words not in artificial but in natural context.

Thus the elementary teacher can emphasize in a variety of ways the effective use of vocabulary in any of the books listed above. The teacher might note the phrasing used by certain characters. For example, here are a few examples of the imaginative use of words found in *Dorp Dead* by Julia Cunningham:

"This story starts and middles and ends with me."   (p. 3)

"ferociously intelligent"   (p. 4)

"overstuffed woman"   (p. 5)

"bongs that bounce off my eardrums"   (p. 7)

"one gulp of reading"   (p. 20)

"wilderness of puzzlement"   (p. 48)

"calm as a boulder in a blizzard"   (p. 53)

"leaf through my memories"   (p. 56)

"thundery clatter"   (p. 58)

"barrenness of the nothinglandscape"   (p. 62)

"tufts of eyebrows"   (p. 68)

Children's Literature and Word Origin

A significant aspect of word study as it relates to general language development is the origin or history of words. Word history often makes interesting reading for young students. Films, filmstrips, and slides on word history are available in many school and college film libraries.

Perhaps the most productive way to have elementary students study word origins, as a technique for building vocabulary and critical awareness about what is read, is through the study of children's literature. A fifth- or sixth-grade teacher might read aloud some well-known nursery rhymes and then ask her students to analyze their vocabulary. (This activity might be labeled "Words in Poetry.") For example, in the rhyme "Little Miss Muffet sat on a tuffet eating her curds and whey," what is a tuffet? What is whey? *Tuffet* (a diminutive of *tuft* meaning a small stool) and *whey* (the watery part of milk) are not known by most twelfth-graders.

In "Mary, Mary, quite contrary," what does *contrary* mean? (The teacher might note that its meaning of opposed to or against is formed from two words that the ancient Romans used — *contra,* against + *dictum,* spoken. That is, a person who *contradicted* you spoke against you, or had the opposite opinion.)

Although the prime purpose of poetry reading is not for word study but for enjoyment and meaning, key words in certain poems can be selected for discussion about their meaning and origin.

The elementary teacher might also use stories in literature as a point of departure for word origin. Short, original stories by the children may be used as an exercise in creating new words or presenting fanciful origins for established words. For example, the teacher may make up a story about the origin of a word or phrase:

In ancient times there was a bird called the *awk.* It was famous for the crazy way it walked. People used to laugh when an awk walked by because it seemed so clumsy. Sometimes it took a few steps forward and then a step backward. People used to say, "Look at the *awk walk backward.*" Later this phrase was shortened to our word *awkward,* meaning clumsy, not graceful.

The students may be invited to try writing and then telling their own "made-up" word origins about familiar objects: household items, people's names, animals' names, kinds of boats, buildings, tools, etc. The class may later want to find out the true origins (if available in the dictionary or encyclopedia) and compare them with their own creations.

After reading Helen F. Orton's *Mystery in the Apple Orchard* the reader may be asked to find the origin of such words as *haunted, treasure, detective, mystery.* Will James's *Smokey the Cowhorse* or Marguerite Henry's *King of the Wind* may lead the reader to look for the origins of such words as *palomino, mesa, mesquite, lariat, mustang,* and *fetlock.*

The Lone Hunt by William Steele may be the basis for the teacher's suggesting that the student find the history behind certain words used in connection with hunting the buffalo in the Cumberland Mountains. Steele's *Winter Danger* offers the teacher an opportunity to have the class search for Indian words taken into our language: *moccasin, tobacco, succotash, skunk,* etc. The teacher might note that many states have Indian names: Delaware, Dakota, etc.

Animal stories give the teacher an opportunity to discuss the origins of the names of animals. The teacher may illustrate on the chalkboard the relationship between the words *leopard* and *lion:* Latin *leo* (lion) + Greek *pardos* (panther, leopard).

Uncle Ben's Whale by Walter Edmonds uses canalboat terms and provides the origin of such words as *harpoon.*

Fanciful tales (such as the excellent story *The Wind in the Willows* by Kenneth Grahame) provide the teacher and her students with a great number of words to analyze in terms of their meaning and origin. Grahame's context will often enhance the student's interest in an otherwise flat word. He says, at one point, that Mole (tunneling up through the ground) "scraped and scratched and scrabbled." Other phrases in the story include: "Something up there was calling him *imperiously*" (from the Latin *impero,* command), related to *imperative* mood and to *emperor* (commander); "fond of a *bijou* riverside residence" (*bijou* is French for a jewel, or trinket); drawing after them a last *nightcap* of *mulled* [heated] ale"; "drawing after them the long bobbing procession of *casks,* like a mile of *porpoises*" (Latin for "hogfish," from *porcus,* pig).

The area of word origin is broad enough to be related to any subject matter being studied. In its relation to children's literature, a great deal of word-origin study can be spontaneous—if the teacher is prepared to encourage it.

However, two key points are necessary for the success of word-history study in the lower grades: (1) The children must be personally involved, suggesting, contributing, experimenting in terms of history or etymology (at their level), and thereby seeing the relationship of word history to their everyday lives. This goal can be reached by encouraging the children to use key words studied in discussion and conversation (for example, making adjectives such as *jovial* from Jove, *solar* from Sol, *lunar* from Luna, etc.). (2) The teacher must become as expert as he can in words and word origin as they relate to general language development. He must, in effect, become "word-conscious," bringing to the classroom a knowledge of the "new" words to be discussed. He must have at his fingertips sufficient background information to sustain the interest of his students as they proceed through a story or poem.

The child who listens to or reads Maxine Kumin's *The Beach Before Breakfast* takes part in a meaningful relationship—a father taking his son on an adventurous, thoughtful expedition to a beach inhabited by interesting sea creatures. The reader easily gets inside the character and identifies with him as he lives his experiences on the sand and water. He meets vivid adjectives such as "creamy" sand, similes such as "the dunes sit up like fat camels." Words such as *dunes, whelks, conch,* form essential parts of the story, within the context of beach surroundings. These words belong in the story. It is no accident that they are there; they are an integral part of the mood and the setting. They are in natural context—an excellent way to learn words.

Underlining Unfamiliar Words in Reading

As noted previously, vocabulary growth is achieved by rich experiences, by conversation, by wide reading of various kinds of literature, and by systematic study. A good part of the systematic study should be devoted to ways of developing a filing system for remembering and retrieving words.

Many students today buy paperback books, perhaps as members of a class book club. To help students become more word-conscious, the teacher should encourage them to underline unfamiliar words they meet while reading their own paperbacks. A marked personal book is not a spoiled book. In fact, it becomes more useful.

In underlining unfamiliar words in reading, there are these points to consider: (1) If the word is a key word, it will occur again. The student will be alerted to it and not skip it. (2) The student becomes conscious of marked words and the way they are spelled. (3) The student becomes uncomfortable if he skips over a hard word without a quick try at inferring its meaning. (4) The student faces a decision—to learn or not to learn a given word. (5) The student becomes conscious of how many important words he does not know. (6) The student may find that word study is a rewarding learning experience, a challenge rather than a chore.

Students can effectively increase their vocabulary skills by wide reading of school magazines. Many such magazines contain interesting word-study games and challenging quizzes. Words may be taken from articles for purposes of definition, noting construction and spelling, and determining their use in the context of the article.

Vocabulary and Periodicals

One way to extend the student's reading horizon is to enrich his recognition vocabulary. The teacher and the class can scan current newspapers and magazines for definitions or explanations of new or unfamiliar words currently used in domestic, scientific, national, and international affairs.

From a newspaper clipping, for example, students may learn that some scientists believed the Apollo 11 astronauts had discovered *biotite* (a form of mica) on the moon. *Biotite* is named after the French mineralogist Jean Biot. Commander Armstrong noted that certain rocks were *vesicular* (having little cavities), from Latin *vesicula* (little blister, bladder). The strange word *gnomon* (a pole or rod with names on it that the Apollo 11 astronauts embedded in the moon's surface) is related to the word *cognomen* (a person's name).

A magazine article may explain that a laser beam is a thin, intense beam of light that can send signals to and from the moon. The teacher may read from an article explaining that the word *laser* is formed from the words *Light Amplification* by *Stimulated Emission* of *Radiation*. He might note that *Mesa* means *Modularized Equipment Storage Assembly* —the moon module's equipment bay from which lunar astronauts remove the TV camera for use on the moon.

The students might want to keep these words and their definitions in a notebook or scrapbook. Here are some additional words and some of their definitions or origins we might find in newspapers and magazines:

They *garnisheed* his wages. (deducted his debt from his pay)

A movie plot revolves around *nepoticide* and *avunculicide*. (killing of a relative and an uncle)

A reporter published a *tendentious* article. (promoting a point of view)

Although the word *ombudsman* is new in U.S. dictionaries, it is already being used by citizens who think that we should, as they do in Sweden, appoint an *ombudsman,* a representative who investigates the complaints of private citizens against public officials. Long established in parts of Europe, the ombudsman is now making his appearance in some cities and universities in the United States.

The Vocabulary of Journalism

Newspapers are a part of our current literature, providing excellent materials for vocabulary and reading growth. Each day a newspaper prints thousands of words, some easy, some hard. Newspapers are responsible for many of the new words appearing in our language. Newspaper reporters often coin words because they need words that are short, to the point, vivid, and graphic.

Students can enrich their vocabularies by noting the way journalists use words. Words in newspapers, especially those in headlines, often have a different flavor from those in books. Because headlines must fit a certain space and tell the story at a glance, headline writers use words and phrases that are short and colorful. Sportswriters have been particularly inventive: "Twins Take Two," "Cubs Cinch Flag," etc.

Below are pairs of words. The student chooses the one a headline writer might be more likely to use. (Correct answers are underlined on this form.)

1. agreement   <u>pact</u>
2. catch   <u>net</u>
3. construct   <u>build</u>
4. <u>curb</u>   restrict
5. <u>hail</u>   welcome
6. <u>hike</u>   increase
7. <u>jolt, quake</u>   earthquake
8. location   <u>site</u>
9. <u>meet</u>   meeting, convention
10. <u>pare</u>   reduce
11. prevent   <u>bar</u>
12. <u>probe</u>   investigation
13. <u>rap</u>   criticize
14. <u>slash</u>   decrease
15. <u>woes</u>   trouble

The teacher might point out that several of the above words, such as *jolt* for *earthquake, hike* for *raise,* etc., are concrete words that get the reader's attention. Note that they are short words.

In the exercises below, the student chooses shorter synonyms from column B for the words in column A. (Answers are provided.)

Column A   Column B

1. _b_ succumb   a. meet   k. ease
2. _f_ consolidate   b. die   l. send
3. _c_ collision   c. crash   m. plot
4. _h_ conflagration   d. pay
5. _m_ scheme   e. rob
6. _k_ alleviate   f. unite
7. _e_ burglarize   g. tell
8. _d_ remunerate   h. fire
9. _a_ encounter   i. try
10. _g_ divulge   j. count

The words used in professions (their vernacular) can provide a basis for discussion about word usage. Here are some words from the vernacular of the newspaperman.

Students might check the words they know and explain them to the class. (Definitions are given below.)

1. ___ art   14. ___ layout
2. ___ banner   15. ___ lead
3. ___ beat   16. ___ makeup
4. ___ boil   17. ___ masthead
5. ___ byline   18. ___ morgue
6. ___ copy   19. ___ obit
7. ___ crop   20. ___ proof
8. ___ cut   21. ___ rim
9. ___ deadline   22. ___ scoop
10. ___ dummy   23. ___ slot
11. ___ deck   24. ___ slug
12. ___ head   25. ___ caption
13. ___ kill

Definitions

1. art: anything that is not copy (pictures, maps, charts, etc.)

2. banner or wordline: a headline extending across a page, usually the front page

3. beat: the particular area a reporter regularly covers

4. boil: to shorten; to take out parts of the copy

5. byline: a line accompanying a story telling the author's name

6. copy: written material to go in the newspaper

7. crop: to cut off or cover up unwanted parts of a picture

8. cut: to shorten

9. deadline: the latest time when newspaper copy can be turned in

250

10. ad or news dummy: sheets representing the pages of the paper on which the news editor indicates the placement of the stories, their length, etc.

11. deck: a smaller headline under the main headline, both for the same story

12. head: one, two, or three lines of type to identify a story

13. kill: to cancel a story after it has been set in type

14. layout: the makeup of an ad

15. lead: the first paragraph of a news article

16. makeup: arrangement of articles in the newspaper

17. masthead: statement giving the name of the paper, the owner, the staff, etc.

18. morgue: a reference library where newspaper clippings and pictures are kept

19. obit: short for *obituary,* a death notice

20. proof: a first print of a story or page to check for errors or make changes

21. rim: the outside edge of the copy desk where the copy editors sit

22. scoop: an important news story appearing in one newspaper before in any others

23. slot: the inside opening of the round copy desk

24. slug: a short phrase at the top of the reporter's copy to indicate what his story is about

25. caption: the descriptive matter under or beside a picture

Words in Literature, Secondary Level

Current and standard literature are excellent vehicles for illustrating the multiple meanings and effective use of words. For example, reading Milton's sonnet "On His Blindness" can be the basis for discussion about the different meanings of a word, its dependence on context for specific meaning. Here the teacher might point out the specialized use of the words *light, spent, days, lodged,* and *bent* in the following lines:

When I consider how my *light* is *spent,*
Ere half my *days,* in this dark world and wide,
And that one talent which is death to hide
Lodg'd with me useless, though my Soul more *bent*
To serve therewith my Maker, . . .

In discussions of the various literary devices used by writers, the teacher can call the student's attention to the effective use of words. For example, he might point out the use of *onomatopoeia* in James Russell Lowell's "Vision of Sir Launfal":

The drawbridge dropped with a surly *clang,*
And through the dark arch a charger *sprang.*

In developing the student's writing style, the teacher can note the use of a variety of words and writing techniques used in prose and poetry. Examples from literature suggest effective use of words, provide excellent models of expression, and may encourage the student to read the whole story or article or poem from which the example came. Thus the teacher might teach the word *rendezvous* in Alan Seeger's lines:

I have a *rendezvous* with Death
At some disputed barricade

The teaching of key words by using illustrative phrases and sentences from a wide range of literature may recall to the student's mind a story, situation, or character he had previously experienced. For example, the teacher may present a few of Mark Twain's phrases, such as: "It got sort of lonesome, and so I went and set on the bank and listened to the current *swashing* along."

Another example might be Huck Finn's remark that

Everything was dead quiet, and it looked late, and *smelt* late.

Or his use of simple, straightforward language:

My heart jumped up amongst my lungs.

Such illustrations may encourage a boy to read again *The Adventures of Huckleberry Finn,* perhaps with greater appreciation than the first time he read it.

The student might also become aware of the poetic sense in Huck as he says:

It's lovely to live on a raft. We had the sky up there, all *speckled* with stars, and we used to lay on our backs and look up at them, and discuss about whether they was *made* or only just *happened.*

In a rereading of certain passages, the student might notice Huck's use of *onomatopoeia:*

and now you'd hear the thunder let go with an awful crash, and then go *rumbling, grumbling, tumbling* down the sky

Perhaps a second or third reading of Twain's novel will make the student more aware of the meaning of Huck's wrestling match with his conscience as he debates whether or not to tell Jim's owner where his slave is. The student may now see more meaning in Huck's thought:

You can't pray a lie—I found that out.

And he may share Huck's decision to befriend Jim even at the risk of his own damnation: "All right, then, I'll go to hell."

The younger student might also have missed the following line (a clue to Huck's humanitarianism, his sympathy, and awareness of life's sadness):

Tom and me got to the edge of the hilltop, we looked away down into the village and could see three or four lights twinkling where there were sick folks, maybe.

Vocabulary and Essay Style

We do not consider the learning of "big" words the goal of vocabulary development, but from time to time there are students who want to increase their vocabularies and who consider the learning of big words important. This desire should not be dampened. Such students can profit greatly from reading Macaulay's *Life of Samuel Johnson.* From its vocabulary alone, high school students can learn the art of using an extensive vocabulary with style (the way we put sentences together).

Macaulay is an excellent model. A look at a few of his pages shows a broad, varied vocabulary: *discernible, morbid, propensity, procrastination, malady, indolent, desultory, opulent, effigy, haranguing, absolving, felons, torpid, squalid, ceruse, extolling, tawdry, munificently, sinecure, rancid, sycophancy, obloquy, septennial, turgid, emendation, scurrilous, triads, casuistry, garrulous.*

Selections from Macaulay's writings can be used to illustrate antithesis and balance in sentence structure—a way of emphasizing a statement by drawing attention not only to what is said but how it is said. For example, he describes Johnson as having "great muscular *strength* but much awkwardness and many *infirmities;* great *quickness* of parts, with a morbid propensity to *sloth* and *procrastination.*" Note the antithesis (contrast of ideas) in *strength* and *infirmities, quickness* and *sloth* or *procrastination. Antithesis* comes from Greek *anti,* against + *tithenai,* to set, and means to set against, to be opposite, as *good* is the antithesis of *evil.*

Contrasting ideas in a balanced construction can be illustrated by selections from Macaulay's *History of England:*

The Puritan hated bear-baiting, not because it gave *pain* to the bear, but because it gave *pleasure* to the spectators.

At the conclusion of his *Life of Samuel Johnson,* Macaulay further illustrates the use of antithesis:

The memory of other authors is kept alive by their works. But the memory of Johnson keeps many of his works alive.

The satirist Swift also uses antithesis effectively:

The two maxims of a great man at court are, always to keep his countenance, and never to keep his word.

Alexander Pope, the master of the epigrammatic couplet (an epigram is sharp, short, and pithy), uses antithesis to express contrasting ideas in short, unadorned words:

To err is human; to forgive, divine.

There is, of course, virtue in short words, and we do not recommend the learning of sesquipedalian words (Horace's term for a long word) just for the sake of learning them. Samuel Johnson sometimes favored big words (as in his novel *Rasselas*) and did not avoid using them when the occasion arose. Macaulay in his biography notes Johnson's natural inclination to use long words and points out that many readers considered Johnson "a pompous pedant, who would never use a word of two syllables where it was possible to use a word of six."

Literary Allusions to the Classics

Prose and poetry are filled with allusions to Greek and Roman mythological and historical characters. In *Paradise Lost,* Milton refers to the Muse, Chaos, Jove, etc. In *The Mayor of Casterbridge,* Thomas Hardy includes classical allusions, such as "the ruined Coliseum," "Aeolian modulations," the "heads of Apollo and Diana in low relief." Knowledge of these allusions produces greater appreciation and enjoyment of an author's writings. Melville describes Billy Budd: "by *Jove*—lugging along his chest—*Apollo* with his portmanteau." The title of Eugene O'Neill's play *Mourning Becomes Electra* reminds us of Sophocles' play *Electra*—named after Electra, the daughter of Agamemnon.

In the following exercise the student covers the answers on the left and fills in the letter spaces after reading each mythological character's statement. Some students will recognize the character. Some may need further explanation of the statements. (Additional information on mythological characters is found on pages 271–274.)

This lesson helps the mature student take stock of his ability to recognize classical allusions. The student is not expected to know all the allusions listed here. Some characters will be well known, others vaguely familiar. Not all of this material should be presented at one time.

Instructions: The student covers the answers and writes the name of the character speaking.

Answers

Oedipus
1. Mother, I'm just as embarrassed as you are.
   O e d _ _ _ s

Sisyphus
2. I could have sworn that stone was up here last night.
   S i s _ _ _ _ s

Icarus
3. Look, Dad, no wings.
   I c _ _ _ s

Hermaphroditus
4. Some say I look like my mother, and some say that I look like my father.
   H e r _ _ _ _ _ _ _ _ u s

Hercules
5. Wow, does this place smell!
   H e r _ _ _ _ s

Narcissus
6. "I wonder who that beautiful creature is down there?" he reflected.
   N a r _ _ _ _ _ s

Procrustes
7. Try this bed for size.
   P r o _ _ _ _ _ _ s

Cassandra
8. I could say, "I told you so."
   C a s _ _ _ _ _ a

Pygmalion
9. That girl has a heart of stone.
   P y g _ _ _ _ _ n

Medusa	10. I just washed my hair and I can't do a thing with it!
	M e _ _ _ a
Ixion	11. Being a big wheel is no fun.
	I _ _ _ n
Tantalus	12. Give me a little boost, will you?
	T a n _ _ _ _ s
Scylla to Charybdis	13. I'll be the devil and you be the deep blue sea.
	S c _ _ _ a to C h _ _ _ _ _ _ s
Charon	14. What do you mean "Travel now, pay later"?
	C h _ _ _ n
Achilles	15. You really know how to hurt a guy!
	A c h _ _ _ _ s
Atlas	16. Why do I have to shoulder the burden alone?
	A _ _ _ s
Centaur	17. *Who's* leading a double life?
	C e n _ _ _ r
Adonis	18. Has anyone seen Venus?
	A d _ _ _ s
Agamemnon	19. Daughter, this hurts me more than it does you.
	A g _ _ _ _ _ _ n
Iphigenia	20. It's an ill wind that blows nobody good.
	I p h _ _ _ _ _ a

Teachers may read short articles to the class while the students make note of unfamiliar words. These words can be discussed in terms of their use in the sentence or their varied meanings. For example, an article might point out that a person or country has achieved a *pyrrhic* victory. At this point the teacher can explain how a pyrrhic victory is one gained at too great a cost, too many lives lost, etc.

Clippings of advertisements with accompanying pictures can be put on the bulletin board. The use of particular words, their connotation, and their effect in connection with the picture may be discussed by the class. For example, the classical name *Atlas* is found in an advertisement for tires, which shows a picture of Atlas holding up the world, thus connoting the product's strength and dependability. Other examples include *Mercury* cars, *Mars* candy bars, *Marathon* gasoline, a Buick *Electra*.

Literary and Historical Allusions

Writers allude to historical or literary characters (1) on the assumption that the reader knows the characters, (2) with the knowledge that the allusion carries with it rich associations, and (3) with the understanding that the allusion will have a dramatic effect, will clarify a point.

In literature we come across such expressions as a "Macedonian cry," "carrying coals to Newcastle," "the silent Sphinx," "the Left Bank," and "castles in Spain." A person may "go to Mecca," be "shanghaied," or "meet his Waterloo." In order to understand these expressions, the reader must have some knowledge about the place itself, and recognition of the metaphorical meaning of the expression.

Therefore, to point up the importance of literary allusions the teacher can discuss the great number and variety of these allusions. Some can be presented in the form of the lesson below to give the student a chance to check his own knowledge of these important characters and phrases. We include below some key biblical allusions.

Biblical Allusions

Instructions: In the space provided, the student writes what he thinks each of the following italicized Biblical words and phrases means. The student's answers need not agree exactly with the suggested answers given for each item.

1. *Adam* literally means <u>man</u>.

2. If you *cast your bread upon the waters* you <u>act charitably with no thought of personal gain</u>.

3. If you go *from Dan to Beersheba* you <u>go from one outermost extreme or limit to the other</u> (the northern and southern limits of biblical Palestine).

4. He was a *Goliath* means he was <u>a huge person, a giant</u> (like the one David slew).

5. When he got his low grades, he *saw the handwriting on the wall*. This means he realized <u>the inevitability of failure or disaster</u> (like the cryptic writing on the wall seen by Belshazzar and interpreted by Daniel).

6. He's another *Judas* means he is <u>treacherous</u> (as was Judas, who betrayed Christ).

7. *As poor as Lazarus* means <u>beggarly, poverty-stricken</u> (as the biblical beggar, Lazarus).

8. The ship was appropriately named *The Leviathan* because it was <u>huge</u> (like the biblical leviathan, a huge sea monster).

9. He's another *Methuselah* means he is <u>old</u> (like the biblical Methuselah, the oldest man).

10. He's a real *Nimrod* means he's <u>a hunting enthusiast</u> (like the biblical Nimrod, a great hunter).

11. Mary has *the patience of Job* means she has <u>great patience</u> (like the biblical Job, who patiently withstood great affliction).

12. In the quotation "Man does not live by *bread* alone," *bread* means <u>food</u>. (The quotation suggests that the spiritual nature of man also needs to be nourished.)

13. People who *kill the fatted calf* are <u>preparing a celebration feast, often to welcome guests</u>. (When the Prodigal Son returned home, his father had the fatted calf killed to celebrate the happy event.)

14. A person described as *a Daniel in the lion's den* is <u>one who overcomes</u> <u>disaster because of his great faith and courage</u> .

15. *An eye for an eye* refers to <u>returning punishment or injury as severe as</u> <u>that received</u> .

16. A *land of milk and honey* is <u>a region of happiness</u> . (The reference is to the Promised Land, Canaan.)

17. *Eden* means <u>Paradise, the Garden of Eden</u> .

18. *Golgotha* means <u>a place of burial; the place where the body of Christ</u> <u>was entombed</u> .

19. A place likened to *Sodom and Gomorrah* is a place of <u>corruption</u> <u>and vice</u> .

20. An *Ishmael* is <u>an outcast</u> . (In the Bible, Ishmael was Abraham's outcast son. Note also the wandering character in *Moby Dick*.)

21. A person described as accepting his *thirty pieces of silver* is <u>a betrayer, an</u> <u>informer for a price</u> (like the apostle Judas who was bribed to betray Christ).

22. A *potter's field* is <u>ground for burying people with no friends or money</u> (burial ground said to be bought by Judas with his bribe).

23. A *Delilah* is a (check the correct answer)
    a. scolding woman. ___
    b. a temptress. <u>X</u>
(She successfully tempted Samson.)

24. *Lucifer* literally means <u>light-bearer</u> (in the Bible, originally the brightest angel. A match is also called a Lucifer.)

25. The *olive branch* is a symbol of <u>peace</u> (the branch the dove brought to Noah showing that the waters were receding).

26. A *Macedonian cry* is <u>a cry for help</u> (from St. Paul's vision of the need for him to go to help the Macedonian people).

27. An *Armaggedon* is <u>any great, final battle</u> (from the biblical description of the final great battle between good and evil at the end of time).

28. A *pharisee* is a person who
    a. considers himself less deserving than others. ___
    b. thinks he is much better than others. <u>X</u>
(The haughty Pharisees, members of a strict religious sect, were said to be very self-righteous.)

29. A *pillar of salt* refers to <u>a punishment</u> . (Lot's wife was turned into a pillar of salt for disobeying an order.)

30. *Doomsday* means <u>last day, Judgment Day</u> .

Mythological Character Quiz

The following lesson emphasizes the importance of being familiar with significant proper nouns found in literature and in history.
    The students circle the appropriate letter. At the end of the lesson the

257

teacher may furnish the answers and discuss the meaning of certain words. Easier or harder proper nouns may be used.

Answers

1. *Mars* represents

c   a. hate.   b. love.   c. war.

2. A *Gordian* knot is

c   a. a deep hole.   b. a crooked branch.   c. a tough problem.

3. *Ulysses* is a symbol of man's

b   a. joy.   b. wanderings.   c. fear.

4. *Mercury* represents

c   a. bad luck.   b. fire.   c. speed.

5. *Pandora's box* represents

b   a. happiness.   b. evils.   c. love.

6. *Pandemonium* indicates

c   a. pleasure.   b. disease.   c. disorder.

7. *Amazons* are

b   a. precious jewels.   b. women warriors.   c. colored stones.

8. *Ambrosia* is

a   a. food of the gods.   b. a thick woods.   c. a shady glen.

Associations in Literature

The teacher may use the following lesson to emphasize the importance of association in learning vocabulary. He might point out that certain people's names bring the name of their partner to mind. Thus, we seldom see the name *Romeo* without thinking of *Juliet,* or vice versa.

Depending on the students' background and interests, the teacher might present one of two closely associated literary characters and ask the student to supply the other. Initial letter clues can be furnished as needed. Many of the following pairs are found in English and American literature.

Primarily, the lesson is meant to help the student remember a word by associating one word with another.

Answers

Cleopatra   1. Antony and Cl _____

Guinevere   2. Lancelot and Gu _____

Knights of   3. King Arthur and the Kn _____
  the Round Table   _____

Adonis   4. Venus and Ad _____

Apollo   5. Daphne and Ap _____

Isolde	6. Tristan and Is_____
Aeneas	7. Dido and Ae_____
Ophelia	8. Hamlet and Op_____
Pythias	9. Damon and Py_____
Icarus	10. Daedalus and Ic_____
Remus	11. Romulus and Re_____
Eurydice	12. Orpheus and Eu_____
Helen	13. Paris and He_____
Leander	14. Hero and Le_____
Penates	15. Lares and Pen_____
Psyche	16. Cupid and Ps_____
Charybdis	17. Scylla and Cha_____
Medea	18. Jason and Me_____
Medusa	19. Perseus and Me_____
Cressida	20. Troilus and Cr_____
Bathsheba	21. David and Ba_____
Beatrice	22. Dante and Be_____
Castor	23. Pollux and Ca_____
Jacob	24. Esau and Ja_____
Philemon	25. Baucis and Ph_____
Sam Weller	26. Mr. Pickwick and S_____ W
Queequeeg	27. Ishmael and Q_____
Albert	28. Queen Victoria and Al_____
Sancho Panza	29. Don Quixote and S_____ P
Brutus	30. Cassius and Br_____
Pocahontas	31. Capt. John Smith and Po_____
Priscilla	32. John Alden and Pr_____
Roxanne	33. Cyrano and Ro_____
Caliban	34. Ariel and Ca_____
Lynette	35. Gareth and Ly_____

Note: These items can also be reversed; e.g., Liza Doolittle and Professor
H_____. Note also that the teacher may use the above form to present
character pairs from stories read by younger students. Here are a few
examples:

Answers

Jill	1. Jack and J_____
Judy	2. Punch and J_____
Huck Finn	3. Tom Sawyer and H_____ F
Delilah	4. Samson and D_____
Mr. Hyde	5. Dr. Jekyll and M_____ H
Watson	6. Holmes and W_____
Tiny Tim	7. Bob Cratchit and T_____ T
Jim	8. Huck Finn and J_____
Chingachgook	9. Hawkeye and C_____
Little John	10. Robin Hood and L_____ J
Captain Hook	11. Peter Pan and Cap_____ H
Jim Hawkins	12. Long John Silver and J_____ H
Marley	13. Scrooge and M_____
Pussy Cat	14. The Owl and the P_____ C

Books may also be listed:

Willows	1. The Wind in the W_____
Beauty	2. Black B_____
Big Woods	3. The Little House in the B_____ W_____

Note: These exercises are not aimed to teach these names to those who have never heard of them. They are rather reminders, revivers of dim memories, and occasionally stimulators to find out more about these persons. Sometimes we may remember one of a pair but can't remember the other.

Nursery Rhyme Quiz

The elementary teacher might test the student's recall of words used in nursery rhymes and other poems and stories.

1. The _king_ was in the counting house.
2. A ten o'clock _scholar_.
3. Simple Simon met a _pieman_.
4. The _sheep's_ in the meadow.
5. Little Miss Muffet sat on a _tuffet_.
6. Little Jack Horner sat in a _corner_.
7. _Pussy's_ in the well.
8. All the king's _horses_ and all the king's _men_.
9. Old King Cole was a _merry_ old soul.
10. She lays eggs for _gentlemen_.
11. There was an old woman who lived in a _shoe_.
12. _Jack_ _Spratt_ could eat no fat.
13. _Jack_ and _Jill_ went up the hill.
14. Little Bo Peep has lost her _sheep_.
15. Mary, Mary quite _contrary_.
16. To _market_ to _market_ to buy a fat pig.
17. Three little kittens lost their _mittens_.
18. The cupboard was _bare_.

Rhymes about Planets

Although rhymes, such as nursery rhymes, are generally used in reading activities, the teacher may also use rhymes to teach or recall words used in other subjects such as health, history, and science. Some astronomy examples are given below.

Answers

	1. If you look up at the stars
Mars	You may see the planet _ _ _ _.
	2. Mercury's closest to the sun,
	Earth is the third closest one.
	The beautiful planet in between us
Venus	The Greeks called Hesperus and we call _ _ _ _ _.

	3. Particles form a circular pattern
Saturn	Around the giant planet S _ _ _ _ _.
	4. The big planet Saturn is noted for its ring,
Jupiter	But the biggest planet, _ _ _ _ _ _ _, is named for a king.
	5. This big planet is hard to see.
Neptune	_ _ _ _ _ _ _ is named for the god of the sea.
Pluto	6. Going outward from the sun, _ _ _ _ _ is the farthest one.
	7. The sun is a star which is large and bright,
satellite	But the moon is only a _ _ _ _ _ _ _ _ _.
	8. The galaxy we live in day by day
Milky Way	is known to us as the _ _ _ _ _ _ _ _.

Choosing the Right Word

Students in composition classes can often learn from models of excellence by noting the words experts use to express an idea, set a mood, a time, a locale, etc. Using selections from literature, the teacher can give students an opportunity to choose concrete, vivid words.

Below are some quotations from *Silas Marner* in the form of a multiple-choice exercise. The student underlines the word he thinks the author used, then checks the answer. Other choices are not necessarily wrong, merely different from those selected by the author. Thus, the teacher may wish to discuss with the class the appropriateness of the author's choice of words to fit the character, setting, mood, etc.

Answers

hummed	1. In the days when the spinning wheel *hummed, droned, sang, buzzed* busily in the farmhouse....
bosom	2. deep in the *center, bosom, heart, core* of the hills, certain
pallid	*wan, pallid, pale, colorless,* undersized men, who, by the
brawny	side of the *strong, muscular, brawny* countryfolk, looked like
remnants	the *fragments, remnants, remainders, residue* of a disinherited race
fiercely	3. The shepherd's dog barked *fiercely, viciously, threateningly* when one of these alien-looking men appeared on the upland....
protuberant	4. these large, brown *bulging, protuberant* eyes in Silas Marner's pale face really saw nothing
rude	5. for the *rude, rustic, crude* mind with difficulty associates the
benignity	idea of power and *goodness, kindness, benignity*
barren	6. Not that it was one of those *sterile, bare, barren, poor* parishes lying on the outskirts of civilization....
vibrations	7. It was never reached by the *blare, vibrations, tooting, call* of the coach horn.

From Emily Brontë's *Wuthering Heights:*

sagacity

1. Oh, indeed! Well, then, I must trust to my own *ingenuity, wisdom, sagacity, discernment.*

degradation

2. He bore his *degradation, disgrace, ignominy, humiliation* pretty well at first, because Cathy taught him what she learnt, and worked or played with him in the fields.

embellishment

3. She gazed concernedly at the dusky fingers she held in her own, and also at her dress, which she feared had gained no *ornament, adornment, embellishment, decoration* from its contact with his.

amiable

4. I urged my companion to hasten now and show his *engaging, charming, lovable, amiable* humor, and he willingly obeyed.

vociferating

5. He entered *bellowing, howling, roaring, vociferating* oaths dreadful to hear and caught me in the act of stowing his son away in the kitchen cupboard.

From Charlotte Brontë's *Jane Eyre:*

audacious

1. but, on hearing this strange and *fearless, bold, audacious, undaunted* declaration, she ran nimbly up the stair

tumult

2. A quarter of an hour passed before lessons again began, during which the schoolroom was in a glorious *uproar, tumult, turmoil, turbulence.*

caprice

3. but harsh *caprice, fancy, humor, whimsy* laid me under no obligation

assiduous

4. and, when the tray came, she proceeded to arrange the cups, spoons, etc., with *assiduous, diligent, attentive, industrious* celerity

tenacious

5. Eight years! you must be *resolute, persistent, pertinacious, tenacious* of life.

From Mark Twain's *The Adventures of Huckleberry Finn:*

whale

1. He used to always *whip, beat, hit, whale* me when he was sober and could get his hands on me.

hifalut'n

2. Who told you you might meddle with such *stuck-up, pompous, haughty, hifalut'n* foolishness, hey?

skiff

3. So he watched out for me one day in the spring, and catched me, and took me up the river about three miles in a *skiff, boat, canoe, raft.*

palavering

4. Well, all right, don't stand there *chattering, prattering, talking, palavering* all day, but about with you and see if there's a fish on the lines for breakfast.

brash

5. When I got to camp I warn't feeling very *impetuous, hasty, brash, rash;* there warn't much sand in my craw.

262

Authors and Characters

The teacher can point up the importance of knowing proper nouns by noting that authors are often associated with certain characters, either fictitious or otherwise, that appear in their books. In the lesson below, the student matches the author with the character portrayed in his book. In each exercise the student writes in the blank one of the three authors listed on the left.

Boswell
James   _Boswell_ and Johnson
Milton

Morley
Strachey   _Strachey_ and Queen Victoria
Huxley

Anderson
Shaw   _Shaw_ and St. Joan
Coward

Marlowe
Coleridge   _Shakespeare_ and Othello
Shakespeare

Lewis
Dickens   _Lewis_ and Arrowsmith
Twain

Wouk
Steinbeck   _Wouk_ and Captain Queeg
Buck

Hawthorne
Melville   _Melville_ and Captain Ahab
Thoreau

Stevenson
Dickens   _Dickens_ and Micawber
Thackeray

Dickens
Stevenson   _Dickens_ and Carton
Dumas

Cather
Brontë   _Brontë_ and Heathcliff
Conrad

Kipling
Doyle   _Doyle_ and Sherlock
Wells

Conrad
Lewis   _Lewis_ and Babbit
Kipling

263

Shakespeare Crossword

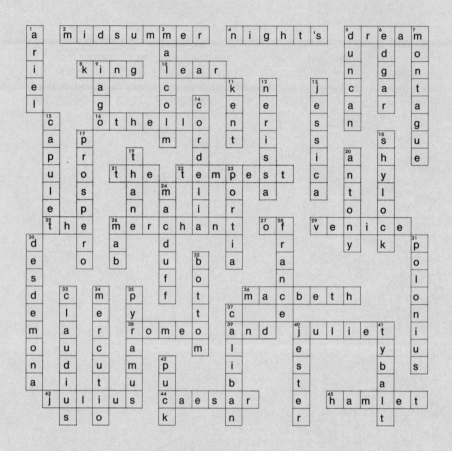

Shakespeare Crossword Clues

Across

1-2- 4-5	A story of fairies and magic love potions
8-10	A tragedy of old age
16	The story of a man ruined by suspicion
21-22	The tale of a king and an enchanted island
25-26- 27-29	Shows the evils of borrowing money
36	Concerns a woman's ambition for her husband
38-39- 40	A pair of star-crossed lovers
43-44	The story of an emperor betrayed
45	The Prince of Denmark

264

Down

1   An airy spirit in 21-22 across
3   A Scottish noble in 36 across
5   He died a horrible death in a Scottish castle
at the hands of 36 across
6   Gloucester's "good" son in 8-10 across
7   The "Hatfield" family of Verona (38-39-40 across)
9   A sergeant who lied to his commander about
the latter's wife in 16 across
11   He kept his loyalty to his sovereign even after the king in 8-10 across
banished him
12   Portia told her just about everything, in 25-26-27-29 across
13   Daughter of "Moneybags," in 25-26-27-29 across
14   Lear's only loyal daughter
15   The "McCoy" family of Verona, in 38-39-40 across
17   The banished Duke of Milan, a first-rate
magician, in 21-22 across
18   Demanded his pound of flesh in 25-26-27-29 across
19   A minor Scottish noble; 36 across was also one
20   He made a funeral speech with a double meaning
in 43-44 across
23   As a judge, she was just as wise as Daniel—at first
24   25-26-27-29 across should have been afraid of him but when he found out,
it was too late
26   The bringer of dreams to folk in 38-39-40 across
28   The country at war with England in many of Shakespeare's plays
30   Her husband was tricked into killing her,
in 16 across
31   His habit of listening in on private conversations
was cured by 45 across
32   The wee folk in 1-2-4-5 across make an ass of him
before the play is over
33   45 across confers with a ghost about removing
this king from the throne
34   A loyal member of Verona's "Hatfield" clan
who is killed by 41 down
35   The lover (in the play within the play)
in 1-2-4-5 across
37   The deformed servant of 17 down
40   Almost every old king had one for entertainment
41   A nasty-tempered "McCoy" who gets his comeuppance before curtain
fall in 38-39-40 across
42   A fairy in the service of Oberon, in 1-2-4-5 across

Recognizing Characters from Shakespeare

In the lesson sample below, the student tests his knowledge of
Shakespearean characters by naming the character suggested by the

description, or by using the clues to complete the crossword puzzle.

To make it easier, initial letters (or additional letters) may be included, as in the exercise below. Abler students may not need the letter clues.

Answers

Duncan	1. He was killed in a Scottish castle. D _ _ _ _ _
Lear	2. A king easily flattered by his daughters. L _ _ _
Othello	3. He was ruined by suspicion. O _ _ _ _ _ _
Shylock	4. Threatened to cut off some flesh. S _ _ _ _ _ _
Romeo & Juliet	5. "Star-crossed lovers." R _ _ _ _ and J _ _ _ _ _
Hamlet	6. Prince of Denmark. H _ _ _ _ _
Macbeth	7. He killed to get the Scottish throne. M _ _ _ _ _ _
Portia	8. A lady lawyer. P _ _ _ _ _
Antony	9. He made a funeral speech. A _ _ _ _ _
Polonius	10. Killed while eavesdropping. P _ _ _ _ _ _ _
Banquo	11. A ghostly guest at the banquet. B _ _ _ _ _
Jaques	12. A philosopher in the woods. J _ _ _ _ _
Prospero	13. First-class magician on an island. P _ _ _ _ _ _ _
Ariel	14. A magician's sprightly servant. A _ _ _ _
Capulet	15. Juliet's family name. C _ _ _ _ _ _
Iago	16. Ruined a general by making him suspicious. I _ _ _
Caesar	17. Stabbed by a good friend. C _ _ _ _ _
Falstaff	18. A gay, robust companion. F _ _ _ _ _ _ _
Caliban	19. Ugly servant on an island. C _ _ _ _ _ _
Cassius	20. A fellow with "a lean and hungry look." C _ _ _ _ _ _

A Vocabulary of Literary Terms

Any evaluation of literature, made either by the student or by a professional critic, is more understandable if the student is familiar with the technical vocabulary of literary criticism and analysis. The items below deal with some of these terms and can be used as both a diagnostic and a teaching device.

Instructions: The student checks one of three choices. Notes in parentheses after certain items are for the teacher's convenience and may be used in class discussion. The teacher should discuss the key words after the lesson.

1. A *ballad* is
   a. ___ meter
   b. _X_ a song (also a narrative poem)
   c. ___ a rhyme scheme

2. A *motif* is
   a. ___ a play acted out
   b. ___ a subplot
   c. _X_ dominant theme (*Romeo and Juliet* has a love motif.)

266

3. A *simile* is
   a. ___ a portrait
   b. _X_ a direct comparison (using *like* or *as*)
   c. ___ a theme

4. A *paradox* is
   a. ___ a rephrasing
   b. _X_ a seeming inconsistency (as in Wordsworth's statement that "The Child is father of the Man")
   c. ___ a strict belief

5. *Alliteration* is (by example)
   a. ___ demise, surprise, realize
   b. _X_ longing, lingering, look (repetition of beginning consonant: "Nor cast one *l*onging, *l*ingering *l*ook behind?" — Gray)
   c. ___ bounce, announce, renounce

6. *Assonance* is
   a. ___ use of the same endings
   b. ___ using words that imitate sounds
   c. _X_ repetition of the same vowel sounds (often in consecutive words: *arm, farm, alarm*)

7. *Onomatopoeia*
   a. ___ unrhymed poetry
   b. ___ an Italian sonnet
   c. _X_ words that imitate sounds (In addition to words such as *buzz, whiz, fizz, murmur,* etc., note words such as *Minnehaha,* Indian name for Laughing Water. Onomatopoetic words set a mood through sound, as in the famous lines by Tennyson in "The Princess": "The moan of doves in immemorial elms, / And murmuring of innumerable bees.")

8. A *threnody* is
   a. _X_ a funeral song (from Greek *threnos,* a lament, and *oide,* a song or ode. Note other *ode* words: ode, mel*ody,* rhaps*ody,* par*ody.*)
   b. ___ a limerick
   c. ___ a love poem

9. *Free verse*
   a. ___ has no rhythm or rhyme
   b. _X_ has neither rhyme nor consistent length (It has rhythms that change with the mood.)
   c. ___ has a regular rhythm pattern

10. *Metonymy*
    a. _X_ The pot boils (using the container for the thing contained)
    b. ___ Man bites dog
    c. ___ Love is blind

11. *Oxymoron*
    a. ___ a brooding storm
    b. _X_ broadly ignorant (words of opposite meaning used together)
    c. ___ hard as nails

12. *Blank verse*
    a. ___ has rhyme but no rhythm
    b. _X_ is unrhymed verse with a meter (the meter is iambic pentameter)

13. *Apostrophe* is
   a. ___ using rhyming couplets
   b. _X_ a kind of personification
   c. ___ a kind of meter

14. An *allegory* is
   a. _X_ an extended metaphor (as Bunyan's *Pilgrim's Progress*)
   b. ___ a refrain or chant
   c. ___ a short stanza

15. An *elegy*
   a. ___ is a lyrical ballad
   b. ___ describes a battle
   c. _X_ laments or honors the dead ("Each in his narrow cell forever laid, / The rude forefathers of the hamlet sleep."—Gray)

16. An *epic* is
   a. _X_ a long poem about a hero's deeds (as *Beowulf* and *Paradise Lost*)
   b. ___ a funeral song
   c. ___ a short poem in free verse

17. *Hyperbole* is
   a. ___ understatement
   b. ___ repetition for emphasis
   c. _X_ exaggeration for effect

18. *Personification* is
   a. ___ characterization
   b. ___ using conversational dialogue
   c. _X_ representing inanimate things as living ("There is a Reaper whose name is Death."—Longfellow)

Oxymorons

One of the literary devices writers use to get an effect is the *oxymoron*. The teacher might use the following form to introduce this figure of speech in which words of opposite meaning are used together.

Have you ever used an *oxymoron*? Maybe you have. Read this phrase: *sweet sorrow*. What's strange about it? For one thing, we don't normally use *sweet* and *sorrow* together. In *Romeo and Juliet*, Juliet says "Parting is such *sweet sorrow*."

Here's another oxymoron: *cruel kindness*. Does it make sense? (A mother may pamper a child and weaken its character.) Many writers use oxymorons for the effect gained from combining contradictory or incongruous (out of harmony) words.

The word *oxymoron* comes from two Greek words, *oxys* (sharp) and *moros* (foolish); *moron* is a related word. So a combining of opposites such as *sharp* or *bright* with *foolish* or *dull* gives us the term *oxymoron*.

Perhaps you can make up some oxymorons or find them in your reading. You'll often find them in poetry. However, before you try writing some of your own, read the oxymorons listed below and check those that have some meaning for you.

___ thunderous silence
___ silent applause
___ orderly confusion
___ studied imprecision
___ fatiguing leisure
___ broadly ignorant
___ laborious indolence
___ a hotbed of apathy
___ sad laughter
___ harrowing calm
___ wonderfully stupid
___ dictatorial democracy
___ open disguise
___ tainted sweetness
___ arrogant simplicity
___ prudent failure
___ narrowly knowledgeable
___ arrogantly humble
___ manageable diversity
___ orderly chaos out of
    disorganized confusion
___ dynamic bore
___ hopeful pessimist

___ successful failure
___ trained incapacity
___ exquisite torture
___ priceless unessentials
___ bittersweet
___ learned ignorance
___ gentle strength
___ wasteful thrift
___ humble pride
___ restless quiet
___ loving hate
___ gilt-edged insecurity
___ bitter fun
___ planned chaos
___ a living corpse
___ sophisticated irrelevancies
___ creative anxiety
___ sublime folly
___ planned spontaneity
___ disciplined relaxation
___ impressive limitations
___ deliberate haste
___ pointedly foolish

Not-So-Famous Second Lines of Poetry

We often look at a famous line of poetry or a well-known phrase as an entity in itself and neglect the line that follows it. For example, we often hear Ben Franklin's aphorism

Experience keeps a dear school

without the second, important thought:

But fools will learn in no other.

In the exercises below (many of which are Pope's couplets) the student covers the often-neglected second line (in parentheses), reads the first, better-known quotation, and then tries to give the lesser-known line. The teacher might use the overhead projector to present the lesson, masking the second line and asking for the student's oral response.

1. A little learning is a dangerous thing;
   (Drink deep, or taste not the Pierian spring.)
      —Pope

2. True wit is nature to advantage dressed—
   (What oft was thought, but ne'er so well expressed.)
      —Pope

3. A thing of beauty is a joy forever:
   (Its loveliness increases; it will never
   Pass into nothingness.)
       —Keats

4. Be not the first by whom the new are tried,
   (Nor yet the last to lay the old aside.)
       —Pope

5. True ease in writing comes from art, not chance,
   (As those move easiest who have learned to dance.)
       —Pope

6. Variety's the very spice of life,
   (That gives it all its flavor.)
       —Cowper

7. Damn with faint praise, assent with civil leer,
   (And, without sneering, teach the rest to sneer.)
       —Pope

8. Some praise at morning what they blame at night,
   (But always think the last opinion right.)
       —Pope

9. And what is so rare as a day in June?
   (Then, if ever, come perfect days.)
       —James Russell Lowell

10. Cowards die many times before their deaths;
    (The valiant never taste of death but once.)
        —Shakespeare

11. Men must be taught as if you taught them not,
    (And things unknown proposed as things forgot.)
        —Pope

12. There is a tide in the affairs of men,
    Which, taken at the flood, leads on to fortune;
    (Omitted, all the voyage of their life
    Is bound in shallows and in miseries.)
        —Shakespeare

13. Hope springs eternal in the human breast:
    (Man never is, but always to be blest.)
        —Pope

14. But love is blind,
    (and lovers cannot see
    The pretty follies that themselves commit.)
        —Shakespeare

15. Worth makes the man, and want of it the fellow;
    (The rest is all but leather or prunella.)
        —Pope

Note: The teacher might also point out that many second lines are more famous than the first:

Errors, like straws, upon the surface flow;
He that would search for pearls must dive below.
    —Dryden

In the Spring a livelier iris changes on the burnished dove;
In the Spring a young man's fancy lightly turns to thoughts of love.
  —Tennyson

A vile encomium doubly ridicules;
There's nothing blackens like the ink of fools.
  —Pope

And still they gazed, and still the wonder grew,
That one small head could carry all he knew.
  —Goldsmith

Know then this truth, enough for man to know,
"Virtue alone is happiness below."
  —Pope

Know then thyself, presume not God to scan
The proper study of mankind is man.
  —Pope

Good-nature and good-sense must ever join
To err is human, to forgive divine.
  —Pope

All seems infected that th' infected spy,
As all looks yellow to the jaundic'd eye.
  —Pope

The hungry judges soon the sentence sign,
And wretches hang that jurymen may dine.
  —Pope

Some Mythological Information

1. *Achilles*   This Greek warrior (hero of the *Iliad*) was invulnerable except in the heel, where he was shot by Paris's arrow. A person's weakness is often called his *Achilles heel*.

2. *Adonis*   A handsome youth loved by Venus, Adonis was killed on a boar hunt. A flower sprang up from his blood—the *anemone,* wind flower (from the Greek *anemos,* wind, as in *anemometer,* a wind gauge).

3. *Aeolus*   The king of the winds, viceroy of the gods. (Note *Aeolian Harp,* one of the foremost symbols of Romantic poetry.)

4. *Aesculapius*   The god of medical skills and healing.

5. *Agamemnon*   Commander in chief of the Greek army attacking Troy, he agreed to sacrifice his daughter in exchange for a good wind for his ships held in port by a calm.

6. *Ajax*   This Greek hero of the Trojan War was second only to Achilles in brave deeds.

7. *Amazons*   Big, warlike, mythical maidens with the strength and battle skill of men.

8. *Antaeus* This giant, son of *Ge* (or *Gaea*) Mother Earth (note *geography, geology,* etc.), possessed unconquerable strength as long as he was touching the earth. Hercules discovered this, lifted him into the air, and overcame him.

9. *Arachne* The proud Arachne was challenged by the goddess Athena to a weaving contest. Punished for her boldness, she was changed into a spider. *Arachne* is the Greek word for spider or web. Note also English *arachnid*—an invertebrate of a class including mites, scorpions, and spiders. Arachnids have eight legs, insects have six.

10. *Argonauts* The Argonauts were led by Jason in search of the Golden Fleece. Argonauts are literally "sailors of the Argo" (from the Latin *nauta,* sailor).

11. *Atalanta* Atalanta, a swift runner, promised to marry the one who beat her in a footrace. Hippomenes challenged her, taking along three golden apples which he tossed near her. Since she could not resist stopping to pick them up, she lost the race.

12. *Atlas* He was condemned to hold up the world on his shoulders.

13. *Aurora* The goddess of the dawn. (Often pictured as driving a chariot drawn by swift horses to announce the arrival of the sun.) The *aurora borealis* is the northern lights.

14. *Bacchus* The god of wine, also called Dionysus.

15. *Capricorn* Capricornus, the goat, a sign of the zodiac ("horned goat," from the Latin *capri,* goat, + *cornu,* horn).

16. *Cassandra* This daughter of King Priam of Troy had the gift of prophecy, but the curse of not having anyone believe her prophecies about the doom of Troy. Hence a Cassandra is a person who prophesies disaster but is not heeded.

17. *Castor and Pollux* Castor was a tamer of horses and Pollux was known for his boxing skill. They were also known as *Gemini* (twins) or *Dioscouri* (from the Greek *Dios,* Zeus + *kouros,* son, boy).

18. *Centaur* A wild, mythological creature, half man and half horse.

19. *Cerberus* This was the three-headed dog that guarded the entrance of Hades.

20. *Ceres* The goddess of grain. Note the word *cereal.*

21. *Chaos* The vast, confused matter before the formation of the universe. The opposite of Chaos is *Cosmos* (order).

22. *Charon* For a fee, Charon carried the dead across the River Styx in the lower world. For this reason the ancients put a coin in the mouth of the corpse.

23. *Cupid* The son of Venus, goddess of love, often went about blindfolded, aiming his arrows indiscriminately.

24. *Cyclops* The Cyclopses were a race of giants, with only one eye in the middle of their forehead. *Cyclops* means round eye. Note *cycle, bicycle, epicycle, encyclical* (a letter that goes around).

25. *Diana* The goddess of the moon.

26. *Dionysus*   Dionysus, also called Bacchus, was the god of wine. He was feted at the Dionysian revels or festivals.

27. *Gemini*   Pollux and Castor, the twin sons of Zeus and also a constellation and the third sign of the zodiac. *Geminus* is Latin for *twin*.

28. *Hercules*   The strongest man on earth, who had to perform twelve great labors after having killed his wife in a fit of madness. One of Hercules' twelve labors was to clean the Augean stables in one day. The stables, which housed 3,000 oxen, hadn't been cleaned for 30 years. Hercules changed the course of the rivers Alpheus and Peneus and let the water run through the stables.

29. *Hermaphroditus*   He inherited the beauty of his father Hermes (Mercury) and his mother Aphrodite (Venus). A nymph fell in love with him and asked the gods to join them together as one. Hence he retained the characteristics of each sex.

30. *Icarus*   One of the first aviators, and the son of the skilled architect Daedalus, who constructed a pair of wings for Icarus and himself. Despite his father's warning, Icarus flew too close to the sun, the wax holding the wings melted, and Icarus fell into the sea and drowned.

31. *Iphigenia*   Obedient daughter of Agamemnon who knew her father planned to have her slain in exchange for a good sailing wind.

32. *Ixion*   When Ixion tried to steal Zeus's wife, Hera, Zeus punished him by having his hands and feet tied to a big wheel.

33. *Jove*   Another word for the Roman god Jupiter.

34. *Mars*   The god of war.

35. *Medusa*   A glance at this lady turned a person into stone. Her head was covered with snakes instead of hair.

36. *Mentor*   He was Ulysses' old, trusted friend and his son's teacher and trusted advisor (his *mentor*).

37. *Midas*   Bacchus gave King Midas his foolish wish—that everything he touched would turn to gold. Since even his food and drink turned to gold, he soon asked to be rid of the *Midas touch.*

38. *Morpheus*   The son of Somnus (Sleep) and the god of dreams. Morpheus is related to Greek *morphe* (form, shape) because of the shapes or forms he presents to the dreamer.

39. *Narcissus*   He fell in love with his own reflection in a pool, stayed there gazing at it until he died, and changed into a flower—the narcissus. Note also the Narcissus complex—love of one's self.

40. *Nemesis*   The goddess of retribution. She also measured out happiness and misery to each person.

41. *Neptune*   Neptune was the god of the sea.

42. *Oedipus*   Unwittingly, he married his own mother, Jocasta. As an infant he had been left on a mountain with his feet pierced and tied together. His name, Oedipus, means swollen foot, from Greek *oidipous* (club foot). From *pous, podos*, foot, we get bi*pod*, tri*pod*, pseudo*pod* (false foot). Note Sophocles' *Oedipus the King.*

43. *Orpheus* Orpheus was the son of the Muse Calliope (note the instrument of the same name). He charmed gods and men with his musical ability, even getting past the gates of Hades to visit his beloved Eurydice. He is often represented as playing the lyre.

44. *Pan* The god of the forest, flocks, and shepherds, who is often portrayed as playing a pipe or reed.

45. *Pandora* In mythology, the first woman on earth. She became curious and opened a box from heaven which released all the evils into the world. Only Hope remained in the box. Pandora means "all-gifted" (from Greek *pan*, all + *doron*, gift).

46. *Paris* Paris abducted Helen and took her to Troy. For revenge, the Greek chiefs attacked Troy, beginning the Trojan War.

47. *Pegasus* Mythological winged horse that flew to the heavens and is now a constellation.

48. *Penelope* She was Ulysses' faithful, patient wife who waited many years for the hero's return.

49. *Phobos* The god of fear, the son and attendant of Mars, god of war. *Phobos* is Greek for *fear* (fear accompanies war). Note also that Phobos still attends Mars. It is one of the moons of Mars. Note the various fears: hydro*phobia*, acro*phobia*, claustro*phobia*, agora*phobia*, etc.

20. *Pluto* The god of the underworld.

51. *Procrustes* In Greek his name means "the stretcher." He made his victims "fit" his bed either by stretching the short ones or by lopping the limbs off the tall ones.

52. *Prometheus* Prometheus and his brother Epimetheus had the job of creating man and the animals and furnishing them with the means of self-preservation—the gifts of speed, strength, etc. Epimetheus gave all his gifts to the animals and had none left for man. So Prometheus stole fire from heaven and gave it to man.

53. *Pygmalion* He fell in love with a statue he had made. The statue came to life. Note Shaw's play *Pygmalion* and the musical version, *My Fair Lady*.

54. *Scylla and Charybdis* Scylla, a mythical monster on one side, and Charybdis, a treacherous whirlpool on the other, menaced ships sailing the narrow strait between them.

55. *Sisyphus* This greedy king of Corinth was punished in the lower world by having to roll a large stone uphill. As he reached the top it would roll back down again.

56. *Tantalus* This king's punishment after death was to have a great thirst and stand in a lake whose water receded each time he tried to drink. Fruit which hung just above his head was always just out of his reach. Note the word *tantalize*, to tease.

57. *Unicorn* This mythological creature resembled a horse with a single long horn in the middle of its forehead (from the Latin *unus*, one + *cornu*, horn).

58. *Vulcan* The god of fire and the blacksmith for the gods.

13

Using
the
Dictionary

What a Dictionary Tells You

Word Entries begin in bold black type. Proper nouns are capitalized. Other words begin with small letters. The first letter of the entry extends into the margin for easy location.

Other Forms of the word may include verb tenses, unusual spellings for plurals, and comparative forms of adjectives. This example shows principal parts of the verb *alembicate*.

Pronunciation, given in phonetic symbols, appears immediately after the word entries. Sometimes several correct pronunciations are listed. This dictionary has a key to its phonetic symbols at the bottom of each right-hand page, and more detailed explanations at the front of the book.

Parts of Speech notations describe the word's grammatical use. Words that may be used as more than one part of speech are defined accordingly. The parts of speech are abbreviated, as in *adj.* for *adjective* and *n.* for noun. Verbs are shown as transitive or intransitive by the initials *v.t.* and *v.i.*

Synonyms that have the same or nearly the same meaning as the word defined appear in a separate paragraph. This note gives the synonyms for the adjective form of *alert*.

Levels of Usage labels, such as *slang* and *informal*, tell whether the word is acceptable English usage. The meaning of the labels is explained at the front of the dictionary.

Usage Notes discuss spelling and grammar, and advise on how to use the word in speaking and writing.

---

a·lem·bic (ə lem'bik), *n.* **1.** a glass or metal container, formerly used in chemistry for distilling. **2.** something that transforms or refines: *Imagination is the alembic of the mind.* [< Medieval Latin *alambicus* < Arabic *al-'anbīq* the still < Late Greek *ámbīx, -īkos* alembic < Greek, vessel narrowing toward the brim]

ALEMBIC

Alembic (def. 1)

a·lem·bi·cate (ə lem'bə kāt), *v.t.,* **-cat·ed, -cat·ing.** to distill in an alembic.

A·len·çon lace (ə len'sən, -son), **1.** a fine needle-point lace made by hand in France.

a·lerce (ə lèrs'), *n.* **1.** a large pine that resembles the California redwood. **2.** the wood used by the Moors in their buildings, obtained from the sandarac tree of Morocco. [< Spanish *alerce* < Arabic *al-'arz* the cedar]

a·lert (ə lèrt'), *adj.* **1.** keen and watchful; wide-awake: *A good hunting dog is alert to every sound and movement in the field.* **2.** quick in action; nimble: *A sparrow is very alert in its movements.* —*n.* **1.** a signal warning of an attack by approaching enemy aircraft or other threatened danger. **2.** the period of time after this warning until the attack is over or the danger has passed: *The rest of the coast as far north as Massachusetts should stand by on a hurricane alert, the bureau said* (Wall Street Journal). **3.** a signal to troops, etc., to be ready for action. **on the alert,** watchful; ready at any instant for what is coming: *A sentry must be on the alert. The Government is on the alert and will take the necessary steps to maintain security and stability* (London Times). —*v.t.* **1.** to warn against an air attack, a hurricane, etc. **2.** to call to arms; notify (troops, etc.) to get ready for action. **3.** to make alert; warn: *Despite alerted anti-aircraft and fighter defenses, the Liberators pressed home low-level attack through oil fires and intense smoke, wrecking the refineries* (Time). [< French *alerte* < Italian *all'erta* on the watch]—**a·lert'ly,** *adv.*—**a·lert'ness,** *n.*

—**Syn.** *adj.* **1.** attentive, vigilant. See **watchful. 2.** brisk, active. —**Ant.** *adj.* **1.** heedless.

à l'es·pa·gnole (à les på nyōl'), *French.* in the Spanish style.

all-right (ôl'rīt'), *adj. U.S., Slang.* very good or excellent of its kind; very dependable: *Don't worry about him; he's an all-right fellow.*

all right, 1. without error; correct. **2.** yes: *All right. I'll come.* **3.** without doubt; certainly. **4.** in good health: *I was ill for a week, but I'm all right now.* **5.** satisfactory; acceptable: *The substitute material should be all right.*

➤ See **alright** for usage note.

al·right (ôl rit'), *adv. Informal.* all right.

➤ **All right** is the correct spelling of both the adjective phrase (*He is all right*) and the sentence adverb meaning yes, certainly (*All right, I'll come*). The spelling **alright** is not used in formal and in most informal writing. Occasionally it is found in advertising and in comic strips, but it is not as yet generally acceptable.

Definitions give the exact meanings of words. When a word has more than one meaning, the definitions are numbered. This dictionary lists the most common meaning first. Some dictionaries present definitions in historical order, beginning with the earliest-known meaning.

Illustrations clarify the definitions. A label shows which meaning of the word is being illustrated. Here, the drawing illustrates the first definition of the word *alembic*.

Derivations tell what language or languages a word comes from, and its meaning in the original language. The symbol < means *comes from*.

Examples point out how to use the word in actual phrases and sentences.

Phrases that include the key word but have special meanings of their own are explained separately.

Quotations from well-known authors or publications often illustrate the meaning of the word. The source of the quotation appears in parentheses.

Antonyms that have the opposite or nearly the opposite meaning to the word defined are included in many entries. *Heedless* is the antonym for the most common definition of *alert*.

Foreign Words and Phrases in common use are identified, and their pronunciation and translation given.

Cross References refer to additional information elsewhere. An arrow marks the note for attention.

Samuel Johnson, who published his *Dictionary* in 1755, says in the Preface, "I applied myself to the perusal of our writers . . . noting whatever might be of use to ascertain or illustrate any word or phrase. . . ." He goes on to say, "[I] do not *form*, but *register* the language. [I] do not teach men how they should think, but *relate* how they have hitherto expressed their thoughts."

The dictionary is more than the recorder of a word's meaning. It is in a sense the depository of man's labeled experiences, and as such is a useful instrument for the teaching of vocabulary. The dictionary gives information on word derivation, meaning, spelling, and pronunciation. Dictionary study increases the student's understanding of general, technical, and literary terms. It also supplies information on the formal and informal use of words, idioms, foreign words, proper nouns, and abbreviations.

A surprisingly large number of students get as far as college without knowing how to use a dictionary to its fullest extent to increase their vocabulary. Unfortunately, the definition of an unfamiliar word (or as much of it as the student cares to read) may be comprehended at the time of reading but quickly fade into obscurity unless the student, through careful analysis of the entire definition, can find sufficient keys to (1) understand it fully, (2) remember it, and most important, (3) use it intelligently.

On the opposite page is a sample dictionary page entitled "What a Dictionary Tells You." This unit will discuss the numbered parenthetical items on either side of the word entries in terms of how they might be taught. Accompanying exercises are intended to test the student's understanding of these items.

1: Word Entries

a·lem·bic (ə lem′bik), *n.* 1. a glass or metal container, formerly used in chemistry for distilling. 2. something that transforms or refines: *Imagination is the alembic of the mind.* [< Medieval Latin *alambicus* < Arabic *al-'anbīq* the still < Late Greek *ámbīx, -īkos* alembic < Greek, vessel narrowing toward the brim]

ALEMBIC

Alembic (def. 1)

a·lem·bi·cate (ə lem′bə kāt), *v.t.*, **-cat·ed, -cat·ing.** to distill in an alembic.

A·len·çon lace (ə len′sən, -son), 1. a fine needle-point lace made by hand in France.

It is important that students be able to find the entry they're looking for quickly. Recognition of word entries should come easily with a little practice, although knowledge of the system of entries will eliminate much trial-and-error searching.

Students should know, for example, that

1. all main entry words are listed in strict alphabetical order.

2. all entries are set in large, boldface type.

3. compound words are listed alphabetically according to the first word.

4. biographical entries are listed according to family name, and alphabetized, if necessary, by given name: *Jackson, Andrew,* followed by *Jackson, Bruce,* and *Jackson, Ralph.*

5. each variant spelling has its own entry in alphabetical order. If two variant spellings are alphabetically close to one another, they may appear together as a joint boldface entry. Variant spellings alphabetically close to the main-entry spelling and pronounced exactly like it are given at the end of the entry block in small boldface.
Example: **par·a·keet**...Also, **paraquet, paroquet, parrakeet, parroket.**
If the two entries are somewhat removed alphabetically, they are cross-referenced.

6. main entries may be single words, compounds, proper nouns, phrases, abbreviations, prefixes, suffixes, or roots.

7. main entries that are spelled alike but are different in meaning and origin (homographs) are entered separately and marked by superscript numbers.
Example: canon[1]
canon[2]

8. entries are syllabified by means of raised dots. The stressed syllable may be indicated by an accent mark ('), which replaces a syllable dot.

9. foreign entries are usually marked in a way that sets them off from English entries. The entry *au naturel* may be preceded by a double dagger (‡) or followed by *Fr* placed in brackets.

Using Guide Words

Although our sample page does not show them, each dictionary page contains two guide words in its top corners, indicating the first and last entries on the page. If, for example, a page contains the guide words *eternal* and *eulogy,* the reader will find *ethics* but not *evaluate.*

Students who need it can be provided with many different guide-word exercises like the sample shown here. Given these guide words and the pages on which they are found, the student is asked to indicate what page he would expect to find the words listed in the second column.

Guide Words and Page	Word	Page
flagpole—flat, 102	gimmick	132
flourishing—flush, 104	hayloft	143
genial—genus, 130	gentle	130
gild—give, 132	flamethrower	102
harmonica—haste, 140	hash	140
hawk—heading, 143	flush	104

a·lert (ə lèrt'), *adj.* 1. keen and watchful; wide-awake: *A good hunting dog is alert to every sound and movement in the field.* 2. quick in action; nimble: *A sparrow is very alert in its movements.*
—*n.* 1. a signal warning of an attack by approaching enemy aircraft or other threatened danger. 2. the period of time after this warning until the attack is over or the danger has passed: *The rest of the coast as far north as Massachusetts should stand by on a hurricane alert, the bureau said* (Wall Street Journal). 3. a signal to troops, etc., to be ready for action.
on the alert, watchful; ready at any instant for what is coming: *A sentry must be on the alert. The Government is on the alert and will take the necessary steps to maintain security and stability* (London Times).
—*v.t.* 1. to warn against an air attack, a hurricane, etc. 2. to call to arms; notify (troops, etc.) to get ready for action. 3. to make alert; warn: *Despite alerted anti-aircraft and fighter defenses, the Liberators pressed home low-level attack through oil fires and intense smoke, wrecking the refineries* (Time).
[< French *alerte* < Italian *all'erta* on the watch]—**a·lert'ly,** *adv.*—**a·lert'ness,** *n.*

When the same word can be used as more than one part of speech, the dictionary will list each definition alphabetically: adjective before noun, etc. Students should notice, for example, that the entry *alert* (above) has quite a different denotation as an adjective than it has as a noun. Should students be unable to distinguish what part of speech the word they are looking for is, they should compare its use in the illustrative sentences (in italics) that a dictionary often provides. If students are weak in parts-of-speech recognition, practicing with simple sentences may help them to learn this skill. Again, using *alert* as a noun, an adjective, and a verb, we can construct these sentences:

1. The *alerts* lasted ten minutes each.
2. The most *alert* boy was first to notice the smoke.
3. They *alerted* us of a change in plans.

We can ask ourselves the following questions:

1. Testing for the noun:
   Can we add *s* to the word and still be understood? (In other words, can we make the word plural?)

2. Testing for the adjective:
   Can we insert *more* or *most* before the word (or add the suffix *-er* or *-est*) and still make sense?

3. Testing for the verb:
   Can we add *ed* (or *ing*) to the word and still make sense? (In other words, can we add a verb inflection?)

Obviously, these tests are inconclusive, but they can often solve problems quickly when students are looking up a word in a dictionary.

a·lert (ə lėrt′), *adj.* **1.** keen and watchful; wide-awake: *A good hunting dog is alert to every sound and movement in the field.* **2.** quick in action; nimble: *A sparrow is very alert in its movements.*
—*n.* **1.** a signal warning of an attack by approaching enemy aircraft or other threatened danger. **2.** the period of time after this warning until the attack is over or the danger has passed: *The rest of the coast as far north as Massachusetts should stand by on a hurricane alert, the bureau said* (Wall Street Journal). **3.** a signal to troops, etc., to be ready for action.
on the alert, watchful; ready at any instant for what is coming: *A sentry must be on the alert. The Government is on the alert and will take the necessary steps to maintain security and stability* (London Times).
—*v.t.* **1.** to warn against an air attack, a hurricane, etc. **2.** to call to arms; notify (troops, etc.) to get ready for action. **3.** to make alert; warn: *Despile alerted anti-aircraft and fighter defenses, the Liberators pressed home low-level attack through oil fires and intense smoke, wrecking the refineries* (Time).
[< French *alerte* < Italian *all'erta* on the watch]—**a·lert′ly,** *adv.*—**a·lert′ness,** *n.*
—Syn. *adj.* **1.** attentive, vigilant. See **watchful. 2.** brisk, active. —Ant. *adj.* **1.** heedless.
à l'es·pa·gnole (á les pà nyŏl′), *French.* in the Spanish style.

Synonyms

Often the dictionary is of little or no help to some students because the definition of a word is harder than the word itself. What good is it, say students, if, in order to look up one word, you have to look up three more to understand the definition? For students with this kind of problem, many dictionary entries include synonyms (and antonyms). Teachers should be aware that for many this provision unlocks doors that formal definitions may never do, and they should promote use of the dictionary to point up the role of synonyms in increasing the student's vocabulary and word skills.

Of course, students may need help in gaining knowledge in the areas of denotation (literal meaning) and connotation (associative or emotional meaning) in order to discriminate between one synonym and another. For example, the teacher might display a still picture of a gorilla with the caption *big* and ask the student to find a synonym that describes the figure in the picture. In his dictionary the student might find such descriptive words as *large, huge, hulking, mammoth,* or *gargantuan.* Because these synonyms are adjectives that can be classified under one topic, they are conceptually related.

Perhaps the caption for another picture is *small, little, tiny.* Additional synonyms from the dictionary might therefore include *wee, diminutive, miniature, lilliputian, minuscule,* etc. Pictures captioned *attractive* or *unattractive* can be displayed and the dictionary can be used to find descriptive synonyms such as *pleasing, pretty, repulsive, gay,* etc.

The colors in a picture or object may elicit descriptive words. Using the dictionary to find a synonym for *red*, the student may find *cherry, scarlet, cardinal, vermilion, crimson, cerise.* The teacher can also discuss the grouping of certain "color" synonyms such as *tint, tinge, shade, tone, hue.*

Experiences involving touch or feeling can sharpen a student's sensitivity to shades of meaning, or nuances, in words. If students are asked to list synonyms connoting wetness, for example, they may find *watery, rainy, flooded,* etc. Some additional related words are *humid, dewy, sloppy, sodden, soaking, muggy, saturated, dripping, dank,* and *drenched.*

The point is that teachers can use the dictionary as a starting point to show students that (1) synonyms provided in the dictionary often unlock the meaning of a word, and (2) synonyms reflect shades of meaning which, when used in context, heighten the accuracy of verbal or written communication.

Antonyms

The study of antonyms is useful in teaching the concept of opposition at all levels of vocabulary and language development. First- or second-graders might learn to conceptualize opposite pairs such as *up* and *down, hot* and *cold, high* and *low;* students at higher levels can study opposites ranging from *dirty* and *clean* to *maculate* and *immaculate, praise* and *blame* to *eulogy* and *dyslogy.*

Students can, for example, use the dictionary to find antonyms for words like these:

near	far	soft	hard
hot	cold	proud	humble
male	female	accept	reject
masculine	feminine	prologue	epilogue
strong	weak	alpha	omega
quick	slow	microcosm	macrocosm
wet	dry	concord	discord

Synonym and Antonym Tests

Students can use their dictionaries to work out tests like the ones provided here. Teachers should be aware, of course, that not all dictionary entries will provide synonym and antonym clues to every one of these words. But students can often use a dictionary synonym, for example, and combine it with what they know about other words on the test in order to arrive at an answer. The point is that students will be able to reinforce their concepts (e.g., "beginning" and "ending") as they proceed through each exercise.

Test 1: *Begin—End*

Instructions: The words below mean *begin* or *end.* If a word means *begin,* write **B** in the blank. If it means *end,* write **E** in the blank. Cover the answer column on the left as you work, and check your answers when you are finished.

Sample: _E_ conclude (end)   _B_ origin (begin)

Answers

1. _B_ launch
2. _E_ finale
3. _B_ initiate
4. _E_ omega
5. _E_ ultimate
6. _E_ expire
7. _B_ primer
8. _B_ alpha
9. _E_ terminal
10. _E_ epilogue
11. _B_ primeval
12. _E_ expiration
13. _B_ incipient
14. _E_ quietus
15. _E_ consummation
16. _B_ preliminary
17. _E_ penultimate

18. _B_ genesis
19. _B_ initial
20. _B_ nascent
21. _B_ debut
22. _B_ prologue
23. _E_ crowning
24. _B_ embark
25. _B_ prime
26. _B_ inaugurate
27. _E_ termination
28. _B_ prelude
29. _E_ finis
30. _B_ broach
31. _B_ commencement
32. _E_ destination
33. _B_ overture
34. _E_ terminus

Test 2: *Large–Small*

Instructions: The words below mean *large* or *small*. If a word means *large*, write **L** in the blank. If it means *small*, write **S** in the blank. Cover the answer column on the left as you work, and check your answers when you are finished.

Sample: _L_ bulky (large)   _S_ tiny (small)

Answers

1. _S_ atom
2. _S_ snip
3. _L_ corpulent
4. _L_ monumental
5. _S_ minutiae
6. _S_ particle
7. _L_ titan
8. _S_ diminutive
9. _L_ colossal
10. _S_ microcosm
11. _L_ herculean
12. _S_ micron
13. _L_ Atlantean
14. _L_ leviathan
15. _L_ macroscopic
16. _S_ mote
17. _L_ titanic

18. _S_ micrography
19. _L_ behemoth
20. _L_ cyclopean
21. _L_ mammoth
22. _S_ mite
23. _L_ massive
24. _S_ morsel
25. _L_ obese
26. _S_ abridgment
27. _S_ microscopy
28. _L_ Goliath
29. _S_ smidgen
30. _S_ molecule
31. _L_ amplitude
32. _S_ bantam
33. _S_ minimal
34. _L_ prodigious

Test 3: Old–Young

Sample: __O__ ancient (old)   __Y__ fawn (young)

Answers

1. __Y__ filly
2. __Y__ juvenility
3. __O__ codger
4. __O__ fossil
5. __O__ archaic
6. __O__ dotard
7. __Y__ stripling
8. __Y__ whelp
9. __O__ elder
10. __O__ Methuselah
11. __O__ patriarchal
12. __Y__ juvenescent
13. __Y__ nymph
14. __Y__ gossoon
15. __Y__ piglet
16. __O__ hoary
17. __O__ senescent

18. __Y__ rejuvenate
19. __O__ antediluvian
20. __Y__ chit
21. __Y__ immature
22. __O__ antiquated
23. __Y__ gosling
24. __Y__ urchin
25. __Y__ vernal
26. __O__ venerable
27. __Y__ neophyte
28. __O__ geriatrics
29. __O__ senile
30. __O__ dowager
31. __O__ doyen
32. __Y__ callow
33. __Y__ fledgling
34. __Y__ eaglet

Section 4: Levels of Usage

all-right (ôl'rīt'), *adj.* *U.S. Slang.* very good or excellent of its kind; very dependable: *Don't worry about him; he's an all-right fellow.*
all right, 1. without error; correct. 2. yes: *All right. I'll come.* 3. without doubt; certainly. 4. in good health: *I was ill for a week, but I'm all right now.* 5. satisfactory; acceptable: *The substitute material should be all right.*
➤ See **alright** for usage note.
al·right (ôl rīt'), *adv.* *Informal.* all right.
➤ **All right** is the correct spelling of both the adjective phrase (*He is all right*) and the sentence adverb meaning yes, certainly (*All right, I'll come*). The spelling **alright** is not used in formal and in most informal writing. Occasionally it is found in advertising and in comic strips, but it is not as yet generally acceptable.

A word may be acceptable in one situation and not in another. *Ain't,* for example, is not generally used in formal speaking and writing. Therefore, the dictionary labels *ain't* as *substandard* or *dialectal.* Entry information also distinguishes between *colloquialisms* (words used in everyday, informal speech) and *slang* (new, flashy, popular words used in special senses, such as *bread* for "money").

Slang Words Used in the Dictionary

Slang is an interesting subject for most students. Basically, slang words are ephemeral, but most good dictionaries include slang because it is a part of a changing language.

Each slang word (often a metaphor) has a chance to become an accepted word if it stands the test of time and utility. Some words make it: *blackmail, lynch,* and *hoax.* But most slang expressions — *twenty-three skiddoo; Oh, you kid,* etc. — soon die out. But *O.K.* or *okay* (all right) is firmly set in the language in an informal sense. *Lousy* (bad, of low quality) has been a permanent slang word for over two hundred years. Slang is not necessarily bad usage. The best speakers and writers find themselves using it for effect.

Students can use the dictionary to trace the origin of certain slang words. For example, why is someone called "a young *punk*" or "an old *geezer.*" *Punk* means rotten. *Geezer* (an odd character) is a variant pronunciation of *guiser* (a masquerader). Slang words are often clipped forms of longer words. The dictionary eventually classifies many of these words as informal: *doc, prof, lab, gym.*

Compounds are another source of slang expressions: *sawbones, headshrinker, sourpuss, knothead, screwball, windbag.* Metaphorization is clearly seen in slang expressions such as "He's a bad egg," "She's a drip," and "She's a peach." A British girl is often called a "bird."

The word *dame* is an example of pejoration in which *dame,* a title originally referring only to a highborn lady, is now applied in a derogatory sense to any woman.

Sports slang readily enters the language: *stymied, up to par, blitz, reddog, muff.*

5: Usage Notes

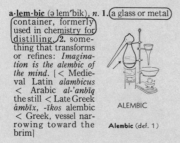

a·lem·bic (ə lem′bik), *n.* **1.** a glass or metal container, formerly used in chemistry for distilling. **2.** something that transforms or refines: *Imagination is the alembic of the mind.* [< Medieval Latin *alambicus* < Arabic *al-'anbīq* the still < Late Greek *ámbīx, -īkos* alembic < Greek, vessel narrowing toward the brim]

ALEMBIC

Alembic (def. 1)

Usage notes in the dictionary help with a variety of language skills. In addition to describing standards for using words grammatically, usage notes can help the student with variant spellings. They may inform him that *data* (information) is the plural of *datum* (an item of information), or that, of the synonyms *harbor* and *port,* the former emphasizes *shelter,* the latter a landing or unloading place.

Examples of Usage

The dictionary also provides examples of how a word is used. For example, the sample dictionary page shows how *alert* is used.

1. "A good hunting dog is *alert* to every sound...."
2. "...stand by on a hurricane *alert*"
3. "A sentry must be on the *alert*."
4. "The Government is on the *alert*...."
5. "Despite *alerted* antiaircraft and fighter defenses...."

Certain words selected from the dictionary can be placed in context and students asked to choose the correct usage, as in the items below. (Key words are underlined.)

1. A sentry must be (a) on (b) at (c) in the alert. **(a)**

2. He shoots well, in addition (a) with (b) of (c) to being a fine rider. **(c)**

3. Beth was not equal (a) with (b) of (c) to the challenge presented by the physics course. **(c)**

4. The queen was oblivious (a) about (b) of (c) in the knight's scorn. **(b)**

5. He refused to cater (a) to (b) in (c) around his daughter's every wish. **(a)**

6. Her hobby of reading coincides (a) with (b) to (c) around her vocation as a bookseller. **(a)**

7. The young man had to serve several years as an apprentice (a) for (b) of (c) to a bricklayer. **(c)**

8. The private boys' school is affiliated (a) by (b) in (c) with the church. **(c)**

6: Words and Definitions

all-right (ôl'rīt'), *adj. U.S. Slang.* very good or excellent of its kind; very dependable: *Don't worry about him; he's an all-right fellow.*
all right, **1.** without error; correct. **2.** yes: *All right. I'll come.* **3.** without doubt; certainly. **4.** in good health: *I was ill for a week, but I'm all right now.* **5.** satisfactory; acceptable: *The substitute material should be all right.*
➤ See **alright** for usage note.
al·right (ôl rīt'), *adv. Informal.* all right.
➤ **All right** is the correct spelling of both the adjective phrase (*He is all right*) and the sentence adverb meaning yes, certainly (*All right, I'll come*). The spelling **alright** is not used in formal and in most informal writing. Occasionally it is found in advertising and in comic strips, but it is not as yet generally acceptable.

One of the greatest sources of vocabulary development lies not so much in learning new words as in learning other meanings for words already known. For example, many students recognize the word *about* as a preposition (She wrote a book *about* dinosaurs), but may not realize that the same word as an *adverb* means "nearly" (The jar is *about* empty). *About* may also mean "somewhere in" (His tame raccoon was always *about* the house). Thus *about* has many meanings, such as in "up and about," "about to leave," "about face."

A first-grader, for example, would know the meaning of *above* in "Put that above the other book." But he is not likely to know the meaning of *above* in the sense of something written before, as in "the *above*-mentioned problem." He would also not understand "She is *above* telling lies," since the literal sense of *above* fails to tell the reader that *above* carries with it the idea of moral superiority and integrity.

The word *battery* has a wide range of dictionary meanings. The young child will know it as something to put in a flashlight or in a car. Perhaps the sixth-grader will know that a battery stores electricity but not know *battery* in "The *battery* for today's game" (the pitcher and catcher). Indeed, many college students do not know the separate and joint meaning of the words in the expression "assault and battery."

The teacher might also select certain words from the dictionary to put on the board, such as the word *bill* (a bird's beak, front part of a cap, theater entertainment, etc.), and ask the students to list the various meanings found in the dictionary. Another word, *bit,* will be known by most students as the past tense of *bite,* or as a small part of something. But its other meanings (something attached to a drill to bore holes; the part of a bridle that is placed in the horse's mouth) may be known to relatively few. The same may be true of the slang expression "two bits."

Keys to Dictionary Definitions

Students using the dictionary to find the meaning of a word often discover that certain key words in the definition are harder than the word they are looking for. These defining, or key, words may be difficult because they involve technical labels for classes: *genus, species, implement, order.* For example, *dogwood* is defined as "any of a *genus* of various trees" — a definition of doubtful help to the student if he doesn't know what *genus* means. Or, some words may be unfamiliar to students at a particular grade level: a fourth-grade student looking in the dictionary for the word *cloth* may find that it is "*material* made from wool, cotton, etc." The key word *material* in this case may be harder for him to understand than *cloth.*

In dictionary work, therefore, the student often needs help with the meaning of certain key words and phrases as they pertain to descriptions of people, places, actions, processes, qualities, geographic location, function, and physical appearance.

In order to alert the teacher to some of these key words, the authors have included here a short list of tested definitions along with key words and grade levels at which we can generally expect students to be familiar with them. (The list is excerpted from a study, as yet unpublished, by Edgar Dale and David Rarick entitled *A List of 364 Key Words Used in Dictionary Definitions,* conducted for the World Book Encyclopedia in 1969.)

Tested Definitions

Word Defined	Key Word and Definition	Grade of Key Word	Known by Students
1. hardware	article made from metal	6	97%
2. ocean	a great body of water	4	55
3. hoop	a flat band in the form of a circle	6	71
4. list	a series of items	6	79
5. cloth	material made from wool, cotton, silk, etc.	6	91
6. gas	matter not solid or liquid	12	71
7. enterprise	readiness to start projects	10	75
8. tool	an implement used for working	8	68
9. gear	a mechanism for starting or changing motion	10	72
10. vat	a large receptacle	10	67
11. Roman	an inhabitant of Rome	10	86
12. monsieur	French title for a man	8	79
13. label (v.)	to identify, put into a class	10	79
14. learn	to obtain knowledge	8	88
15. invent	to originate or create	8	74
16. Liberty Bell	bell in Independence Hall regarded as a symbol of liberty	8	75
17. flag	specially designed colored cloth that represents a country	8	89
18. masterpiece	a perfect production	6	75
19. astronomy	the study of the stars and planets	4	75
20. mammoth	large extinct kind of elephant	8	70
21. post	timber or metal that serves as support	6	74
22. law	body of rules recognized by a state	6	77
23. reptile	any of a class of cold-blooded animals	6	81
24. dogwood	any of a genus of various trees	12	82
25. buggy	a kind of four-wheeled, horse-drawn vehicle	8	74
26. fern	pteridophytes of the order Filicoles	10	79
27. shoveler	a species of fresh-water ducks	6	69
28. science	knowledge of facts in an orderly system	8	76
29. ampere	unit measuring strength of electric current	6	57
30. sea-island cotton	long-staple variety of cotton	6	66
31. plain	flat area of level land	6	63
32. little (adv.)	in a small degree (little-known writer)	8	60
33. bulk	volume (amount held)	8	78

Word Defined	Key Word and Definition	Grade of Key Word	Known by Students
34. plastic	having the <u>character</u> of being easily molded	8	77
35. metallic	<u>characteristic</u> of metal	10	84
36. resemblance	having similar external <u>features</u>	8	62
37. magnetic	having the <u>property</u> of attracting	10	85
38. beauty	the <u>quality</u> that pleases	8	77
39. lace	<u>ornamental</u> pattern of fine thread	8	79
40. Hawaii	U.S. state <u>comprising</u> the Pacific islands of Hawaii, Kauai, etc.	10	68
41. licorice	sweet, black, gummy substance <u>obtained</u> from the roots of an Asiatic plant	6	63
42. Athanasian creed	Christian creed formerly <u>attributed</u> to Athanasius	10	79
43. hardbound (books)	as <u>distinguished</u> from paperback	8	70
44. African	<u>of</u> Africa	10	57
45. French	<u>pertaining</u> to the people of France	10	82
46. brown thrasher	songbird <u>related</u> to the mockingbird	6	70
47. lightning	an electrical <u>phenomenon</u>	10	81
48. map	drawing <u>representing</u> earth's surface features	10	72

Word Choice

Students who seek to exhibit what they consider to be a well-developed vocabulary often fall into the trap of substituting quantity for quality. As a result, their oral and written communications abound with lengthy, cumbersome words and sentence constructions.

The following lessons emphasize the choice of expression available to the dictionary user. The student consults his dictionary to find the simpler word or phrase that could be used instead of the longer one. (Letter clues may be needed to get some students started.)

Answers	Harder Words	Easier Words
shorten	abbreviate	<u>s h</u> _ _ _ _ _
waiting	abeyance	<u>w a</u> _ _ _ _ _
shorten	abridge	<u>s h</u> _ _ _ _ _
total	aggregate	<u>t o</u> _ _ _
share	allotment	<u>s h</u> _ _ _
refer	allude	<u>r e</u> _ _ _
change	alteration	<u>c h</u> _ _ _ _
doubtful	problematical	<u>d o</u> _ _ _ _ _ _
get	procure	<u>g</u> _ _
offer	proffer	<u>o f</u> _ _ _

288

In another form, definitive phrases can be replaced by single words. The student writes the word that fits the italicized phrase by filling in the blanks.

Answers

wired
1. He *sent him a message by wire*.
   He w _ _ _ _ him.

indent
2. At the beginning of a paragraph, we *write the first word of the first sentence about an inch inside the margin*.
   At the beginning of a paragraph, we i n _ _ _ _ _.

biography
3. I read *a story written about a man's life*.
   I read a b _ _ _ _ _ _ _ _.

autobiography
4. Have you ever read *a man's story of his own life*?
   Have you ever read a man's a _ _ _ _ _ _ _ _ _ _ _ _?

biographer
5. He is a *man who writes the life stories* of famous men.
   He is a b i _ _ _ _ _ _ _ _.

7: Derivations

a·lerce (ə lèrs′), *n.* **1.** a large pine that resembles the California redwood. **2.** the wood used by the Moors in their buildings, obtained from the sandarac tree of Morocco. [< Spanish *alerce* < Arabic *al-'arz* the cedar]

Word derivations are statements of how new words are made from old ones by the use of prefixes, suffixes, compounds, etc. For example, one dictionary lists the derivation of *eugenics* as follows: [Gk *eugenes,* wellborn; fr. *eu + genes*]. Notice that word-derivation statements are usually enclosed by brackets; *fr.* is an abbreviation for *from* or *derived from* (some dictionaries use the symbol <); the word parts (also referred to as combining forms) *eu* and *genes* are italicized.

Dictionary derivations can be the basis for useful word-skill activities on word structure and comprehension. In an exercise on word analysis, the students can use the dictionary to write down the literal meaning of certain word parts (roots, prefixes, and suffixes) listed in the derivation of a given word. Below is one form that might be used. The student writes the prefix and root of each word, along with their meanings, in the appropriate blanks below. (Answers are provided.)

Word	Prefix	Meaning	Root	Meaning
conduct	con	together	duct	lead
predict	pre	before	dict	say
repel	re	back	pel	push
contradict	contra	against	dict	speak
eject	e	out	ject	cast

Word	Prefix	Meaning	Root	Meaning
post mortem	post	after	mort(em)	death
subaqueous	sub	under	aque(ous)	watery
distant	dis	apart from	stant	stand
inaudible	in	not	aud(ible)	hearable

In this exercise, the student looks up the derivation and fills in the blank.

Answers

not	1. In the word *invisible, in* means _____
forward	2. In the word *provident, pro* means _____
not	3. In the word *improvident, im* means _____
over, above	4. In the word *supervise, super* means _____
two	5. In the word *bicycle, bi* means _____
one	6. In the word *monocycle, mono* means _____
three	7. In the word *tricycle, tri* means _____
through	8. In the word *permit, per* means _____

8: Phrases in the Dictionary

a·lert (ə lėrt′), *adj.* **1.** keen and watchful; wide-awake: *A good hunting dog is alert to every sound and movement in the field.* **2.** quick in action; nimble: *A sparrow is very alert in its movements.*
—*n.* **1.** a signal warning of an attack by approaching enemy aircraft or other threatened danger. **2.** the period of time after this warning until the attack is over or the danger has passed: *The rest of the coast as far north as Massachusetts should stand by on a hurricane alert, the bureau said* (Wall Street Journal). **3.** a signal to troops, etc., to be ready for action.
on the alert, watchful; ready at any instant for what is coming: *A sentry must be on the alert. The Government is on the alert and will take the necessary steps to maintain security and stability* (London Times).
—*v.t.* **1.** to warn against an air attack, a hurricane, etc. **2.** to call to arms; notify (troops, etc.) to get ready for action. **3.** to make alert; warn: *Despite alerted anti-aircraft and fighter defenses, the Liberators pressed home low-level attack through oil fires and intense smoke, wrecking the refineries* (Time).
[< French *alerte* < Italian *all'erta* on the watch]—**a·lert′ly,** *adv.*—**a·lert′ness,** *n.*

Many word entries list special meanings that depend on usage. The word *account* assumes different meanings in each of these phrases:

a. to take into *account* (make allowance for)
b. to turn to *account* (make profit from)

c. to call to *account* (reprimand)
d. to *account* for (give a reason for)
e. on your own *account* (for yourself)
 f. on no *account* (under no conditions)
g. on *account* of (because)
h. on *account* (on credit, part payment)
 i. of no *account* (of no use)

In the dictionary, these phrases are defined and often placed (in italics) in sentence context.

Phrases like these can be used by the teacher for teaching the concept of metaphor. The word *card,* for example, might be metaphorized in several ways in dictionary phrases:

a. He has a card up his sleeve (holding back a plan).
b. Put your cards on the table (be perfectly frank).
c. It's in the cards (likely to occur).

Word Pairs in the Dictionary

Illustrative phrases and sentences found in the dictionary often associate an entry word with certain other words. For example, the adjective *bumper* often appears with *crop* in "a bumper crop." *Brand* may appear with *new* in "brand new." Such associations may be the basis for class discussion. Here is a sample list:

spick-and-span: neat and clean (short for spick-and-span-new)

kith and kin: friends and relatives (from Old English *cythth*, native land; kinsfold, from *cunnan*, to know)

null and void: not binding (from *nullus*, not any; French *voide* and Latin *vacuus*, empty)

flotsam and jetsam: things thrown overboard and floating on the sea, articles that drift ashore (*flotsam*, floating; *jetsam*, jettisoned or cast overboard)

assault and battery: successful carrying out of a threat to do physical harm (*assault*, to threaten to beat; *battery*, to beat)

Reduplications

Word combinations such as *helter-skelter, lickety-split, dilly-dally, wishy-washy, flip-flap*, and *tip-top* are called *reduplications*. These are combinations of words or syllables whose sound is reduplicated or repeated for effect. They appeal to the ear.

One of Shakespeare's witches in *Macbeth* uses the phrase "hurly-burly." ("When the hurly-burly's done, / When the battle's lost and won.") It means *tumult* or *uproar*.

The following are additional reduplications that the class can discuss:

bonbon	tsetse (fly)	okey-dokey	papa
teeny-weeny	razzle-dazzle	palsy-walsy	hustle-bustle
tom-tom	knickknack	mama	killer-diller

10: Foreign Words and Phrases in the Dictionary

aircraft and fighter defenses, the Liberators pressed home low-level attack through oil fires and intense smoke, wrecking the refineries (Time).
[< French *alerte* < Italian *all'erta* on the watch]—**a·lert′ly,** *adv.*—**a·lert′ness,** *n.*
—**Syn.** *adj.* **1.** attentive, vigilant. See **watchful. 2.** brisk, active. —**Ant.** *adj.* **1.** heedless.
à l'es·pa·gnole(à les pá nyŏl′), *French.* in the Spanish style.

Since many words in our language originated in different parts of the world, we might say that there is a "geography" of words. Although we have anglicized the majority of these words, there are still many that have retained aspects of their original spelling and pronunciation. The sections that follow provide the teacher with exercises and lists as a starting point in promoting student interest in commonly used foreign (mainly French and Latin) words and phrases. The lists we have provided are intended to be merely examples, but from them, teachers can suggest many activities involving the dictionary.

Food Terms

In the following exercises, the student fills in the blanks with the nationality of the people who originated the food or the name of the country it comes from.

The student is not expected to recognize the source of every food listed here. Dictionaries can be used as an aid during the test or can be consulted afterwards to check answers.

1. *Tortilla* is a __Mexican__ word for pancake.
2. *Zwieback,* twice-baked bread, got its name from __Germany__.
3. Cookies known as *macaroons* were first baked by the __Italians__.
4. Whipped egg whites baked on the top of a lemon pie are called *meringue.* *Meringue* is a __French__ word.
5. __Italians__ gave us *minestrone,* a thick vegetable soup.
6. *Chocolate* is a __Spanish__ word that came from the Nahuatl Indian language.
7. A __French__ dessert served in tall glasses is a *parfait.*
8. Milk is *pasteurized,* a process named after a __French__ man.
9. *Ravioli,* dough filled with meat, is a popular __Italian__ dish.
10. Toasted cubes of bread called *croutons* are a __French__ contribution.
11. A small piece of meat is called a *cutlet. Cutlet* (small rib) is a __French__ term.
12. *Eclairs* are __French__ pastry.
13. *Filet mignon,* a __French__ term, is a "dainty slice."
14. The __Hungarians__ gave us *goulash.*
15. A city in __Germany__ is the home of the *frankfurter,* a smoked sausage of beef or pork.

In another form of this kind of test, the student matches the foods in column A with the places (most usually associated with the food) in column B. Some places may be used more than once. Students should check their answers in the dictionary.

Answers	Column A	Column B
c	1. ___ tamale	a. Italy
g	2. ___ plum pudding	b. Denmark
c	3. ___ enchilada	c. Mexico
e	4. ___ sukiyaki	d. India
h	5. ___ clam chowder	e. Japan
g	6. ___ Yorkshire pudding	f. Hawaii
b	7. ___ smorgasbord	g. England
f	8. ___ poi	h. New England
a	9. ___ vermicelli	i. Scotland
g, i	10. ___ kippered herring	
g	11. ___ crumpet	
c	12. ___ tortilla	
a	13. ___ pasta	
i	14. ___ oatmeal	
d	15. ___ curry	

Dance Terms

The names of dances can also help emphasize the geography of words. Dictionaries and encyclopedias provide the student with information on a dance and the country where the dance originated. Sometimes the geography of the dance name becomes somewhat involved. The Parisians use the word *Apache* (American Indian) to describe a band of rough criminals in Paris. They gave the name "Apache dance" to a dance done by a supposedly underworld character and his girl partner. The samba is an African dance popularized in Brazil. The schottische, now danced in many countries, was originally a German round dance; the name comes from the German word *Schottische,* meaning "Scottish."

In the following exercise the student matches the dance with the nationality of the people who created it. Note that one nationality name may be used for more than one dance term. After completing the exercise the student can check his answers by consulting his dictionary.

Answers	Column A	Column B
b	1. cancan	a. Spanish
g, e	2. polka	b. French
d	3. Highland fling	c. Hawaiian
b	4. minuet	d. Scottish
l	5. square dance	e. Czech
g	6. mazurka	f. Japanese
a	7. flamenco	g. Polish
c	8. hula	h. Irish
n, b	9. ballet	i. Argentine
j, r	10. waltz	j. Austrian
l	11. Charleston	k. Brazilian

Answers	Column A	Column B
q	12. cha-cha	l. American
k	13. bossa nova	m. Haitian
b	14. Apache	n. Italian
l	15. Virginia reel	o. Mexican
q	16. rumba	p. English
l	17. rock 'n' roll	q. Cuban
l	18. jitterbug	r. German
o	19. hat dance	

French Words in English

The following lesson tests the student's knowledge of certain French words and phrases found in most good dictionaries.

Word	Meaning
1. adroit	clever
2. attaché	diplomatic member
3. au courant	well-informed
4. avenue	street, approach
5. blasé	bored, tired
6. bon ami	good friend
7. bon vivant	lover of luxury
8. bon voyage	pleasant trip
9. boulevard	wide street
10. bourgeoisie	middle-class people
11. café	restaurant
12. chalet	mountain house
13. chapeau	hat
14. chargé d'affaires	substitute diplomat
15. château	castle
16. chic	stylish
17. clairvoyance	mental perception
18. cliché	used over and over
19. connoisseur	an expert
20. coterie	a social set
21. coup	brilliant move
22. coupe	two-door car
23. debonair	carefree
24. debutante	girl entering society
25. devotee	has special interest
26. élite	upper class
27. émigré	a refugee
28. ensemble	all together
29. entrée	main course
30. entrepreneur	a manager
31. envelope	covering for letter
32. envoy	sent as representative
33. essay	short piece of writing

34. façade	front of building
35. fiancé	engaged man
36. fiancée	engaged woman
37. flâneur	an idler
38. gendarme	policeman
39. ingénue	naïve girl
40. liaison	linking
41. maître d'hôtel	headwaiter
42. maladroit	awkward
43. martinet	strict disciplinarian
44. naïve	childlike
45. nonchalant	seemingly indifferent
46. nouveau riche	newly rich
47. passé	out of date
48. protégé	person under patronage
49. raconteur	a storyteller

In the exercise below, context clues (sentences 1-6) help the student match column A with column B.

1. Capturing the fort was a *tour de force* for the rebels.
2. He found himself *tête-à-tête* with the president.
3. Her *gauche* manners embarrassed us.
4. Mark Twain was Samuel Clemens's *nom de plume*.
5. The crowd moved *en masse* to the platform.
6. His *bon mot* made us laugh.

Answers	Column A	Column B
b	1. ___ tour de force	a. clumsy
e	2. ___ tête-à-tête	b. skillful feat
a	3. ___ gauche	c. witty remark
d	4. ___ nom de plume	d. pen name
f	5. ___ en masse	e. face to face
c	6. ___ bon mot	f. as a whole

Other French phrases the class might look up include:

1. pièce de résistance: chief dish of a meal; something outstanding
2. hors de combat: disabled, literally "out of the fight"
3. carte blanche: full authority, literally "white paper"
4. hors d'oeuvres: appetizers, literally "apart from the main work"
5. coup d'état: sudden, decisive political move, literally a "stroke of state"
6. joie de vivre: joy of living, enjoyment of life
7. apropos: fittingly; opportunely; to the purpose
8. vis-à-vis: opposite; in relation to; literally "face to face"

Latin Words in the English Dictionary

The English language abounds with words of Latin origin, as these sentences illustrate:

1. When this *actor* visited the *campus* last *December,* a *doctor* told him that the pain *in* his *abdomen* was caused by an infected *appendix.*

2. In all *candor,* the *senior senator* reminded *me* of the Roman *orator* Cicero as he stood on the *rostrum* and, like a *castigator,* blamed his opponent for the *squalor* in the cities.

In the exercise below, the student uses the ten sentences containing Latin phrases as context clues to help him match the phrases in column A with their meanings in column B.

1. In the field of politics, the senator was a *rara avis.*
2. They postponed the meeting *sine die.*
3. Taste is the *sine qua non* in fashion.
4. Repeat the announcement *verbatim.*
5. Conservative politicians favor maintaining the *status quo.*
6. The diplomat was *persona non grata* when relations between the two countries worsened.
7. The group met *sub rosa* in the cellar.
8. *De jure* segregation is less common than *de facto* segregation.
9. He forgot his prepared speech and proceeded *ad libitum (ad lib).*
10. The speech seemed to go on *ad infinitum.*

Answers	Column A	Column B
c	1. ___ rara avis	a. absolutely necessary
h	2. ___ sine die	b. as one pleases
a	3. ___ sine qua non	c. rare person or thing
		d. actual
k	4. ___ verbatim	e. unacceptable person
g	5. ___ status quo	f. by law
e	6. ___ persona non grata	g. way things are
j	7. ___ sub rosa	h. indefinitely (without setting
f	8. ___ de jure	a day)
		i. without end
b	9. ___ ad libitum (ad lib)	j. secretly
i	10. ___ ad infinitum	k. word for word

Additional exercises can be constructed from this short list:

Latin	English
ab incunabulis	from the cradle
ab initio	from the beginning
ad absurdum	to show the absurdity
ad astra per aspera	to the stars through difficulties
addendum (-a)	to be added; an appendix
ad hoc	for this purpose
ad hominem	to the individual; personal
ad infinitum	to infinity
ad interim	in the meanwhile
ad lib(itum)	at pleasure
ad litteram	to the letter; exact
ad modum	in the manner of
ad nauseam	to the point of nausea
ad rem	to the purpose; to the point

ad summum	to the highest point
ad valorem	according to the value
agenda	things to be done
alias	otherwise
alibi	elsewhere
alma mater	fostering mother
alter ego	another self
anno Domini	in the year of our Lord (A.D.)
ante bellum	before the war
ante meridiem	before noon
annuit coeptis	(God) has favored our undertakings (on the back of a dollar bill)
a priori	from the cause to the effect
artium magister	master of arts (M.A.)
biennium	a period of two years
bona fide	in good faith
casus belli	events provoking war
caveat emptor	let the buyer beware
cave canem	beware of the dog (found in front of Roman thresholds)
compos mentis	of sound mind
corpus delicti	facts that prove a crime (literally "body of the crime"; popularly known as "the murdered person")
datum (-a)	a fact or principle granted (from *dare*, to give)
de jure	by right; by the law
delenda est Carthago	Carthage must be destroyed (Rome's rival city; Cato ended every speech with this phrase)
de mortuis nil nisi bonum	of the dead say nothing except good
de novo	anew
de profundis	out of the depths
dictum	a saying; a decision
dramatis personae	characters of the play
emeritus	retired but holding rank and title
errare est humanum	to err is human
erratum (-a)	an error
et alii (*et al.*)	and others (*people*) [Use *etc.* for other *things.*]
et cetera (etc.)	and the rest
ex cathedra	from the chair; spoken with authority; by virtue of one's office
exempli gratia (e.g.)	for the sake of an example
exit	he (she, it) goes out
ex officio	by virtue of one's office
ex post facto	after the deed is done; after the fact; retrospective
ex tempore	without preparation; offhand
facsimile	an exact imitation
fiat	let it be done; a decree
finis	the end
in flagrante delictis	in the very act (of the crime)
post hoc ergo propter hoc	after this, therefore, on account of this

Note: The teacher might also present a list of ten to twenty English words (some of which are on this list) and ask the student to find five, eight, or ten *Latin* words in his *English* dictionary. These activities make the student aware of the association of one language with another and alert him to the foreign-language aspects of English. Note that the same approach can be used with French, Italian, Spanish, German, etc., to help integrate vocabulary study as it relates to foreign-language instruction in the curriculum. A more complete list of Latin words used in English can be found in the Appendix.

Additional Information in the Dictionary

Certain sections of the dictionary are devoted to explaining the abbreviations used by writers and printers. An understanding of these abbreviations should be considered an important part of a student's vocabulary skills.

In writing a research paper, there is often a need to refer to certain publications or to provide additional information. Some of these references will be in the form of footnotes; some of them will appear in context, preceded by certain abbreviations. Instead of saying *for example* we can write *e.g.* (from Latin *exempli gratia,* meaning for the sake of an example). Another word commonly used in such writing is *viz.,* short for Latin *videlicet.* The translation of this Latin term is "it may be seen; it is clear." The usual meaning of the word is "namely," or "to wit."

In the following exercise on manuscript abbreviations, the student may test his knowledge of these items and gain an understanding of their use in books and periodicals. Answers are provided for the teacher's convenience.

Instructions: Write the meaning of each abbreviation in the blank. Use the dictionary to check your answers when you have completed the exercise.

Abbreviation	Word
1. p.	**page** (from Latin *pagina,* page)
2. pp.	**pages**
3. anon.	**anonymous** (from Greek *a* + *onym,* without a name)
4. ff.	**following** (pages)
5. cf.	**compare** (from Latin *conferre*)
6. e.g.	**for example** (from Latin *exempli gratia,* for the sake of an example)
7. i.e.	**id est** (Latin "that is")
8. ibid.	**ibidem** (Latin "in the same place")
9. loc. cit.	**loco citato** (Latin "in the place cited")
10. n.b.	**nota bene** (Latin "note well")
11. non seq.	**non sequitur** (Latin "it does not follow")
12. op. cit.	**opere citato** (Latin "in the work cited")

13. pseud.	**pseudonym** (false name)
14. ref.	**reference**
15. viz.	**namely** (abbreviation for Latin *videlicet,* it may be seen)
16. q.v.	**quod vide** (Latin "which see")
17. Q.E.D.	**quod erat demonstrandum** (Latin "which was to be demonstrated or proved")
18. et al.	**et alii** (Latin "and others")
19. vol.	**volume** (from Latin *volumen,* a roll, scroll, hence a book written on a parchment)

Additional Word-Skill Aids

In addition to material previously discussed, many dictionaries also include information on the following:

1. common abbreviations

2. signs and symbols used in many fields, such as astronomy, $\oplus$ (earth); biology, ♂ (male); mathematics, π (pi); medicine, ℞ (take, from Latin *recipe*)

3. biographical names with their pronunciations, as well as information about famous men and women

4. a pronouncing gazetteer that lists names, locations, populations, and other information about important geographical features, countries, regions, cities, etc.

5. common first names of men and women, including the literal meaning of each name

6. a vocabulary of rhymes, helpful in writing verse (*ace, base, bass, brace, case, chase*)

7. the correct use of punctuation, capitals, compounds, parts of speech, etc.

8. the preparation of bibliographies, including correct form for author names, book titles, magazines, etc.

9. preparing manuscript for publication

10. proofreaders' marks and their meanings: ℘ (delete); ⊂ (close up); ⸿ (paragraph); etc.

11. where to divide a word in writing (*aer·i·al*)

12. what syllables are stressed (accented), shown by the symbol [′]; the use of the schwa [ə] in unaccented syllables

13. archaic words (old-fashioned words) used in poetry and in the Bible, such as *avaunt* (begone), *abide* (wait for), *agone* (gone away), *belike* (probably), *methinks* (it seems to me), etc.

14. illustration of word entries by means of drawings and diagrams

15. differentiations in usage between words such as *respectively* and *respectfully; continual* and *continuous; uninterested* and *disinterested; luxurious* and *luxuriant, flaunt* and *flout*

16. run-on entries (words derived from entry words by the addition of suffixes): *figure, figurative, figuratively*, etc.

17. pronunciation, using a pronunciation key often found at the bottom of each page

18. variant ways of pronouncing words such as *leisure, ideology, ration, status, aunt*, etc.

19. irregular inflectional forms: *spectrum, spectrums* or *spectra; fungus, funguses* or *fungi; children, oxen, geese, beaux*, etc.

20. the degrees of an adjective: *high, higher, highest; good, better, best*

21. regional pronunciations: *suthun* for *Southern* (in the South); *hahd* for *hard* and *Hahvahd* for *Harvard* (in Boston)

14

Using
Word
Games

An important objective of vocabulary instruction is to develop an interest in words. The student whose curiosity about words is aroused is likely to increase his vocabulary and to become more discriminating.

Students generally enjoy games and exercises involving the use of *puns, riddles, crossword puzzles, anagrams,* and *palindromes.* Each of these categories is discussed and illustrated in this unit. In general, it is believed that these lessons will

1. point up the element of enjoyment or challenge in language study and encourage word play;

2. require the student to look carefully at words—an important aspect of vocabulary building;

3. give the student practice in calling up words on the basis of given clues;

4. require the student to match words with definitions;

5. provide spelling practice and compel close attention to word formation;

6. show the student how the letters of many words can be manipulated to form other words;

7. emphasize the importance of letter position in relation to word meaning;

8. encourage students to classify and generalize concepts.

The grade level is important in deciding the kinds of exercises the teacher will use. Some of the exercises require mature thinking; others can be done at a lower grade level. However, by using appropriate words the teacher can fit the techniques of the exercises to any desired grade level.

Using Anagrams

The teacher may use anagrams (words made by transposing letters of one word to form another) to give students practice in word formation and spelling. The word *anagram* comes from Greek *ana* (back) + *gramma* (letter). Anagrams may be used to build students' interest in words, offering them the opportunity to concentrate on the manipulation of letters to form words.

Instructions:

The student transposes the letters of the key word and writes in the blank another word appropriate to each definition. For example:

Key word: <u>nail</u>
Definition: past participle of *lie*
New word: <u>lain</u>

Shorter words may be made by omitting some letters of the key word and transposing the rest. For example:

Key word: <u>nail</u>
Definition: article used before words beginning with a vowel
New word: <u>an</u>

The student follows the procedure described above in the following exercises:

1. Key word: <u>rail</u>
   Definition: a lion's den
   New word: <u>lair</u>

2. Key word: <u>rail</u>
   Definition: one who lies
   New word: <u>liar</u>

3. Key word: <u>rail</u>
   Definition: what you breathe
   New word: <u>air</u>

4. Key word: <u>bear</u>
   Definition: uncovered
   New word: <u>bare</u>

5. Key word: <u>bear</u>
   Definition: what you hear with
   New word: <u>ear</u>

6. Key word: <u>bear</u>
   Definition: plural of *is*
   New word: <u>are</u>

7. Key word: <u>rate</u>
   Definition: rip
   New word: <u>tear</u>

8. Key word: <u>rate</u>
   Definition: gnawing animal
   New word: <u>rat</u>

Anagrams in Context

Another approach is to use the anagrams in context. For example, the student rearranges the letters in each italicized word below and writes the appropriate anagram in the spaces provided. The teacher will note that these exercises can be reversed:

Example: *Untied* we stand, divided we fall. <u>u n i t e d</u>

Answers

untied	1. His shoelace is *united*. _ _ _ _ _ _
mace	2. The knight slew his opponent with his *acme*. _ _ _ _
sword	3. The guardsman drew his *words*. _ _ _ _ _
ambled	4. The old man *blamed* around the park. _ _ _ _ _ _
swine	5. The swineherd tended the *wines*. _ _ _ _ _
tinsel	6. They decorated the tree with *silent*. _ _ _ _ _ _
luster	7. The paint on the new car had an attractive *rustle*. _ _ _ _ _ _
heart	8. To reach the mind we first must touch the *earth*. _ _ _ _ _
care	9. He didn't seem to *race* whether he won or not. _ _ _ _
evil	10. Love of money is the root of all *vile*. _ _ _ _
bleat	11. He could recognize the *table* of a lamb. _ _ _ _ _
wolf	12. Mythology tells us that Romulus and Remus were nursed by a *fowl*. _ _ _ _
ample	13. There is *maple* room for dancing. _ _ _ _ _
mite	14. The parson considered her offering a widow's *time*. _ _ _ _
tastes	15. There is no disputing about *states*. _ _ _ _ _ _
stripes	16. The sergeant had three *sprites*. _ _ _ _ _ _ _

Anagrams—Days and Months

The student gets practice in spelling by writing in the blanks the names of the days and months hidden in the words and phrases below (Column A). The answers in Column B are for the teacher's convenience and should be deleted before duplicating the exercise for the class.

Column A	Column B
1. yam	May
2. ah sturdy	Thursday
3. bear fury	February
4. fay rid	Friday
5. rip la	April
6. ausgut	August
7. say duet	Tuesday
8. jury a an	January
9. be peers mt.	September
10. do many	Monday
11. cede berm	December
12. den say dew	Wednesday
13. me on verb	November
14. a sturdy a	Saturday
15. or be cot	October
16. say dun	Sunday
17. charm	March

The students may be asked to find the colors hidden in the words and phrases below.

1. gore an	orange
2. lube	blue
3. we hit	white
4. balk c.	black
5. i dingo	indigo
6. genre	green
7. rule pp.	purple
8. low lye	yellow
9. in k.p.	pink
10. quit rouse	turquoise
11. a man a quire	aquamarine
12. gary	gray

A variation of this exercise may be school subjects:

1. tar	art
2. shingle	English
3. chair met it	arithmetic
4. pen gills	spelling
5. ring wit	writing
6. egg ray hop	geography
7. he halt	health
8. i scum	music

Mixed Fruits

1.	lump	plum
2.	one rag	orange
3.	reap	pear
4.	he cap	peach
5.	la pep	apple
6.	i cop rat	apricot
7.	nab an a	banana
8.	gaper	grape
9.	pure fig rat	grapefruit
10.	lone m	lemon or melon
11.	eel not warm	watermelon
12.	to moat	tomato
13.	lo men	melon or lemon
14.	a ted	date
15.	count co	coconut
16.	plain peep	pineapple

Instructions: The student forms other words from the key words.

	Key word	Words formed from key word
1.	turn	urn, nut, run, rut, tun, etc.
2.	lead	deal, led, lad, ad, lea, etc.
3.	mean	man, men, am, name, me, an, etc.
4.	tear	tar, tea, eat, ear, are, rat, era, etc.
5.	chesty	chest, yet, sty, scythe, etc.
6.	cheat	heat, eat, hat, cat, tea, hate, etc.
7.	course	sour, our, rose, core, us, sore, use, etc.
8.	pearl	pear, pare, leap, reap, real, pale, ale, etc.
9.	listen	tinsel, enlist, list, ten, tin, tile, let, lint, etc.
10.	fortune	fort, forte, tune, turn, turf, route, tone, etc.
11.	vowel	love, low, wove, owe, owl, woe, etc.
12.	father	fat, her, fate, feat, rat, rate, far, fear, etc.

Hidden Animals

The teacher might call attention to words, syllables, and letters by pointing out the chance arrangement of letters in sentences. For example, in the sentence "I saw Bob at home," the student tries to find the animal (bat).

Students read the sentences, find the name of the animal (or bird) and write it in the blank. Levels of difficulty can be varied by using different categories, such as colors, trees, flowers, etc.

In the sample exercise below, the key letters have been underlined and the answers provided for the teacher's convenience.

1. This is an uncommon key. monkey
2. They will be arriving soon. bear
3. Move the box. ox
4. Eskimos try to keep igloos warm. pig

305

Concept Association

Vocabulary can be taught by concept association. In the examples that follow, the student is asked to figure out the name of an animal from the description of the animal or of its activity. In doing this he relates one concept to another; for example, he may associate *gnawing* with *rat*. He also learns the correct spelling of the word, since he is limited by the number of letters he can use in completing the exercise.

The student looks first at the clue in column A and then fills in the blanks in column B. The teacher may ask certain students to write some of their answers on the board while the other class members check their own papers. Answers are provided on the left.

Answers	Column A	Column B
rat	1. gnaws through things	_ a _
cat	2. scratches	_ a _
crab	3. pinches	_ _ a _
whale	4. largest animal	_ _ a _ _
goat, seal	5. has whiskers	_ _ a _
bear	6. furry	_ _ a _
elephant	7. trunk	_ _ _ _ _ a _ _
giraffe	8. tall	_ _ _ a _ _ _
kangaroo	9. jumps	_ _ _ _ a _ _ _
rabbit	10. eats carrots	_ a _ _ _ _
zebra	11. has stripes	_ _ _ _ a
antelope	12. runs fast	a _ _ _ _ _ _ _
robin	13. a sign of spring	_ o _ _ _
crow	14. black	_ _ o _
dove	15. coos	_ o _ _
owl	16. often called wise	o _ _
stork	17. has long legs	_ _ o _ _
ostrich	18. largest living bird	o _ _ _ _ _ _
sparrow	19. often called "English"	_ _ _ _ _ o _
goose	20. web-footed bird	_ o _ _ _
oriole	21. Baltimore	o _ _ _ _ _
dodo	22. not living now (extinct)	_ o _ _

Beginnings and Endings

Adding to Beginnings of Words

Instructions: The student adds a letter or letters to the beginning of each word to make another word that fits the clue. For example: _and, plus the clue "on the beach" = sand.

Answers	Word	Clue
aboard	_board	on a ship
afire	_fire	on fire
amaze	_maze	surprise
arrest	__rest	take prisoner
arrival	__rival	reaching home
ashamed	_shamed	sorry for doing
ashore	_shore	on land
attack	__tack	strike with force
award	_ward	prize
baboon	__boon	large monkey
bark	_ark	tree "skin"
bawl	_awl	cry
beaten	_eaten	defeated
blast	_last	sudden sound
bled	_led	lost blood
blink	_link	flutter eyelids
block	_lock	stop something
blot	_lot	dry ink
boat	_oat	to sail in
boldness	_oldness	courage
bore	_ore	make weary

Adding Letters to Endings of Words

Instructions: The student adds either one or two letters to the end of each word to make another word that fits the clue. For example: it__ plus the clue "scratchy skin" = itch.

Answers	Word	Clue
kneel	knee_	bend down
lately	late__	not long ago
loafer	loaf__	lazy person
locket	lock__	jewelry
madam	mad__	a lady
menu	men_	list of food
muffin	muff__	small cake
nickel	nick__	hard, white metal
palm	pal_	inside of hand
pinch	pin__	to squeeze
plank	plan_	a board
plump	plum_	round and full
poppy	pop__	flower
replant	replan_	plant again
robot	rob__	manlike machine
rocker	rock__	chair
rodeo	rode_	cowboy contest
ruby	rub_	a red jewel

Riddles

Riddles which use puns in the question or answer are called *conundrums*, as in the exercise below. A variety of approaches may be used, but the student will best learn and reinforce certain concepts if the material is structured, that is, classified or grouped for study. As with the material used previously in puzzle exercises, words or concepts can be chosen that represent given categories: foods, trees, flowers, animals, occupations, etc. The following exercise is an example.

Finding Flowers

Instructions: The student fills in the blanks with the names of flowers.

1. What flowers do you use for kissing? <u>tulips</u>
2. What flower is seen in the eye? <u>iris</u>
3. A nation with a lot of cars is a <u>carnation</u>.
4. Ben Franklin was happy when his kite <u>rose</u>.
5. How did he know she would go with him? He <u>aster</u>.
6. What flower wants to be remembered? <u>forget-me-not</u>
7. When does a pin hurt most? When it <u>'s in ya (zinnia)</u>.
8. What did the mother dragon say to the boy dragon that wanted her son to come out to play? "It's taking it <u>its nap, dragon (snapdragon)</u>."
9. The boy watched the cow cross the ice because he wanted to see the <u>cowslip</u>.
10. When do sheep look like a flower? When they come in <u>phlox</u>.
11. What plant is a fake stone? <u>shamrock</u>

Note: Additional riddles and puns can be presented in a variety of forms. Students can help collect riddles or construct various exercises involving the use of puns and homonyms.

The materials can be grouped according to sound, meaning, or spelling. For example, exercises involving puns or homonyms provide practice in spelling discrimination: *pear, pare,* or *pair; need, kneed,* or *knead.*

Various words and word parts have similar sounds and can be used as the basis for puns or riddles. We illustrate a few of these in the following lessons. The material is presented as a matter of interest, not as serious word analysis, although a student, by observing certain word endings or recurring syllables, might better remember how to spell a word, classify, and remember it. For example, finding a *rat* in *separate* might help remind the student not to spell it "seperate."

Riddles and Word Endings

1. How can you help a *lemon*? <u>Give it lemonade.</u>
2. What *log* moves around? <u>a travelog</u>
3. What *age* does a ship have? <u>anchorage</u>
4. What *age* do all birds have? <u>plumage</u>

5. What is the *age* of a duke? peerage
6. A stamp is what *age*? postage
7. The *Canterbury Tales* is about what *age*? a pilgrimage
8. What was King Lear's *age*? dotage
9. What's the opposite of a girl *ant*? a buoyant
10. What's the opposite of a boy *ant*? a gallant
11. What *ant* is proud? arrogant
12. What *ant* lives in a house? an occupant
13. What *ant* repels? a repellant

Harder Hidden Words

The words in the following exercise all contain an additional "hidden" word. Clues are given; the student finds the additional word and writes it in the letter space on the right. For example, in the word *avoid* there is a word meaning empty or vacant (*void*).

The exercise is in general directed toward students at the higher levels, though the elementary teacher can select the easiest items for use with his students.

The exercise gives the student practice in letter discrimination and word recognition, and tests his ability to call up a word on the basis of its definition. In doing this exercise the student will also get a chance to learn new words or review words that are in his "twilight zone"—words he sees or hears but seldom uses because he is unsure of their meaning. Note: The student may find more than one word in some items (for example, No. 9, *invent,* contains two words: *in* and *vent*), but he is asked to choose only the word that fits the definition.

Answers				Definition of Hidden Word
lute	1.	The word *flute*	contains _ _ _ _.	stringed musical instrument
lobe	2.	The word *globe*	contains _ _ _ _.	lower part of ear
rift	3.	*drift*	_ _ _ _	a split or break
lance	4.	*glance*	_ _ _ _ _	to cut open
raze	5.	*graze*	_ _ _ _	destroy completely
rill	6.	*grill*	_ _ _ _	little brook
rove	7.	*grove*	_ _ _ _	wander
ail	8.	*hail*	_ _ _	be ill
vent	9.	*invent*	_ _ _ _	opening
oaf	10.	*loaf*	_ _ _	clumsy person
ilk	11.	*milk*	_ _ _	kind or sort
addle	12.	*paddle*	_ _ _ _ _	make confused
alms	13.	*palms*	_ _ _ _	charity
bran	14.	*brand*	_ _ _ _	outer coat of wheat kernel
coo	15.	*coon*	_ _ _	dove sound
coup	16.	*coupon*	_ _ _ _	brilliant move
din	17.	*diner*	_ _ _	loud noise
fro	18.	*frown*	_ _ _	back again

309

Answers			Definition of Hidden Word
duct	19.	The word *abduct* contains _ _ _	a tube
loon	20.	*balloon* _ _ _ _	a bird
abash	21.	*calabash* _ _ _ _ _	embarrass
canter	22.	*decanter* _ _ _ _ _ _	easy gallop
earl	23.	*early* _ _ _ _	nobleman
simile	24.	*facsimile* _ _ _ _ _ _	comparison
amorous	25.	*glamorous* _ _ _ _ _ _ _	passionate
rue	26.	*imbrue* _ _ _	be sorry for
yak	27.	*kayak* _ _ _	Asian ox
lama	28.	*llama* _ _ _ _	Buddhist monk
baste	29.	*lambaste* _ _ _ _ _	sew loosely

Crossword Puzzles

The crossword puzzle is still the most popular word game. Although the ones provided here are merely examples of what can be devised, we have provided clues, beginning on page 312, should the teacher wish to reproduce them.

Fish Crossword

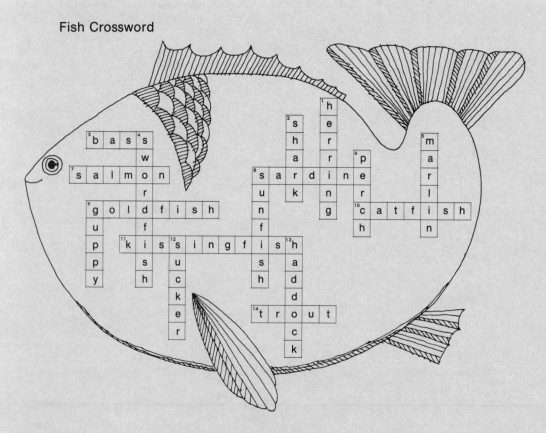

Sports Crossword

Animal Crossword

Clues for Fish Crossword

Across

3. It has a name like a male singer.
7. They swim upstream to spawn.
8. It is really packed in tightly.
9. A common pet.
10. It has whiskers.
11. It likes to kiss.
14. Some have the colors of the rainbow.

Down

1. What a sardine might grow up to be.
2. One of the greediest eaters and a killer.
4. It is named for its long, sharp upper jaw.
5. It has pointed spears and lives in the ocean.
6. What a bird stands on.
8. It is small and brightly colored and likes the sun.
9. Its name rhymes with young dog. It multiplies quickly and often.
12. It sucks up animal and plant life on bottom of lakes.
13. It rhymes with horses' pen at a race track.

Clues for Sports Crossword

Across

6. It is played with a ball and paddles at a table.
8. It is played with a mallet.
10. Its players dribble the ball.
12. Riding waves on a board.
13. Use of a bow and arrow.
16. Riding on the water.
17. Its players hit a puck while ice skating.
19. Its players don't like bogeys.
22. Game played by men on horseback.
23. Its players move a ball with their feet, head, or body into the opposing team's goal.
25. He rides on a bridle path.
27. Taking a short trip on foot.
29. A birdie is used in it.
30. It is played between wickets.

Down

1. Rod and reel are used in it.
2. A gun is used in it.
3. Players compete in forty-yard dash on it.
4. The ball is hit with the hand.
5. All its players wear helmets.
7. The backstroke is used.
9. Its players use a racket to hit a ball over a net.
10. It is played on a diamond.
11. Its players use cues.
14. Its players use a stick with a net at one end.
15. Its players hit a ball over a net with their hands.
18. You can sit or lie on it to go down a snow slope.
20. Swords are used in it.
21. Skimming along on top of the water.
24. Player knocks pins down in it.
26. Moving on little wheels.
28. Gliding across a frozen pond.

Clues for Animal Crossword

Across

1. I have fins to swim with.
4. I am the biggest animal in the ocean.
6. I look like a deer, but I am bigger.
8. I look like a butterfly. I like to fly at night near the light.
9. I am the largest land mammal.
14. We lived a long time ago.
18. A cat says _ _ _ _.
19. I am a baby dog.
21. I am the king of the beasts.
22. I have the longest neck of all.
23. I look like a mouse, but I am larger.
25. I am a mother chicken.
26. I am a lady tiger.
27. We are the smallest unit in everything living, from a plant to you.
29. Bambi is one of my kind.
32. Daniel Boone and Davy Crockett made hats out of my tail.
35. I am a donkey.
36. We are man's best friends.
37. I am the largest American deer, with great big horns.
40. I can pull my head, legs, and tail into my shell.
41. I am the official bird of the United States.
43. Donald is one of my family.
44. I live in my shell at the bottom of the sea.

2. I swoop down and catch chickens.
3. I am the smartest animal in the ocean. Flipper is one of my kind.
5. I run like a deer, but I live on the plains, not in the woods.
7. I am a big spotted cat that lives in the jungle.
10. We are city birds and message carriers.
11. I am the father of kittens.
12. I am the queen of the jungle.
13. I am a bird that comes out at night. Some say I'm very wise.
15. I am a sea animal with eight long, grabby legs.
16. I am a long crawling animal.
17. I look like a big monkey with no tail.
20. We have bright feathers and talk a lot.
24. I am a large jungle cat with stripes.

27. We eat grass and give milk.
28. I have horns and a little beard.
30. I am a male sheep.
31. Man likes to ride me.
33. I am a young horse.
34. I am the largest bird, but I can't fly.
38. I am a mother deer.
39. We are really slow. We carry our houses along with us.
42. I am a baby sheep.

Overlapping-Word Puzzles

Using the "opposites" concept and a variation of the crossword puzzle, the teacher can provide the student with practice in word recognition skills.

Using the synonyms and antonyms of given concepts such as shortness and length, the teacher may place given words in rectangular or square form as we have done in the puzzle form which follows.

The advantage of this technique over that of the crossword puzzle lies in the ease with which it can be constructed. There are no blank spaces or numbers to contend with. The words are run together horizontally and vertically.

These puzzle forms may be used in several ways:

1. The student finds animals, colors, or plants in the puzzle.

2. The student finds certain parts of speech: verb, noun, preposition, etc.

3. Other categories may include the names of the days of the week, months, school subjects, birds, flowers, space terms, etc.

4. The student finds proper nouns: cities, states, countries, famous people, etc.

5. The student finds certain kinds of activities: trades, professions, sports, hobbies, etc.

6. The student finds synonyms for a key word such as *hot, cold, big*.

7. The teacher may also combine both antonyms and synonyms in the puzzle as we have done in the following suggested lesson.

In this lesson and others like it, the student may enjoy working the puzzle and also gain practice in reviewing synonyms and antonyms. For example, in the lesson following, the student has a chance to review the various words that stand for the concepts of shortness or length.

"Short" and "Long" Hidden Words

Instructions: Go across or down to form words that have something to do with longness or shortness. (There are at least forty words.) The student may circle each word as illustrated below.

Short & Long

```
c  o  n  c  i  s  e  t  a  b  l  o  i  d  s
u  c  u  r  t  u  p  r  u  n  e  a  n  p  e
r  a  n  g  y  c  i  u  a  p  l  b  t  r  s
t  e  r  s  e  c  t  n  p  r  i  r  e  o  q
a  e  s  t  l  i  o  c  e  e  s  i  r  t  u
i  l  y  u  i  n  m  a  r  c  i  d  m  r  i
l  i  n  n  d  c  i  t  c  i  o  g  i  a  p
e  s  c  t  e  t  z  e  u  s  n  e  n  c  e
d  i  o  c  b  o  e  d  r  s  q  u  a  t  d
l  o  p  r  a  n  g  y  s  t  u  b  b  e  a
a  n  a  o  l  a  b  r  i  d  g  e  l  d  l
c  l  t  p  r  o  l  o  n  g  a  t  e  b  i
o  a  e  p  r  o  l  i  x  i  t  y  t  r  a
n  n  d  e  l  o  n  g  a  t  e  d  s  e  n
i  k  e  d  l  o  n  g  e  v  i  t  y  v  e
c  o  m  p  e  n  d  i  u  m  b  r  i  e  f
a  b  s  t  r  a  c  t  s  t  r  i  n  g  y
```

Answers

Across

concise	squat	long	compend
tabloids	lop	prolix	compendium
curt	stub	prolixity	brief
prune	abridge	elongate	abstract
rangy	prolong	elongated	stringy
terse	prolongate	longevity	

315

curt	syncopated	epitomize	interminable
curtail	stunt	truncated	protract
curtailed	crop	apercu	protracted
laconic	cropped	précis	breve
lank	elide	elision	sesquipedalian
syncopate	succinct	abridge	

Hard "Small" Hidden Words

Instructions: Go across or down to form words related to "small."

```
m  e  a  g  e  r  m  i  n  i  a  t  u  r  e
i  o  t  a  l  l  i  e  p  i  t  o  m  e  l
c  j  o  t  i  s  c  a  n  t  d  w  a  r  f
r  s  m  a  l  l  r  m  o  l  e  c  u  l  e
o  u  t  i  n  y  o  p  o  i  n  t  w  r  x
c  n  h  o  m  u  n  c  u  l  u  s  e  u  i
o  d  u  r  c  h  i  n  t  l  t  e  e  n  g
s  e  m  i  c  r  o  b  e  i  e  s  s  t  u
m  r  b  s  w  e  e  m  r  p  y  g  m  y  i
i  s  a  t  d  i  m  i  n  u  t  i  o  n  t
n  i  n  u  u  m  i  n  u  t  e  l  f  o  y
i  z  t  n  m  a  r  u  d  i  m  e  n  t  m
m  e  a  t  p  c  e  t  o  a  t  h  i  n  i
u  a  m  e  y  r  l  i  o  n  f  i  n  e  t
m  l  o  d  e  o  p  a  r  t  i  c  l  e  e
```

Answers

Across

meager	scant	homunculus	minute
germ	dwarf	urchin	elf
miniature	small	microbe	rudiment
iota	molecule	wee	thin
epitome	tiny	pygmy	fine
jot	point	diminution	particle

Down

microcosm	bantam	Lilliputian	elf
minimum	stunted	ant	exiguity
undersize	dumpy	wee	mite
atom	micron	runt	
Tom Thumb	minutia	runty	

316

Hidden "River" Words

Instructions: Go across or down to form names of rivers.

```
m  i  s  s  i  s  s  i  p  p  i  n  d  u  s
a  r  e  r  i  o  g  r  a  n  d  e  o  r  a
c  n  i  a  g  a  r  a  r  h  i  n  e  a  l
k  a  n  g  a  a  h  w  a  n  g  h  o  y  t
e  r  e  d  n  m  i  a  r  n  o  u  h  a  e
n  k  l  u  g  a  n  d  p  o  n  d  i  n  n
z  a  m  b  e  z  i  d  r  e  i  s  o  g  n
i  n  r  a  s  o  u  y  e  l  l  o  w  t  e
e  s  o  n  o  n  r  e  d  o  e  n  a  z  s
a  a  c  g  m  l  e  u  p  h  r  a  t  e  s
s  s  k  i  m  e  k  o  n  g  s  n  a  k  e
t  h  a  m  e  s  t  l  a  w  r  e  n  c  e
```

Answers

Across

Mississippi	Rhine	Po	Mekong
Indus	Hwang Ho	Zambezi	Snake
Rio Grande	Red	Yellow	Thames
Niagara	Arno	Euphrates	St. Lawrence

Down

Mackenzie	Rock	Irawaddy	Ohio
East	Ubangi	Red	Yangtze
Arkansas	Ganges	Nile	Salt
Seine	Somme	Hudson	Tennessee

Consonant-Vowel Substitution

The teacher can build interest in word formation by challenging students to make words by manipulating letters within a prescribed form.

As we have previously pointed out, word interest may be heightened by various kinds of word games. The following game requires close attention to letter discrimination and can be a means of providing practice in concentration on words and spelling. Many of the key words used are antonyms.

In this exercise the student must change only <u>one</u> letter at a time to form a new word. For example, moving from *like* to *hate* in four steps or from *well* to *sick* in five steps, thus:

like	well
lake	will
late	sill
hate	silk
	sick

The following exercises may be duplicated for the student to fill out. For the teacher's convenience in checking the answers or for self-checking by the student, the answers are on the pages immediately following these exercises.

The teacher will note that most of the beginning items are composed of words likely to be known by younger students. Some of the later material, involving more steps, or more difficult words, is suitable for the higher grade levels. The number of steps used is not important. One student may take more or fewer steps than another but he must take only one step (a change of one letter) at a time. Words going from one key word to another may differ. For example, the student may move from *dog* to *cat* in at least two ways:

dog	dog
cog	dot
cot	cot
cat	cat

A beginning group of key words might include the names of the animals below.

Animal Exercise

1. pup		4. calf			
_ _ _		_ _ _ _			
_ _ _		_ _ _ _			
dog		bull			

2. worm	5. pig
_ _ _ _	_ _ _
_ _ _ _	_ _ _
_ _ _ _	_ _ _
_ _ _ _	_ _ _
fish	sty

3. hare	6. deer
_ _ _ _	_ _ _ _
_ _ _ _	_ _ _ _
_ _ _ _	_ _ _ _
_ _ _ _	_ _ _ _
bear	lion

Answers

1. pup	4. calf
p u g	c a l l
d u g	b a l l
dog	bull

2. worm	5. pig
w o r e	b i g
w i r e	b a g
w i s e	s a g
w i s h	s a y
fish	sty

3. hare	6. deer
h e r e	d e a r
h e r d	d e a n
h e a d	l e a n
b e a d	l e o n
bear	lion

Antonym Exercise (Answers are on the right)

1. cool	2. work		1. cool	2. work
_ _ _ _	_ _ _ _		w o o l	p o r k
_ _ _ _	_ _ _ _		w o o d	p o r t
_ _ _ _	_ _ _ _		w o r d	p o s t
_ _ _ _	_ _ _ _		w a r d	p e s t
warm	rest		warm	rest

3. wet	4. talk		3. wet	4. talk
_ _ _	_ _ _ _		b e t	t a c k
_ _ _	_ _ _ _		b a t	s a c k
_ _ _	_ _ _ _		b a y	s i c k
_ _ _	_ _ _ _		d a y	s i n k
dry	sing		dry	sing

5. give	6. find		5. give	6. find
_ _ _ _	_ _ _ _		g a v e	f i n e
_ _ _ _	_ _ _ _		c a v e	l i n e
_ _ _ _	_ _ _ _		c a k e	l o n e
take	lose		take	lose

7. well	8. heat		7. well	8. heat
_ _ _ _	_ _ _ _		w i l l	h e a d
_ _ _ _	_ _ _ _		s i l l	h e l d
_ _ _ _	_ _ _ _		s i l k	h o l d
sick	cold		sick	cold

9. hard	10. bug		9. hard	10. bug
_ _ _ _	_ _ _		h a r e	b o g
_ _ _ _	_ _ _		b a r e	b o y
_ _ _ _	_ _		b o r e	t o y
_ _ _ _	_ _ _		s o r e	t r y
_ _ _ _	_ _ _		s o r t	f r y
soft	fly		soft	fly

Adding Letters To Form New Words

The student can practice calling up words in games involving the addition or transposition of a letter or letters of a given word to form another word. A variety of rules may be set up, such as requiring the student to add a letter each time he writes a new word: *able, table, tablet; ice, lice, slice, splice;* or *read, rated, prated.* (Note that all the letters in the previous word must be used in addition to the new letter or letters. The letters may or may not be transposed, as in the last group above.)

One procedure divides the class into two or more teams; each adds a letter (or two letters) to make additional words. The first team to make four, five, or six words wins the game.

If the teacher wishes, he may set a time limit for each game. On the whole, mere inflectional endings such as *run, runner, running* should not be counted as new words, although a teacher in the lower grades might try this approach to provide practice in using endings. Likewise, the teacher might decide to accept the addition of prefixes to form new words: *migrate, emigrate, immigrate.*

A few word groups suitable for various levels are included below. The teacher might write the first word of a group on the chalkboard and have the teams proceed as indicated in the exercises below. A student from the winning team may write his group's words on the chalkboard for the class to see. If neither team writes the required number of words, the team with the most words may be considered the winner.

Instructions: The first word of each exercise is given in row 1. The student fills in rows 2, 3, 4, etc., horizontally, by adding either one or two letters to form a longer word for each succeeding row.

Example Words

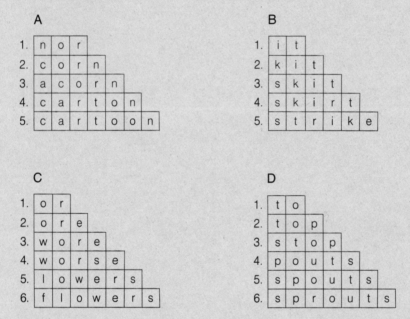

Below are additional words the teacher might use. (The added letters are underlined.)

E	F	G	H
1. or	1. an	1. and	1. sad
2. for	2. and	2. darn	2. shad
3. fort	3. land	3. drain	3. shade
4. forte	4. leaned	4. rained	4. dashed
5. forest	5. cleaned	5. strained	5. reshaded

I	**J**	**K**	**L**
1. pal	1. had	1. man	1. lad
2. laps	2. hard	2. mean	2. lead
3. slaps	3. heard	3. maned	3. dealt
4. lapses	4. thread	4. manned	4. dilate
5. pleases	5. thrashed	5. mannered	5. trailed

M	**N**	**O**	**P**
1. at	1. in	1. cad	1. mad
2. fat	2. fin	2. card	2. made
3. feat	3. fine	3. cared	3. tamed
4. fated	4. define	4. braced	4. teamed
5. fatted	5. refined	5. breached	5. mediate

Q	**R**	**S**	**T**
1. dam	1. it	1. cram	1. vie
2. dram	2. fit	2. cream	2. vile
3. dream	3. rift	3. camera	3. liver
4. ramped	4. first	4. cameral	4. livery
5. revamped	5. firths	5. bicameral	5. delivery

Homonym Crossword

The student writes in the puzzle a *homonym* of each word below. We include only one puzzle; the teacher, perhaps with the help of some students, can use the homonyms in Unit 4 to develop additional puzzles. (For the teacher's convenience, answers to the puzzle are included.)

Crossword solution grid:

¹b		²s	³t	e	e	⁴l		⁵a	⁶i	⁷r
e		⁸f		h		⁹s	e	w		n	e
	¹⁰b	a	r	e		¹¹g	a	t	¹²e		d
	l	r		i			d		¹³w	e	
	u	e	¹⁴t	r				¹⁵s	e	e	¹⁶n
¹⁷t	e		e		¹⁸f	e	e	t		¹⁹s	o
o			a		²⁰w	r	i	t	e		t

Across

2. steal
5. heir
9. sow
10. bear
11. gait
13. wee
15. seen
18. feat
19. sew
20. right

Down

1. bee
3. there
4. led
6. inn
7. read (*past*)
8. fair
10. blew
12. you
14. tee
16. knot
17. too

321

Palindromes

This lesson may be introduced in a variety of ways. One procedure is suggested below. The teacher might present the following palindromic phrases and ask students what they notice about them:

Draw pupil's lip upward
Walsh's law

A careful look will reveal that each example can be read backwards and forwards with the same result. This curious combination of words or letters is called a *palindrome,* from the Greek meaning "running back again," from the Greek word *dromos* (running course). Note other words such as *airdrome, dromedary, hippodrome* (from the Greek word *hippos,* horse).

Here are some one-word palindromes:

Hannah   Otto   rotor   level   sees

In sentence form:

Red root put up to order.   Name no one man.

After he lost his power and was exiled to the island of Elba, Napoleon might have said:

Able was I ere I saw Elba.

Here are some other palindromes:

gold log
stops spots
goldenrod adorned log
a man, a plan, a canal—Panama

Can you guess what the following palindromes are? Remember they must read the same backwards as forwards.

1. A female sheep: e w e
2. Paper showing ownership of land: d e e d
3. Shortened word for a yellow flower: m u m
4. Help me p u t u p the curtain.
5. A baby wears one: b i b
6. Used for defense against aircraft: r a d a r
7. A joke: g a g
8. Eskimo boat: k a y a k
9. You see with it: e y e
10. A girl's name: A n n a
11. A boy's name: B o b
12. An exclamation: a h a
13. Add a vowel and make a slang word out of Bob: b o o b
14. The sound a tugboat makes: t o o t
15. A short word for father: d a d

Note: Students might enjoy keeping their own lists of palindromes which they make up themselves or encounter in their reading. Perhaps the teacher could hold a contest in which the lists would be judged for both length and originality.

Suggested List of Word Games

The teacher can get many ideas for word game exercises from many commercial word games. One excellent source of word games (and games in general) is Darwin A. Hindman's *The Complete Book of Games and Stunts*, Part I, "Indoor Games and Stunts" (Prentice-Hall, Inc., 1962).

For the teacher's convenience we include below a list (published by the International Reading Association[1]) of commercial word games.

Alphabet, Childcraft ($3.00)

ABC Lotto, Childcraft ($1.25)

Consonant Lotto, Garrard Publishing Company ($1.00)

Easy Crossword Puzzles for People Learning English, Walter P. Allen, English Language Services

Fun With Rhymes, Instructo Products Company ($3.95)

Go Fish, A Consonant Sound Game, Remedial Education Center ($1.25)

Go Fish, A Consonant Blend Game, Remedial Education Center ($1.25)

Grab, Dorothea Alcock (Deck 1, $1.75; Deck 2, $1.75; Senior, $1.75)

Group Sounding Game, Garrard Publishing Company ($1.59)

Group Word Teaching Game, Garrard Publishing Company ($1.59)

Judy's Match-Ettes (for use at the reading-readiness level), Judy Company ($3.95)

Junior Scrabble, Selchow and Righter Company ($3.00)

Match, Sets I and II, Garrard Publishing Company ($1.50)

The Monkey Game, Dorothea Alcock ($2.50)

My Puzzle Book, I, II, Garrard Publishing Company ($.56)

Object Lotto, Childcraft ($1.25)

Pay the Cashier, Garrard Publishing Company ($3.95)

Phonetic Quizmo, Milton Bradley Company ($1.50)

Picture Dominoes, Childcraft ($1.25)

Picture Readiness Game, Garrard Publishing Company ($.75)

Picture Word Builder, Milton Bradley Company ($.75)

Pirate Keys (for phonics instruction), Antioch Bookplate Company

Read and Say Verb Game, Garrard Publishing Company ($1.50)

Rummy: Phonic Rummy; Junior Phonic Rummy; Phonic Visual Products ($1.25/set)

Scrabble, Selchow and Righter Company ($4.00)

Sentence Builder, Milton Bradley Company ($1.00)

Spill and Spell, Childcraft ($2.00)

Show You Know Then Go, Teaching Resources, Inc. ($7.50)

The Syllable Game, Garrard Publishing Company ($1.00)

Take, Garrard Publishing Company ($1.50)

Vowel Dominoes, Remedial Education Center ($1.35)

Vowel Lotto, Garrard Publishing Company ($1.00)

What the Letters Say, Garrard Publishing Company ($1.98)

Who Gets It? Garrard Publishing Company ($1.59)

[1]Lillie Pope, *Handbook for the Volunteer Tutor* (Newark, Del.: International Reading Association, 1969), p. 91.

Appendix

List of Common Prefixes and Derived Words

Prefix	Meaning	Example Words
a	on	ashore, aboard, afire, atop, afoot
a, an	not, without	atom, anemia, aseptic, apathy, atheism
ab	from	absent, abduct, abdicate, abnormal, abstain
ac (*form of* ad)	to	accident, acquire, accept, accessory, accommodate
ad	to	adhere, adjoin, adverb, adjacent, adjunct, admit
af (*form of* ad)	to	affair, affirm, affect, afferent, affix
ag (*form of* ad)	to	aggression, aggravate, aggregate, agglutinate, agglomeration
am (*form of* ambi)	both, around	amputate, amputee, amplectant, amplexicaul
ambi	both, around	ambidextrous, ambiguous, ambivalent, ambient, ambilateral
amphi	both, around	amphibious, amphibian, amphitheater, amphibiology, amphipod
an (*form of* ad)	to	annotate, announce, annul, annihilate, annex
ana	back, again, up	anachronism, analysis, anabasis, anapestic, Anabaptist
ante	before	antedate, anteroom, antewar, antecedent, antechamber
anti	against	antifreeze, antisocial, antidote, antislavery, antiseptic
apo	away from, from	apogee, apostle, apostasy, apocryphal, apotheosis
as (*form of* ad)	to	ascribe, assist, aspersion, aspect, assault
auto	self	autograph, automobile, automat, automatic, autobiography
be	make	belittle, becalm, bedim, benumb, becloud
be	thoroughly, all around	bespatter, besplash, besmatter, besmirch, besprinkle
bene	well, good	benefit, beneficial, benediction, benefactor, benevolent
bi, bin, bis	two, twice	bicycle, binocular, bimonthly, bigamy, biceps, biscuit
by	near, aside, from	bystander, bypass, bypath, byplay, byroad
cata	down, against, back	catalog, catapult, cataract, catacomb, catastrophe
cent	hundred	century, centenary, centipede, centigrade, centimeter
circu	around	circus, circuit, circular, circuitous
circum	around	circumnavigate, circumference, circumpolar, circumlocution
cis	on this side	cis-Alpine, cis-Jordan, cislunar, cismontane, cispontine
co	with, together	coworker, cooperator, coequal, coexist, coalition
col	together, with	collect, collaborate, college, collide, colloquial
com	together, with	combine, companion, compact, compose, combat
con	together, with	connect, concentrate, conference, congress

contra, contro	against	contrast, contradict, contrary, contraband, contravene, controversy, incontrovertible
counter	against, in return	counterclockwise, counterattack, counterbalance, counteract, counterrevolution
de	down	descend, degrade, depress, dejected, debase
de	away	depopulate, deflect, detract, dehydrate, deter
dec	ten	decade, decimal, December, decathlon, decagon
deci	tenth	decimal, decimate, decimeter, decibel, decigram
demi, hemi, semi	half, partly	demigod, demigoddess, demitasse, hemisphere, semiconscious, hemidemisemiquaver
di	two	diphthong, dioxide, divalent, dilemma, digamy
dia	through, between	diameter, diagonal, dialogue, diaphragm, diagnosis
dis	not	dishonest, distrustful, discontent, disobey, disable
dis	apart from	dismiss, discard, disarm, dislocate, disassemble
dis	opposite	disarrange, discomfort, disconnect, disown, discontent
du	two	dual, duet, duplex, duplicate, duologue
dys	bad	dyspepsia, dysfunction, dysentery, dystrophy, dysphasia
e (*form of* ex)	out	eject, emit, erupt, elicit, elevate
ec	out	ecstasy, eccentric, eclipse, eclectic, ecdysis
ecto	outside	ectoplasm, ectoderm, ectoblast, ectopia, ectomorph
ef (*form of* ex)	out	effect, efferent, effulgent, effort, efficient
em	in	empathy, embrace, embark, embalm, empiric
en	in	encircle, enfold, encase, enchain, enslave
endo	inside	endoderm, endogamy, endogenous, endoskeleton, endocrine
enter, entre (*form of* inter)	among, between	entertain, entertainer, enterprise, entremets
entero	intestine	enterology, enterovirus, enterococcus, enterotomy, enterostomy
ento	within	entogastric, entophyte, entozoon, entoblast, entoptic
epi	upon, in addition	epilogue, epidermis, epitaph, epithet, epidemic
eu	well, good	eulogy, euphemism, euphonious, eugenics
ex	out	exit, extract, exclude, excerpt, exaggerate
exo	out	exoderm, exoskeleton, exocentric, exodontist, exogamous
extra	outside, beyond	extramural, extravagant, extraordinary, extracurricular, extradite
for	to prohibit, omit, thoroughly	forfend, forget, forgo, forlorn, forswear
fore, for	in front	foresee, foretell, foreground, forecastle, forward
forth	forward, onward	forthcoming, forthgoing, forthright, forthwith, forthputting

hept, sept	seven	heptagon, heptangular, heptarchy, septennial, September
hetero	different	heteronym, heterogeneous, heterodox, heterosexual
hex, sex	six	hexagon, hexameter, hexahedral, sextillion, sexcentenary
homo	same	homogenized, homonym, homogeneous, homocentric, homogenesis
hyper	over, beyond	hypersensitive, hyperacidity, hypercritical, hypertension, hyperbole
hypo	under, too little	hypoactive, hypothyroid, hypochondriac, hypodermic, hypotenuse
il	not	illegal, illogical, illegible, illiterate, illaudable
im	into	immerse, immerge, immigrate, implant, impale
im	not	immovable, immobile, immaculate, immaterial, impartial
in	into	intake, inhale, include, incision, incorporate, incentive
in	not	inactive, incorrect, indecent, informal, incorrigible
infra	below	infrared, infrahuman, infraglacial, infrastructure
inter	between, among	international, interurban, intermission, interjection, intercede
intro, intra	within	introduce, introvert, introspective, intramural, intracoastal
ir	not	irregular, irresistible, irreverent, irrational, irrelevant
iso	equal, same	isobar, isometric, isosceles, isotope, isochronous
kilo	1,000	kilocycle, kilogram, kilometer, kilowatt, kilovolt
macro	large, long	macron, macroscopic, macrometer, macrocosm, macrofossil, macrobiotic
mega	large	megalomania, megaphone, megapod, megascope, megalith
meso	middle	mesoderm, mesocephalic, mesocolon, Mesozoic, mesoseismal
meta	change	metaphor, metamorphosis, metabolic, metabolism, metastasis
meta	beyond	metaphysics, metapsychosis, metabiological, metachrome
micro	small	microscopic, microphone, micrometer, microfilm, microcosm
mid	middle	midday, midnight, midship, midwestern, midstream
milli	1/1,000	millimeter, milligram, millisecond, millivolt, milliwatt
mis	wrong	misspell, misstep, misdeed, misinterpret, misbehave, misgiving
mono	one	monarch, monocle, monoplane, monorail, monochrome
multi	many	multitude, multimillionaire, multicolored, multilateral, multiform
myriad	10,000	myriad, myriapod, myriorama, myriagram, myrialiter
ne, neg	not	never, nefarious, neuter, negative
neo	new, modern	neologism, neophyte, neolithic, neoteric

non	not	nonstop, nonsense, nonpolitical, nonflowering, nonentity
novem, non	nine	November, novena, nones, nonagon, novennial
ob	against	objection, obstacle, obstruct, obdurate, objurgate
oct	eight	octopus, October, octagon, octave, octopod
off	from	offshore, offshoot, offspring, offset, offcenter
olig	few	oligarch, oligarchy, oligopoly, oligochrome, oligocarpous
omni	all	omnipotent, omnivorous, omnipresent, omniscient, omnibus
on	on	oncoming, ongoing, onflow, onshore, onside
out	surpassing	outreach, outrun, outstanding, outwear, outsell
out	outside of	outskirts, outlying, outfield, outsider, outcast
over	above, beyond	overheat, overactive, overdone, overshoot, overage
pan	all	pandemonium, pan-American, pandemic, panorama, pansophy
para	beside	paragraph, parallel, parasite, paraphrase, paradigm
pen, pene	almost	peneplain, peninsula, penannular, penultimate
penta	five	pentagon, Pentecost, pentameter, pentasyllable, pentacle
per	throughout	pervade, perpetual, permanent, permit, perforate
peri	around, near, about	periscope, perimeter, periphery, peripatetic, perigee
poly	many	polygon, polysyllable, polygamy, polytheism, polygyny
post	after	postscript, postpone, postdate, posterity, post-bellum
pre	before	predict, presume, precede, premeditate, predecessor
preter	beyond	preternatural, pretermit, preterition, preterit, preterlegal
pro	before	prognosis, program, progenitor, prophesy, prophet
pro	in place of	pronoun, pronominal, proconsul
pro	forward	project, propel, progress, promenade, profuse
pro	in favor of	proslavery, pro-American, pro-liberal, proponent, pro-Western
pro	in front	prologue, proboscis, program, proseminar
pros, proso	toward, forward	proselyte, prosody, prosodetic, prosodemic, prosencephalon
proto	first	protozoa, prototype, protoplasm, protocol, protomartyr
pseudo	false	pseudohistoric, pseudoclassic, pseudonym, pseudopod, pseudoscience
quad, quatr, quart	four	quadruplet, quadruped, quadrilateral, quatrain, quarter
quasi	seemingly	quasi-humorous, quasi-historical, quasi-judicial, quasi-legislative
quin	five	quintet, quintuplet, quintuple, quintessence
re	back	refund, retract, repay, remit, return
re	again	reread, rearrange, rediscover, reabsorb, readmit

retro	back	retrorocket, retroactive, retrograde, retrospection
se	aside	secede, seduce, seclude, segregate, secret
semi	half	semicircle, semiannual, semifinal, semiconscious, semiformal
sept	seven	September, septennial, septet, septuagenarian, septangular, Septuagesima
sesqui	one and a half	sesquilateral, sesquicentennial, sesquioxide, sesquipedalian
sex	six	sexagenarian, sexennial, sextet, sexagonal, sexennium
sext	sixth	sextet, sextant, sextain, sextillion, sextuple
sub, subter	under, below	submarine, subsoil, submerge, subnormal, subterfuge
super, supra	over	supersede, supernatural, superannuated, superheat, superfine, supraorbital
syl (*form of* syn)	together, with	syllable, syllabicate, syllabus, syllapsis, syllogism
sym	together, with	sympathy, symphony, symmetry, symposium, symbiosis
syn	together, with	synonym, synthesis, synopsis, synchronous, synapse
ter	thrice, threefold	tercentenary, terchloride, terdiurnally, ternary, tertiary
tetra	four	tetragonal, tetrameter, tetrarchy, tetrachromatic, tetrachloride
thorough	through	thoroughfare, thoroughgoing, thoroughbred, thoroughpaced
trans	cross, over	transfer, transmit, transit, transcontinental, translate
tri	three	triangle, tricycle, trigonometry, trivial, triarchy, triad
twi	two, double	twice, twilight, twilit, twi-nighter
ultra	beyond	ultraviolet, ultramodern, ultranationalism, ultrasonic
un	not	unsafe, uncomfortable, unsure, unreliable, unadorned
under	below	underline, underscore, underrate, understatement, underage
uni	one	unit, unicycle, unicorn, universe, uniform, unify
ut, utter	out, outer	utmost, uttermost, utter, utterance, utterly
vice	in place of	vice-president, vice-principal, vice-admiral, viceroy, vice-chancellor
with	back, away, against, with	withdraw, withhold, withstand, within, without

List of Common Suffixes and Derived Words

Suffix	Meaning	Example Words
able, ble, ible	can be done	readable, credible, soluble, eatable, lovable
able, ble, ible	inclined to	peaceable, perishable, terrible, voluble, durable
ac	descriptive of	maniac, demoniac, hypochondriac, elegiac
aceae	denotes families	Ulmaceae, Liliaceae, Roscaceae, Rubiaceae, Frankeniaceae
aceous	having appearance of	arenaceous, cretaceous, crustaceous, herbaceous, ulmaceous
acious	tends to be	spacious, loquacious, pugnacious, fallacious, mendacious
acy, cy	office, rank of, state of	agency, candidacy, infancy, celibacy, privacy
ad	in the direction of	dorsad, ventrad, cephalad, caudad
ad	aggregate	myriad, monad, triad, dyad, pentad
ade	result, product, thing made	orangeade, lemonade, grapeade, limeade, marmalade
ade	process, action	parade, blockade, escapade, cannonade, promenade
ae	Latin feminine plural	alumnae, formulae, algae, vitae, larvae
age	place of	orphanage, parsonage, anchorage
age	collective	percentage, average, mileage, peerage, baggage
age	action, process	ravage, pillage, marriage, carnage, pilgrimage
age	result of	damage, wastage, shrinkage, coinage
al	relating to	filial, natural, ornamental, royal, hypocritical
an	relating to	veteran, Korean, American, sylvan, Anglican, European
ana	collection of	Americana, Shakespeariana, Lincolniana, Johnsoniana, Leeana
ance	state of	variance, resistance, avoidance, annoyance, importance
ancy	state of	vacancy, truancy, occupancy, ascendancy
and, end	to be done	multiplicand, addend, dividend, subtrahend, reverend
ant (*adj.*)	state of, condition of	variant, defiant, radiant, vacant, buoyant
ant, ent (*noun*)	person who	immigrant, resident, student, emigrant, assistant, regent
ar	characterized by, relating to	popular, muscular, circular, linear, polar
ard, art	person who	drunkard, braggart, dullard, sluggard, coward, wizard
arian	person who, place where, thing which	grammarian, librarian, humanitarian, libertarian, agrarian
ary	person who, place where, thing which	secretary, sanctuary, dictionary, infirmary, statuary
ary	characterized by, relating to	literary, military, reactionary, exemplary, customary
ate (*verb*)	to make, cause to be	fascinate, annihilate, liberate, radiate, venerate
ate (*adj.*)	state of, quality of, condition of	fortunate, desolate, desperate, dispassionate, collegiate
ate (*noun*)	function, office, person who, thing which	magistrate, advocate, mandate, potentate, episcopate

ation	process, action	narration, continuation, visitation, computation, alteration
ation	state of, quality of, result of	occupation, moderation, decoration, refrigeration, exhilaration
ator, itor	person who, place where, thing which	editor, orator, refrigerator, incubator, incinerator
atory	process, action, place where	oratory, reformatory, laboratory, conservatory, lavatory
cule	small	minuscule, molecule, denticule, animalcule, pedicule
cy	state of, condition of	accuracy, diplomacy, lunacy, despondency, bankruptcy
cy, y	process, action	piracy, idiocy, inquiry, vagrancy, truancy
dom	region, collectivity	kingdom, dukedom, earldom, heathendom, Christendom, officialdom
dom	state of	freedom, martyrdom, serfdom, wisdom, boredom
ectomy	surgical removal	tonsillectomy, gastrectomy, appendectomy, thoracectomy, thyroidectomy
eme	denoting basic structural unit	phoneme, morpheme, grapheme, prosodeme
emia	condition of the blood	leukemia, anemia, toxemia, pyremia, septicemia
en	made or consisting of	earthen, ashen, golden, wooden
en	to render or induce	lengthen, shorten, blacken, weaken, frighten
ence	state, quality, condition of	dependence, insolence, confidence, competence, absence
ency	quality of, state of	potency, despondency, clemency, frequency, expediency
ene	double-bonded hydrocarbons	benzene, ethylene, pentene, butyrene, acetylene
eous	composed of	aqueous, igneous, vitreous, arboreous, nauseous
er	comparative degree	faster, lighter, clearer, prettier, tighter
er, or	person connected with	carpenter, islander, grocer, barber, officer, garner
er, or	process, action	recover, discover, murder, plunder, waiver
ern	direction	eastern, western, northern, southern
ery, ry	place where	laundry, bakery, vinery, rookery, bindery
ery, ry	product of action	pottery, poetry, tapestry, heraldry
ery, ry	state of	bravery, angry, snobbery, tomfoolery, priggery, imagery, savagery
ery, ry	act, trade, occupation	archery, robbery, sorcery, surgery, skulduggery
ese	derivation, language	Japanese, Maltese, Chinese, Nepalese, Cantonese
esque	in the manner, style of, like	picturesque, arabesque, burlesque, Romanesque, statuesque
ess	feminine ending	songstress, poetess, shepherdess, actress, countess
et, ette	little, small	islet, cigarette, kitchenette, statuette
eth	Middle English verb ending	knoweth, thinketh, doeth, sayeth, wanteth
eth	numbers	twentieth, thirtieth, fortieth, fiftieth, eightieth
etic	adjective ending	genetic, energetic, sympathetic
eur	state or quality	grandeur, hauteur, rigueur
eur	agent	amateur, entrepreneur, chauffeur, masseur, raconteur, saboteur, connoisseur
fer	bearing, carrying	conifer, Lucifer, Jennifer

ferous	bearing, yielding, producing	coniferous, auriferous, odoriferous, cruciferous
fic	making, causing	scientific, sporific, odorific, sudorific, honorific
fold	increase, multiplication	manifold, manyfold, threefold, severalfold, thousandfold
form	in the shape of	calciform, oviform, solidiform, theiform, cuneiform
ful	characterized by, full of	beautiful, successful, skillful, thankful, unmerciful
ful	enough to fill	cupful, spoonful, pailful, mouthful, handful, armful
fy	make or form into	satisfy, amplify, dandify, Frenchify, deify, qualify
gram	something written, a record	telegram, chronogram, diagram, cablegram, radiogram
graph, graphy	writing, an instrument for writing	telegraph, phonograph, photography, cryptograph, paragraph
hood	state of, quality of, condition of	knighthood, manhood, childhood, likelihood, falsehood, brotherhood
ial	characterized by, related to	connubial, fluvial, pluvial, commercial, remedial
ian	characterized by, related to	Christian, physician, Parisian, barbarian, Jeffersonian
iana	product, collection of	Johnsoniana, Christiana, Peruviana, omniana, mediana
iasis	process, action, diseased condition	odontiasis, pogoniasis, psoriasis, hypochondriasis, mydriasis
iatric, iatry	healing art	psychiatry, pediatric, gyniatrics, hippiatry, physiatric
ic	of the nature of, characterized by	angelic, iambic, apostolic, volcanic, quixotic
ic	to form nouns	magic, classic, public, rhetoric, music, arithmetic
ical	of the nature of, characterized by	critical, fantastical, comical, apostolical, political
icle	little	canticle, denticle, particle, cuticle, article
ics	scientific and social systems	acoustics, dramatics, athletics, gymnastics, politics
id	of the nature of, characterized by	solid, acid, morbid, splendid, frigid, rancid, lucid, candid
id	a member of	parotid, pyramid, Leonid, allergid, cystid
idae	patronymic, group families of animals	Homeridae, Seleucidae, Alcmaeonidae, Aphididae, Equidae
ide	chemical suffix	chloride, sulfide, iodide, hydride, bromide
ie, y	diminutive suffix	birdie, Jeanie, Jimmy, dearie, Natalie, calorie
ier (yer *after* w)	person who, place where, thing which	cashier, gondolier, cavalier, grenadier, chiffonier, brazier, financier, clothier, lawyer, sawyer
ile, il	capable of, suitable for, pertaining to	docile, mobile, virile, civil, fossil, utensil
in	noun suffix	dolphin, cousin, vermin, goblin, bulletin
ina	feminine suffix, orders and suborders	czarina, Wilhelmina, Regina, Acarina, Monadina
inae	subfamilies	Felinae, Meliponinae, Sardinae, Gallinae, Tyranninae
ine	like, characterized by, pertaining to	canine, feline, bovine, Florentine, feminine
ine	noun-forming suffix	discipline, medicine, rapine, ravine, quarantine

333

ine	feminine suffix	heroine, Caroline, Josephine, valentine, Clementine
ine	chemical suffix	chlorine, fluorine, bromine, calcine
ing	present participle	sleeping, walking, writing, acting, playing
ing	material	roofing, bedding, siding, quilting, sheeting
ings	noun associated with the verb form	sweepings, earnings, shavings, windings, furnishings, filings
ion	act, process	construction, rebellion, solution, revolution, electrocution
ion	state of	ambition, dominion, subjection, suspicion, cushion
ious	characterized by	gracious, ambitious, invidious, various, infectious
ish	to form adjectives	Scottish, Turkish, clownish, whitish, bluish, eightish
ish	verb ending	flourish, abolish, cherish, furnish, finish
ism	action, process	baptism, ostracism, plagiarism, despotism, heroism
ism	state of, condition of	hypnotism, barbarism, mysticism, racism, pacifism
ism	doctrine, system	stoicism, Quakerism, Americanism, realism
ist	person who	biologist, monopolist, theorist, botanist, hedonist, socialist
ite	mineral or rock	granite, anthracite, chlorite, pyrite, syenite
itis	inflammatory disease	bronchitis, phrenitis, arthritis, encephalitis, meningitis
ity	state of	calamity, felicity, necessity, acidity, fecundity
ium	scientific names	geranium, androecium, uranium, sodium, helium
ive	having the nature or quality of, tending to	affirmative, active, passive, conclusive, corrective
ization	state of	civilization, hybridization, standardization, verbalization, localization
ize, ise	subject to, make, carry on	baptize, sterilize, civilize, temporize
kin	small	manikin, lambkin, napkin, pumpkin
le	repeated action	hobble, crackle, twinkle, mumble, prattle
ent	full of	pestilent, succulent, fraudulent, purulent, corpulent
less	without	witless, childless, fatherless, doubtless, careless
less	beyond the range of	resistless, dauntless, quenchless, tireless, ageless, ceaseless
let	small	streamlet, ringlet, leaflet, armlet, bracelet
like	like	homelike, lifelike, apelike, tigerlike, ghostlike
ling	small	duckling, gosling, hireling, nestling, darling, princeling
logy	science of	anthropology, biology, zoology
logy	speaking	eulogy, tautology, doxology
long	direction, duration	headlong, endlong, sidelong, lifelong, livelong
ly	characteristic of, in the manner of	fatherly, kingly, manly, timely, daily
lysis, lytic	a loosing, dissolving	analysis, paralytic, autolysis, hydrolytic, electrolysis
man	native, one engaged in, an operator	countryman, dairyman, gasman, camerman, coachman, craftsman
ment	concrete result or thing	entanglement, increment, fragment, instrument, ornament

ment	action or process	development, abridgement, government, embezzlement, cantonment
ment	state of	amazement, adornment, arrangement, puzzlement, refinement
mony	resulting thing	acrimony, matrimony, alimony, ceremony, testimony
most	superlative ending	aftermost, utmost, hindmost, topmost, outermost
ness	state of, quality of, condition of	goodness, greatness, sickness, kindness, wilderness, dimness
ock	small, little	hillock, haddock, tussock, paddock
oid	like, resembling	adenoid, colloid, asteroid, spheroid, planetoid
ol	denotes an alcohol	phenol, glycol, methanol, cresol, ethanol
oma	tumor	sarcoma, fibroma, lymphoma, angioma, leucoma
oon	big	balloon, cartoon, bassoon, harpoon
opia	eye condition	amblyopia, myopia, presbyopia, photopia, ectopia
or	state, quality	error, fervor, pallor, candor, rigor
or, ore	person who	auditor, donor, elevator, creditor, executor, commodore, stevedore
orium	place for, thing used for	auditorium, natatorium, haustorium, emporium, conservatorium
ory	place where	laboratory, conservatory, consistory, purgatory
ose	state of, quality of, condition of	verbose, globose, comatose, bellicose, jocose
ose	chemical suffix	cellulose, fructose, dextrose, glucose
osis	abnormal condition, state, process	hypnosis, psychosis, osmosis, neurosis
ous	possessing the qualities of	poisonous, riotous, joyous, polygamous, bulbous
parous	bearing	oviparous, biparous, viviparous, ovoviviparous
ry	collection of	jewelry, revelry, yeomanry, laundry, citizenry, masonry, poetry
s	to form plural	theaters, streets, volumes, wheels, offices
ship	type of ship	airship, battleship, flagship, warship
ship	state of	hardship, friendship, censorship, worship, ownership
ship	office, profession	clerkship, chancellorship, lordship, authorship, partnership
ship	art, skill	horsemanship, marksmanship, seamanship, swordsmanship, penmanship
sis	state, condition	peristalsis, synopsis, catharsis, symphysis, chassis
some	like, same	awesome, bothersome, cumbersome, meddlesome, quarrelsome, wholesome
some	a group of	twosome, threesome, foursome, fivesome, sixsome, eightsome
some	body	acrosome, chromosome, plastosome, throphosome, mitosome
ster	one belonging to, characterized by	mobster, gangster, trickster, huckster
th	part of	tenth, eleventh, fourth, eighteenth, thirty-sixth

trix	woman who	administratrix, aviatrix, executrix, mediatrix, narratrix
tron	instrument	cyclotron, biotron, vibratron, magnetron, fusetron
tude	state of	amplitude, platitude, gratitude, altitude, fortitude
ular	characterized by	regular, popular, secular, circular, cellular
ule	little, small	capsule, molecule, plumule, spicule, tubule
ulent	abounding in	corpulent, florulent, fraudulent, truculent, succulent
ulose	characterized by	granulose, tuberculose, coagulose, venulose, stimulose
und	of the nature of	jocund, rotund, moribund, fecund
uous	of the nature of	fatuous, impetuous, sensuous, contemptuous, tempestuous
ure	act, process	censure, culture, exposure, enclosure, failure, picture
ure	rank	judicature, prefecture, legislature, magistrature, corporature
ward, wards	course or direction	toward, backwards, homeward, forward, westward
ways	manner	sideways, always, slantways, crossways, longways
wise	way, manner, respect	clockwise, counterclockwise, lengthwise, slantwise, bookwise
wright	workman, craftsman	wheelwright, playwright, shipwright, wainwright, millwright
y	characterized by, inclined to	dreamy, chilly, lumpy, sleepy, windy
yer	person who	lawyer, sawyer, bowyer

List of Common Roots and Derived Words

In the list below, Levels 1, 2, and 3 refer to the general difficulty level of the root and its derived words. A root marked Level 1 forms words found at the elementary, junior- and senior-high levels. Level 2 includes roots forming words often used at high school and college levels. Level 3 contains roots generally appropriate to higher college-level students, including words used in various disciplines such as biology, zoology, and anthropology.

The levels are not meant to represent a distinct trichotomy, since words from certain roots may range from easy to hard. However, the rating may be useful to a teacher who wishes to construct lessons on roots for a given class. For example, a glance at the list will show that roots such as *act* (do), *equ* (equal), *cent* (100) can be taught to either elementary students or high school students. But the roots *hem* (blood) or *leuco* (white) are more likely to be useful for students at the higher levels of learning.

Level	Root	Meaning	Derived Words
2	acer, acr	sharp, bitter	acrid, acrimony, acerbity, exacerbate
2	acet, aceto	vinegar	acetic, acetate, acetone, acetylene
1	acro	highest	acrobat, acronym, acropolis, acrophobia
1	act	do, move	actor, activate, react, enact
3	actin	ray	actinal, actinic, actinoid, actiniform
2	acu	a point	acute, acuity, acuteness, cute
3	aden, adeno	gland	adenalgia, adenectomy, adenoid, adenoma
1	aer	air	aerial, aerialist, aeroplane, aerate
1	ag	do, move	agenda, agile, agitate, agility
1	ag, agogue	to lead	synagogue, demagogue, pedagogue, anagogue
2	agon	a contest	agony, antagonist, protagonist, deuteragonist
3	agora	assembly	agora, phantasmagoria, paregoric, agoraphobia
1	agr	field, land	agriculture, agrarian, agronomy, agrology
2	aisthesis	sensation	esthete, esthetics, aesthetic, anesthesia
1	akademia	plot of ground in Athens	academic, academe, academy, academician
3	akanthos	thorn	acanthus, acanthoid, acantha, acanthology
2	akoustikos	related to hearing	acoustic, acoustician, acoustics, acoumeter
3	aktis	a ray	actinal, actinism, actinoid, actenoscopy
2	alb	white	albumen, albino, albatross, alb
2	alg, algos	pain	nostalgia, analgesic, neuralgia, algesic
2	ali	another	alias, alien, unalienable, alienate
3	allos	other	allegory, allonym, allopathy, allotrope
1	alpha	beginning	alphabet, alphabetize, alpha particle, alpha ray
1	alt	tall, high	altitude, alto, altimeter, exalted
1	alter	other	alteration, alternate, altercation, subaltern

1	ama, ami	love	amateur, amiable, amity, amorous
2	ambi	to go around	ambience, ambient, circumambient, ambit
1	ambul	walk	amble, ambulance, somnambulist, perambulator
3	amoibe	change	amoeba, amoebic, amoeboid, amoebocyte
3	amphi	on both sides	amphigory, amphitheatre, amphisexual, amphibian
3	ander	man	philander, polyandry, androgynous, androphobia
2	anemos	wind	anemograph, anemology, anemometer, anemone
3	angeion	vessel	angiocarpous, angiology, angiosperm, hydrangea
1	angul, angle	corner	angle, rectangle, angular, quadrangle
1	anim	life, spirit	animal, animate, animator, inanimate
1	animus	soul, mind	animosity, unanimous, equanimity, animadversion
1	annu	year	anniversary, annual, biannual, annuity
3	annulus	ring	annulus, annulet, annulate, annular
1	antiq	ancient	antique, antiquity, antiquarian, antiquated
2	aoide	song	melodeon, melodic, melody, nickelodeon
3	Aphrodite	Greek goddess of love	aphrodisiac, aphrodisian, hermaphrodite
1	api	bee	apiary, apiculture, apian, apiarian
1	apt	fit	adapt, aptitude, apt, inept
1	aqua	water	aquarium, aquatic, aqueduct, aqueous
2	arachn	spider	arachnean, arachnida, arachnid
1	arbitr	consider, judge	arbitrary, arbitrator, arbitrate, arbiter
1	arbor	tree	arboreal, arborist, arboriculture, arboresque
1	arc	bow	arc, arch, archery, arcade
3	arca	chest, box	ark, arcane, arcanum
1	arch	chief	architect, monarch, archbishop, oligarchy
1	arch, arche	ancient, beginning	archaeology, archaic, archive, archetype
3	argent	silver	Argentina, argentiferous, argentum
1	aristo	best	aristocracy, aristocrat, aristocratic, aristogenesis
1	arithmos	number	arithmetic, logarithm, arithmometer
1	arm	weapon	arms, armor, armory, armistice
1	art	skill, art	artist, artificial, artful, artifact
3	arteria	artery, windpipe	artery, arterial, arteriosclerosis, arteriotomy
3	arthron	joint	arthritis, arthritic, arthralgia, arthropathy
3	asper	rough	asperity, exasperation, asperous, asperifoliate
1	aster, astro	star	asterisk, astronomy, astronaut, disaster
1	athl, athlon	prize, contest	athlete, athletic, decathlon, pentathlon
1	atmos	vapor	atmosphere, atmospherics, atmospheric
1	auct, auth	increase, be responsible for	auction, auctioneer, author, authority
1	aud	hear	auditorium, audience, audible, audiovisual
2	aurum	gold	aureole, aureate, auriferous, oriole
1	authen	absolute master	authentic, authenticate, authenticity

1	auto	self	autobiography, autocracy, autograph, automat
1	avi	bird	aviator, aviary, aviatrix, aviculture
3	bacill	staff, rod	bacillus, bacilliform, bacillophobia, bacillicide
2	bacteria	rod	bacteria, bactericide, bacteriology, antibacterial
1	baptein	to dip	baptize, baptism, baptistry, Anabaptist
1	barba	beard	barb, barber, barbate, barbule
1	barbar	barbarous	barbarian, barbaric, barbarous, Barbara
1	baro	weight	barometer, barograph, barogram, isobar
2	basilikos	royal	basilic, basilica, Basil, basil
2	bathos, bathys	depth	batholith, bathometer, bathysphere
2	beat	blessed	beatitude, beatify, beatific, beatification
1	belli	war	belligerent, bellicose, ante bellum, rebellion
1	bene	good, well	benediction, benefit, beneficiary, benevolent
2	beta	B, second letter	alphabet, beta, beta particle, beta ray
2	bibl	book	Bible, bibliography, bibliophile, bibliomania
1	bio	life	biology, biography, biochemist, biopsy
3	blastos	sprout	blastogenesis, blastoderm, endoblast, mesoblast
2	bolbos	bulb	bulb, bulbar, bulbous, bulbiferous
1	bombos	hollow, booming sound	bomb, bomber, bombard, bombardier
1	botane	plant	botany, botanical, botanist, botanize
2	brach	arm	brace, embrace, brachiopod, bracelet
1	brev	short	brevity, breviary, abbreviate, breve
3	bromos	stench	bromide, bromate, bromine, bromic
2	bronch	windpipe	bronchitis, bronchial, bronchotomy, bronchia
2	bursa	bag, purse	bursar, bursitis, reimburse, disburse
2	byssus	bottom	abysm, abysmal, abyss, abyssal
2	cad, cas	to fall	cadence, cadaver, cascade, decadence
1	cal	hot	calorie, caldron, scald, caloric
1	calc	lime, stone	calculate, incalculable, calcium, calculus
2	calli, kali	beautiful	calligraphy, calisthenics, calligram, kaleidoscope
1	campus	field	camp, campaign, campus, encamp
1	cand	glow, white	candle, candidate, candelabra, incandescent
1	cant	song	cantata, canto, incantation, chant
1	cap	head	captain, cape (headland), capital, decapitate
2	caper	goat	caper, caprice, capricious, Capricorn
1	capt	take, receive	captive, incapable, capacity, captivate
2	carbo	coal	carbon, carbuncle, carbohydrate, carborundum
2	cardi	heart	electrocardiogram, cardiac, cardiograph, cardiectomy
1	carn	flesh	chili con carne, incarnation, carnivorous, carnal
3	carp	fruit	endocarp, schizocarp, monocarpus, carpology

2	cast, chast	pure	caste, chastize, chasten, chastity
2	caust, caut	burn	caustic, cauterize, holocaust, cautery
1	cav	hollow	cave, cavern, cavity, excavate
1	ced	go, yield	precede, recede, antecedent, concede
1	celer	swift	accelerate, accelerator, celerity, decelerate
1	cell	small room	cell, cellar, cellular, cellulose
1	cend	set fire to	incendiary, incensed, incense, censer
1	cens	judge	censor, censorship, census, censure
1	center, centr	center	central, eccentricity, centrifugal, egocentric
1	centum	one hundred	cent, centennial, century, percentage
3	cephal	head	acephalous, cephalic, encephalitis, brachycephalic
1	cept	take, receive	reception, conception, accept, receptive
1	cert	perceive clearly	certain, certificate, certify, ascertain
1	cess	go, yield	process, recession, accession, cessation
2	charis	favor	charism, eucharis, Eucharist, charisma
1	charta	leaf of paper	card, chart, cartoon, charter
2	chir	hand	chirognomy, chiromancy, chiropody, chiropractor
2	chlor	light green	chlorophyll, chlorine, hydrochloric, bichloride
2	chole	bile	choleric, melancholy, cholera, cholesterol
2	chorde	string	chord, clavichord, harpsichord, chordate
2	choreia, chorus	dancing	choreography, chorus, choir, chorister
1	christos	anointed	Christ, Christmas, Christian, christen
2	chrom	color	monochrome, chromatic, chromosome, achromatic
1	chron	time	anachronism, chronicle, chronic, chronology
1	cide	kill	suicide, insecticide, homicide, genocide
1	cil	call	council, conciliate, reconcile, conciliatory
1	cin	ashes	cinders, Cinderella, incinerator, cinerarium
1	cine, kine	move	cinema, Cinerama, cinematography, Cinemascope
1	cip	take, receive	recipe, participate, incipient, recipient
1	circ	ring	circle, circus, circular, circuitous
1	cis	cut	scissors, incision, incisive, incisor
1	citare	rouse, call forth	citation, excitement, incite, recite
1	civ	citizen	civilization, civil, civic, civilian
1	clam, claim	shout	exclamation, proclamation, acclamation, clamor
1	clar	clear	declare, clarify, declaration, clarity
1	class	class, group	classify, classical, classics, neoclassic
1	clin	lean	declination, decline, recline, incline
1	clud	shut	include, conclude, exclude, seclude
1	cogn	know	recognize, cognitive, incognito, cognate
2	coll, col	glue	collage, collagen, protocol, collochemistry
1	colo (cultus)	cultivate	agriculture, culture, cultivate, floriculture
1	color	color	discolor, colorful, Colorado, coloration

1	commun	common	community, communism, communion, excommunicate
1	cord	heart	cordial, accord, discord, concord
1	cornu	horn	unicorn, cornucopia, corner, cornet
1	coron	wreath	coronation, coronate, coronet, corona
1	corp	body	corporation, corps, corpuscle, corpse
1	cosm	universe	cosmopolitan, microcosm, macrocosm, cosmic
2	cotyl	hollow	cotyledon, monocotyledon, dicotyledon, epicotyledon
1	cran	skull	cranium, craniology, craniectomy, craniometry
1	crat	rule	democratic, aristocrat, bureaucrat, plutocrat
1	crea	make, create	recreation, creature, creator, creativity
1	cred	believe	credit, incredible, discredit, credulous
3	crep	to crack, crackle	crepitate, decrepitate, decrepit, decrepitude
1	crim	judge, accuse	crime, criminal, incriminate, discriminate
1	crit	separate, judge	critic, criticize, critical, critique
1	cruc, crux	cross	crucify, crucifix, crucial, excruciating
2	crypt	secret	cryptic, crypt, cryptogram, cryptography
2	culp	fault, blame	culpable, exculpate, culprit, mea culpa
1	cum	pile up	accumulate, cumulative, cumulate, cumulus
2	cumb	lie, recline	incumbent, succumb, recumbent, incumbency
1	cur	care	cure, manicure, pedicure, accurate
1	cur	run	current, excursion, recur, concurrent
1	cuss	shake, strike	discussion, concussion, repercussion, percussion
1	cycl	ring, circle	tricycle, bicycle, cyclone, cyclist
2	dactyl	finger, toe	dactyl, dactylic, tridactyl, pterodactyl
2	daimon	divinity, spirit	demon, demonic, demonolatry, eudemon
1	dat	give	date, data, mandate, antedate
1	deb	owe	debt, indebted, debtor, debit
1	decor	proper, fitting	decoration, decor, decorum, decorous
1	dei	god	deity, deify, deism, deicide
1	demn	harm, damage	condemn, condemnation, indemnity, indemnify
1	demos	people	democracy, epidemic, demography, demagogy
2	dendr	tree	rhododendron, philodendron, dendrology, dendrite
1	densus	thick	dense, densify, condensation, density
1	dent	tooth	dentist, dental, dentifrice, trident
1	derm	skin	hypodermic, dermatology, epidermis, pachyderm
1	despotes	master	despot, despotic, despotism
2	deuteros	second	deuteragonist, deuterogamy, deuterium, Deuteronomy
2	dia, diu (dies)	day	diary, diurnal, diet, diuturnal
1	dic, dict	say	predict, abdicate, verdict, contradict
2	dicho	in two, divided	dichotomy, dichotomous, dichoptic, dichogamy
2	digit	finger, toe	digit, digital, digitate, prestidigitation
1	dign	worth	dignity, dignitary, indignant, dignify

341

1	diskos	round plate	disk, discus, discography, disk jockey
1	div	separate	divide, divisor, dividend, divorce
1	do	give	donate, donor, donee, pardon
1	doc	teach	doctor, doctrine, indoctrinate, documentary
1	dogma	opinion	dogma, dogmatic, dogmatism, dogmatist
1	dol	grief	condolence, doleful, dolorous, dolor
1	domin	master	domineering, dominate, dominant, dominion
1	dorm	sleep	dormitory, dormant, dormer, dormition
2	dors	back	endorse, dorsal, dorsoventral, dorsolateral
3	doxa	belief, teaching	doxology, unorthodox, heterodoxy, orthodoxy
2	drakon	serpent	dragon, dragonet, dragonfly, dragoon
1	drama	deed, play	drama, dramatize, dramatic, melodrama
1	drom	running course	airdrome, syndrome, palindrome, hippodrome
1	dub	doubt	dubious, indubitable, dubiety, dubitative
1	duc	lead	conduct, educate, abduct, aqueduct
2	dulc	sweet	dulcimer, dulcet, dulcify, dulciana
2	duplo	double, twofold	duplicate, reduplicate, duplicity, duplex
1	dur	hard	durable, endurable, endure, duress
1	dynamis	power	dynamite, dynamic, dynasty, dynamo
2	echo	echo	echo, echoic, echogram, echolalia
1	ego	I	egotistic, ego, egoism, egocentric
2	eikon	image	icon, iconic, iconoclast, iconolatry
2	elegos	lament	elegiac, elegy, elegize, elegiast
2	elektron	amber	electric, electrocute, electrolysis, electron
2	elephas	ivory	elephant, elephantine, elephantiasis
2	eco, ecu	environment, habitat	economy, economics, ecology, ecumenical
2	em, empt	buy, obtain	exempt, caveat emptor, redemption, preempt
1	emia, hemia	blood	anemic, anemia, leukemia, hemoglobin
2	end, enda	must be done	addenda, dividend, agenda, subtrahend
1	enni	year	biennial, centennial, perennial, bicentennial
2	enter	intestines	dysentery, enteritis, enterectomy, enteralgia
1	equ	equal	equality, equator, equation, equilateral
1	erg	work	energy, erg, ergmeter, synergy
2	erotikos	desire, love	erotic, eroticism, Eros, erogenous
1	err	wander	error, erratic, erroneous, aberration
1	esse	be, exist	essential, essentialism, essence, quintessence
2	esth	feeling	esthetic, anesthetic, anesthetist, anesthetize
1	ether	upper air	ethereal, ether, etherialize, ethane
2	ethn, ethnos	nation	ethnic, ethnocentric, ethnologist, ethnography
2	etym	true meaning	etymology, etymologist, etymon, etymography
1	fac	make, do	manufacture, factory, benefactor, facsimile
1	facil	easy	facility, facilitate, facile, facilities
1	fall	deceive	false, fallacy, infallible, fallacious

3	fatu	foolish	fatuous, fatuitous, infatuate, fatuity
1	fatum	fate	fatal, fatalism, fateful, fatality
1	favor	favor	favorite, unfavorable, favoritism, disfavor
2	feas	do	feasible, infeasible, feasance, malfeasance
1	feder	alliance, bond	federal, confederation, federation, federalist
2	felic	lucky, happy	felicity, felicitate, felicitous, felicitation
3	felis	cat	feline, felinity, felid
2	femina	woman	female, feminine, effeminate, femme fatale
1	fen, fend	ward off	fence, fender, defend, offense
1	fer	carry, bear	transfer, refer, infer, ferry
1	ferv	be hot	fervent, fervid, fervor, effervesce
1	fic	do, make	efficient, efficacious, sufficient, proficient
1	fict	invent, form	fiction, fictitious, fictional, fictive
1	fid	faith	confide, fidelity, infidel, bona fide
1	fig	form	figure, disfigure, figment, effigy
1	fili	son, daughter	filial, affiliate, affiliation, unfilial
1	fin	end	final, finish, finite, infinite
1	firm	steady	confirm, infirm, affirm, firmament
1	fisc	purse	fiscal, fisc, confiscate
1	fiss	split	fission, fissionable, fissure, fissiped
1	fix	fasten	fixation, suffix, fixture, prefix
1	fla	blow, puff	inflate, inflation, deflation, flatulent
1	flagr	blaze	conflagration, flagrant, flagration, deflagrate
1	flam	blaze	flame, inflammable, flammable, flamboyant
1	flect	bend	reflect, reflector, deflect, inflection
1	flex	bend	reflex, flexible, circumflex, flexor
1	flor	flower	flora, floral, florist, florid
1	flu	flow	fluid, fluent, influx, affluent
1	fol	leaf	portfolio, foliage, folio, bifoliate
1	form	shape	uniform, reform, formation, transform
1	fort	strong	fort, fortify, fortitude, forte
1	fortu	chance, fate	fortune, fortunately, fortuitous, fortuity
1	foss	dig, ditch	fossil, fossilize, fossilology, fossiliferous
1	fract	break	fraction, fracture, infraction, refract
1	frank, franch	free	frank, franking, franchise, disenfranchise
1	frat	brother	fraternity, fraternal, fraternize, fratricide
2	frica, frict	rub	friction, affricate, fricative, dentifrice
2	frigor	cold	frigid, frigidity, frigotherapy, refrigerator
1	front	front	confront, affront, effrontery, frontier
1	fru	enjoy	fruit, fruitful, frugal, fruition
1	fug	flee	fugitive, refuge, refugee, centrifugal
2	fulg	shine	fulgent, fulgid, refulgent, effulgence
1	fumus	smoke	fume, fumigate, perfume, fumitory
2	funct	perform	functional, malfunction, functionary, dysfunction
1	fund, found	bottom	profound, fundamental, fund, profundity
2	fus	pour	transfusion, fusion, diffuse, profuse
2	gala	milk	galaxy, galactic, galactose
2	gam	marriage	monogamy, bigamy, trigamy, polygamy
2	gastr	stomach	gastric, gastritis, gastrectomy, gastronomic

1	gel	freeze	gelid, congeal, gel, gelatin
1	gen	race, birth	generation, progeny, genocide, miscegenation
1	gentilis	of the same class	genteel, gentle, gentlemen, gentry
1	geo	earth	geography, geology, geometry, geophysical
2	geras	old age	geriatrics, geriatrician, geratology, gerontology
3	glauco	gray	glauconite, glaucous, glaucoma
2	globus	globe	globe, globular, globoid, globulin
2	glomer	ball, cluster	agglomeration, conglomeration, glomerate, glomerule
2	gloss, glott	tongue	gloss, glossary, polyglot, epiglottis
2	glut	swallow	glut, glutton, gluttony
2	glyphe	carving	glyph, hieroglyph, petroglyph, anaglyph
2	gnos	know	gnostic, agnostic, diagnostic, prognosticate
1	gon	angle	trigonometry, octagonal, agonic, pentagon
2	gonos	birth	cosmogony, theogony, gonad, homogony
1	grad	step	degrade, graduation, retrograde, gradual
1	gram	letter, written	monogram, telegram, grammar, epigram
1	gran	grain	grain, granary, granulated, granule
2	grand	great	aggrandize, grandiose, grandiloquent, grandeur
1	graph	write	autograph, paragraph, phonograph, biography
1	grat	please, thank	grateful, congratulate, gratitude, gratuity
2	gravis	heavy	grave, gravity, aggravation, gravitate
1	greg	herd	congregation, gregarious, aggregation, segregation
2	gust	taste	disgust, gust, gusto, gustatory
2	gymnos	naked	gym, gymnast, gymnastic, gymnasium
2	gyn	woman	monogyny, polygyny, gynecologist, misogynist
1	hab, habi	to hold	prohibit, exhibit, habitual, inhabit
2	hagio	sacred, holy	hagiocracy, hagiolith, hagiology, hagiolotry
2	haima, hemo, hema	blood	hemoglobin, hemorrhage, hemorrhoid, hematosis
1	harmon	harmony	harmonica, harmony, philharmonic, harmonious
2	hedon	pleasure	hedonics, hedonism, hedonist
2	hedr	side, seat	polyhedron, tetrahedron, cathedral, ex cathedra
1	heir	heir	heiress, heirloom, inherit, disinherit
2	heli	sun	helium, heliotrope, heliocentric, heliograph
1	helix	spiral	helicopter, helicoid, heliport, helical
3	hepar	liver	hepatitis, gastrohepatic, hepatic, hepatectomy
1	here, hes	stick	adhere, cohere, adhesion, adhesive
2	herpein	to creep	herpes, herpetology, herpetic, serpent
2	hetero	different	heteronym, heterosexual, heterogeneous, heterodoxy
2	hieros	sacred	hierarchy, hieroglyphics, hierology, hieratic

2	hippos	horse	hippopotamus, hippopod, hippodrome
3	histo	tissue, web	histology, histophysiology, antihistamine, histozoic
1	histor	knowing	history, story, prehistoric, historian
2	holos	whole	holotype, catholic, holocaust, holograph
1	hom	man	homage, *Homo sapiens*, homicide, hombre
3	homeo	similar	homeoid, homeomorphous, homeopathy, homeostasis
1	homo	same	homogenized, homonym, homograph, homocentric
1	honos	respect	honor, dishonest, honorable, honorific
2	hora	hour	hour, horoscope, horologe, horoscopy
2	hort	urge	exhort, exhortation, hortative, hortatory
1	hosp	host	hospital, hospitable, hospice, hostess
1	hum	earth, soil	humus, humiliate, exhume, inhume
1	humanus	human	human, humane, humanitarian, inhumanity
1	humid	moist	humidity, humidor, humidify, dehumidifier
1	hydr	water	hydrant, hydrogen, hydrophobia, dehydrate
2	hygieia	health	hygiene, hygienist, hygienics, Hygeia
3	hygr	moisture	hygrometer, hygrograph, hygroscope, hygrology
2	hymnos	hymn	hymn, hymnal, hymnody, hymnology
1	hypnos	sleep	hypnotism, hypnosis, hypnoid, autohypnosis
2	hystera	womb	hysteria, hysterical, hysterectomy, hysteroid
2	iatrik	healing art	pediatrician, psychiatric, podiatry, geriatrics
3	ichthys	fish	ichthyosis, ichthyosaur, ichthyology
2	icon	image, idol	iconoclast, iconography, iconic, iconophile
1	ident	same	identity, identical, identification, identify
2	idio	peculiar	idiot, idiom, idiomatic, idiosyncrasy
1	ign	fire	ignite, ignition, igneous, ignis fatuus
1	ign	not know	ignore, ignorant, ignorance, ignoramus
1	imagin	imagine	image, imagination, imaginary, imagery
1	imperi	command	imperative, empire, emperor, imperial
1	insul	island	peninsula, insulate, insular, insularism
1	integ	whole, untouched	integrity, integrate, integral, integer
1	ir	anger	irritate, irate, ire, irascible
2	iris, irid	rainbow	iris, iridescent, iridectomy, iritis
1	it	go	exit, initial, initiate, adit
2	itera	say again	iterate, reiteration, reiterative
2	itiner	journey, route	itinerary, itinerant, itinerate, itinerancy
2	jace	lie	adjacent, circumjacent, jacent, subjacent
1	ject	throw	project, projector, reject, eject
1	jocus	joke	joke, jocose, jocular, jocund
1	journ	daily	journal, journalism, journey, journeyman
1	ju, jud	law, right	judge, judicial, adjudicate, judicious
1	junct	join	junction, conjunction, juncture, adjunct
1	jur, jus	law, right	jury, perjury, jurisdiction, jurisprudence
1	juven	young	juvenile, juvenescence, rejuvenate, juvenility

1	kamara	vault, chamber	bicameral, camera, chamber, chamberlain
3	karpos	fruit	acrocarpous, gymnocarpous, pericarp
2	keras	horn	carat, dinoceras, keratose, rhinoceros
1	kilo	one thousand	kilometer, kilogram, kilowatt, kilocycle
2	klasis	breaking	iconoclastic, anaclastic, osteoclasis, synclastic
1	klima	region	climate, acclimate, clime, climatology
3	kokkos	berry	coccus, micrococcus, pneumococcus, streptococcus
1	komos	festival, revel	comic, comedian, encomium, tragicomedy
3	kytos	hollow, cell	cytology, leucocyte, phagocyte, cytolysis
1	labor	work	collaborate, laboratory, elaborate, belabor
3	lact	milk	lactic, lactic acid, lactation, lactose
3	lana	wool	lanolin, lansdowne, laniferous
2	laps	slip	elapse, relapse, collapse, prolapse
3	laryng	windpipe	larynx, laryngoscope, laryngitis, laryngeal
1	lat	side	lateral, unilateral, bilateral, collateral
2	latrea	service, worship	idolatry, diabolatry, theolatry
1	laud	praise	laud, laudatory, laudable, laudability
1	lav	wash	lavatory, lavage, lavation, lavabo
1	lect	gather, choose	collect, elect, select, electoral
1	leg	law	legal, legacy, legitimate, legislate
1	leg	read	legend, legendary, legible, illegible
1	lega	appoint	delegation, legate, delegate, relegate
2	lens, lent	seed-shaped, two sides curved	lens, lenticular, lentil, lenticel
1	leon	lion	lion, chameleon, leopard, leonine
3	lep, lepido, lepra	peeling, scaly	leprosy, leper, Lepidoptera, leproid
3	leuco	white	leucoderma, leukemia, leucoplast, leucocyte
1	lev	raise	elevator, leverage, levee, levy
2	lev	light	levity, alleviate, alleviation, levitation
2	lex, lexis	word	lexicon, lexicography, lexical, dyslexia
1	liber	free	liberty, liberate, liberal, libertine
2	liber	book	library, librarian, librettist, libretto
2	lig	to bind	ligature, ligament, obligation, religion
3	lignum	wood	lignin, lignite, ligneous, lignose
2	limin	threshold	eliminate, liminal, preliminary, subliminal
1	lin	thread	line, linear, lineage, delineate
2	lingu	tongue	lingual, linguistics, linguist, bilingual
1	linguere, lic	leave behind	relinquish, relict, relic, dereliction
2	lip	to leave	eclipse, ecliptic, ellipse, elliptical
3	lipar	fat, grease	liparous, lipase, lipoid, lipoma
1	liqu	liquid	liquor, liquefy, liquidate, liquidity
1	liter	letter	literature, literary, literate, literal
2	lith	stone	monolith, paleolithic, neolithic, lithograph
2	litig	dispute	litigant, litigation, litigable, litiguous
2	lob	rounded projection	bilobate, trilobite, lobe, lobectomy
1	loc	place	local, location, dislocate, localize
2	locu	speak	locution, elocution, circumlocution, interlocutor

1	log	speech	dialogue, prologue, epilogue, eulogy
1	longus	long	elongate, longevity, longitude, prolong
1	lop	run	elope, interloper, elopement, lope
2	loqu	speak	eloquence, soliloquy, colloquial, loquacious
2	lu	wash	deluge, antediluvian, ablution, dilute
2	lubric	slippery	lubricant, lubricate, lube, lubricious
2	luc	light	lucid, translucent, elucidate, Lucifer
1	lud	play	interlude, prelude, postlude, ludicrous
1	lum	light	illuminate, luminous, luminescent
1	luna	moon	lunar, lunatic, sublunar, lunule
1	lus	play	illusion, delusion, elusive, allusion
1	lustra	shine	luster, lustrous, lackluster, illustrious
2	lys, lyt	to loosen	analysis, paralysis, catalyst, hydrolysis, electrolysis
2	macul	spot	immaculate, maculate, macular, maculation
1	magister	master	magistrate, magistry, maestro, majesty
1	magni	great	magnify, magnitude, magnificent, magnanimous
1	magnes	attracting stone	magnetic, magnetism, magnesia, electromagnetic
3	maha	great	mahajan, maharajah, mahatma
1	mal	bad	malice, malady, malign, malignant
1	mall	hammer	mall, mallet, malleable, malleus
1	mamma	breast	mammal, mammary, mammillary, mamma
1	man	hand	manual, manuscript, manipulate, manacle
1	man	remain, dwell	manor, mansion, permanent, remnant
1	mand	order	command, demand, remand, mandate
1	mania	mad	mania, maniac, kleptomania, bibliomania
2	mantia	divination	necromancy, chiromancy, hydromancy
2	mantum	cloak	mantle, mantel, mantilla, manteau
1	mare	sea	marine, submarine, mariner, maritime
1	marg	edge	margin, marginal, submarginal
1	maritus	husband	marital, marriage, intermarriage, premarital
2	mastos	breast	mastectomy, mastoid, mastodon
1	mater, matri	mother	maternal, maternity, matricide, matrix
1	math	learning	mathematics, mathetic, biomathematics, mathesis
1	matur	ripe	mature, immature, maturity, premature
1	maxima	greatest	maxim, maximum, Maximilian, maximize
1	mechan	machine	machine, mechanic, machination, photomechanics
1	med	middle	medium, mediate, median, mediocre
1	medicus	healing	medical, medicine, remedial, remedy
1	meditari	to ponder	meditate, premeditated, meditation
2	melan	black	melancholy, melanism, melanite, Melanesian
2	melior	better	ameliorate, meliorate, amelioration, meliorative
2	mell	honey	mellifluous, melliferous, mellivorous
1	melos	song	melody, melodrama, melodeon, philomel
1	memoria	memory	commemorate, immemorial, memorandum, memorial

347

1	mend	fault, error	amend, emend, mend, amendment
3	menin	membrane	meninges, meningitis, meningospinal, meningorrhea
3	mensis	month	menses, mensual, menstruation, trimester
2	mensura	measure	mensurable, commensurate, dimension, immensely
1	ment	mind	mental, demented, memento, mention
1	merc	trade	merchant, merchandise, commerce, mercantile
1	merg	plunge, dip	merge, submerge, emerge, immerge
1	mers	sink, dip	immerse, emersed, submerse, submersion
1	meter	measure	diameter, barometer, perimeter, centimeter
1	metr	measure	metric, geometric, metrics, diametrically
2	metro	mother, womb	metropolis, metropolitan, metrorrhagia, metralgia
2	mezzo	middle	mezzanine, mezzosoprano, mezzoforte, mezzograph
1	mid	center	amidships, midmorning, middle, midterm
1	migr	move	migrate, emigrate, immigrate, migratory
1	mil	soldier	militant, military, militia, militarism
1	mim	imitate	mimic, mimeograph, pantomime, mime
2	min	to jut out, threaten	prominent, eminent, imminent, commination
1	min	small	minute, minus, minor, minuscule
1	ministrare	officer, servant	minister, ministry, ministrate, administrate
1	minuere	lessen	diminutive, minuet, minuend, minutia
1	mir	to wonder at	admire, admirable, miracle, mirage
2	misan	hate	misanthrope, misanthropy, misogamist, misogynist
1	miscere	mix	miscible, immiscible, promiscuous
1	miser	wretched	miserable, miser, misery, commiserate
1	miss	send, let go	mission, missionary, missile, dismiss
1	mit	send, allow	admit, remit, transmit, permit
2	mnem	memory	amnesia, mnemonic, amnesty, paramnesia
1	mob	move	automobile, mobile, mobility, mobilize
1	mod	manner, measure	model, modest, moderate, mode
2	moll	soft	mollify, emollient, mollusk, emolliate
2	mon	advise, warn	admonish, monitor, admonition, premonition
1	mone	money	monetary, monetize, money, monetarily
1	mons	mountain	mountain, amount, transmontane, surmount
1	monstr	show, point out	demonstrate, demonstrable, remonstrate, monstrance
1	mor	custom	moral, morality, morale, mores
1	morb	disease	morbid, morbidity, morbidness, morbose
2	mord	bite	mordacious, mordant, morsel, remorse
1	moron	stupid	moronic, oxymoron, sophomore, sophomoric
2	morph	shape	metamorphosis, morphology, amorphic, anthropomorphic
2	Morpheus	god of sleep	Morphian, morphine, morphiate, morphinism
1	mort	death	mortal, immortal, mortician, mortuary

1	mot	move	motion, motor, promote, demote
1	mov	move	movable, remove, immovable, movement
2	mucus	mucus, slime	mucid, mucilage, mucilaginous, mucous
1	mun	fortify	munition, ammunition, muniment, praemunire
1	mun, muner	gift, service	immunity, remuneration, munificent, municipal
2	mund	world, earth	mundane, supermundane, intermundane, submundane
2	mur	wall	mural, intramural, extramural, intermural
1	mut	change	mutual, commute, immutable, mutation
3	myc	fungus	mycology, mycelium, actinomyces, mycetous
3	myel, myelo	marrow	myelitis, myelin, poliomyelitis, osteomyelitis
3	myo	muscle	myocardiograph, myogen, myocyte, myology
1	mystes	silent, closed	mystery, mystic, mysterious, mysticism
3	narco	numbness	narcotize, narcolepsy, narcotic, narcosis
2	nas	nose	nasal, nasalize, nasoscope, nasturtium
1	nat	born	native, nativity, natal, innate
3	natare	float, swim	natant, natation, natatorium, naiad
1	naut	ship	nautical, aeronautics, astronaut, Argonauts
1	nav	ship	navy, navigate, circumnavigate, navigable
2	necro	dead	necrology, necrologist, necromancy, necropolis
1	nect, nex	bind	connect, annex, disconnective, connection
1	nego	to say no	abnegate, negation, negative, renege
1	negro	black	Negro, Negrito, Negroid, denigrate
1	neo	new, modern	neoclassic, neolithic, neophyte, neologism
3	nephros	kidney	nephralgia, nephrectomy, nephric, nephritis
1	nervus	nerve	enervate, nervous, unnerved, nervy
2	nes	island	Indonesia, Polynesian, Peloponnesus, Micronesia
1	neur	nerve	neuralgia, neuritis, neurotic, neurectomy
1	neuter	not either	neutral, neutrality, neutron, neuter
1	nihil	nothing	nihilism, nihilistic, annihilate, nil
2	noc, nox	do harm	innocence, innocuous, noxious, obnoxious
1	noctis	night	nocturnal, nocturne, noctambulate, equinox
1	nodus	knot	node, nodal, knot, nodule
1	nom	law	astronomy, economy, autonomy, taxonomy
2	nomen	name	nomenclature, denomination, ignominious, nominate
1	norma	pattern, rule	norm, normal, enormous, abnormality
3	noso	disease	nosology, nosocomium, myonosus, nosographer
1	nounce, nunci	declare	pronounce, announce, denounce, enunciate
1	nov	new	novel, novelty, novice, innovate
2	nucis	nut, kernel	nucleus, nuclear, nucleolus

349

1	nullus	none, not any	null, annul, nullify, nullity
1	numer	number	numeral, supernumerary, numerous, enumerate
1	nutrix	food	nutrition, nutriment, nurture, malnutrition
2	obit	going away	obituary, obital, obituarian
1	ocul	eye	ocular, oculist, binocular, monocular
1	oda	song	ode, melody, parody, rhapsody
3	odonto	tooth	odontitis, odontopathy, odontoscope, orthodontist
3	ontos	being, existing	ontology, ontogeny, ontography, paleontology
1	onym	name	antonym, synonym, pseudonym, acronym
3	oö	egg	oöblast, oöcyst, oöcyte, oöspore
3	ophthalmos	eyes	ophthalmologist, ophthalmodynia, ophthalmagra, ophthalmia
2	ops	power, wealth	copious, cornucopia, opulent, copiosity
2	opsis	appearance	autopsy, synopsis, thanatopsis, necropsy
1	opt	sight	optic, optometrist, optical, optician
1	opt, optio	choose, wish	option, optional, opt, adopt
1	opus	work	opera, operate, cooperate, opus
1	orare	speak	oral, oracle, oratory, adoration
2	orbis	circle	orb, orbit, suborbital, exorbitant
1	ordinis	arrange	order, ordinance, ordinary, ordinal
1	organ	organ	organic, organism, organology, microorganism
1	oriri	rise	origin, originate, orient, orientation
3	ornithos	bird	ornithology, ornis, ornithine, ornithoid
3	oros	mountain	orogeny, orology, orographic, orometer
2	ortho	right, straight	orthography, orthodontic, orthopedic, orthodox
2	oscilla	swing	oscillate, oscillation, oscillograph, oscilloscope
3	osmo	push	osmosis, osmotaxis, endosmosis, exosmosis
2	osteo, oss	bone	osteopath, osteomyelitis, ossuary, ossify
2	otos	ear	otitis, otologist, otolaryngologist, otoscope
1	ov	egg	oval, ovum, ovary, oviparous
1	pacis	peace	pacific, pacify, *pax Romana*
1	paed, ped	child	encyclopedia, pedantic, pedagogue, orthopedics
2	paleo	ancient	paleography, paleolithic, Paleozoic, paleozoology
2	palin, palim	back again	palindrome, palimpsest, palingenesis, palinode
1	pallidus	wanting in color	pallid, pale, appalling, pallor
1	palpare	to feel, stroke	palpable, palpitate, palpus, palpation
1	panis	bread	companion, *pain* (Fr.), appanage, pantry
1	papas	father	papal, papacy, pope
2	par	give birth	parent, oviparous, viviparous, parturition
1	par	equal	compare, comparable, disparity, parity
1	parare	be ready, stop	prepare, parapet, parry, repair
1	parl	talk	parley, parlor, parliament, parlance
1	partis	part, division	part, partial, bipartisan, partition
1	passus	step	pass, passage, impassable, impasse

1	passus, pati	suffer	passion, compassionate, compatible, patient
1	pasta	paste	paste, pastry, pastel, pasty
1	pastum	shepherd, to feed	pastor, pastoral, pasture, repast
1	pater	father	paternal, patriarch, patronymic, patricide
1	path	feeling	sympathy, empathy, antipathy, apathy
2	patri	father, fatherland	unpatriotic, expatriate, compatriot, patriotism
1	ped	foot	pedal, pedestrian, pedestal, biped
1	pel	drive	compel, repel, expel, propel
1	pen	punishment	penal, penance, penitentiary, penalty
1	pend, pens	hang	pendulum, appendage, suspend, appendix
2	penna	feather	pennant, pennate, pennon, bipinnate
2	peptein	to cook, digest	peptic, dyspepsia, eupepsia, pepsin
1	persona	mask	person, personality, impersonate, personnel
2	petalon	leaf	petal, apetalous, monopetalous, bipetalous
1	petr	rock	petrify, petroleum, petrol, Peter
2	phag	eat	esophagus, anthropophagous, sarcophagous, phagocyte
2	phant	appearance, image	phantom, phantasm, phantasmagoria, fantasy
2	pharmakon	drug	pharmaceutical, pharmacology, pharmacy, pharmacist
3	pharynx	chasm, throat	pharyngeal, pharyngitis, pharynopathy, pharyngoscopy
2	phasis	appearance	emphasis, phase, anaphase, metaphase
1	phil	love	philharmonic, philosopher, philatelist, philology
3	phlebos	blood vessel, vein	phlebalgia, phlebitis, phlebotomy, phlebosclerosis
2	phobos	fear	necrophobia, xenophobia, agoraphobia, claustrophobia
1	phon	sound	symphony, phonics, saxophone, xylophone
2	phor	to carry	euphoria, dysphoria, metaphor, semaphore
1	photo	light	photocell, photosynthesis, photography, photostatic
1	phrazein	to speak	paraphrase, phrase, periphrasis, phraseology
2	phren	brain	frenzy, frenetic, phrenology, schizophrenia
2	phyllon	leaf	chlorophyll, cataphyll, phyllade, phylliform
1	physis	nature	metaphysics, physiognomy, physical, physique
3	piscis	fish	piscary, piscatology, Pisces, piscine
2	plac	please	placate, placid, implacable, placebo
2	planeta	wander	planet, planetary, planetoid, plankton
1	planus	level, flat	plain, plane, plan
2	plasma	form	metaplasm, chromoplasm, protoplasm, cytoplasm
2	plastos	formed	plastic, euplastic, osteoplastic, rhinoplasty
1	plaudere	clap the hands	applaud, plaudit, explode, implode
2	plebis	common people	plebe, plebeian, plebiscite, plebs
1	plen	full	plenitude, plenty, plentiful, plenary
3	pleura	rib, side	pleura, pleurisy, pleuropneumonia, pleurotomy

1	pli, plic	fold	multiplication, duplicate, implicate, explicate
1	pluma	feather	plume, plumage, plumate, deplume
1	plumb	lead	plumb bob, plumber, plumbing
1	plutos	wealth	plutocracy, plutarchy, plutolatry
3	pnea	breathing	dyspnea, hyperpnea, orthopnea, tachypnea
2	pneumon	air, lung	pneumatic, pneumonia, pneumococcus, pneumectomy
1	pod, podos	foot	podium, bipod, tripod, chiropodist
1	poiein	to make	onomatopoeia, poem, poet, poetics
1	polis	city	acropolis, metropolis, police, politician
1	polos	pivot, axis	pole, polarity, Polaris, polarization
1	pomum	fruit	pome, pomegranate, pomade, pomace
1	pon	place	postpone, exponent, component, opponent
1	popul	people	popular, populate, depopulate, populous
1	porcus	pig, swine	porcupine, porcine, pork
1	port	carry	transport, import, export, portfolio
1	porta	gate	port, seaport, portal, porter
1	pos	place	deposit, preposition, apposition, composition
1	posse, potes	able	possible, potential, potent, impotence
1	possessum	sit in power	possess, depossess, repossessed, possessive
3	potamos	river	potamic, potamology, potamometer, hippopotamus
1	praktikos	practical, effective	practicable, practice, practitioner, chiropractor
1	press	force	pressure, suppress, oppress, compress
1	privus	one's own	private, deprive, privilege, privacy
1	probare	test, prove	probe, probate, approbation, probation
3	proktos	rectum, anus	proctalgia, proctectomy, proctologist, proctoscope
2	proles	offspring	prolific, proletariat, proletary, proliferate
1	propr	one's own	appropriate, propriety, proprietor, proper
1	proxim	near	proximity, approximation, proximal, proximolingual
3	prurire	itch	prurient, prurigo, pruritis, pruriency
2	psyche	soul, mind	psyche, psychiatry, psychological, psychoanalysis
2	pter	wing	helicopter, pterodactyl, apteryx, lepidopterous
3	pteridos	fern	pteridious, pteridium, pteridology, pteridophyte
3	ptych, ptyx	fold	diptych, triptych, anaptyxis, polyptych
1	pubes	adult	pubic, pubescent, puberty, public
3	puer	child, boy	puerile, puerilism, puerility, puerperal
2	pugil, pugn	fight	pugilist, pugnacious, repugnant, impugn
2	pulmo	lung	pulmonary, pulmometer, pulmocardiac, pulmonitis
1	puls	urge	impulse, repulse, expulsion, compulsory
2	punct	point	punctual, punctuate, punctilious, puncture
1	punir	punish	punish, punishment, punitive
1	pup	child	pupil, puppet, puppy, pupa
3	puru, puster	pus	purulent, pus, pustulant, pustulous
2	purus, purg	clean	pure, purge, purgative, purgatory
2	puter	rot	putrid, putrify, putresce, putricide

3	pyelo	basin, pelvis of kidney	pyelitis, pyelogram, pyelonephritis, pyeloscopy
3	pyla	gate	pylorus, pyloric, micropyle, pylon
3	pyo	pus	pyocyst, pyodermia, pyogenesis, pyolymph
2	pyr	fire	empyrean, pyre, pyromaniac, pyrotechnics
1	quadr	four	quadrangle, quadrant, quadruple, quadrilateral
1	quaero, quest	seek	inquest, request, query, question
2	quantus	how much	quantity, quantify, quantitative, quantum
1	quartus	fourth	quart, quarter, quarterback, quarter horse
3	quater, quatr	four	quaternary, quatrain, quatrefoil, quatercentenary
3	queri	to complain	querimonious, querulous, querulity, querimony
1	quin	five	quintet, quintessence, quintuplets, quincentennial
3	rachios	spine	rachitis, rachialgia, atelorachida, rachiodont
1	radius	ray, spoke of wheel	radial, radius, radium, radiation
1	radix	root	radix, radical, radish, eradicate
2	rama (orama)	view	panorama, cinerama, cyclorama, diorama
1	ramp	climb, rage	ramp, rampant, rampage, rampancy
2	ramus	branch	ramify, ramification, ramose, ramiform
2	ranc	bad odor	rancid, rancor, rancidity, rank
1	rapere	seize and rush away	rape, rapacious, rapt, rapture
1	rarus	seldom	rare, rarity, rarefied, *rara avis*
1	ras	scrape	erase, abrasive, rase, razor
1	ratus	reason	ration, irrational, rationale, ratiocination
1	rect	straight, right	correct, rectify, erect, rectangle
1	referre	carry back	refer, reference, referendum, referent
1	reg, regn, regul	guide, rule	regal, regime, regulate, interregnum
1	regesta	write down	register, registrant, registration, registrar
3	renes	kidneys	renal, adrenal, adrenalin, suprarenal
1	reptum	creeping	reptile, reptilian, reptilarium, reptant
2	resina	pitch, gum	resin, resinate, resinous, resiniferous
3	rete	net	reticule, reticle, reticular, retina
1	revereri	to respect	revere, reverence, irreverence, reverend
2	rheos, rrhea	current, flow	diarrhea, pyorrhea, rheostat, rheoscope
2	rhetor	orator	rhetoric, rhetorician, rhetorical, rhetorize
2	rheum	flow, discharge	rheumatic, rheumatism, rheumatoid, rheum
2	rhinos	nose	rhinoceros, rhinitis, rhinoscope, rhinoplasty
3	rhize	root	rhizopod, rhizoid, rhizophagous, rhizogenic
2	rhodon	rose, red	rhododendron, Rhode Island, rhodora
1	rhym	verse, beat	rhyme, rhymester, rhythm, eurythmic
2	rid, ris	laugh	deride, derisive, ridiculous, ridicule
1	rigare	stiff	rigid, rigidity, rigor, *rigor mortis*
1	ritus	ceremony	rite, ritual, ritualistic, *rites de passage*
2	robota	compulsory servitude	robot, robotry, robotism, robotization

1	rodere	to gnaw	rodent, erode, corrode, corrosive
3	roentgen	intensity of X-rays	roentgenology, roentgenograph, roentgenogram, roentgenometer
2	rogare	ask	interrogate, derogatory, abrogate, subrogate
1	rosa	rose	rose, rosary, roseate, *sub rosa*
1	rota	wheel	rotate, rotary, rotation, rotund
3	rrhag	burst, discharge	hemorrhage, bronchorrhagic, menorrhagia, myelorrhage
1	rub, rud, rus	red	ruby, ruddy, russet, rust
2	ruga	wrinkle	corrugate, rugose, rugate, rugosity
1	rupt	to break	abrupt, rupture, erupt, interrupt
1	rus, rur	country	rustic, rural, rusticity, rusticate
1	sabbatum	day of rest	sabbath, sabbatic, sabbatical, Sabbatism
3	saccus	bag	sac, sacciform, saccule, saccoderm
1	sacr	holy	sacrifice, sacrament, sacred, sacrilege
3	sagitta	arrow	Sagittarius, sagittoid, sagittal, sagittoform
1	sal	salt	salt, salary, saline, desalinate
2	sal, sult	leap	desultory, insult, assault, sally
1	salu, salut	health, greeting	salute, salutary, salubrious, salutation
1	san, sanus	healthy, sound	sane, insane, sanitary, sanitarium
1	sanct	holy	sanctuary, sanctity, sanctify, sanctimonious
2	sanguin	blood	sanguine, consanguine, sanguinary
1	sap, sip	juice, taste	sap, sapling, sapid, insipid
2	sapere	to know	sapience, sapient, *Homo sapiens*
3	sapo	soap	saponify, saponification, saponaceous, saponite
3	sarmentum	twig	sarment, sarmentaceous, sarmentose, sarmentiferous
3	sarx, sarkos	flesh	sarcophagous, sarcasm, ectosarc, endosarc
1	sat, satis	enough	satisfy, satiety, sate, satiate
2	satanas	adversary	Satan, satanic, Satanism, satanist
1	saur	lizard	dinosaur, tyrannosaurus, brontosaurus, saurian
1	scabr	rough	scabrid, scabrous, scabrin, scabrescent
1	scala	ladder, staircase	scalar, scale, escalate, escalator
2	scapulo	shoulder	scapula, scapular, scapuloclavicular, scapulalgia
1	scena	stage	scene, scenario, scenery, scenic
1	scend	climb	descend, descendant, ascend, transcend
1	schema	shape, figure	scheme, schema, schematic, schematism
3	schiz, schis	split, cleave	schism, schismatic, schizophrenic
1	schole	school	school, scholastic, scholasticism, scholar
1	sci	know	conscience, science, scientific, omniscience
2	scind, sciss	cut, split	scissors, scissile, scission, rescind
2	scintilla	spark	scintillometer, scintillant, scintillate, scintillescent
3	sclero	hard	sclerosis, scleroid, scleroderm, arteriosclerosis
1	scope	to watch	scope, telescope, microscope, periscope

1	scrib, script	write	describe, inscribe, scripture, manuscript
3	scrupus	sharp stone, anxiety	scruple, scrupulous, unscrupulous, scrupulosity
1	sculptus	carve	sculpture, sculptor, sculptress, sculpt
1	sect	cut	sect, dissect, insect, intersect
2	seculum	age, time, world	secular, secularism, secularize, secularity
2	sed	sit, settle	sedative, sedimentary, sedentary, sedate
3	seismos	earthquake	seismograph, seismology, seismometer, seismic
3	selene	moon	selenic, selenium, selenocentric, selenology
2	sema	sign	semantic, semantics, semaphore, sematic
2	semin	seed	seminary, disseminate, seminar, seminal, semen
1	sen	old	senator, senior, seniority, senile
1	sens	feel	senses, sensitive, sensation, sensory
1	sent	feel	consent, assent, sentiment, presentiment
2	seps, sept	decay	antiseptic, septic, sepsis, septic tank
1	sequ	follow	consequence, sequence, subsequent, sequel
1	serenus	calm	serenade, serene, serenity, serenador
1	seria	in a row	serial, series, serialize, seriate
2	serpens	creep	serpent, serpentine, serpenticide, serpentile
2	serr	saw-toothed	serrate, serration, serriform, serratus
3	serum	liquid	serum, serocyst, serofluid, serology
1	serv	save, keep	reservoir, reserve, preserve, conserve
1	servus	slave	serve, service, servant, servile
1	severus	strict	severe, perseverance, asseveration, severity
1	sexus	division	sex, sexual, sexuality, bisexual
3	siccus	dry	siccate, siccimeter, desiccant, desiccation
3	sidus, sideris	star	siderostat, sidereal, sideromancy
3	sigma	S	sigma, sigmate, sigmation, sigmoid
1	signi	mark, indicate	significant, signify, signal, signature
1	signum	token	assign, signate, signet, sign
1	silere	to be quiet	silence, silencer, silent, silentium
2	silicis	flint	silica, silicate, siliceous, silicon
2	silva	woods, grove	sylvan, Sylvania, Silvester, Sylvia
1	similis	like	similar, simile, simultaneous, simulate
1	simplex	single	simple, simplicity, simpleton, simplistic
1	singuli	one each	single, singular, singleton, singularity
2	sinistr	left hand	sinister, sinistrad, sinistral, sinistration
2	sinus	bend, curve	sine, sinus, insinuate, sinusoidal
3	sitos	food	parasite, sitomania, sitophobia, sitology
1	situs	place	site, situation, homesite, campsite
1	skandalon	stumbling block	scandal, scandalize, scandalmonger, scandalous
3	skatos	dung	scatology, scatological, scatophagous
1	skeptis	reflect, think, doubt	skeptic, skeptical, skepticism, skepticize
1	socium	comrade	associate, society, social, sociology
1	sol	alone	solo, solitude, desolate, soliloquy
1	solicitus	arouse, stir up	solicit, solicitation, solicitor, solicitous
1	solidus	solid	solid, solidarity, solder, solidify

1	solv	loosen	solve, dissolve, resolve, absolve
2	soma	body	somatic, chromosome, somatology, psychosomatic
1	somn	sleep	insomnia, insomniac, somnambulist, somnolent
1	son	sound	unison, resonant, sonata, sonorous
1	soph	wise	philosopher, sophisticate, sophomore, sophist
3	sopor	deep sleep	sopite, soporific, soporose, sopition
2	sorb	suck in	absorb, adsorb, absorbent, sorbose
2	soror	sister	sorority, sororal, sororate, sororicide
3	spasm, spast	draw up, convulsion	spasmodic, spastic, angiospasm, myospasm
2	spatium	space	spatial, spacial, expatiate, spacious
1	species	appearance, kind	special, species, specific, specious
1	spect	look	inspector, spectator, spectacular, spectacle
3	speleon	cave	speleology, spelunk, spelunker, spelean
1	sperare	hope	prosper, despair, desperate, desperado
3	sperm	seed, spore	sperm, spermatophore, spermatozoan, endosperm
1	sphaira	ball, sphere	atmosphere, hemisphere, sphere, spheroid
2	spica	sharp point	spike, spicose, spiculate, spicule
2	spina	thorn	spinal, spine, spiniform, spinulose
1	spir	breathe	conspirator, inspire, respiration, expire
2	spira	coil, twist	spiral, spire, spiriferous, spireme
1	splendor	to shine	splendor, splendid, splendent, resplendent
1	spolium	booty	spoil, spoliate, despoil, despoliation
1	spond, spons	promise	responsibility, respond, response, sponsor
3	sporos	sowing, seed	spore, sporozoan, macrospore, endospore
3	spuma	foam	spume, spumescent, spumoid, spumous
1	sta	stand	stationary, stability, status, stagnant
1	stalag, stalact	drip	stalagmite, stalactite, stalactiform, stalagmometer
2	stamin	thread	stamen, stamina, staminate, staminiferous
3	stannum	tin	stannous, stanniferous, stannary, stannic
3	staphyle	bunch of grapes, uvula	staphylococcus, staphylodema, staphyloplasty, staphylotomy
3	stear, steat	fat	stearic acid, steariform, steatite, stearin
3	stegos	roof	stegocarpus, stegosaurus, stegodon, stegomyia
1	stella	star	stellar, interstellar, stellate, Stella
1	stenos	short, narrow	stenographer, stenotype, stenopetalous, stenophyllous
2	stephan	crown	stephane, stephanoceros, Stephanie, Stephen
1	stereo	solid, three-dimensional	stereo, stereophonic, stereograph, cholesterol
3	sterno	breastbone	sternum, sternomancy, sternoclavicular
3	stethos	breast, chest	stethoscope, stethometry, stethospasm, stethophone
2	stigma	spot, mark	stigma, stigmatize, astigmatism, stigmata
1	stimul	goad, prod	stimulus, stimulate, stimulant, antistimulant

1	stoicus	porch	stoa, Stoic, Stoicism, stoical
3	stoma	mouth	stomach, peristome, macrostomia, stomatoplasty
3	strabos	distorted, squinting	strabismus, strabismic, strabometer, strabotomy
1	strait	narrow, limited	straits, straitened, strait jacket, straitlaced
2	strat	spread, layer	stratify, stratification, stratum, stratocumulus
2	stratos	army	stratagem, strategic, strategy, stratocracy
2	streptos	twisted	streptococcus, streptomycin, streptothricin, streptothricosis
3	striden	harsh-sounding	strident, stridulent, stridulate, stridulous laryngitis
3	strobos	whirling	strobic, strobila, stroboscope, strobe light
2	strophe	a turning	apostrophe, catastrophe, strophe, anastrophe
1	stru	build	construct, structure, instruct, destruction
1	studeo	be eager	student, studious, study, studio
1	stylus	writing instrument	style, stylish, stylize, stylus
2	suadeo, suasi	to advise	persuade, assuage, persuasion, dissuade
3	sudor	sweat	sudarium, sudatorium, sudorific, sudorous
1	sume, sumpt	take, take up	assume, consume, resume, subsume
1	summus	total, highest	sum, summary, summit, summation
1	surg, surr	rise	resurrection, resurge, insurrection, insurgent
2	syco	fig	sycamore, sycoma, sycophant, sycosis
1	syllaba	take together	syllable, syllabus, monosyllabic, multisyllable
1	tabula	board, tablet	table, tablet, tableau, tabulate
2	tacere	be silent	tacit, taciturn, reticent, taciturnity
3	tachy	swift, quick	tachycardia, tachygenesis, tachometer, tachistoscope
1	tain	hold	attain, retain, detain, contain
1	tang, tact	touch	tangent, tangible, tangential, tactile
1	tardus	slow	retard, retarded, tardy, tarry
3	tarsos	flat of the foot	tarsus, tarsal, tarsius, metatarsus
2	taurus	bull	taurine, tauricide, toreador, torero
2	tax, tact	to arrange, order	tactics, tactician, taxis, taxonomy
1	techne	art, skill	technical, technician, technique, technology
1	tele	distant	telephone, telegraph, telescope, televise
3	tellus	earth	tellural, tellurium, tellurian, tellurism
1	temp	time	temporary, contemporary, temporal, extemporaneous
1	temperare	be moderate	temper, distemper, temperance, temperate
1	tempto	to try	attempt, tempt, temptation, temptress
1	ten	hold	tenacious, tenure, detention, retention
1	tend	tend, stretch	tendency, tend, tendon, tensile
2	tenu	thin	tenuous, attenuate, extenuate, tenuity
1	terg	wipe off	deterge, detergent, detergency
1	termin	end	terminate, exterminate, terminal, interminable

1	terra	earth	terrace, territory, terrain, terrestrial
1	terrere	to frighten	terrify, terror, terrible, terrific
1	testare	to witness	testify, testimonial, testament, intestate
3	thanatos	death	thanatism, thanatophobia, thanatopsis, thanatosis
2	the	god	theism, atheism, theology, monotheism
1	thea	view	theatre, theatrics, theorem, theory
2	them, thes, thet	thing set down	theme, thesis, antithesis, epithet
2	therapeutos	to treat medically	therapeutic, therapeusis, therapy, therapist
1	thermo	heat	thermos, thermometer, thermal, thermostat
3	thorax	chest	mesothorax, thoracectomy, thoracid, thoracoplasty
3	thrombos	clot	thrombin, thrombocyte, thrombogen, thrombosis
3	tibia	shinbone	tibia, tibial, tibialis, tibiotarsus
1	ting	to wet	tincture, tinge, tint, stain
1	Titan	mythological giant	Titan, titanic, titanium, Titanosaurus
1	toler	endure	tolerable, tolerance, intolerant, tolerate
2	tom	cut	appendectomy, tonsillectomy, anatomy, atom
1	tonos	tone, tension	baritone, monotone, overtone, atonal
2	topos	place or spot	topical, topographical, Utopia, toponym
2	torp	stupor, numbness	torpid, torpedo, torpor, torpidity
1	tort	twist, turn	distort, extort, tortuous, torture
1	totus	whole, entire	total, totalitarian, totality, totalize
2	tox	poison	toxin, antitoxin, toxic, intoxication
1	trachia	windpipe, trough	trachea, tracheitis, trachoma, tracheotomy
1	tract	pull	tractor, abstract, detract, extract
1	tranquillus	calm	tranquil, tranquilize, tranquilizer, tranquility
2	trauma	injury, wound	traumatic, traumasthenia, traumatism, traumatology
1	tremere	to shake	tremulous, tremor, tremble, tremendous
2	trigon	three angles	trigonometry, trigon, trigonous, trigonocerous
3	trochos	wheel, running	trochee, troche, trochanter, trochophore
1	trope	turning	trophy, tropical, troposperm, tropism
3	trophos	feed	trophic, dystrophy, atrophy, eutrophy
2	trudere	to thrust	intrude, protrude, obtrusive, abstruse
2	tubor	lump, swelling	tuber, tuberculosis, tubercle, protuberant
1	tubus	pipe	tube, tuba, tubing, tubular
2	tuitus	watch over	tuition, intuition, tutelage, tutor
2	turb	confusion	turbine, turbid, turbulent, perturb
2	turg	swell	turgid, turgescent, turgor, turgent
2	tympanon	drum	tympanum, tympany, tympanic bone
1	typ	print	typist, typography, typical, prototype
1	tyrannos	tyrant	tyranny, tyrannicide, tyrant, tyrannosaur
2	ubi	where	ubiquitous, ubiety, ubiquitary, ubiquity
3	ulna	elbow	ulna, ulnar, ulnoradial, ulnocarpal
2	ultimus	last	penult, antepenult, ultimate, ultimatum
2	umber	shadow	umbrian, umber, umbrage, somber
2	umbilicus	navel	umbilical cord, umbilicate, umbiliform, umbilicus

1	umbra	shade	umbra, umbrella, adumbrate, penumbra
3	uncus	hook	unciform, uncinnate, uncinariasis
2	unda	wave	undulate, undulous, inundate, abundant
2	ungue	anoint	anoint, ointment, unction, unguent
3	unguis	nail	unguis, ungula, ungular, ungulate
3	uranos	heaven	uranography, uranium, uranology, Uranus
1	urb	city	urban, urbane, suburb, conurbation
2	urina	urine	urinal, urine, urinate, urinalysis
2	ursus	bear	ursa, Ursa Major, ursiform, ursine
1	usus	use	use, abuse, usual, usage
1	uter	either	neuter, neutral, neutrality, neutron
2	uterus	womb	uterine, uterus, uterectomy, uteralgia
1	utilis	useful	utilitarian, utilitarianism, utensil, utilize
3	uva	grape	uvea, uvula, uvular, uvulitis
3	uxor	wife	uxorious, uxorial, uxoricide
1	vaca, vacu	empty, hollow	vacate, vacant, vacation, evacuate
1	vacca	cow	vaccinate, vaccination, vaccinal, vaccine
2	vacill	waver	vacillate, vacillator, vacillant
1	vad	go	invade, evade, pervade, vademecum
1	vag	wander	vagrant, vagabond, extravagant, vagary
2	vagin	sheath, pod	vagina, vaginate, vaginectomy, vaginitis
1	val	strong	value, invalid, validity, convalesce
1	vallis	valley	vale, valley, avalanche, vallecula
1	van	empty	vanish, vain, vanity, evanescent
1	van	front, forward	vanguard, caravan, avant-garde, vantage
1	vapor	steam	vapor, vaporous, evaporate, evaporator
1	vari	different	vary, various, variety, variegated
2	vas	vessel	vase, vascular, intravascular, vasotomy
1	vassus	servant	valet, varlet, vassal, vassalage
1	vast	empty, vast, waste	devastate, vast, waste, wastrel
2	vectum	carry	vector, vection, convection, convex
1	veh	carry	vehicle, convey, vehicular, conveyance
2	velox	swift, quick	velocity, velocipede, velocimeter
1	velum	sail, covering	veil, reveal, envelope, develop
1	ven	come	convention, convent, convene, advent
2	ven	sale	vend, vendor, venal, venality
2	ven	vein	venous, intravenous, venular, venasection
2	venenum	poison	envenom, venom, venomous, veneniferous
2	venter	belly	ventricle, ventriloquism, ventrodorsal
1	ventus	wind	vent, ventiduct, ventilation, ventilator
1	ver	true	verdict, verify, aver, veracity
1	ver, verer	fear, awe	reverence, reverend, revere, irreverent
1	verb	word	adverb, verbal, proverb, verbatim
2	verd	green	verdant, verdure, Vermont, viridescent
2	verg	bend, incline	verge, converge, diverge, convergent
3	verm	worm	vermiculate, vermilion, vermin, vermicelli
2	vernus	spring	vernal, vernation, vernal equinox, vernant
1	vers	turn	reverse, conversation, adverse, inverse
1	vert	turn	convertible, convert, revert, subvert
3	vesica	bladder	vesica, vesicle, vesicular, vesical

3	vespa	wasp	vespiary, vespid, vespiform, vespacide
2	vesper	evening star	vesper, vesperal, vespers, Hesperus
1	vest	clothing	vest, vestment, divest, investiture
2	vestig	footprint, trace	investigate, vestige, vestigial, vestigium
1	veter	old, experienced	vet, veteran, veterinarian, inveterate
1	vexare	agitate	vex, vexed, vexation, vexatious
1	vi	force	violent, violate, vim, inviolable
1	via	way	via, trivial, deviate, viaduct
1	vibra	vibrate	vibrate, vibrant, vibraharp, vibraphone
1	vice	substitute	vicar, viceroy, vicarious, vice-president
1	vict	conquer	victory, convict, evict, victor
2	vicus	neighboring	vicinity, vicinage, vicine, vicinal
1	vid	see	video, provide, evidence, providence
1	vig	lively, strong	vigor, invigorate, vigorous, reinvigorate
1	vigil	awake	vigil, vigilant, vigilante, surveillance
2	vil	cheap	vilify, vile, vilipend, revile
1	villa	farmhouse	village, villager, villain, villatic
2	villus	tuft of hair	villi, villous, velvet, villiform
1	vin	wine	vine, vinegar, vineyard, vintage
1	vinc	conquer	vincible, invincible, convince, vanquish
1	vindex	avenger	avenge, vengeance, vendetta, vindicate
1	viol	stringed instrument	viola, violin, violincello, violinist
1	vir	man	virile, virility, triumvirate, decemvir
2	virga	twig, rod	virgule, virgate, virgulate, virgation
1	virtu	virtue, strength	virtue, virtuous, virtually, virtuoso
3	viru	poison	virulent, virus, viruliferous
1	vis	see	television, visual, visit, visa
2	visco	sticky, thick	viscid, viscosity, viscous, viscosimetry
3	viscus	bowels	eviscerate, viscera, visceral, viscerate
1	vit	live	vitamin, vitality, vital, vitalize
1	viti	fault	vice, vicious, vitiate, vituperation
3	vitrum	glass	vitreous, vitreous humor, vitric, vitrify
1	viv	live	survive, revive, vivid, vivacious
1	vo	vow, wish	vote, vow, devote, devout
1	voc	call	vocal, vocalize, evocative, convocation
1	void	empty	avoid, devoid, avoidance, voided
1	voke	call	provoke, revoke, invoke, evoke
1	vol	wish, will	volunteer, voluntarily, benevolent, volition
1	vol	fly	volleyball, volley, volatile, volplane
1	volv	roll, turn	revolve, revolution, revolver, involve
1	vor	eat	omnivorous, carnivorous, herbivorous, voracious
1	vul	to tear	convulse, divulsion, revulsion, vulture
1	Vulcan	god of fire	Vulcan, volcano, vulcanite, vulcanize
1	vulg	common people	vulgar, vulgarity, divulge, Vulgate
1	vulnus	wound	vulnerable, vulneral, invulnerability
3	vulpes	fox	vulpine, Volpone, vulpecular, vulpicide
3	xenos	stranger	xenogamy, xenolith, xenon, xenophobia
3	xer, xero	dry, arid	xerography, xeroprinting, xeromorph, xerotherm, xerox
2	xylo, xyl	wood, woody	xylophonist, xylophone, xylograph, xylene
1	zo	animal	zoo, zoology, protozoa, zodiac
3	zygo	yoke, pair	zygosis, zygote, zygoma, zygodactyl
3	zym	ferment	enzyme, histozyme, zymology, zymurgy

A Short List of Latin Words Used in English

abdomen
aborigines
acceptor
accumulator
actor
acumen
adit
administer
administrator
advocator
aggressor
agitator
album
albumen
alibi
alias
altar
alter
animal
animus
annotator
anterior
apex
Apollo
apparatus
appendix
aquarium
arbiter
arbitrator
arbor
arbutus
ardor
arena
assertor
assessor
auditor
augur
basilica
basis
benefactor
biceps
bicolor
bonus
cadaver
caesura
calculator
calculus
calumniator
campus
cancer
candelabrum
candor
cantor
caper
captor
castigator
celebrator
censor
census
cervix
chorus
circulator
circus
clamor
clangor
cognomen
collector

color
commentator
communicator
compendium
competitor
complex
compositor
compressor
conciliator
conductor
confessor
confiteor
consensus
conservator
consul
contaminator
contemplator
contractor
copula
cornucopia
corpus
corrector
corruptor
cortex
creator
creditor
credo
crocus
cumulus
curator
curriculum
data
December
declamator
decor
decorum
dedicator
defector
deliberator
delirium
dementia
demonstrator
depositor
deprecator
depreciator
designator
desolator
detector
detractor
devastator
deviator
dictator
dictum
discolor
discriminator
disseminator
dissimulator
dissipator
distributor
divisor
doctor
dominator
duplex
duplicator
editor
educator
ego

elector
elevator
emancipator
emeritus
error
excelsior
exemplar
exit
exhibitor
exonerator
expiator
expositor
extempore
exterior
extra
fabricator
factor
fauna
favor
femur
fervor
fetus
flora
focus
forceps
formula
forum
fulcrum
fungus
furor
genius
genus
gladiator
gladiolus
gratis
gusto
habitat
herbarium
hernia
hiatus
homunculus
honor
honorarium
horror
humus
ignoramus
illuminator
illustrator
imitator
immolator
impetus
impostor
incognito
incubator
incubus
incunabula
index
indicator
inductor
inertia
inferior
initiator
inquisitor
insignia
inspector
instigator
institutor

instructor
integer
intercessor
interest
interim
interior
interpellator
interpolator
interregnum
interrogator
inventor
investigator
irrigator
item
janitor
junior
Jupiter
labor
lacuna
languor
larva
legislator
lens
liberator
liquor
litigator
locus
major
malefactor
Mars
matrix
maximum
me
mediator
meditator
medium
memorabilia
memorandum
militia
minimum
minister
minor
minus
miser
moderator
modicum
modulator
momentum
monitor
motor
mucus
murmur
narrator
nasturtium
navigator
negotiator
neuter
nominator
nostrum
November
nucleus
numerator
objector
October
odium
odor
omen

omnibus
onus
opera
operator
oppressor
opprobrium
opus
orator
ovum
pabulum
pallor
panacea
papyrus
par
participator
pastor
pauper
pelvis
pendulum
penetrator
peninsula
perpetrator
persecutor
placebo
plaudit
plus
Pluto
pollen
pontifex
posse
possessor
posterior
postulator
prior
procreator
procurator
professor
progenitor
prolocutor
promulgator
propagator
propitiator
prospector
prospectus
protector

proviso
proximo
pus
quantum
quarto
quietus
quorum
quota
rabies
radius
rancor
ratio
rebus
recipe
rector
referendum
regalia
regimen
remunerator
renovator
repressor
repudiator
residuum
rhinoceros
rigor
rostrum
rumor
saliva
sanctum
sarcophagus
scintilla
sculptor
sector
selector
semen
senator
senior
separator
September
series
sexagesima
sic
Silvia
simile
simulator

sinister
sinus
siren
sol
solarium
spatula
species
specimen
spectator
spectrum
speculator
speculum
splendor
sponsor
squalor
stadium
stamen
status
Stella
stimulator
stimulus
strata
studio
stupor
subpoena
substratum
successor
sulphur
super
superior
supplicator
suppressor
supra
tandem
tenet
tenor
tergiversator
terminus
terror
testator
thesaurus
thorax
toga
torpedo
torpor

transactor
transgressor
translator
tremor
tribunal
triumvir
trivium
tuber
tumor
tutor
tyro (tiro)
ulterior
ultimatum
ultra
vacuum
valor
vapor
vector
venerator
ventilator
Venus
versus
vertebra
vertex
vertigo
vesper
veto
via
vice versa
victor
Victoria
video
vigil
vigor
villa
vim
vindicator
violator
virago
virus
viscera
visor
vitiator
vituperator
vociferator

362

Index

Index of Words and Phrases

365

introspective, 154
invaluable, 57
invisible, 93
Iphigenia, 273
Irene, 72
iridescence, 83
iridescent glow, 83
iris, 72, 75, 83, 226
irrational, 96
irreclaimable, 96
irredeemable, 96
irrefutable, 41
irregular, 96
irreligious, 95
irreplaceable, 96
irresistible, 96
irresponsible, 96
irreverent, 96
irreversible, 96
Ishmael, 275
islet, 130
isn't, 199
it'd, 199
it'll, 199
it's, 198, 199
its, 198
Ivan, 70
I've, 199
Ixion, 273

January, 76
jet, 138
jettisoned, 138
Job, 256
John, 70, 72
joie de vivre, 295
Joiner, 73
Joseph, 72
joust, 209
Jove, 79, 273
jovial, 79, 85, 247
jovial mood, 82
Judas, 256
Judith, 72
July, 77
June, 77
Juno, 80, 88
Junoesque, 80
Jupiter, 85
jute, 31

kaleidoscope, 7, 150
Kathleen, 72
Kaufman, 73
Keeler, 73
kerchief, 86
kill, 251
Kilner, 73
king, 199
kitchenette, 37, 130
kith and kin, 291
Kleenex, 211
knave, 212
knight, 166, 211

Labyrinth, 80
labyrinthian, 80
laconic, 75
laconically, 40
laconic reply, 83
Ladd, 73
lady, 199, 211
Lambert, 73

Lane, 71
laryngitis, 129
laser, 201, 248
latitude, 32
Laura, 72
lavaliere, 75
layout, 251
Lazarus, 256
lead, 251
leader, 118
leaflet, 130
leak, 202
lean, 202
Leech, 73
LEM, 201
Leninism, 75
lens, 226
Leo, 72, 80
leonine, 80, 229
leopard, 246
leopardine, 229
lethal, 80
lethargic, 80
Lethe, 80
let's, 199
leviathan, 256
Leyden jar, 75
liaison, 295
lilliputian, 31–32
limousine, 75
linen, 77
lingerie, 212
lion, 246
liquefy, 131
listener, 118
Lister, 73
litotes, 237
little, 54–55
Lloyd, 71
loc. cit., 298
loco citato, 298
loganberry, 75
loony, 200
loquacious, 162
lord, 199, 212
Louis, 72
lousy, 284
lovable, 132
lox, 201
Lucifer, 257
Luna, 79, 85
lunar, 85, 247
lunar month, 82
lunatic, 85
Lunik, 88
lupine, 229
lynch, 75
lynx-eyed, 83
lyric, 199

macaroons, 292
Macedonian cry, 257
mackinaw, 75
mackintosh, 75
macrobiotic, 158
macrocosm, 158
Magna Carta, 34
magnifying glass, 131
magnolia, 75
maid, 210
maître d'hôtel, 295
makeup, 251
maladroit, 295

malapropism, 75, 186
malaria, 162
malediction, 162
malefactor, 162
malevolent, 162
man, 53
manicure, 153
manila paper, 75
maniple, 154
mansion, 212
manual, 154
manufacture, 139
manuscript, 154, 211
March, 77
Margaret, 72
Marner, 73
Mars, 79, 83, 85, 258, 273
marshal, 212
Martha. 72
martial law, 83
Martin, 72
martinet, 75, 295
Marxism, 75
Mary, 72
maser, 201
masthead, 251
mastoiditis, 129
material, 286
matriarchal, 156
matricide, 161
matriculate, 33
matrimony, 161
matron, 161
Matthew, 72
Maureen, 72
maverick, 74, 77
May, 77
Mediterranean, 157
Medusa, 273
megalith, 150
megalomaniac, 150
megalopolis, 150
megaphone, 150
Melissa, 72
Mellor, 73
mend, 199
meningitis, 129
mentor, 273
Mercer, 73
mercurial, 80, 85
Mercury, 32, 80, 85, 88, 258
meridian, 161
meringue, 292
mesmerize, 74
metaphor, 224
metathesis, 217
meteorological, 89
meteorology, 127
methinks, 299
Methuselah, 256
metonymy, 234, 267
metropolis, 78, 161
Michael, 72
microcosm, 158
micrometer, 153
microphobia, 136
microphone, 150
microscope, 7
Midas, 273
Midas touch, the, 83

middies, 200
mightn't, 199
might've, 199
migrant, 147
migrated, 147
migration, 146, 147
migratory, 147
Milner, 73
mineralogy, 126
minestrone, 292
minister, 76
minuscule, 130
misanthrope, 152
misanthropy, 152
misogamist, 152
misogynist, 152
Miss, 200
mob, 200
mobile, 22
mobocracy, 159
modify, 131
module, 89
molecule, 130
monarch, 102, 156, 161
Monday, 77
monk, 102, 161
monolith, 161
monolog, 161
monopoly, 161
monotheism, 103
monotone, 103
monotonous, 161
monoxide, 103
month, 77
moon, 29
moonstruck, 85
morgue, 251
Morpheus, 273
morphology, 171
morris chair, 75
Morse code, 75
Morta, 79
motel, 84, 202
motif, 266
mulled, 247
multiflorous, 137
musicology, 126
muslin, 77
mustang, 77
myelitis, 129
mystifying, 131

naïve, 295
narcissistic, 80
Narcissus, 80, 273
Narcissus complex, 80
NASA, 201
natatorium, 155
NATO, 201
Naylor, 74
n.b., 298
nectar, 81
nectarean, 81
nectareous, 81
nectarine, 81
Nemesis, 273
nephritis, 129
nepoticide, 248
Neptune, 273
neuritis, 129

368

375

376